Pristine Affluence

Daoist Roots in the Stone Age

Livia Kohn

Three Pines Press
P. O. Box 530416
St. Petersburg, FL 33747
www.threepinespress.com

9 8 7 6 5 4 3 2 1

Printed in the United States of America
This edition is printed on acid-free paper that meets the American National Standard Institute Z39.48 Standard.
Distributed in the United States by Three Pines Press.

Cover Art: "The Yongcheng Emperor Dressed as a Daoist." Anonymous, Qing-dynasty painting, 52x45 cm. Collection of the Palace Museum, Beijing. Found in the exhibition catalog 清世宗文物大展: *Harmony and Integrity: The Yongcheng Emperor and His Times* (Taipei: Palace Museum, 2009).

Library of Congress Cataloging-in-Publication Data
Names: Kohn, Livia, 1956- author.
Title: Pristine affluence : Daoist roots in the Stone Age / Livia Kohn.
Description: First [edition]. | St. Petersburg : Three Pines Press, 2017.
Identifiers: LCCN 2016051110 (print) | LCCN 2016057243 (ebook) | ISBN 9781931483360 (alk. paper) | ISBN 9781365505638
Subjects: LCSH: Taoism--China--History--To 1500. | Taoism--Customs and practices.
Classification: LCC BL1910 K638 2017 (print) | LCC BL1910 (ebook) | DDC 299.5/14440932--dc23
LC record available at https://lccn.loc.gov/2016051110

Contents

Acknowledgments

This work grew out of a chapter in my book *Science and the Dao* on the evolution of consciousness as described in the *Zhuangzi*, interpreted in relation to paleo-anthropological studies of the evolution of language and culture. Also, encountering the work of David Pankenier and realizing that a number of Daoist cosmological concepts went back well into the Neolithic, I became curious about just how many aspects of the religion could be traced back into prehistory.

Learning a lot about how humanity used to live before agriculture and civilization, I came to appreciate the Daoist tradition in an entirely new dimension, often inspired by economics, anthropology, and sociology, as ceaselessly and insistently promoting prehistoric patterns, health-enhancement, and joyful living.

This understanding would not have been possible without the numerous scholars who have studied prehistory in so many different dimensions. I am deeply indebted to them all. More specifically, I wish to thank Greg Colgan, grandmaster of interlibrary loan at Eckerd College, for his unfailing support, Shih-shan Susan Huang for helping with the cover illustration, and the organizers of the Third International Symposium on Quanzhen Daoism and Lao-Zhuang Studies at Wuhan University for the opportunity to present my findings. Finally, I am deeply grateful to my husband for always being up for new adventures. His amazing enthusiasm for exploring unchartered territories and openness to often weird propositions make life truly enchanting.

Introduction

Scholars have long debated when and how Daoism originated. Those who see the religion more strongly in communal and ritual terms have tended to place the starting point in the Later Han dynasty, with the arising of various millenarian movements. Their key focus has been organization of the Celestial Masters (Tianshi 天師) under the leadership of Zhang Daoling 張道陵, who allegedly received the founding revelation from Lord Lao on Mount Heming in Sichuan in 142 CE.[1]

Those who understand Daoism to focus on philosophy and personal cultivation have typically placed its origin in the Warring States period (479-221—all dates in this book, unless marked "CE" are BCE), linking it to early thinkers such as Laozi, Zhuangzi, Liezi, Yang Zhu, and the like. Appreciating that philosophers at the time held a strong interest in social application and were also practitioners of self-cultivation techniques, they see the beginning of the religion in small groups of like-minded seekers who later evolved into more complex ritual and communal structures.[2]

Early Dynasties

Looking further back in history, however, the picture changes. Even before the Warring States, under the Shang (ca. 1550-1046) and Western Zhou (1046-771) dynasties, Chinese society had already established patterns that continued to pervade Daoist beliefs and practices, embedding the religion deeply in the culture. Most notable among them are worship of nature deities, a hierarchical understanding of the otherworld, extensive ancestral sacrifices, and widespread use of divination in various modes.

That is to say, populated by nature deities such as sun, moon, rain, and thunder as well as a plethora of ancestors—most importantly those of the ruling house and its original founder, known as the High God or Thearch (*shangdi* 上帝)—the otherworld in early China had a major impact on all events and occurrences on earth.[3] Ancestors not only served as intermediaries to the great nature deities but also influenced social and personal events by bestowing either blessings or curses on human actions.

---

[1] See Hendrischke 2000; Kleeman 1998; Strickmann 1980.

[2] See Kirkland 2004; Puett 2002; Roth 1999.

[3] Allan 1991; Chang 1983; Keightley 2000.

As a result, all activities involving the ruler, from the most mundane to the most decisive, had to be submitted to the ancestors' inspection and were either supported or rejected. All events likely to occur were posted to the ancestors for their prediction and guidance. Different ancestors, moreover, held different ranks and were responsible for different areas of life, giving rise to an extensive otherworldly bureaucracy.[4] They received regular offerings based on a complex ritual schedule that followed the so-called sexagenary cycle, a calendar consisting of a ten-day week and twelve-year system (Keightley 2000, 37-43).

Divination, unlike fortune-telling from palms, playing cards, or dreams, is the reading of divine guidance through natural or external signs. Shang rulers employed the so-called oracle bones, carapaces of turtles and shoulder blades of cattle that had holes drilled into them and were heated over a fire. Professional diviners, possibly of shamanic background, would then interpret the resulting cracks to mean either yes or no. Questions asked could be both simple and more complex, including particular weather patterns on given days, the outcome of warfare, the birth of son or daughter, the relief for the king's toothache, and more (Chang 1980; Keightley 1978a; 2000).

Daoists incorporated a heavy dose of Shang religion into their beliefs and practices. The Daoist otherworld is hierarchically organized and populated by nature deities and ancestors, joined in due course by pure divine emanations of Dao and lofty spirit immortals. Regular rituals to these various deities are essential to maintain harmony in the cosmos. The gods have to be appeased to prevent disasters, but they can also be enticed to give guidance to human beings. Communication with them is a bureaucratic act that involves the written language, no longer in the form of oracle-bone cracks but through petitions, contracts, mandates, and other documents. Daoist priests are intermediaries of the divine realm and occupy official positions in the otherworld; equipped with special passports and sacred passwords, they can—like shamans—travel into the spheres beyond (Benn 2000; Bumbacher 2012).

Another early feature of Chinese culture that exerted a strong impact on Daoism is the notion of Heaven (*tian* 天), the central deity of the Zhou and ultimate arbiter of nature gods and ancestors. Unlike the High God of the Shang, this was not a former human being and thus not guided by personal whims and moods. Rather, Heaven was a process, an abstract representation of the cycles and patterns of nature, a nonhuman force that interacted closely with the human world in an impersonal way.

Reacting to good rule and upright social behavior, it would show its pleasure by creating harmony through appropriate weather patterns, fertility, and general wellness. Should the ruler be dissolute or society in discord, however, it would reveal its displeasure by sending along floods, droughts, earthquakes, locust plagues, epidemics, and the like. Heaven thus represented the

---

[4] Keightley 2000, 101; Shahar and Weller 1996.

sum-total of human and natural activities, matching their impulses with appropriate responses (Eno 1990).

The concept that humanity and nature or Heaven exist in a close, if not immediate, relationship has remained central to Chinese thinking, and even in 1976 it was clear to all Chinese that the massive earthquake in August was a harbinger of the death of Chairman Mao in September—both equally signifying upheaval and major change. The understanding has thoroughly pervaded Daoism, and the entire complex of Daoist ethics revolves around it (Kohn 2004a).

Divination

A yet different early feature of early Chinese culture that has shaped Daoism is the *Yijing* 易經 (Book of Changes), a divination manual that, rather than providing yes/no answers as the oracle bones did, helps people determine the tendencies inherent in the course of Heaven and aids them in making good decisions through formal judgments and advice. Allegedly compiled into a coherent book by Confucius around 500, its system claims to go back to prehistory when a mythical ruler named Fu Xi 伏羲 discerned its original symbols from constellations in the stars. King Wen, the mastermind behind the Zhou conquest, supposedly first standardized its basic judgments (Wilhelm 1950).

The *Yijing* utilizes the two cosmic forces yin and yang as symbolized by an unbroken and a broken line, then combined in sets of two and three to form four symbols (*sixiang* 四象) and eight trigrams (*bagua* 八卦). The latter are further joined into a set of sixty-four hexagrams that form the bulk of the work. Each hexagram comes with an explanation of its image, a judgment, an explanation of the judgment, and a fortune for each individual line.

All these provide advice, often couched in rather ambiguous and vague terms yet closely reflecting the concrete reality of Zhou-dynasty life, where family relations were important, travel and communication were hard, the key relationship was with the lord or great man, and inner sincerity was valued highly. It is accessible today through commentaries, both traditional and modern, and often has to be read with a good dose of intuition and personal feeling (Smith 1991).

Daoists as much as other Chinese literati have used the *Yijing* for millennia to give guidance and to support them in their decision-making. More specifically Daoists have used the hexagrams in alchemy to symbolize the waxing and waning of yin and yang through the seasons, placing them in a series of twelve hexagrams:

This sequence shows the rising of yang between the winter and summer solstices—the latter located in the center of the line and symbolized by the six-yang hexagram "Heaven"—followed by the rising of yin as the year once again moves toward winter. It allows a subtle, pictorial description of seasonal change, pinpointing optimal times for the concoction of an elixir or the growth of the immortal embryo. Besides applying the *Yijing* in its originally intended mode as a divination manual, Daoists have thus also employed its symbols to express subtle cosmological and internal transformations.

Taking all this together, the entire complex of Daoist interaction with the otherworld—its deities, administration, functioning, as well as the major ways of discerning its patterns and communicating with it—has deep roots in early China, going back far beyond the ancient thinkers and even farther beyond the first communities of the religion. Seen from this perspective, the Daoist movements of the Later Han that eventually gave rise to the full-fledged organized religion appear as a historically and sociologically specific manifestation of a pervasive Chinese way of dealing with life in and beyond this world. The philosophical exploits of Warring States thinkers and the proto-Daoist self-cultivation and alternative social communities that reflected their ideas, moreover, in this light appear as particular superstructures that punctuate and modulate, but never fundamentally change, the overall flow of dominant religious attitudes and behaviors.

The Golden Age

What is more, Daoists are quite aware of this fact. They—both thinkers and priests—as much as all Chinese philosophers, are backward looking, postulating a golden age in the murky past when Dao was whole, the world was in harmony, and life was good. While scholars have been well aware of this tendency, the overall assumption has been that this golden age was entirely fictional, a figment of the collective imagination, a well-intentioned fantasy. But what if it is more than that?

The texts are fairly specific, after all. Confucians speak clearly about the ideal sage kings Yao 堯, Shun 舜, and Yu 禹. While all three were thought to be mythical paragons, recent archaeological excavation suggests differently. There is some speculation today that the Xia dynasty, allegedly founded by Yu, was in fact a historical force with one of its capitals, Wenyi 文邑, located at Erlitou 二里頭 in Henan (Liu and Chen 2012, 253). There is evidence for several great floods that the Erlitou state controlled as part of its rise to local dominance (2012, 251). Prior to that, as some scholars suggest, glyphs written in red on a pottery vessel found at Taosi 陶寺 in the Linfen Basin 臨汾盆 of the Yellow River, indicate the name of Yao. This would identify him as the ruler of this important economic, political, and religious center, a hub of early urbanism, with Shun as his chosen, nonhereditary successor (Liu and Chen 2012, 226).

Taosi dates to 2600-2000, while Erlitou flourished right afterwards, 1900-1500, overlapping with the rising Shang by about a century (Chang 2005, 126).

The time saw the transition from copper to bronze technology as well as the consolidation of about 10,000 to 3,000 local centers through increasingly institutionalized warfare and the accumulation of wealth and amassing of power in the hands of smaller elites (2005, 127).

In other words, the golden age later Confucian thinkers look back to is the Chalcolithic, the Copper Age, when technology was advanced enough to work with metal, but had not yet developed the mining and smelting of tin—nor yet the social organization and political clout—needed for the production of bronze (McIntosh 2006, 55). The earliest bronzes appear in very late Taosi and, more extensively, in Erlitou, indicating a more stratified and controlled society, where personal relationships were secondary to institutional governance and moral integrity gave way to power mongering—the exact trends Confucian thinkers bemoan and want to reverse.

Daoists, on the other hand, do not share this vision. Their ideal is "a small country with few people" (*Daode jing* 80), where folk live in contained, settled communities with dogs and chickens, grow their own food, weave their own cloth, make their own pots, and generally are self-sufficient and contented. This reflects Chinese reality at an earlier period, i.e., in the early Neolithic or Mesolithic, around 9000-5000, during the Mid-Holocene climatic optimum, when the weather had turned warm and wet (Liu and Chen 2012, 123).

People in the Chinese heartland at the time, while maintaining many aspects of the Paleolithic lifestyle, were no longer itinerant but lived in year-round settlements, as evidenced by remnants of dwellings, storage pits, and burials. They were practicing some elementary plant cultivation in conjunction with hunting and gathering, as testified in the remains of various food animals—both wild and domesticated— as well as of large numbers of vermin, plant parts, functionally specific vessels, and secondary refuse (2012, 125). Villages were about 5-20 acres in size and housed around a hundred people. They were not close, but surrounded by uncultivated land—only two acres being occupied in every 30 square miles (Shelach-Levi 2015, 70-71).

In other words, early Daoist thinkers, saw the Mesolithic as their golden age, a time when agricultural cultivation began and communities were settled, but still matched Paleolithic and hunter-gatherer patterns by living in small, egalitarian communities, their life closely following the cycles of nature. This is most blatant in their primitivist strand, which adopted the Divine Farmer (Shennong 神農) as its mythical hero, the sage ruler who allegedly first developed agriculture, animal husbandry, weaving, and pharmacology.[5] After him, this group was called the Agriculturists or School of Tillers (*nongjia* 農家). Around 315, under the leadership of Chen Xiang 陳相, they established a withdrawn utopian community in the state of Teng, which consisted largely of farmers and craftsmen (Graham 1990a, 68-69, 101; Vervoorn 1990, 60).

[5] Graham 1990a, 81; Campany 2005, 99; Lee 2014, ch. 4.

Their ideal was to achieve alignment with Dao by living in small, self-administered communities free from social stratification and outside pressures. Sedentary, they would rest contented with enough food, clothing, and shelter and have no desire for migration, expansion, or outside contacts (Lee 2007, 600-01). They believed that the "inner nature" (*xing* 性) or inherent tendencies of everything, including people, animals, and natural objects, formed a set ontological reality that needed to be uncovered and preserved but not cultivated or transformed, and certainly not altered or manipulated by instruments or techniques (Lee 2007, 602-03, 608; Brindley 2010, 80-81).

Reclaiming Simplicity

They—as much as many later Daoists—accordingly rejected the hallmarks of civilization, such as boats, carriages, and armor (Sarkassian 2010, 314), as well as all forms of expert craftsmanship. "If we must use curve and plumb line, compass and square to make something right," the primitivists note, "that means cutting away its inner nature; if we must use cords and knots, glue and lacquer to make something firm, this means violating its natural potency" (*Zhuangzi* 8; Watson 1968, 100). Claiming that "works of art derange the senses and generate unnatural desires" and that "any advance in sophistication and laws only creates more trouble" (Sarkassian 2010, 316-17), they pursued the ideal of the "uncarved block" (*pu* 朴) (Lee 2007, 601). This also involved a rejection of knowledge and critical awareness, achieved in the legendary age of He Xu 赫胥: "People stayed home but did not know what they were doing, walked around but did not know where they were going. Their mouths crammed with food, they were merry; drumming their bellies, they had a good time" (*Zhuangzi* 9; Watson 1968, 106; Sarkassian 2010, 220).

Believing that "we once lived in better balance not because we had better desires or better leadership but because we lacked the means to let our desires run amok and cause strife" (Sarkassian 2010, 322), the primitivists proposed a radical program of purging the world. They strove to obliterate all artifice and silence all those who promoted it, in other words, returning as closely as possible to Mesolithic conditions, recovering a time that was long gone but remained hidden and submerged in their subconscious memory.

Going even beyond this, Daoist recluses and immortality seekers pursued a time when human beings were not settled and did not practice agriculture, but lived off the land and were even more closely connected to nature. Unlike Confucian hermits who left society because they put personal integrity, health, and peace of mind before the demands of politics and society, Daoists pursued total independence, a state beyond harm, the freedom to wander wherever they pleased, easily and joyfully (Vervoorn 1984, 280; Berkowitz 1989, 101-03).

Leaving all civilization behind, they moved into the mountains, where wild animals and indigenous tribes roamed, seeking to follow simpler, even animal ways of life (Goh 2011, 118). Immortals, called *xian* 仙, a graph that shows a man next to a mountain, were closely associated with the untamed and threatening parts of the natural world. Living alone or in very small groups, always on the move in full alignment with the natural cycles and partaking of its most potent parts, they attained extended old age and strong vigor as well as all sorts of healing and exorcistic powers.

Seen from the perspective of prehistory, these Daoists reclaimed a time before settled communities and agriculture, when humans lived in small groups, roaming the land, hunting and gathering, and enjoying their lives—the Paleolithic. As both archaeological evidence of temporary settlements and anthropological fieldwork among modern hunter-gatherers document, the itinerant life was one of "pristine affluence" (Sahlins 1972, 29). Secure in a deep "trust in the abundance of nature's resources," people had few needs and minimal possessions, with lots of space to gather and hunt and play. There was plenty of food to go around, so that their workdays were short and interspersed with breaks and fun. They were tall, healthy, and long-lived, enjoying their small communities, yet also meeting with other bands at regular intervals to exchange news, goods, and marriage partners (Mithen 2004, 43; Christian 2008, 101).

Life was sweet—and there is every reason to be suspicious of civilization with its social organization, power structure, and repressive administration. Early Daoist recluses, therefore—and monastics and self-cultivation practitioners in their wake—chose to recover a golden age of the even more distant past, besting their community-centered fellows by another 5000 or so years. However, both have in common that they do not pursue an empty illusion but seek something humanity did in fact have at some time in history, working to recover a state that is rightfully ours. The roots of Daoism, in other words, go far beyond the Celestial Masters and the *Daode jing*, into the Stone Age, the early stages of humanity on earth.

Chapter One

The Stone Age

> In the most ancient of times birds and beasts were numerous while human beings were few. People built nests in trees to avoid them. During the day, they gathered acorns and chestnuts, at night they climbed back up into the top of the trees. For this reason, they are called the people of the nesting clan.
>
> Following this, in high antiquity, people knew nothing about clothes and garments. In the summertime, they would collect great piles of firewood to burn in the winter to keep warm. For this reason, they are called the people who knew how to live.
>
> In the age of the Divine Farmer, the people lay down peaceful and easy, woke up wide-eyed and blank. They knew their mothers but not their fathers, and lived side by side with the elk and the deer. They plowed for their food, wove for their clothing, and had no thought in their hearts of harming one another. This was perfect potency at its height! (*Zhuangzi* 29)[1]

The Stone Age began with the first use of tools, about 3.3 million years ago, encompassing the vast majority of human history.[2] Dominated by the use of stone for handiwork and construction, it ended around 2000, when metal became the main source of technology, leading in turn to the Bronze, Iron, and Steel Ages.

Shrouded in mystery for most of history, it has become much better known over the past few decades, mainly due to new methods and technologies in fieldwork and laboratory analysis. These include the systematic use of the flotation method in recovering macrofaunal and macrofloral remains; full-coverage regional survey methods in the study of settlement patterns—incorporating geoarchaeology, geographic information systems (GIS), and re-

---

[1] Similar passages are also found in other early texts, such as the *Huainanzi* 淮南子 (Book of the Master of Huainan; trl. Major et al. 2010), *Hanfeizi* 韓非子 (Book of Master Han Fei; trl. Liao 1959), and *Liji* 禮記 (Book of Rites; trl. Legge 1967). See Birrell 1993, 49; Campany 2005, 99-100.

[2] Schick and Toth 1993; 2013; Pettit 2011, 2.

mote sensing; mineralogical studies of archaic jade and other minerals; the development of interdisciplinary approaches such as zooarchaelogy, archaeobotany, and environmental archaeology; as well as the application of advanced laboratory technology such as the accelerator mass spectrometry dating method, genetic studies, and the specific analysis of phytoliths, starch, isotopes, and stone tools (Liu and Chen 2012, 19; Jones 2007, 13). More specifically, DNA and isotope ratio mass spectrometry allowing the sexing of skeletons and the tracing of genetic alleles (Bramanti 2013, 102) as well as the dating of materials and determination of food intake and age of weaning (Eriksson 2013, 126, 130, 135). In addition, scholars use methods of human behavioral ecology, analyzing the cost-benefit ratio of certain ways of dealing with the environment and food supplies (Shelach-Levi 2015, 65). Overall, this has led to an increasingly higher level of sophistication of study and more detailed appreciation of human prehistory.

Major Phases

The Stone Age is typically subdivided into two main periods, an old and a new, i. e., the Paleolithic and the Neolithic, the dividing line being the end of the last ice age around 9600 (Mithen 2004, 27; Bellwood 2005, 20). The transition involves "an economic transformation, in which people exploited food differently from hunting-gathering communities, including particularly the domestication of plants and animals. This new economic model further interrelates with a range of changes in tool technology, settlement patterns, and social organization" (Liu and Chen 2012, 46). The Neolithic, then, has transitional stages both before and after. They are the Mesolithic or Middle Stone Age, in some regions also called the Epipaleolithic or Late Old Stone Age, signifying the transition from old to new, and the Chalcolithic or Copper Age that marks the beginning of metal work and the transition to the Bronze Age.

Another way of dividing human history is into Paleolithic, Agrarian, and Modern. Here the criterion is not the kind of tools used but the main means of subsistence, i. e., hunting and gathering, farming, and manufacturing (Christian 2008, 99). The dividing lines are accordingly the beginning of sedentism and agriculture around 10,000 plus the Industrial Revolution in 1800 CE. This means, in terms of time, humanity has lived to 96 percent as hunter-gatherers, 4 percent by agriculture, and only very little through manufacturing (Cohen 1977a, 1; Lee and Devore 1968, 3). In terms of the total number of human beings ever alive, 80 billion all told, 12 percent were hunter-gatherers, 68 percent farmers, and 20 percent manufacturers (Christian 2008, 100).

Throughout their existence, humans have been amazingly ingenious, always making the best of the resources at hand. Accordingly, they moved at various speeds and through diverse technologies at different times. Thus, the so-called Neolithic Revolution, which involved becoming sedentary and developing agriculture, animal husbandry, and pottery (not necessarily in this order), occurred first in the Near East, in the so-called Fertile Crescent (Clark 2007, 37; Jones 2007, 143). It did not happen until later in Mesoamerica, partly due to geographical constraints (Diamond 1997). In Australia and various other, often tropical places, on the other hand, it never occurred, and indigenous people there have remained hunter-gatherers to the present day (Christian 2008, 118).

We now know that this was not because they did not know how to cultivate plants or tame animals, but because they *chose* to maintain this particular lifestyle (Harris 1977, 27). That is to say, the transition to agriculture was not inevitable, nor was it truly a "revolution," however much it changed the shape of life on earth (McBrearty and Brooks 2000). It was also, most definitely, not progress in many respects, such as quality of life, affluence, health, and life expectancy. Some even consider it "the worst mistake in the history of the human race" (Diamond 1987). Still, it dominated the world—to such a degree that the fundamental mode of food production did not change in any significant way until the 19th century, while the standard of living for peasants and workers continued to decline (Clark 2007, 1).

The Stone Age, in other words, laid the foundation for life on earth until very recently, providing both good and bad models for how to live.

Early Hominins

The first traces of the species *homo* go back to around 6 million years ago, a tiny drop in the huge bucket of the overall history of the earth of close to 14 billion (Leakey and Lewin 1977). The earliest hominins evolved from primates, eventually developing into as many as twenty different types (Corballis 2011, 182; Baumer 2012, 20). Known as *Australopithecus*, they were the first to walk upright and develop great throwing capability (Leakey 1994, 24). With a body height of 1.1 to 1. 4 meters and a brain capacity of about 450 cc, they shared sensory, bodily, and brain systems with all mammals.[3]

Early hominins were vegetarians.[4] They tended to congregate and live in bands of about thirty members, formed as "a genetic adaptation for protection against predators."[5] In that, they matched primates who clearly show group integration. "A thirsty baboon, for example, does not leave the group and go seeking water; it is the whole group that moves or none. Thirst is satisfied within the patterned activity of the group. And so it is with other needs and situations" (Jaynes 1990, 127).

---

[3] Toth and Schick 2005, 59. See also Anderson 2005, 14-15; Montagu 1965, 48; Wightman 2015, 139-41.

[4] Barnicot 1969, 526. See also Hart and Sussman 2005, 227; Schmid 2015, 18; Schoeninger et al. 2001, 182; Teaford and Ungar 2000.

[5] Jaynes 1990, 126. See also Anderson 2005, 16; Birdsell 1968, 235; Franks 2010, 25; trout 2011, 101; Petzinger 2016, 75; Williams 1968, 131.

Prehistoric humans as much as primates today lived in a state of constant vigilance, lest they be hunted and devoured by hundreds of species of predators—big cats, hyenas, bears, venomous snakes, birds of prey, and more.[6] Highly attuned to environmental change, they could feel—and immediately react to—changes as they occurred (Lee 1979, 117). Thus even today, animals are alert when predators draw near, get nervous before an earthquake, seek higher ground before a tsunami, gather more food when a particularly cold winter approaches, and so on. Their behavior is instinctual and, in modern terms, highly intuitive. Paying attention largely to the here and now, early hominins, too, worked on an energetic level of immediacy, bypassing complex processing and without recourse to conscious awareness (Franks 2010, 25).

The main reason they did not perish under the numerous threats lies in their unique coping strategies: developing larger size, bipedalism, vocalization, intelligence, threat behavior, and group coordination (Hart and Sussman 2005, 165, 173). The first creature generally regarded as properly human is *Homo habilis*, representing a slightly more technologically advanced group than the Australopithecines. Emerging after the receding of an ice age about 2.3 million years ago, they used Oldowan stone tools found over much of Africa, the Near East, Asia, and Europe.[7] More scavengers than hunters, they stood about 1.5 meters tall, had brains of about 800 cc, and lived in slightly larger groups.[8]

While they continued to plod along, a new evolutionary strain developed at 1.8 million years ago: *Homo ergaster*, the maker of the Acheulean stone tools. Archaeological evidence suggests that these early humans lived as hunter-gathers and had some control over fire.[9] Being able to cook food, they scavenged and hunted animals and became partial meat eaters, as documented in the Nariokotome hominid (Noble and Davidson 1996, 174, 213). As a result, they gained a great deal of energy and underwent various genetic mutations. Their jaws and teeth grew smaller (Teaford et al. 2002, 145), they developed greater hand coordination, and their digestive tract shrank (Noble and Davidson 1996, 218; Foley 2001, 322). "In fact, modern man has a 60 percent shorter digestive tract than predicted for a great ape of our size" (Gazzaniga 2008, 89; see also Anderson 2005, 16).

---

[6] Hart and Sussman 2005, chs. 4-7; Trout 2011, 31-60; Valkenburgh 2001.

[7] Christian 2008, 86. See also Anderson 2003, 12-13; Gibson 2007, 73; Lake 1998, 134-36; Petzinger 2016, 25; Toth and Schick 2005, 61.

[8] Anderson 2005, 19; Anton 2013, 500; Corballis 2011, 192; Greenspan and Shan-ker 2004, 141; Montagu 1965, 75; Outram 2007, 41.

[9] On early man and fire, see Bellah 2011, 84; Gamble 2007, 233; Jaynes 1990, 129; Jones 2007, 77-79; Hart and Sussman 2005, 224; Marshack 1991, 112-13; Noble and Diamond 1996, 205-06; Silk 1993, 221; Teaford and Ungar 2000; Walter 2006, 50-51; Watts 2014, 215; Wrangham 2009; Zihlman 2013, 28. The active use of fire, beyond general control, dates back about 350,000 years.

They also developed a larger brain of 1100 cc, combined with a higher forehead and flatter face, but were as yet without a prefrontal cortex.[10] As calculated from skeletal remains, they grew to heights of up to two meters (over 6 feet), and their females expanded to allow for giving birth to the larger heads.[11] Born earlier, infants were more helpless, requiring more care, so that overall "social connectivity increased" (2004, 218; Franks 2010, 27; Montagu 1965, 122). This connectivity also led to cooperative child care, in contrast to apes, who never let anyone else handle their infants, opening the path to greater social flexibility and cultural specialization.[12]

Another early group that was human but not a direct forerunner of *Homo sapiens*—with whom they intermingled and share four percent of genetic material—was the Neanderthals.[13] They lived from about 300,000 to 40,000 years ago, like all Paleolithic people mostly under ice-age conditions—so that the most ancient word for summer in northern Europe literally means "thaw time" (Barber 1994, 47). Similarly tall and with a rather large brain, they left the so-called Mousterian stone tools behind, including also in various Central Asian sites, but show little variation or adaptation in technology, still dominantly shaping their tools by reduction, i.e., "making a functioning form by reducing or lessening the mass of a natural material.[14]

Although neither of these early humans had speech, it is quite likely that they evolved beyond instinctual reactions common to all mammals and created a variety of complex signals, sounds, or memes (Jones 2007, 60), leading over time to increasingly sophisticated systems of mimetics. The foundation of language, this is a form of "attention manipulation" compounded into a complicated system of signs and symbols.[15] It can still be observed among Pygmys and the !Kung San today and serves as an essential communication tool in their immediate-return society, where people use objects and food the very day they produce them.[16]

Mimetics, moreover, activates the same processing centers in the brain for comprehending distinctions and creating meaning as spoken and written language. These are particularly Broca's area for speech creation and Wernecke's

---

[10] Franks 2010, 27. See also Foley 2001, 312; Petzinger 2016, 29; Walter 2006, 103; Watts 2014, 211.

[11] Greenspan and Shanker 2004, 139. See also Pechenkina, Ma, and Fan 2013, 450; Silk 1993, 223.

[12] Power 2014, 200-01; Baumer 2012, 22; Zihlman 2013, 33.

[13] Anderson 2014, 17. See also Baumer 2012, 24; Christian 2008, 95; Cochran and Harpending 2009, 61; Gamble 1999, 423-24; Harvati-Papatheodorou 2013, 547; Jones 2007, 75-93; Kimura 2015, 36; Pettit 2011, ch. 5; Petzinger 2016, 37; Pfeiffer 1982, ch. 6; Svoboda 2015, 25.

[14] Oswalt 1982, 61; see also Baumer 2912, 27; Christian 2008, 95; Pettitt 2005, 125; Speth anfd Tchernov 2001, 53, 68.

[15] Tomasello 1999, 133; Corballis 2011, 161-65; Christian 2008, 92.

[16] Lee 1979, 118; Lawlor 1991; Lewis 2014.

area for language reception (Joordens 2011, 56). In other words, as early humans, primed by expanded brain capacity, developed a complex mimetic system, they also primed themselves for the development of speech (Walter 2006, 89; Ardila 2009, 160).

Homo Sapiens

Speech, one of the major factors to distinguish humans from primates, first evolved with *Homo sapiens*, who split from other early humans about 500,000 years ago and whose first clear manifestation appears in *Homo helmei*, dated to 250,000 years ago and signaling the beginning of the Upper Paleolithic (Christian 2008, 97). As found in the Blombos Cave in South Africa, these humans made delicate stone tools, undertook complex hunts, adapted to their environment by expanding their diet to include shellfish, and used ochre coloring on their bodies, signifying body awareness and possibly ritual activity.[17]

Homo sapiens is the source "from which all modern genetic mitochondria descend" (Cavalli-Sforza 2000, 79), originating in Africa and spreading over the world in several migratory waves (Kimura 2015, 38-39; Collard and Dembo 2013, 558). With rounder skulls, higher foreheads, and receding jaws, they also had an enlarged pharynx, a cone-shaped 4.5" long cavity behind the nose and mouth, which allowed the larynx or voice box to drop.[18] This in turn made the formation of subtler sounds possible and gave rise to early orality, i. e., more complex oral signals developing from intentional calls in imitation of natural sounds. These were particularly necessary due to the darkness of the European caves—and of the fourth ice age—which replaced the open brightness of the African savannas.[19]

Humans gradually modified sounds to signal specifically whether a given danger was near or far, big or small, required immediate or delayed action. Over thousands of years, these particular calls became standardized within a given group. They also, through epigenetic transmission and biological evolution, established themselves in particular areas in the brain, thus gradually forming part of the fundamental make-up of humanity.[20]

Eventually sounds and signals developed into more intricate language. "Language dramatically extends the possibility-space for interaction, facilitates the profiling and navigation of joint attentional scenes, enables the sharing of

---

[17] Pettitt 2005, 132, 143. See also Baumer 2012, 29; Cochran and Harpending 2009, 35; Kuhn and Stiner 2007, 45; McBrearty and Brooks 2000; Outram 2007, 42; Petzinger 2016, 58-66; Watts 2014.

[18] Walter 2006, 90; Ardila 2009, 163; Christian 2008, 94; Hart and Sussman 2005 185. The same still happens in infants between two and four months of age (Huber 2007, 61).

[19] Greenspan and Shanker 2004, 157; Mithen 2006, 246. Tomasello 1999, 3.

[20] Dor and Jablonka 2014, 21. See also Cochran and Harpending 2009, 26-27; Jaynes 1990, 133; Pagel 2012, 280.

situation models and action plans, and mediates experimental the cultural shaping of interacting minds" (Dor and Jablonka 2014, 26). Expanding the ability for symbolic thinking (Mellars 2015, 14), this led to a new level of culture as seen in drawings of animals in caves, such as those at Altamira, Lascaux, and Vogelherd, and stone statues of human figures, such as the Lion Man of Hohlenstein and the Venus of Willendorf (Cochran and Harpending 2009, 38-39). Dated to 40,000—although early traces of advanced tools, body ornamentation, and pictographic art go back much further, as far as 230,000—these are related to the rise of modern humans or Cro Magnon man, an event commonly called the Human Revolution or "creative explosion."[21]

"The most fundamental change in human behavior that the archaeological record may ever reveal,"[22] it came with a rapid spread of human populations into farther reaches of the planet (Petzinger 2016, 75) and manifested in an increased frequency of blade production, extensively shaped bone and antler tools, the use of perforated animal teeth, and the appearance of marine shells, traded in wider-ranging distribution networks (Gamble 2007, 170-74). For the first time, there are extensive personal ornaments as well as instances of complex, naturalistic art (Mellars and Stringer 1989, 9).

Marking the beginning of the Upper Paleolithic—divided into the Aurignacian (30-20,000) and the Magdalenian (20-9,000)—the period also saw greater group cooperation) and the appearance of new tools and technologies.[23] For the first time, people created tools by conjunction, "combining two or more technounits to create a compound or complex form," such as adding a shaft to a stone to make an ax. Around 13,000, moreover, they began to form tools by replication and linkage, i. e., "crafting two or more separate structural units that were nearly identical in form and adding them as one part to other units" (Oswalt 1982, 61). This, moreover, allowed the combination of several independent units to function together, such as bow and arrow (Mellars 1989, 351; Otterbein 2004, 63-64).

With enhanced technology, humans improved their hunting and came to consume a greater amount of meat.[24] This in turn led to genetic changes evident from the same period, notably the mutation of the MCPH1 gene that regulates brain size and of the FOXP2 gene in chromosome 7, responsible for

[21] Baumer 2012, 28. See also Cauvin 2000, 13; Clottes and Courtin 1996, 63; Gamble 2007, ch. 2; Keeley 1996, 37; Mellars 2007, 4-5; Pfeiffer 1982, 13, 40; Svoboda 2015, 29; Wightman 2015, 232. The earliest female figure is a rock engraving found in a cave in Berekhat Ram, Israel, and dated to 230,000 (Petzinger 2016, 34). Use of ochre as body ornamentation similarly goes back to 160,000, as found in the cave at Pinnacle Point in South Africa (2016, 43).

[22] Klein 1999, 524. See also Cochran and Harpending 2009, 29; Greenspan and Shanker 2004, 167-70; Jaynes 1990, 133; Lieberman 1989; Montagu 1965.

[23] Chase 1989, 323; Mellars 1989, 339-41; Pfeiffer 1982, 42-47.

[24] Schmid 2015, 19. See also Hart and Sussman 2005, 230; Steward 1968, 325.

speech production.[25] Increased brain capacity and a new level of language development not only enhanced people's ability to think about things as separate, but also gave rise to initial forms of memory.

Language in due course came to modulate sensory experience and related processing, determining how humans thought, the particular way they conceived and classified the world (Boroditsky 2009, 119). As a result, even today people from different cultures pay attention to different sets of distinctions, see colors differently, and envision the flow of time as vertical or horizontal, thick or thin, big or small. Some cultures even have no words for "right" and "left," using geographical directions instead (2009, 121-24). Gendered nouns create different perceptions of objects, such as a perfectly ordinary "key" being seen as hard, heavy, and jagged by German speakers and as intricate, lovely, and shiny by Spanish natives (2009, 127).

Paleolithic perceptions at the time of the Human Revolution are best documented in early cave art, which indicates a new level of overall awareness, a new acculturation of self and environment.[26] Beads and other ornaments—pierced or perforated animal teeth, ivory and bone fragments, stones and shells, some from longer distances away (Mellars 2015, 13; Sørensen 2000, 195)—came to be used as pendants or attachments on clothing. Besides extensive rock art and murals of hunters and animals, first full human figures appeared, such as the Venus of Willendorf, Germany, and various statues found in France.[27] Contrary to stereotyped visions of the caveman or "other" as hairy and unkempt, only few men among the figures show facial hair and women commonly possess elaborate hairdos (Berman 1999, 292-93; McIntosh 2006, 340), indicating that early humans took good care of themselves.

Paleolithic Life

Equipped with basic memory, able to communicate, socially aware, and personally caring, people in the Upper Paleolithic lived in small bands, surviving by combining hunting and fishing with foraging for various plant foods (Cohen 1977a, 27). This is evident both from archaeological excavations (Binford et al. 1983) and the linguistic analysis of the most ancient vocabulary surviving today, studied in particular by Björn Collinder for Uralic languages (1977; see Barber 1994, 47-51).

According to this, Paleolithic people had a wide variety of tools, made from wood, grass, vines, and bone—including nets, baskets, and cradles (Barber 1994, 48; Oakley 1967)—as well as elementary forms of pottery. The oldest

---

25 Ardila 2009, 167; Cochran and Harpending 2009, 63; Corballis 2011, 70-72; Pagel 2012, 277; Petzinger 2016, 175.

26 Sørensen 2000, 193, 196. See also Barber 1994, 42; Eller 2002, 121; White 1989.

27 Goodison and Morris 2013, 266-67; Markale 1999, 51; Petzinger 2016, 94-96; Pfeiffer 1982, 9.

ceramic fragments, part of human figurines, go back to 25,000, found at Dolní Věstonice in the Czech Republic.[28] The earliest parts of pottery vessels were discovered in a cave in Hunan called Yuchanyan 玉蟾岩, dating back to about 18,000, followed closely by shards from the Japanese Jōmon culture.[29] Made from clay and only lightly fired, they were not very hard or durable, but easily discarded and refashioned—used for cooking rather than storage.

Beyond this, people applied stone to a plethora of purposes. While early tools, dating back well over two million years, were made by breaking off the edges of stone cores to create crude points or rough cutting surfaces, late Paleolithic hunters "had achieved total control over the process of fracturing, chipping, and shaping crystalline rocks." The "master stoneworkers of all times," they produced, among others, "finely chipped 'laurel leaf' knives, eleven inches long but only four-tenths of an inch thick, that cannot be duplicated even by modern industrial techniques" (Harris 1977, 9).

Using these tools, they created a lifestyle that provided them with "high standards of comfort and security" (1977, 9). They made artificial shelters, often set in shallow pits and covered densely with animal-skins—traces of which remain in southern Russia and the Czech Republic (1977, 10). They lived to a large extent on animal protein, as shown by Paleolithic kill sites that contain enormous quantities of animal bones, the remnants of vast herds of mammoth, horses, deer, reindeer, and bison that roamed across Europe and Asia, the so-called Pleistocene megafauna (1977, 10, 23).

Their main habitat was the forest steppe, the dominant landscape during the ice age, consisting of "grasses, shrubs, and flowers growing lushly below thinly scattered trees." In addition to animals, it offered an immense diversity of plant foods, including "the wild relatives of the first domesticated crops: wheat, barley, peas, lentils, and flax," as well as fruits, berries, seeds, and nuts (Mithen 2004, 21). Adding fish and shellfish as well as a variety of birds and mushrooms to this mix, often made into stews, soups, and porridge, Paleolithic people consumed a varied and healthy diet.[30]

They lived on wild, lean animal foods, with quite a high protein intake (Conklin-Brittain et al. 2002, 70; Milton 2002, 112). All their carbohydrates came from nonstarchy wild fruits and vegetables, while their main fats were healthful, monounsaturated, polyunsaturated, and omega-3. They ate no dairy and hardly ever cereal grains. Nor did they need to salt their food, since most of it came from animals. If they had a sweetener, it was in the form of wild

---

[28] Bolger 3013b, 168; Joyce 2008, 6-7; Petzinger 2016, 105.

[29] Liu and Chen 2012, 59, 68. See also Barnes 2015, 93; Aikens 1995; Oswalt 1982, 62; Tsutsumi 2002, 242; Yan 2002, 154.

[30] Cochran and Harpending 2009, 33. See also Barber 1994, 49; Dunn 1968, 223; Lawlor 1991, 60; Mithen 2004, 24; Sahlins 1972, 18; Yudkin 1969, 548.

honey, a rare delicacy.[31] This provided them with ample nourishment. "Median food consumption in contemporary foraging societies is 2,340 kilocalories per day, implying that hunter-gatherers and subsistence agriculturists ate as many calories as the median person in England or Belgium circa 1800 CE. Primitive man ate well compared with one of the richest societies in the world in 1800—people typically had less protein and much less variety" (Clark 2007, 51).

As a result, they were muscular and fit and grew tall in stature, to about 6 feet (180 cm) and showed no tooth decay or any signs of major ailments.[32] "The medical evidence shows that their body fat, aerobic fitness, blood cholesterol, blood pressure, and insulin metabolism are always superior to that of the average modern couch potato" (Cordain 2011, 6). This holds true also for isolated and indigenous communities today, as documented in the work of Weston Price (1870-1948), a dentist from Ontario who traced dental issues to dietary habits. Studying fourteen different groups, including Lötschental Swiss, Scottish Gaels, New Zealand Maoris, Canadian Inuit, Australian aborigines, and more, he found that, despite using widely varying cuisines, they all had excellent health, straight teeth, clear vision, and good posture, and were highly socially adept, with little or no aggression.[33]

Similarly, "the Tahitians of 1760, still in the Stone Age, seem to have been as tall, or taller, than their English visitors with all their marvelous European technology. Polynesians in the period before contact with the outside world were tall by preindustrial standards" (Clark 2007, 60-61). Living in an economy without metals, the Polynesians fashioned fishhooks from bone or coral, fought with wooden clubs, and made canoes from tree trunks by using fire and stone axes. "There was little or no earthenware. There was no system of writing. Cloth was made from tree bark, but little clothing was required in the equatorial climate" (2007, 61). Still, as much as their Paleolithic forebears, they were perfectly healthy, strong, vigorous, and free from deformations, malaria, infections, or other debilitating diseases.

Their life expectancy was short, around 35 years, but their life was joyful and largely stress-free (Harris 1977, 14; Lawlor 1991, 60). Living in areas rich in natural resources and moving every so often in alignment with the seasons and the migratory patterns of animals, they only needed to work about four hours a day.[34] Even this work was relatively leisurely: not physically demanding, it commenced at ease, involved diverse tasks, and was punctuated by frequent

---

31 Cordain 2011, 10-11, 28. See also Anderson 2005, 24; Eaton et al. 20002, 13; McIntosh 2006, 347; Schmid 2015, 19.

32 The average height of skeletons found in Upper Paleolithic caves in France and Italy (dated to 25,000), is around 6 feet, many being taller. Their muscular insertions show that they possessed ample vigor and power, their lower limbs being more developed than the upper (Clottes and Courtin 1996, 44).

33 Price 1989, 14, 419, 452; Schmid 2015, 26-28, 62-63.

34 Harris 1977, 11; Cohen 1977a, 30; Lawlor 1991, 65; Lee 1979, 259.

breaks and play—more like a picnic outing than a work gang.[35] Off-time, moreover, also allowed for ritual and social activities, involving music, dance, story-telling, and the like—reflecting that early life was "not merely subsistence but enmeshed in complex social and ritual behavior" (Asouti and Fuller 2013, 331).

This still holds true for the ninety-six groups of hunter-gatherer societies surviving today. They include most prominently the !Kung San in Botswana, the Hazda in Tanzania, the Yanomamo in the Amazon jungle, as well as various aboriginal tribes in Australia.[36] As anthropological documentation shows, their foraging mode of production has five distinct characteristics: (1) overall mobility over a rather wide area; (2) limited group size; (3) flexible social structures; (4) limited wealth and possessions; and (5) clear rules about access to resources (Lee 1979, 117).

Generally, using homespun products, their wants are easily satisfied, their resources free to take, their tools common, their knowledge equal, and their division of labor simple.[37] Living a life predicated on abundance, they feast on whatever they hunt or gather in a given day, free from "the market obsession of scarcity"—a post-agricultural invention—and without the urgency to accumulate or hoard.[38] Whether then or now, land belongs to all, and "to the hunter, wealth is a burden" (Sahlins 1972, 11). Without even a word for "ownership" (Lawlor 1991, 237, 383), primitive cultures find the amassing of material possessions detrimental. Everything has to be mobile, light-weight, and portable as well as easily fashioned from commonly available materials.[39] Since movement "rapidly depreciates the satisfactions of property" (Sahlins 1972, 11), hunter-gatherers are extremely apt at making any sort of tool on the spur of the moment. They can build shelters quickly and efficiently and collapse or condense their belongings at a moment's notice (Lawlor 1991, 64-65). They have few possessions and maintain a low standard of living, but they are certainly not poor or deprived, rather following the "Zen road to predicated affluence."[40]

---

[35] Sahlins 1972, 17-18, 30; Lawlor 1991, 308; Lee 1979, 120, 156; Mountford 1960, 2:150.
[36] For a comprehensive list, see Keeley 1995, 250-53. On these specific groups, see Bunn 2001; Lee 1979; Marlowe 2010; O'Connell et al. 2002; Woodburn 1968a; 1968b; Schwartz and Englebert 1995. For Australia, see Grey 1841; Lawlor 1991; Mountford and Specht 1960.
[37] Sahlins 1972, 10; Cohen 1977a, 31; Ridley 1997, 93.
[38] Sahlins 1972, 2, 7. See also Fabbro 1978, 81; Fried 1967, 34; Kelly 2000, 16; Mithen 2004, 31; Otterbein 2004, 78.
[39] Lee 1979, 119; Pfeiffer 1982, 157; Washburn and Lancaster 1968, 298.
[40] Sahlins 1972, 2, 37. While this is the dominant tendency, there is also evidence that some hunter-gatherer societies develop a certain degree of social complexity, working toward the establishment of social status and accumulation of wealth. For examples in Japan and North America, see Koyama and Thomas 1981.

Social Structure

This emphasis on mobility and lightness of possessions requires the consideration of "diminishing returns at the margins of portability, minimum necessary equipment, and elimination of duplicates" (Sahlins 1972, 34). While not entirely precluding basic dominance structures and incipient social complexity (Price and Brown 1985, 12), it typically manifests in two major social facets, key characteristics of Paleolithic life: population control and egalitarianism.

Population control satisfies two requirements. For one, women need to be able to move around, both to gather food and to move camp, and they can only carry one infant at a time without exhausting themselves (Barber 1994, 76). For another, any increase in overall population would throw the delicate equilibrium between human consumption and nature's provisions out of balance and endanger the entire group (Mithen 2004, 47; Clark 2007, 79).

To resolve this dilemma, hunter-gatherers today extend their breast-feeding period to prevent conception and have babies only once every 4-5 instead of 1-2 years.[41] Lessening the fertility rate of women, this also maintains their health and stabilizes the population (DiCosmo 2002, 23). Beyond that, they practice abortion and infanticide, using a "large repertory of chemical and mechanical means" to lessen the overall birth rate and thereby reduce fertility and limit population growth (Harris 1977, 15; Lawlor 1991, 163). While this is not a dominant method for the most part, in 19th-century Polynesia, "between two-thirds and three-quarters of all children born were killed immediately by suffocation, strangulation, and breaking of the neck" (Clark 2007, 109-10).

At the other end of the life cycle, mobile hunter-gatherers cannot afford to carry the sick, the old, and the dying, and accordingly practice geronticide (Birdsell 1968, 237; Dunn 1968, 225). Thus, for example, among the Murngin of the Australian aborigines, old people "are being treated as if they were already dead when they become sick; the group begins to perform its last rites, and the old person responds by getting sicker" (Harris 1977, 16).

The other social consequence of mobility and portability is egalitarianism. While there tends to be some division of labor according to gender among contemporary hunter-gatherers—men hunting, women gathering—this is neither pervasive nor evaluative (Sahlins 1972, 35, 95; Lee 1979, 118). That is to say, a strong, muscular, vibrant woman may well go out hunting while a slim, weaker man might join the gatherers. It also means that "women's work" is no less important or valued lower than that commonly done by men (Christian 2008, 101).

---

[41] Cohen 1977a, 43-44. See also Harris 1977, 16; Huber 2007, 79; Lawlor 1991, 162; Lee 1979, 312. This, however, does not hold true for early hunter-gatherers. Contrary to common assumptions, as isotope radio mass spectrometry has shown, they breast-fed just as long as early farmers, to age two (Eriksson 2013, 130).

No accumulation, moreover, means that there is no social rank or supremacy built on material objects or possessions; on the contrary, a hunter who preserves his kill and hoards objects is considered incompetent and loses face. In other words, while hoarding is "technically feasible, it is economically undesirable and socially unachievable" (Sahlins 1972, 32). Nor does it make any sense to design, produce, and store fancy ornamental or ritual items beyond what can be easily used and carried. For all material goods—utensils, tools, clothes, and decorations—the basic rule applies: the fewer and smaller, the better. This leaves no room for self-aggrandizement through the possession of objects (Huber 2007, 99).

Besides leading to a pervasive lack of dominance and coercion in leadership and a tendency toward anarchism (Cochran and Harpending 2009, 105), this also eliminates a major reason for conflict and war. So does the overall tendency toward "maximum dispersion" (Sahlins 1972, 97), the "absence of sharply defined territorial boundaries" (Harris 1977, 34). Still, bands came in contact with each other, not only holding regular gatherings and exchanges (Christian 2008, 101), but also to engage in battle—verbal and physical (Lee 1979, 371). Intergroup violence was common, as evidenced by mutilated and severed skulls dating back half a million years as well as in early depictions of killed or injured men.[42] Since even primates, especially males, engage in aggressive behavior and kill each other on a regular basis, it is not surprising that "foragers were inveterate raiders" and often set up combat between selected champions.[43]

As Gregory Clark notes, "In the mobile forager societies there were heightened risks of death from encounters with dangerous animals, drowning, thirst, and falls. But homicide was an even more common killer than such accidents. Despite romantic notions of the noble savage, violent conflict within and between bands of foragers seems to be frequent" (2007, 124). He points out further that death by homicide per 1000 was 1.4 in Neolithic France but 15.0 among the modern Ache tribe (1900-1970) and in New Guinea hovered around 7.0. In contrast, in 1999, it lay at 0.07 in the United States and 0.01 in England (2007, 125).

Still, Paleolithic violence was a far cry from proper war, i. e., infantry battles and mass slaughters executed by professional, state-run military forces on the basis of organized "unit training, hierarchical subordination, and physical compulsion" (Keeley 1996, 42; Otterbein 2004, 5). As described for aborigines in northern Australia, two hostile groups might line up at daybreak across a clearing. They hurled insults and shouted obscenities at each other, then individuals came forward and threw spears, usually with "highly inaccurate marksmanship." If someone got hurt, often "some innocent noncombattant or one

[42] Cochran and Harpending 2009, 104; Clottes and Courtin 1996, 157; Penchenkina et al. 2013, 315)

[43] Keeley 1996, 29, 46; Otterbein 2004, 3; Wrangham and Peterson 1996.

of the screaming old women who weaved through the fighting men," all hostilities stopped until this new situation could be assessed, then the process resumed (Harris 1977, 35). Not only small in overall scale, therefore, combat was not continuous but would be interrupted for food procurement to prevent general famine—what we today call humanitarian reasons (Keeley 1996, 44).

End of an Era

Hunting and gathering in the Paleolithic was relatively easy, allowing a way of life oriented toward quality and sufficiency. It provided low living standards, yet was full of leisure and social interaction—simple but not poor. While it lasted many thousands of years, it came to an end after the last ice age, due to a variety of factors.

The first is climate change, predicated by the rotating orientation of the earth to the sun, generally responsible for a reduction in the strength of the magnetic field (Lawlor 1991, 125) and the increase of greenhouse gases, volcanic activities, and atmospheric and oceanic currents (Baumer 2012, 17). After the last glacial maximum around 20,000, when temperatures barely reached over 10^0 C (50^0 F) in the summer, the climate gradually became milder, with a major trend toward warmer and wetter seasons starting around 12,500 (Bellwood 2005, 20; Cochran and Harpending 2009, 67). This ended around 11,000, leading to another cold and dry period known as the Younger Dryas, which lasted until 9,600, the date marking the end of the Paleolithic.[44]

Warmer climate meant that steppe changed toward woodland with luscious undergrowth, encouraging the growth of fruit trees, wild cereals, and various vegetables (Guilday 1967, 125; Wright 1977). It also meant the rise of sea and river levels due to the collapse of the North American ice sheet and thus a widening of aquatic resources (Mithen 2004, 48). At the same time, the Pleistocene megafauna lost its habitat and moved toward colder regions. As Mark N. Cohen says, "It is well established that the open tundra environment of Pleistocene Europe was gradually replaced by more closed forest vegetation after the retreat of the last glaciation. [This also meant the] decline or migration of the large herds of reindeer and other species which had provided the subsistence base for Paleolithic hunters" (1977a, 126).

Another factor is demographics or population growth. Mitochondrial DNA analysis shows a great rate of maternal linage expansions at the time (Wang et al. 2016, 1), so that humans, in a process of continuous extensification (Christian 2008, 105), came to spread over the entire planet and reached

---

[44] Cohen 1977a, 30; Baumer 2012, 40; Bellwood 2005, 52; Cauvin 2000, 12; Higham 1995, 127. The period is named after a plant, *Dryas octopetala.* A low, downy perennial, it today grows in the mountains, but during cold, dry periods spreads everywhere—characterizing ice-age conditions. The last ice age is accordingly known as the Older Dryas (Jones 2007, 142).

even the Arctic Circle. As a result, they required larger quantities of food to maintain life (Edwards 1967, 146; Cohen 1977a, 41). The third factor is cultural: human over-exploitation, particularly in Europe and Asia. Greatly improved hunting techniques—better weapons, stronger group coordination, more sophisticated control of fire (Edwards 1967, 149; Cohen 1977a, 127)—and more people to feed meant mass killings of big game, documented in extensive sites with massive piles of animal bones (1977a, 122, 133; Otterbein 2004, 66-67).

Combined with a reduction in feeding grounds due to climate change, this resulted in the extinction of over 200 species of big game, typically animals over 50 kilograms in weight, needing long periods of gestation, and dependent on other species for food.[45] Thus, North America lost its entire population of elephants, yaks, mammoths, camels, tapirs, ground sloths, pronghorn, mountain goats, giant beavers, and more (Guilday 1967, 125; Cohen 1977a, 181-82). 70 percent of all large Australian mammals—including giant versions of kangaroos, wombats, and possums—became extinct (Christian 2008, 106; Lawlor 1991, 125). Africa, on the other hand, being closer to the equator and not as affected by magnetic field changes, suffered less severe climate restrictions. As a result, it continued to provide abundant sources of vegetable food and was not impacted as strongly, so that large game still survives today (Jelinek 1967, 193).

Known as the Pleistocene overkill, this change signals the "terminal Pleistocene extinction of migratory megafauna" (Harris 1977, 23). Observable in many regions, it had a widespread "tendency to alter economic strategies and promote sedentism and population growth" (Cohen 1977a, 11). The following period, the Holocene or Mesolithic, saw "expanding forest binomes, hunting of solitary forest animals, as well as heavy dependence on small game, avifauna, and aquatic resources." These included "elk, aurochs, deer, and wild pigs as well as ducks, swans, grebe, coot, heron, cormorants, gulls, razorbills, and gannets," plus all kinds of aquatic life, even stranded whales (1977a, 122-24).

Sedentism

Having less large game to hunt and more vegetables and fruit to pick predicated economic shifts that "seem to have entailed increasingly sedentary behavior" (Newell 1973). In other words, rather than following herds of large game over an extended territory and living in temporary camps, people set up more permanent living quarters, typically on hillsides near rivers, lakes, or oceans. Sedentism afforded them several advantages: a reduced mobility strain, especially burdensome for mothers carrying children; a cut in labor cost associated with

[45] Martin 1967, 75. See also Christian 2008, 106; Pfeiffer 1982, 60-61; Slaughter 1967, 163. Pleistocene life was characterized by enormously large predators, from killer cats such as cave lions and sabre-tooth tigers through dire wolves, huge crocodiles, and giant fish to monster birds such as the teratorns and harpagornis (Trout 2011, 31-60).

transport; a reduction of danger and injuries on the road; as well as the opportunity to store food for leaner times and accumulate capital goods.[46]

Signaling the beginning of the Mesolithic, people at the time shifted their subsistence strategy from foraging to collecting—using terminology coined by Lewis Binford (1980). That is to say, when resources were plentiful, mobility was residential and people foraged, moving base camp frequently to cope with resource exhaustion at one location. When resources became more seasonal or were at times unavailable, mobility became logistic and people moved to collecting, sending out small, organized task groups to assemble food resources, which were then brought back to residential areas, processed, and stored for later use.[47]

Besides sending out parties of hunters to procure meat, people in the Mesolithic also made increasing use of boats to go further off-shore and increasingly processed nuts and seeds (Mithen 2004, 33; Nishida 2002, 232). Thus, in Europe the most important plant species was the hazelnut, while in China the acorn became a major staple (Cohen 1977a, 125; Jones 2007, 161). In the Near East, on the other hand, people began to harvest wild grains, efficiently using newly developed sickles. As Jack Harlan has shown (1967), even with a primitive sickle blade, people could harvest as much as one kilogram of edible grain per hour, being able to feed a family for one year with a mere three weeks' worth of work.[48]

Use of these resources "was for the most part *not* based on new technology, but rather signaled a shift in emphasis" (Cohen 1977a, 124). In other words, "sedentism was within the technological capability of man long before he adopted it as a way of life, . . . and large group aggregations were achieved in many parts of the world without agriculture, and often in fact without any evidence of significant new technology" (1977a, 37). Based on the increasingly intensive use of vegetable foods and coastal and river resources, sedentism became a necessity, maybe even a "necessary evil," since it also entailed cramped living, exposure to parasitic diseases as well as a restriction in the range of dietary resources, and often led to an increase in social disorder.[49]

The first people known to have adopted sedentism were the Natufians, a group centered in the Levant, in what is today Israel (Caldwell 1977, 78). Numerous villages spread through the area, best known among them being Ain Mallaha in the Jordan valley, excavated by Jean Perrot in 1954, and Hayonim on the Sea of Galilee, unearthed by Ofer Bar-Yosef in 1964.[50] They became sedentary during the first warming period around 12,500, living in wooded hills

---

[46] Cohen 1977a, 36; Cochran and Harpending 2009, 70.

[47] Cohen 1985, 103; Liu and Chen 2012, 45; Price and Brown 1985, 5-6.

[48] Cohen 1977a, 142; Shelach-Levi 2015, 61.

[49] Cohen 1977a, 37; 1985, 100. See also Bellwood 2005, 32.

[50] Bar-Yosef 2002, 44-46. See also Cauvin 2000, 15-21; Christian 2008, 120; Jones 2007, 130; Mithen 2004, 29, 32; Pettit 2011, 253.

above rivers and lakes (Keeley 1995, 268; Henry 1985, 371). Villages of over a hundred people contained numerous structures: dwellings, workshops, storage pits, and graves (Bellwood 2005, 51). Tools included stone mortars, bows and arrows, flint knives, and sickles; food involved a wide variety of vegetable and plant resources.[51]

Among animal remnants there are notably dogs, already domesticated around 20,000,[52] and gazelles—the latter killed at different times of the year and stages of their development, showing that they were gradually bred toward smaller stature (Mithen 2004, 47). Bones of rats, mice, and sparrows indicate the presence of refuse and vermin. Remnants of cereals and seeds show that they were well able to manage wild plans, had in fact begun active cultivation.[53]

In addition, burials reveal the presence of intricate ornaments, made from bones, clay, and fox teeth, as well as seashells from the distant Mediterranean Sea, presumably acquired from still mobile hunter-gatherers in exchange for food. Signaling wealth and power, these objects may indicate a gradual development of social stratification and the tendency toward accumulation (Mithen 2004, 33). However, villages tended to stick to themselves—a different site, only twenty kilometers away, shows similar material culture but a vast difference in genetics (2004, 32).

Natufian sites spread widely during the first warming—all through western Asia, the Arab peninsula, and the Euphrates valley—probably due to population pressure that led to groups splitting off and migrating elsewhere (Mithen 2004, 47). Seventy-four locations in the Levant and twenty-six in Anatolia are known today (Bellwood 2005, 51). However, their lifestyle did not last. With the beginning of the Younger Dryas around 11,000, colder and dryer weather came to dominate, the woodland died from lack of rain and warmth, and food resources receded. As a result, people abandoned their villages and returned to a foraging way of life—which also meant again a more portable and egalitarian society with no ornaments or seashells as status symbols (Mithen 2004, 48, 50).

---

[51] Mithen 2004, 32; Watson 1995, 29; Harlan 1977, 363.

[52] McIntosh 2006, 112. See also Barber 1994, 73; Mithen 2004, 35; Powers and Powers 1984, 48.

[53] Mithen 2004, 34, 36; Bar-Yosef and Kislev 1989, 634.

Chapter Two

Agriculture and Civilization

> The courts are exceedingly splendid
> While the fields are exceedingly weedy
> And the granaries are exceedingly empty.
> Elegant clothes are worn,
> Sharp weapons are carried.
> Food and drink are enjoyed beyond limit,
> Wealth and treasures accumulated in excess.
> (*Daode jing* 53)

Egalitarianism and freedom from accumulation ended permanently for most people with the beginning of civilization in the Neolithic, predicated on the development of agriculture. After the climate changed again, and more permanently, to a warmer level around 9600, various peoples in the Near East, including also the Natufians, settled down permanently and formed farming communities (Bellwood 2005, 51). In due course, they came to sustain as many as 4000 to 6000 people in one place, moving toward greater social complexity and expansive economic institutions (2005, 52). Other areas followed, changing the face of the earth and opening the path for technological and cultural progress.

Agriculture

A multi-layered complex of activities and factors,

> Agriculture is not a single unified concept or behavior, but a combination of behaviors, any one of which may be either inadvertent or purposeful. They include such things as the creation of clearings in which certain plants strive, the enrichment of soils, the planting of seeds, the irrigation of plants, the removal of competing species, the practice of conservation measures, the transporting of species beyond their original ecological boundaries, or the selection of preferred types. None of these behaviors alone constitutes agriculture; taken together they *are* agriculture. (Cohen 1977a, 23; see also Price and Gebauer 1995, 17)

Usually defined as the intentional control and modification of plants and animals into a symbiotic relationship with humans, agriculture is a form of *intensification* of production, enhancing the food yield per land area by as many as fifty to a hundred times beyond that reached by hinter-gatherers who use land *extensively*.[1] In addition, it provides increased predictability of food supplies, the option to explore a much greater variety of food sources, and ways of experimenting with new and different ways of treating food and other material objects, such as tools, pottery, and ornaments (Shelach-Levi 2015, 66). Evolving gradually, agriculture depends on, yet is clearly distinct from, resource management, cultivation, and domestication.

More specifically, resource management is "any technique that propagates, tends, or protects a species, reduces competition, prolongs or increases the harvest, insures growth at a particular place and time, extends range, and modifies nature, density, or distribution" (Bellwood 2005, 12). It is not consciously planned, but done spontaneously, serving as a common way of dealing with nature and material reality.

Cultivation, on the other hand, is a conscious activity, a planned and intentional series of actions, usually done in close coordination with the seasonal cycles. Most obvious in gardening or horticulture, it involves a clear sequence of human activity in a prepared plot: sow, plant, protect, harvest, and sow again (Bellwood 2005, 13). Domestication, in turn, a development of cultivation, is yet different in that it morphologically changes the plant (or animal) away from its wild phenotype, often making it dependent on humans in a symbiotic relationship (Barber 1994, 74). Domesticated animals thus show indisputable signs of human control and breeding: food on the hoof (Barber 1994, 75), they are usually smaller and more compliant than their wild counterparts (Bellwood 2005, 14) or, as David Christian puts it, increasingly "stupid, fat, and incapable of defense" (2008, 110).

Domestication appears when there are "indisputable signs of human control and breeding" (Bellwood 2005, 13). It can be unintentional or incidental, as a side effect of resource management. In that case, people may favor a plant or animal most pleasing or useful, leading to selection toward this type, which in turn causes evolution, i. e., genetic change (Watson 1995, 31; Rindos 1984, 184, 138-39). It can also be intentional or specialized, moving toward agroecology and transforming hunters into herders (Price and Gebauer 1995, 8). This means, people make the conscious choice to breed or cull particular members of a given species, thus developing a fundamentally different relationship with them. Agricultural domestication or agropastoral production, finally, occurs when plants and animals are fully adapted to human needs, giving rise to a clear symbiosis. "The relationship between people and plants undergoes a fundamental change" (Rindos 1984, 165; Asouti and Fuller 2013, 303).

---

[1] Harris 1977, 4; Christian 2008, 111; Cochran and Harpending 2009, 69; Lee 1979, 118.

Theories of Origination

How agriculture developed within a few thousand years of the end of the last glaciation is a hotly debated topic. While the development is one of great complexity and involves numerous aspects and dimensions (Price and Brown 1985, 8-9), scholars tend to focus on the same three factors that led to early sedentism—climate change, population growth, and cultural or technological transformation (Reed 1977, 885-88). Or, as Gideon Shelach-Levi puts it, the three factors were "push, pull, and social"—pressures due to climate change and a reduction in natural resources, the attraction of more efficient ways of feeding large populations, and the strife for prestige and culture (2015, 62). Another way of putting it is in terms of the cultural-ecological theory versus the socio-economic competition model (Liu and Chen 2012, 118). Different scholars place primary importance on different aspects (Watson 1995, 23-34).

To give some examples,[2] V. Gordon Childe (1951), who first coined the expression "Neolithic Revolution" in 1923, proposes the propinquity theory. An increasing desiccation after the ice age caused people to crowd together near water and seek out local plants and animals, which they duly managed, tamed, and domesticated. David Harris (1977), Herbert E. Wright (1977), and David Christian (2008), too, appreciate climate change in conjunction with population pressure as the key stimulant.

Robert Braidwood (1967) sees a geographic component in that the main area of first agriculture was the hilly flanks of the Near East, clearly showing signs of climate change in the early Holocene, but overall focuses more on cultural factors such as technology and environmental knowledge, whose growth allowed people to realize the full potential of local flora and fauna.

Lewis Binford (1968), Bennet Bronson (1977), Philip Wagner (1977), and Mark N. Cohen (1977a; 1977b; 1981) tend to emphasize the demographic issue of population growth. Semi-sedentary groups would increase in size, then fission before reaching regional capacity. The splinter groups further impinged on indigenous inhabitants outside of the optimum zone, putting pressure on food resources. Agriculture, then, developed on the fringes as a new method due to the need to find alternative ways of procuring food.

Kent Flannery (1969) basically agrees with this so-called marginality or edge hypothesis, noting that plant cultivation came about as a deliberate attempt to produce food artificially, around optimal zone margins. But he sees it also as part of a broad-spectrum revolution and emphasizes the eclectic nature

---

[2] For more summaries of key theories, see also Asouti and Fuller 2013, 299; Barker and Janowski 2011; Bellwood 2005, 21-23; Cohen 1977a, 7-10; Cohen 2002; Gamble 2007, ch. 1; Graeme and Janowski 1977, 1-2; Harris 1977; Huber 2007, 104; Pechenkina, Ma, and Fan 2013, 444; Otterbein 2004, 92-96; Price and Brown 1985; Price and Gebauer 1995, 4-5; Schelach-Levi 2015, 63-64; Yasuda 2002a.

of economies. Some, such as Carl Sauer (1952) and Richard and Patty Jo Watson (1969) see sedentism as a precondition for the development of agriculture. Others point out that in Mesoamerica people intentionally planted crops—corn, beans, squash, and manioc—yet remained mobile for several millennia (Harris 1977, 25; Christian 2008, 109). Their agriculture, moreover, stayed manual since there were no cattle or horses to pull plows, llamas being not suitable as draft animals (Diamond 1997).

Brian Hayden (1990; 1995; 2011) considers social elements as predominant, linking the purposeful accumulation of domesticates with prestige seeking by individual aggrandizers rather than with subsistence needs of the populace. In support, he emphasizes the fact that, "in many areas the first domesticate was a nonedible plant or specialty food, such as hemp, bottle gourd, chili pepper, cardamom, and other condiments. This suggests that early domesticated edible plants were prestige goods or luxury foods rather than subsistence materials and that competitive feasting for increase in status and prestige was the driving force behind the transition to farming."[3]

This holds particularly true for rice, which required enormous time and labor as well community organization and carried heavy cosmological implications.[4] Along a similar vein, Daron Acemoglu and James Robinson (2012)—and Niall Ferguson (2013) in their wake—claim that institutions were primal and preceded social and economic change, while Jacques Cauvin (2000) contends that cognitive and symbolic transformation was the primary mover.

Typical Development

There is today no question that agricultural knowledge is common among hunter-gatherers, and by extension was part of Paleolithic life (Graeme and Janowski 2011, 13). They all know the connection between seeds and plants (Flannery 1968, 68) and judge accurately which parts are edible when, and how best to process them. Being "expert ecologists" (Cohen 1977a, 22) and "superb botanists" (Lee 1979, 158), hunter-gatherers know very well how to propagate and manage plants to their best advantage, often imbuing them with symbolic or ritual significance.[5]

"Pre-agricultural men commonly created pathways, village clearings, dump heaps, and recently burned areas, which provided open habitats for colonization by new plants" (Anderson 1952, 36). They also often transported plants to other places, thus leading to cross-fertilization and genetic evolution (Ho 1969, 26). That is to say, systematic cultivation, and by extension agricul-

---

[3] Hayden 1995, 282. See also Liu and Chen 2012, 119; McCauley 1990, 17; Underhill 2002, 1.
[4] Graeme and Janowski 2011, 7; Hanks 1972, 53-54; Hayden 2011, 75-79; Ho 1969, 25-56. See also Lu 1999; Ohnuki-Tierney 1993.
[5] Asouti and Fuller 2013, 331. See also Bronson 1977, 30; Christian 2008, 102; Lawlor 1991, 311; Ridley 1997, 47.

ture, was not something newly discovered after the ice age but a choice people made due to particular circumstances (Lawlor 1991, 59). It was "about choosing to sow, not about learning that seeds grew into plants" (Anderson 2014, 33).

This choice, moreover, was secondary to sedentism. As recent excavations and paleobotanic studies have documented, "settled, well-fed life preceded agriculture" (2014, 33). Its development required a life in a prolonged period of peace, free from war in both its basic forms, i. e., hunter-gatherer raids and city-state siege operations (Otterbein 2004, 10-11). Disproving earlier assumptions, recent studies have conclusively shown that agriculture occurred first in plentiful, stable environments as opposed to marginal areas: here risk was affordable and people could experiment with new methods (Price and Gebauer 1995, 8).

In addition, recent research outlines the typical unfolding of these methods. Hunter-gatherers, having meat supply issues and facing population pressure, i. e., reaching their "carrying capacity" (Baumhoff 1981), tend to supplement their protein intake through nuts and seeds, processing them in a variety of ways (Matsuyama 1981). "The food quest becomes more diversified and more specialized—more diversified in the numbers of new species and habitats that are exploited and more specialized in terms of technology and organization of procurement activities" (Price and Brown 1985, 11). Narrowed geographically by competition, "niches broaden in the economic and technical sense" (Cohen 1985, 102).

Some, to stimulate plant growth, intentionally set fire to vegetation, moving from collecting to resource management. They then sow seeds to grow the cereals they desire—in fact developing a form of swidden or slash-and-burn agriculture.[6] This sequence is common enough to be a necessary but not sufficient condition for the development of agriculture. Moreover, it tends to occur in warmer climates: the higher the latitude, the less important plants are in the human diet and the more people rely on fish and meat (Keeley 1995, 249).

In other words, ecological productivity, annual precipitation, and population pressure are the three key factors for the beginning of agriculture. As local fertility decreases while there are more mouths to feed, people have "little choice but to intensify the use of plants" (1995, 249; Cohen 1985, 101). The greater the importance of plant food in their diet, moreover, the greater is the likelihood that they make ample use of seeds and use periodic fires to encourage growth (Keeley 1995, 250). People at this level of slash-and-burn, then, such as certain groups among Australian aborigines, are still socially egalitarian, with no accumulation, competitive feasting, expropriating classes, or heavy workloads (1995, 255; Lawlor 1991, 65). While population pressure is an important "kicker variable" that eventually leads to socioeconomic complexity, in the early stages "social demand is completely irrelevant" (Keeley 1995, 256-57).

6 Christian 2008, 106, 120; Hayden 2011, 80-81; Keeley 1995, 248; Lee 1979, 147.

Geographical Distribution

This changes later, as agriculture develops fully. According to some scholars, this occurred independently only in two prime locales, the Fertile Crescent in the Near East and Mexico in Mesoamerica—the remainder of the world receiving it by diffusion (Keeley 1995, 267). A few see the Near East as the single place of origin (Carter 1977), but most acknowledge three or four major areas of origination, also including China, as well as Africa and/or the Peruvian Andes.[7] Yet others acknowledge New Guinea as an independent location of agriculture, although the prime focus here is on tubers—sago, taro, yams—rather than grains, and there is no animal domestication.[8] All agree that certain areas remained without agricultural development, most importantly Australia, but also Japan. "Jōmon Japan presents a situation, in which maritime exploitation and the harvesting of nuts and tubers were generally so successful that cereal agriculture, while certainly not absent, was treated as something of an irrelevancy."[9]

In terms of timing, the Fertile Crescent came first, with clearly domesticated species beginning around 9000, followed by China around 8000, New Guinea around 4000, and Mesoamerica around 2000 (Christian 2008, 109). All other areas developed agriculture due to diffusion, a pattern clearly documented for Europe where it moved both east and west over several millennia, mostly along rivers.[10] More specifically, as borne out by genetic and linguistic evidence (see Bellwood and Renfrew 2002), farming reached Turkey in 6500, Greece in 6000, Romania in 5500, Hungary in 5400, and England in 4000. Moving east, it appears in the Caucasus and Pakistan by 7500, and is documented in the ancient city of Mehrgarh around 7000. From there, it reached northern India (Harappa) in 3500, eastern India in 3000, central India in 2000, and Sri Lanka around 1500.[11]

Each area, moreover, was unique in its geographical setting, and people accordingly domesticated different plants and animals, often combining the qualities of several wild variants into one plant.[12] In the Near East and in India, they included emmer, einkorn, wheat, barley, rye, peas, lentils, and chickpeas as

---

[7] Cohen 1977a, 23. See also Harlan 1977, 357; Otterbein 2004, 113; Outram 2007, 51; Wang et al. 2016, 1.

[8] Christian 2008, 109. See also Anderson 2014, 30; Bellwood 2005, 42; Barton and Denham 2011, 17; Fernandez-Armesto 2002, 79-81; Larsen 2002, 19.

[9] Bellwood 2005, 114. See also Higham 2005, 260; Barnes 2015, 103-14; Kotani 1981; Ohnuki-Tierney 1993, 31; Temple and Larson 2013.

[10] Childe 1958, 43. See also Barber 1994, 73; Cohen 1977a, 130-31; Jones 2007, 146-47; McIntosh 2006, 26.

[11] Bellwood 2005, 68-69; Harlan 1977, 371; Shinde 2002, 91-93.

[12] Asouti and Fuller 2013, 232; Cochran and Harpending 2009, 48.

well as goats, sheep, pigs, and cattle.[13] Chinese agriculture focused on millet and rice plus pigs. In New Guinea, people cultivated taro, manioc, and bananas, while those in Mesoamerica worked dominantly with corn, beans, squash, and various small animals (Christian 2008, 109). In all cases, this resulted in a genetic change among the domesticated species, making animals smaller and more compliant and plants less likely to scatter their seeds and easier to harvest.

Among humanity, agriculture eliminated the two main characteristics of Paleolithic life: population control and social equality. That is to say, the end of the need for mobility combined with a higher percentage of plant calories in the diet, increasing from next to none to 42 percent in the Neolithic, reduced the time of lactation and increased the birth rate (Harris 1977, 24, 29; Lee 1979, 319). Thus, by 3000, the world's population had increased from 6 to 60 million, in Southwest Asia alone rising from 100,000 to 5 million, that is, at a rate of 1,600 percent.[14]

Genetic Mutations

This had a variety of consequences. For one, it led to a vastly accelerated growth in paternal lineages and male populations, typically within about 1,000 years after the advent of agriculture (Wang et al. 2016, 3). Not only encouraging patrilocality and male dominance patterns, it also opened the doors to all sorts of new ideas and methods. "A larger area in population means more potential inventors, more competing societies, more innovations available to adopt—and more pressure to adopt and retain innovations, because societies failing to do well will be eliminated by competing societies."[15]

It also predicated a great increase in genetic change. With hundreds of thousands of people serving as potential mutants, adaptive change happened a hundred times more rapidly than in the Pleistocene (2009, 74). "Mutations that had previously occurred every 100,000 years or so were now showing up every 400 years" (2009, 31), allowing more rapid developments and increased spread of new genetic components (Pagel 2012, 23).

Thus, for example, the lactose allele or gene variant that allows adults to digest milk is entirely absent in 6000, appears in 25 percent of Near Eastern people in 3000, and today has risen to 95 percent among Europeans.[16] The gene that helps people conserve salt over long periods, on the other hand, was gradually phased out as humans settled further north where sweating was not as much of an issue. Today, while common in Africa, it is present elsewhere only

---

[13] Bellwood 2005, 42. See also Anderson 2014, 31; Fernandez-Armesto 2002, 96; Jones 2007, 145; Smith 1995, 49; McIntosh 2006; Outram 2007, 54; Renfrew 1973; Shinde 2002.

[14] Bellwood 2005, 15. See also Barber 1994, 72; Christian 2008, 119; Cochran and Harpending 2009, 65; McIntosh 2006, 348; Wang et al. 2016, 3.

[15] Diamond 1997, 407; Cochran and Harpending 2009, 66.

[16] Cochran and Harpending 2009, 83; Harris 1985, 137-48.

in its null variant, i.e., without a particular function (Cochran and Harpending 2009, 71).

The lighter skin and blue eyes of northern people, too, are due to a genetic adaptation, a mutation in the way vitamins are transported to cells, allowing the absorption of vitamin D even under conditions of sparse sunlight and little meat (2009, 78, 92; Anderson 2014, 18). The increased consumption of carbohydrates, furthermore, enhanced the absorption of sugars in agricultural people. Populations that never farmed, if adopting a Western diet, are at a much higher risk to develop type-2 diabetes—Navajo Indians twice, Australian aborigines four times as much (Cochran and Harpending 2009, 80). By the same token, there are hundreds of genes still undergoing sweeps today that began thousands of years ago, affecting changes in metabolism and digestion, defenses against infections, and modification in reproductive systems (2009, 75).

In terms of bone structure, too, humans have undergone major genetic mutations. Thus, the brow ridges, typical of early humans, have all but disappeared today, found only among certain Australian aborigines. People today are much lighter in their skeleton, have smaller, more receding jaws, and overall longer and lighter bones (2009, 94). Their skulls are 10 percent less in volume while their frontal-lobe area has increased—even over the past 500 years (2009, 95). This, together with ongoing mutations in the dystrophin protein complex that controls muscles, reveals an overall genetic trend of sacrificing skeletal volume and muscle strength in favor of higher intelligence (2009, 99).

Another dimension of change is the area of human perception and cognition, moods and emotions. For one, agriculture predicated a new level of language, a major milestone in human development (2009, 26). More complex syntax, expressions, and metaphors increased perception and attention, but did not yet lead to full individual awareness and personal identity, which emerged after the invention of writing and the spread of literacy (Kohn 2016, 64-65).

Also, the more agriculture demanded organized cooperation and greater population density required interpersonal consideration, the more the independent-minded personality became obsolete. Distinctive genetic changes occurred that were "almost entirely the result of self-domestication caused by the determination of breeding patterns by rising cultural imperatives" (Bednarik 2008, 14). Thus, in the same way as the Green Revolution reduced the competition between members of domesticated plant and animal species, the genetic mutations since the Neolithic have lowered individuality and bred people increasingly for submission to authority.

One example is the 7 repeat allele of the dopamine D4 receptor gene. Today linked with ADHD and biologically associated with aggression and combativeness, it has increasingly become a liability rather than a benefit for top survival fitness. As a result, it has been reduced significantly and is practically unknown in East Asia (Cochran and Harpending 2009, 111-12). On the other hand, traits of self-denial, dependence on others, and childlike behavior patterns (neoteny) have been on the increase worldwide (2009, 112-14).

Invading Parasites

In another dimension of physiological change, "through the long agrarian passage man became biologically better adapted to the modern economic world" and developed "resistance to epidemic diseases that arise with concentrated populations" (Diamond 1997, 18-22; Clark 2007, 187), such as measles that do only occur in dense populations over half a million (Cochran and Harpending 2009, 86).

In the initial stages, however, there was no resistance in the face of a massive exposure to various bacteria, viruses, and parasites invading human space, another consequence of the agricultural lifestyle (Barnicot 1969, 525; Larsen 2002, 29). Parasites multiplied partly due to the increased density of living quarters and a pervasive lack of hygiene, partly because of the proximity of life stock—notably pigs and cattle, but also dogs, poultry, horses, goats, and rats.[17] Human beings share from twenty-six (poultry) to sixty-five (dogs) diseases with them, pigs and cattle ranging between forty and fifty (McNeill 1976, 45-46; Upex and Dobney 2012, 197).

The infectious environment of mass settlements with their closeness to animals, accumulation of waste, and large rodent and vermin populations (Cochran and Harpending 2009, 86), moreover, was exacerbated by the dominantly grain-based diet (Temple and Larson 2013, 359). "The hunter gatherers of the early Mesolithic used at least 120 seed foods, but by the end of Neolithic, the farmers used only 5 seeds, 3 cereals, and 2 pulses" (Spencer 1993, 35). Partly due to social conditions, which allowed only elite members to have a varied diet, this reduction in variety may also be due to the higher sweetness of grains (Outram 2007, 54)—which in itself caused a plethora of new diseases.[18] In addition, grains contain exorphins, a morphine-like compound that makes them addictive, leading people to prefer them to fresh vegetables and meat (Gedgaudas 2009, 15).

If not addicted and given free choice, people generally tend to eat meat and fruits as much as they can, cereals and tubers only if they must. "Grasses are not food that people prefer" (Cohen 1977a, 146). This is because they tend to be bland and tasteless—requiring the addition of salt—and low in nutrition (Outram 2007, 57). It is also because "human beings are very poorly adapted to digest cereals," often reacting with allergies to the phytate they contain, which "interferes with the proper assimilation of calcium by the body and is conducive to rickets" (Yudkin 1969, 549, 551; Cohen 1977a, 146).

---

[17] Barber 1994, 76; Diamond 1997; Huber 2007, 109; McIntosh 2006, 347.

[18] Christian 2008, 121. See also Coatsworth 1996; Eaton et al. 2002, 10-11, 13; Schmid 2015, 16.

Archaeological excavations show that, unlike their Paleolithic forebears, people in the Neolithic lived largely on grains and beans, and used meat that was pickled, salted, or smoked—fresh fruits and vegetables increasingly becoming luxuries (Cordain 2011, 45). As a result, they suffered widely from skeletal malformations due to beriberi, scurvy, and rickets caused by insufficient vitamins B, C, and D, which the human body does not produce internally.[19] They also exhibit lathyrism, spina bifida, and lower-leg paralysis as the result of toxins in beans and pulses as well as goiters due to iodine deficiency. Having to add salt to their food, they began to consume too much sodium, leading to a more acidic diet, which leads to high blood pressure, bone and muscle loss, as well as an increased risk of cancer (Cordain 2011, 54). Being weakened, they came to suffer from various other ailments, including malaria, osteomyelitis, rheumatism, kidney stones, polio, diabetes, eye problems, ear infections, and tumors (McIntosh 2006, 348).

In addition, farmers experienced many problems with their teeth, their grain-based diet encouraging dental caries, while the minute pieces of grit that resulted from the grinding of the grain caused the teeth to become worn and chipped. Abscesses, gum disease, and tooth loss are also known."[20] Overall, they were in "an atrocious state of dental health" (Penchenkina, Ma, and Fan 2013, 460), women more so than men (McIntosh 2006, 347). These findings match the contemporary contrast between ailing and deformed people eating refined foods and healthy specimens who maintain a more traditional, whole-foods diet (see Price 1989). To make matter worse, a diet heavy in gluten overloads the intestines, clogs the skin, and impacts the nervous system (Perlmutter 2013, 53). Over time, it may well lead to a variety of mental and psychological issues, such as anxiety, chronic stress, depression, epilepsy, difficulty concentrating, insomnia, and weak memory (Perlmutter 2013, 10)—all features that made Neolithic man that much more pliable to social control, economic exploitation, and political suppression.

A further consequence of agriculture, combining genetic evolution with dietary shortcomings is that Neolithic people were considerably shorter than early hunter-gatherers, rarely reaching a height above five feet (150 cm).[21] This indicates not only the lack of meat but also shortages in fruit and fresh vegetables for large portions of the population (Outram 2007, 52).

Besides being plagued by disease and nutritional shortages, people suffered yet another consequence of agriculture in that they had to labor harder and for longer hours (Christian 2008, 121). Farming was monotonous and routine work that lasted all day long for much of the year, eliminating hunter-

---

[19] Cohen 1977a, 29; Cordain 2011, 44; Ortner 2012, 258.

[20] McIntosh 2006, 347. See also Brothwell 1969, 532-37; Cochran and Harpending 2009, 79; Larsen 2002, 22-23; Pechenkina et al. 2013, 301; Temple and Larson 2913, 344.

[21] Schmid 2015, 16. See also Cordain 2011, 44; Larsen 2002, 24-25; Pechenkina, Ma, and Fan 2013, 459.

gatherer leisure (Harris 1977, 11). In addition, agriculture required more stringent social organization, especially when it depended on irrigation (McNeill 1976, 38) and allowed the accumulation of goods, forming the fundamental condition for social segmentation and stratification, i. e., the unequal access to resources (food, tools, weapons), and in due course ending hunter-gatherer egalitarianism.[22]

The majority of people were no longer free agents, but subject to the commands and whims of a ruling class who established social supremacy through competitive feasting and conspicuous consumption, often to mark major life transitions.[23] They also controlled the production and distribution of highly valued prestige goods, notably finely made food containers, personal ornaments, embellished clothing, and fancy weapons—some so delicate they were of no practical use and became hypertrophic (Underhill 2002, 4).

This stratification had a permanent impact. Through agriculture humans entered a symbiotic relationship of mutual exploitation with plants and animals, changing the quality of both, and adjusted to the presence of disease-bearing parasites in their midst. In the very same way, as they established social stratification (Johnson 1997, 47), they entered a relationship of "modulated macroparasitism" with wealthier and more powerful members of their community, "other men who, by specializing in violence, are able to secure a living without themselves producing the food and other commodities they consume" (McNeill 1982, vii, 6).

These nonproductive elites, moreover, "were not formed in response to some societal need: they took because they could" (Cochran and Harpending 2009, 70). As a result, societies moved into stable patterns of exploitation, individuals increasingly willing "to participate in systems that determined and guaranteed access to resources and promised to provide homeostatic buffers" (Cohen 1985, 102). Rulers came to seize a substantial part of the harvest from their subjects, "leaving just enough behind to allow the plundered community to survive indefinitely. . . Only later and by slow degrees did reciprocal services between town and countryside develop importance enough to diminish the one-sidedness of tax and rent collection" (McNeill 1976, 6), providing law and order in exchange (Cochran and Harpending 2009, 109).

Statehood

All this caused the freedom of Paleolithic hunter-gatherer bands and the ease of Mesolithic village life to vanish gradually in favor of larger and more stratified communities that eventually consolidated into states (Harris 1977, 69)—societies with a centralized and specialized institution of government (Haas

---

[22] Fox 1999, 26-28. See also Fried 1983, 478; Haas 1982, 91, 93; 1990, 173; Huber 2007, 57; Johnson 1997, 46-47; McCauley 1990, 11; Spencer 1993, 33.

[23] Asouti and Fuller 2013, 330; Harris 1977, 71, 73; McIntosh 2006, 336; Underhill 2002, 1.

1982, 3), whose elite members exercised control over agricultural production, including land, irrigation, storage, finance, and transport (Underhill 2002, 6). Before reaching this level, however, human society grew through several distinct stages.[24]

In the beginning, humans formed bands, "small, politically autonomous groups of twenty to fifty people—usually a few related extended families—with an informal head person" (Keeley 1996, 26). For a few weeks each year, they might join to form a macro-band of several hundred people for ceremonies, marriage alliances, and exchange, but their basic identity was with the small group and the social organization largely egalitarian (Service 1971, 60).

As population increased, they began to grow into tribes, i.e., "pyramids of social groups that trace descent to a common hypothetical or mythological ancestor" (1996, 26; Haas 1990, 176)—under sedentary conditions localized in clan-based villages. Joined by association of multiple fraternal interest groups into a single social organization, notably for war or ceremonial purposes, tribes are led by big men or chiefs, who tend to exercise influence rather than power and are responsible to a council of elders.[25] Despite their larger numbers and increasing social structure, they show little specialization and are still largely egalitarian communities. Linked by marriage, ceremonial interactions, and the sharing of resources, tribes constitute a powerful form of human networking (Lawlor 1991, 279).

The next stage is that of chiefdom, a "multicommunity political unit" that "unites many thousands or tens of thousands of people under formal, full-time political leadership."[26] Here society is fully stratified, divided into hereditary ranks or incipient social classes, notably rulers, warriors, and commoners (Carneiro 1990, 2000). The chief is in charge of overall organization, controlling both the means of production and all economic surpluses (Earle 1991b, 71). "Access to chiefship is hereditary, permanent, and justified on religious or magical grounds" (1996, 27). However, the chief does not have the pervasive power to coerce people into obedience (Carneiro 1981, 43; Haas 1982, 213).

This changes with the arrival of statehood. Typically arising in areas where people could not easily escape (Anderson 2014, 46), "in regions where plants were grown and there was no war" (Otterbein 2004, 97), states "have a central government empowered to collect taxes, draft labor for public works or war, decrees laws, and physically enforce those laws" (Keeley 1996, 27), wielding

---

[24] Jones and Kautz 1981, 19. See also Carneiro 1990, 190; Fried 1967; Haas 1990, 172; Kristiansen 1991, 23; Li 2013, 21; Liu 2004, 13; Otterbein 1970, 20; 2004, 105; Service 1963; 1975.

[25] Fried 1983, 471; Otterbein 2004, 102; Service 1971, 111.

[26] Carneiro 1981, 37; 1990, 190, See also Earle 1991a, 1; Keeley 1996, 26; Service 1971, 143.

"centralized power in an order of socioeconomic stratification."[27] Fundamentally despotic in nature (Otterbein 2004, 109), states established penalties and penitentiaries of various sorts. Thereby they systematically taught people to "bow, grovel, kneel, and kowtow," signifying the "descent from freedom to slavery" (Christian 2008, 123). Maintaining "a monopoly of deadly force" (Keeley 1996, 27), some eventually consolidated through conquest and suppression of neighboring units into ever larger units and even turned into empires.

Early states come in one of four major forms. City-states are the earliest and most recurrent, beginning the Near East and spreading from there, China being "the latest of the seminal culture centers to produce the state."[28] Governed by a single, often divinely anointed ruler or god-like king (Christian 2008, 130; Stein 2001, 211), they are class-stratified political units, centered in densely populated cities with control only over relatively small territories (Haas 1981, 83). They typically have a three-tiered settlement hierarchy, including the capital, small centers, and villages (Chen and Liu 2003, 15).

Segmentary states, second, have political control only in their core domain but exert ritual suzerainty over an extended yet flexible, changing periphery (2003, 17). Territorial states, next, are controlled by a single ruler, but consist of multiple local centers housing elite administrators. Surrounded by farmers living in dispersed homesteads and villages, these states work with a two-tiered society and economy (2003, 18-19). Last but not least, village-states are "royal, administrative, and cultic centers surrounded by a sea of peasant villages" (2003, 20). Rather than focused on a single ruler, they depend on clans and lineages for organization and leadership.

Historically, both chiefdoms and states developed under the impact of agriculture, leading to the beginning of civilization with complex societies and standardized, increasingly mass-produced goods (Underhill 2002, 8-9). As Gregory Clark describes it,

> Agrarian societies differed in two crucial ways from their forager predecessors. Agriculture allowed for much higher population densities, so that, instead of living in communities of twenty to fifty, people now lived in communities of hundreds to thousands. By 2500 BCE, the cities of Sumer and Babylonia are estimated to have been already as large as 40,000 people.
>
> Agrarian societies also had large stocks of assets owned by specific people: land, houses, animals. The sizes of these societies allowed the extensive use of money as a medium of exchange. Their size, and the importance of the income streams from these assets, created a need for enduring records of property ownership and transfers. Thus a mass of clay

---

[27] Jones and Kautz 1981, 14. See also Barnes 2015, 161; Ferguson 1991, 170; Haas 1982, 142-43; Otterbein 2004, 104; Underhill 2002, 4. Statehood also comes with a marked increase in human sacrifice. See Chang 2005, 26; Bell 2016; Watts et al. 2016.

[28] Maiseld 1999, 267; Anderson 2014, 58; Cauvin 2000, 117.

tablets recording leases, sales, wills, and labor contracts survive. (2007, 184-85)

The first city of record is Jericho, already a regional node of commercial and ritual activity around 7000 (Asouti and Fuller 2013, 330). Established in a fertile oasis west of the Jordan, today located in the West Bank and called Tell es Sultan (Mithen 2004, 56), it was the first place in human history where a viable population lived and worked together (Christian 2008, 120).

Discovered in 1867 by Charles Warren and excavated by Kathleen Kenyon in the 1950s (Kenyon 1957), it was the also the first fortified city. The entire structure was surrounded by major walls, 3.6 meters thick and 1.8 meters wide at the base, and dominated by a tall tower, 8 meters high and 9 meters wide with a weight of a thousand tons. The construction indicates the need for strong defenses as well as stringent social control that allowed the mobilization of a large labor force, revealing all the signs of statehood (Cauvin 2000, 35-38; Mithen 2004, 58). Still, there was no fully developed pottery in Jericho—the technique gradually spreading from the Far East (Anderson 2014, 49)—only vessels and bricks from fire-hardened clay that served to build houses and increasingly specialized workshops (Christian 2008, 120).

Specialization increased further with the development of extensive and ever more densely settled cities—here as much as in other parts of the world. Excavations show increasingly separate districts, including those of palace, temple, tomb, workshop, and servitor housing, all spatially distinct and in parts even walled off, so that the ancient hub was in many ways a collection of functionally distinct villages forming a settlement cluster and not a city in the modern sense (Maisels 1999, 330). It supported full-time specialists, notably craftsmen, transport workers, merchants, officials, and priests, increasingly centering on war and ritual as the key official focus (Harris 1977, 60).

At the same time, male supremacy enhanced a gender-based division of labor, tying women to the house (Christian 2008, 129; Huber 2007, 106), so that today among all the various tribes and peoples on the planet, patriliny is five times more common than matriliny and polygamy a hundred times more common than polyandry.[29]

Stratification

Specialization and gender division are both aspects of the increasing stratification of human society, due to the rise of an increasingly powerful ruling class. This is documented widely in graves that place certain groups and individuals in special locations and contain decorated skulls, various ornaments, and increasingly lavish grave goods (Christian 2008, 121, 128). Unequal access to food, moreover, is evident from sites that contain food discards and remains of well-

[29] Harris 1977, 58; 1993, 69; Hart and Sussman 2005, 198.

nourished upper-class members buried with sacrificial servant victims who show distinct signs of malnutrition (Haas 1982, 94-95)—a major break with the Paleolithic that yet set the pattern for most of human history since.

> All hunter-gatherer societies are egalitarian. Material consumption varies little across the members. In contrast, inequality was pervasive in the agrarian economies that dominated the world to 1800 [CE]. The riches of a few dwarfed the pinched allocations of the masses. Jane Austen may have written about refined conversations over tea served in china cups. But for the majority of the English as late as 1813 conditions were no better than for their naked ancestors of the African savanna. The Darcys were few, the poor plentiful. (Clark 2007, 1)

The king and his minions—arranged in a hierarchy of officials, priests, and retainers—held absolute power. Having great reproductive advantage (Chagnon 1990, 94), they fathered numerous children and continued to spread their network of dominance—to the point where even today 2 to 3 million men of Irish descent have the Y-chromosome of King Niall (r. 379-405 CE) whose clan ruled Ireland until 1609, and all of 16 million Central Asians are direct descendants of Genghis Khan (Cochran and Harpending 2009, 106).

The ever-growing elite owned all surplus, created by an indentured if not actually enslaved peasantry—living in conditions close to "the minimum required for biological survival" (McNeill 1982, 4). They paid a tax-rent and had to provide living labor, duly used to erect monumental palaces and ritual structures.[30] All technical expertise served the goals of the ruling class, increasing wealth and creating weaponry and ritual objects, while the mode of food production remained essentially the same. This trend, moreover, persisted for the next 3000 years, through the entire Agrarian period, to end only with the Industrial Revolution.

Thus, in China, "no significantly new technological invention has been archaeologically documented from the Neolithic into the Bronze Age: the same stone, bone, shell, and presumably digging, earth turning, weeding, and harvesting implements were used during both periods. The emergence of Bronze Age civilizations in China was not accompanied, insofar as our available archaeological record suggests, by a significant use of metal farming implements, irrigation networks, or the use of the plough" (Chang 1986, 364; Maisels 1999, 313). By the same token,

> The average person in the world of 1800 was no better off than the average person of 100,000 BCE. Indeed, in 1800 the bulk of the world's population was poorer than their remote ancestors. The lucky denizens of wealthy societies such as eighteenth-century England or the Netherlands managed a ma-

[30] Maisels 1999, 332. See also Anderson 2014, 55; Christian 2008, 123; Haas 1982, 214.

> terial lifestyle equivalent to that of the Stone Age. But the vast swath of humanity in East and South Asia, particularly in China and Japan, eked out a living significantly poorer than those of cavemen.
>
> The quality of life also failed to improve on any other observable dimension. Life expectancy was no higher in 1800 than for hunter-gatherers: thirty to thirty-five years. Stature, a measure both of the quality of diet and of children's exposure to disease, was higher in the Stone Age than in 1800.
>
> And while foragers satisfy their material wants with small amounts of work, the modest comforts of the English in 1800 were purchased only through a life of unrelenting drudgery. Nor did the variety of material consumption improve. The average forager had a diet, and a work life, much more varied than the typical English worker of 1800, even though the English table by then included such exotics as tea, pepper, and sugar. . . . So, even according to the broadest measures of material life, average welfare, if anything, declined from the Stone Age to 1800. The poor of 1800, those who lived by their unskilled labor alone, would have been better off if transferred to a hunter-gatherer band. (Clark 2007, 1-2)

The Malthusian Trap

Settlements being cramped, bodies getting sick, and life becoming increasingly harder, agriculture—the beginning of "a massive crescendo of plunder, massacre, enslavement, and dispossession" (Lawlor 1991, 51)—seems an odd choice to make. The question arises, "If agriculture provided neither a better diet, nor greater dietary reliability, nor greater ease in the food quest; if it did not of itself confer the capability of sedentism, but conversely provided a poorer diet, less reliably, at equal or greater labor costs: why did anyone become a farmer?"[31]

It is much more likely that people would try hard to retain the easier life of nomadic foraging. As R. Hitchcock puts it, "Considering all the problems incurred by sedentism, it comes as no surprise that many hunter-gatherer groups would attempt to keep moving if at all possible."[32] Similarly, it makes sense that aborigines would refuse planting, clothing, architecture, writing, and more, and even intentionally return to simpler ways, as in the case of the Tasmanians (Lawlor 1991, 61, 79-83), and that herders would object to participating in World Bank schemes to streamline their production by making them sedentary and part of a greater economic structure, as seen among the Sheikhanzai in Afghanistan in the 1970s (Tavakokian 1982, 104-06).

The assumption is likely that, as David Christian says, "people were first forced into it, then born into it" (2008, 119; Huber 2007, 96), making the decision that "it was better to live on their knees than die on their feet" (Cochran and Harpending 2009, 110). Or, as Gregory Clark notes, "Agriculture was

---

[31] Cohen 1977a, 39. See also Cohen 2002, 218; Pfeiffer 1982, 121; Shelach-Levi 2015, 61.
[32] Hitchcock 1982, in Bellwood 2005, 32; Lee 1968, 33.

adopted because it was initially a better technology, which generated higher incomes. But those higher incomes inevitably led to larger populations and a decrease of living standards to a new Malthusian equilibrium, seemingly one less favorable than that for the previous hunter-gatherer societies" (2007, 38).

As first pointed out by British cleric and scholar Thomas Robert Malthus (1766-1834) in his *Essay on the Principle of Population* (1798), human populations if left unchecked tend to grow exponentially while food production increases arithmetically. "Even moderate rates of population growth can rapidly catch up with all plausible improvements in food production" (Cochran and Harpending 2009, 101). This means that within a few generations any benefit gained from improving the modes of production and thus increasing nutritional resources would be used up by the larger number of people to feed. This creates first an overall state of poverty and misery for all, then leads to wide-spread unrest, epidemics, and famines—war, pestilence, and starvation (2009, 102)—until such time when new innovations improve production yet again.

This scenario is known as the Malthusian trap. It has played out innumerable times in many parts of the world over the ten thousand years of the Agrarian period (Clark 2007, 5). While it can be avoided by the systematic control of population growth, time and again people have chosen quantity over quality, accumulation over happiness, population growth over higher standards of living, increase in power over spiritual and cultural advances. The result has been a life of poverty, scarcity, and misery for the vast majority of human beings—states that are by no means intrinsic to the human condition but "systematically instituted by the market-industrial system" (Sahlins 1972, 4-5; Bronson 1977, 39). This is why Jared Diamond has called the Neolithic Revolution "the worst mistake in the history of the human race," arguing that when "forced to choose between limiting population or trying to increase food production, we chose the latter and ended up with starvation, warfare, and tyranny" (1987, 66; Lawlor 1991, 60-62).

Institutional Dynamics

Another way of looking at the absolute power and pervasive social control of the elite that allowed them to build complex societies and massive monuments (Christian 2008, 124) is in terms of extractive versus inclusive institutions. As economists Daron Acemoglu and James Robinson note,

> Extractive political institutions concentrate power in the hands of a narrow elite and place few constraints on the exercise of this power. Economic institutions are then often structured by this elite to extract resources from the rest of the society. The two are mutually interdependent: extractive economic institutions must inherently depend on extractive political institutions.
>
> Inclusive political institutions, on the other hand, vest power broadly, and tend to uproot economic institutions that appropriate the resources of

> many, erect entry barriers, and suppress the functioning of markets so that only a few benefit. Inclusive economic institutions, in turn, are forged on foundations laid by inclusive political institutions, which make power broadly distributed in society and constrain its arbitrary exercise. . . .
>
> They make it harder for others to usurp power and undermine the foundations, creating a more equitable distribution of resources and facilitating the persistence of inclusive political institutions. (2012, 81-82)

As long as groups are small, such as the bands, tribes, and villages of the early part of the Stone Age, institutions have to remain inclusive, protecting the well-being of each member to ensure survival of the whole. While there may be some division of labor, guidance by a council of elders, and leadership by a headman, power is never centralized or absolute. Once population increases and the mode of production requires authoritarian organization and creates a surplus that allows accumulation, stratification begins and the elite establishes extractive institutions—first economic then increasingly political.

They, moreover, hang on to these institutions with all their might due to a pervasive fear of what economist Joseph Schumpeter has called "creative destruction." It is the natural way of the world that "economic growth and technological change replace the old with the new: new firms take over, new technologies make existing skills and machines obsolete. The process creates losers as well as winners, endangers old privilege and power structures," potentially toppling governments and upending social patterns (Acemoglu and Robinson 2012, 82). Thus "fear of creative destruction is often at the root of the opposition to inclusive economic and political institutions" (2012, 82), leading elites to "stifle growth, tighten taxes, and make war" (Christian 2008, 161).

While inclusive institutions tend to create affluence for all and allow a focus on quality of life rather than quantity of possessions, extractive institutions, too, can be and have been powerful engines of growth and prosperity. For example, the Bushong, a tribe on the eastern bank of the Kasai River in the Congo, underwent a political revolution led by Shyaam in 1620. Forging the Kuba Kingdom, he built a state and a pyramid of political institutions that were not just more centralized but also involved highly elaborate structures. He created a bureaucracy to raise taxes as well as a legal system and police force to administer the law. Leaders were checked by councils, which they had to consult before making decisions. There was even trial by jury. The result was a tremendous surge of productivity and prosperity for all. "Nevertheless, the centralized state that Shyaam constructed was a tool of extraction and highly absolutist," bound to fail eventually (Acemoglu and Robinson 2012, 134-35).

There may be—as is the case in China today—a "vigorous market exchange system," reflective of inclusive economic institutions, "operating underneath the official command structure," thus enhancing the flexibility of the economy, increasing wealth and expanding the resources of the country. There may even be a functioning legal and civil administrative system guaranteeing security and basic rights. However, unless political institutions become inclusive, under any form of authoritarian government, the market will never "displace officialdom from its controlling position." On the contrary, all wealth and economic improvements will enhance elite power (McNeill 1982, 49).

The bottom line is that the ruler and his elite, since they want to extract taxes and wealth from the people, have to enable them to produce a surplus above what they consume themselves and keep them functioning at least at a minimum level. They realize very well, as David Christian puts it, that "parasites that are lethal never last" (2008, 124). They thus allow innovation within limits yet program themselves to fail in the long run. Profits gained under extractive institutions lack the crucial quality of renewal through creative destruction. Sooner or later the system grows rigid and oppressive to the point of collapse, becoming the dominant reason "why nations fail" (Acemoglu and Robinson 2012; see also Ferguson 2013, 27).

The Daoist Agenda

On the other hand, there is no inevitable process or compulsive reason why exponential population growth or the establishment of extractive institutions must occur. They arise historically as the consequence of agriculture, but they do so by choice, not necessity. Agriculture in itself is just a technology, a complex mixture of techniques and methods, but a mere means nonetheless. It enables but does not inevitably bring forth more people or domineering elites.

Daoists, uniquely in human history, have recognized this fact and strongly affirm that not only was the choice avoidable historically but that *it can be avoided or reversed at any time by anyone in any social situation*! "We are all capable of repudiating the distorting influences of civilization and recovering our original nature" (Ames 1994, 8). We as individuals have the power to limit procreation, reduce accumulation, refrain from exercising power, and refuse to give in to economic, political, and social pressure. We can live in pristine affluence even in an agricultural or industrial setting, even under the auspices of statehood, even within a stratified society. We can practice peaceful coexistence, cultivate ourselves to perfect health, eat a simple and nutritious diet, and live in sufficiency, peace, and moral integrity, spending our free time leisurely in cultural and spiritual pursuits. We can, moreover, create communities that embrace these values and develop a form of life on earth that is as close to perfection as imaginable at this level in human development.

The Daoist agenda, in all its different dimensions, has focused on achieving just this, recovering Paleo- and Mesolithic values and lifestyle choices under the most varied social, economic, political, and historical conditions.

Chapter Three

Early Chinese Cultures

> The more taboos and prohibitions there are,
> The poorer the people will be.
> The more sharp weapons the people have,
> The more troubled the state will be.
> The more cunning and skill man possesses,
> The more vicious things will appear.
> The more laws and orders are made prominent,
> The more thieves and robbers there will be. (*Daode jing* 57)

The development of culture and civilization, from the first hominins to the great states of the early dynasties, underwent a very similar trajectory in China. Human beings settled the area around two million years ago, as documented in the finds of the hominids at Yuanmou 元谋 (Yunnan) and Lantian 蓝田 (Shaanxi).[1] While only two incisors remain of the former, dated as far back as 1.7 million years, the latter has left behind numerous bones at a number of different sites, including a cranium and a mandible, dated to between 1.6 million and 530,000 years ago.

Stone artifacts include cores, flakes, choppers, hand axes, and scrapers, in many ways similar to the Acheulean stone tools associated with *Homo ergaster* in Africa (Barnes 2015, 55-56). This suggests a closer connection between different strands of early human development than assumed earlier and overcoming the 1940s division established by Harvard archaeologist Hallam L. Movius (1907-1987) of hand-axe technology in the West versus chopper-chopping tools in the East (Gao 2013, 359).

The great star of early Chinese anthropology is Peking Man 北京猿人, a clear member of *Homo erectus*, discovered at Zhoukoudian 周口店 near Beijing in 1923, then excavated variously, until the bones were lost in 1941, in the up-

[1] See Scarpani 2000, 20; Yan and Wang 2005, 19; Barnes 2015, 51-52. Another early site that contained various tools and bone fragments is Longgupo 龙骨坡 near Chongqing, dated 1.7-1.3 million years ago (Shelach-Levi 2015, 22).

heaval of World War II—only one incisor being rediscovered in a box in Uppsala, Sweden, in 2011.[2]

A deep cave with multiple layers and various locations, the site yielded 15 partial skulls, 11 mandibles, many bone fragments, and thousands of stone tools (Yan and Wang 2005, 16). Dated to 780,000 to 680,000 years ago, Peking Man had a robust skeleton, short and stocky, with a brain of about 1050 cc. His face was large with a low, sloping forehead, a massive brow ridge and a broad, flat nose, while the skull tended to be more angular than that of modern humans, the jaw thicker and the teeth bigger (Howells 1983, 298). Using a variety of stone tools, he foraged, scavenged, and hunted, living largely on meat, supplemented with some plant foods. Charcoal and ash deposits clearly indicate the use of fire (Anderson 2014, 16; http://australianmuseum.net.au/homo-erectus).

Paleolithic Developments

While these early traces belong to the Lower Paleolithic, usually dated from 3.3 million to 300,000 years ago, the next phase, the Middle Paleolithic, all the way to the Human Revolution presents hundreds of Chinese sites (Gao 2013, 361). However, technological change is relatively small, and Chinese paleoanthropologists agree that the European division into three distinct stages does not apply to China and it is better to speak of Early and Late Paleolithic—the dividing line being the year 40,000 (2013, 359; Kei 2012, 619; Li 2014, 1303).

Sample sites include caves on Jinniushan 金牛山 and Miaohoushan 庙后山, near Yingkou 营口 and Benxi 本溪 (Liaoning), dated to 300,000-140,000. Discovered in the 1970s, they yielded various artifacts such as cores, flakes, and retouched stones, as well as human remains (Yan and Wang 2005, 18). At Zhoukoudian, notably Locality 15, the successors of Peking Man, between 140,000 and 110,000 years ago, left behind thousands of stone artifacts, including chopping tools, side scrapers, knives, points, awls, notches, and burins, largely made from locally available quartz.

In Shaanxi, sites include Dali 大荔, discovered in 1978, and Dingcun 丁村, first found in 1953, dating as far back as 380,000 and 260,000 years, respectively. Both yielded human skulls and bones plus hundreds of stone tools. Further south, there are over 300 sites in the Luonan 洛南 Basin of southern Shanxi, dating back to 800,000, as well as Lingjing 灵井 near Xuchang 许昌 (Henan), Jigongshan 鸡公山 near Jingzhou 荆州 (Hubei), and Sanxia 三峡 near Chongqing 重庆 (Gao 2013, 361-64).

In all cases, technology is characterized by the exclusively local (under three miles) procurement of raw materials, the production of stone tools by

[2] Shelach-Levi 2015, 27. See also Anderson 2014, 15; Lei 1996, 219; Oosterzee 2000.

lithic reduction—i. e., trimming the edges around a core—the ongoing retouching of stone tools through soft hammering and pressure flaking, and the creation of a specific typology of tools (Liu and Chen 2012, 621-23; Gao 2013, 359; Barnes 2015, 79). The simple and local nature of the artifacts and the quality of site remains indicate that settlements were seasonal and only occupied for short periods, characteristic of a hunter-gatherer lifestyle (Gao 2013, 367). Two major regional areas can be distinguished: the north working dominantly with small flakes and the south using large pebbles—the dividing line being the Huai River 淮河 and the Qingling Range 清灵山 (2013, 367; Barnes 1993, 97).

The period was not stagnant, however, progress overall being slow and conservative. Gradually behavior became more flexible and complex, and both raw materials and techniques used improved in quality, so that types of tools increased (Wang 2015, 257). There were more drills and points, retouching was more delicate, and flakes became more regular (Gao 2013, 367). By 40,000, Chinese sites too exhibited the characteristics of the Mousterian stone tools and Levallois blade technology—smoother and subtler flaking techniques, the careful preparation of cores, as well as the creation of triangular and disk-shaped cores (Svoboda 2015, 25). This in turn led to a greater variety of instruments, notably side scrapers, hand axes, knives, saws, hammers, and bolas (a ball-shaped stone used as a weapon) (Keates and Kuzmin 2015, 715).

This transition (part of the Human Revolution) is obvious in several sites in the Zhengzhou region of Henan, including one cave (Zhijidong 织机洞) and some open-air sites (Laonainaimiao 老奶奶庙, Zhaozhuang 赵庄, and Xishi 西施). Dated to 50,000 to 26,000 years ago, they have yielded over 20,000 stone artifacts and cultural remains (Wang 2015, 250). Except for quartz and sandstone, many raw materials were transported over longer distances, showing an increase in trade networks. Bone remnants, including some from large prehistoric bovines, come from numerous different animals, revealing a widening in the scope of hunting. Fire was commonly used, and camps were occupied repeatedly over the years, indicating a settling of paths and modes of production (Wang 2015, 252, 254).

Typically site occupation increased whenever the climate got warmer and nature more productive, that is, during milder phases of the late Upper Paleolithic, 130,000-14,000 years ago. Dated through the examination of deep-sea core samples, this period divides into five marine isotope stages (MIS): beginning at 130,000 years ago, stage 5 goes to 71,000; 4 to 57,000; 3 to 29,000; 2 to 14,000; and 1 to the present. Among these, the odd numbered stages are warm, with MIS-5 being further subdivided into five alternating phases, so that 87-82,000 and 109-97,000 were cold periods, the remainder was warmer.[3]

---

[3] Morgan et al. 2011, 366. See also Barnes 2015, 50; Jones 2007, 65.

Occupation in the Central Loess Plateau of the Yellow River dates back to the MIS-5 interglacial, but settlements are few and finds are scarce. A much larger number appears in MIS-3, notably along the Qingshui 清水 and Shuiluo 水落 Rivers. They reveal a clear relationship between climate shift and human behavior and technology, the wetter and warmer weather producing abundant resources for hunter-gatherer populations (Morgan et al. 2011, 376). This is evident in an increasing sophistication of tool making, reduction in artifact size, and growing numbers of large-animal bones, notably of bison, horse, and deer (2011, 372). Even though colder periods led to a resource depression and a matching reduction in population size, the various novel technologies and behavior patterns remained entrenched in later populations, leading to an overall progressive development (2011, 376).

Dietary Expansion

At the end of the Pleistocene, 20,000 years ago, although the climate was still cold and dry, and the landscape was dominantly steppe with shrubs,[4] a distinct change in behavior is evident, signaling a gradual move toward sedentism, defined as a "settlement system, in which at least part of the population remains at the same location throughout the entire year" (Liu and Chen 2012, 125). It is evident in architectural construction, the use of heavy materials, as well as the presence of storage pits, cemeteries, and remains of vermin. Sites show thick and dense deposits, an increasing variety of food stuffs, both plant and animal, more functionally specific and less portable pottery, as well as more secondary refuse, indicated by increased efforts at systematic disposal (2012, 125).

In the process, foragers began to "broaden their resource base to encompass a wide array of plant and animal foods," including particularly wild grains, beans, tubers, and nuts (Liu et al. 2013, 5380). The earliest grinding stones (*mopan* 磨盘) in central China appear at Longwangchan 龙王辿 near Yichuan 宜川 (Shaanxi), on the west bank of the Yellow River (Barnes 2015, 88). Dated to 18-13,000, the site yielded 20 hearths, as well as 20,000 artifacts, animal bones, and ground-edge stone tools (Liu and Chen 2012, 48).

Over 25 other early sites appear in the Xiachuan 下川 Basin and at Shizitan 柿子滩 on the banks of the Qingshui River (Shanxi) (Shelach-Levi 2015, 51-53; Highham 2005, 238). Location 14 of the latter dates back as far as 23,000. Excavations in 2000, 2003, and 2005 CE, unearthed 1645 lithic artifacts and 2776 animal bone fragments as well as 17 ash pits and burnt areas (Liu et al. 2013, 5380). This is clear evidence of extensive, if not yet permanent, settlements with houses, grave yards, and fire places, despite the fact that the climate at the time was still dry and cold. A yet similar site appears at Hutouliang 虎头

[4] Higham 2005, 237; Yan 2005, 27; Barnes 2015, 76; Whyte 1983, 9.

梁 on the banks of Sanggan 桑干 River (Hebei). Dated to 12,300-10,700, it was the home of a highly mobile hunter-gatherer group who were dominantly foragers, yet had some pottery and used grinding stone.[5]

Grinding stones show that these people processed food, grinding it to flour while moving their hands in various directions and with different pressures (Liu et al. 2013, 5381). Those found in Shizitan contain residue of 136 starch granules from six main vegetable food groups. They include wild cereals (wheat, barley, rye) to 33 percent; tubers and yams to 18 percent; beans and legumes to 15 percent; various kinds of millet to 13 percent; snakegourd root to 11 percent; and nuts and acorns to 10 percent (2013, 5382). Especially acorns and snakegourd root—still used in traditional medicine today—needed to be ground into flour and cooked before being digestible. Overall, this shows that in the very late Paleolithic, human beings in China began to expand their dietary selection to include increasing amounts of starchy foods, supplementing and replacing the meat that dominated their diet before then (2013, 5384; Anderson 2014, 36).

In central China, the main matching site is Yuchanyan 玉蟾岩 near Daoxian 道县 (Hunan). Dated to 16-12,000, it is an extensive cave, 46 m^2 in size, complete with fireplaces, stone tools, and animal bones. The latter belong to 27 avian and 28 mammalian species, mostly deer. In addition, the cave yielded various spiral shells, 17 types of plants, seeds, fruits, and rice phytoliths. It also contained fragments of potsherds—roughly made with charcoal and coarse sand. They are the earliest in world, right before those found in Jōmon Japan.[6]

In south China, two further sites date from approximately the same period, i. e., around 13,000-11,000. They are Xianrendong 仙人洞 and Diaotonghuan 吊桶环 in Wannian 万年 County, northeast Jiangxi. Excavated in the 1960s, they contained numerous stone implements, bone, shell, and pottery pieces as well as thousands of animal and plant remains, including early rice phytoliths. Pottery in particular was made either by direct molding or by piling clay on baskets, the latter leaving unique markings and designs (Zhang 2002, 186-88; Anderson 2014, 16).

In addition, several caves at Changbin 長濱 in eastern Taiwan have yielded a variety of Paleolithic stone tools, indicating a copper-chopping culture matching mainland patterns—not entirely surprising since massively lower sea levels allowed a land passage at the time (Jiao 2007, 90).

---

[5] Shelach-Levi 2015, 54; Barnes 2015, 88; Guo and Li 2002, 199.

[6] Liu and Chen 2012, 58-59; Shelach-Levi 2015, 57. See also Higham 2005, 241; Mithen 2004, 359; Yasuda 2002b, 121; Yuan 2002, 160; Zhang 2002, 189.

Sedentism

Around 12,000, a warming trend began, which saw oak, elm, and willow replace the thinly scattered pine and spruce combined with a thick undergrowth of ferns. This reversed around 10,500 back to dryer and colder weather during the Younger Dryas. After this, global warming and wetter seasons starting around 9,600 mark the beginning of the transition toward sedentism in China as well as the rise of sea levels and separation of Taiwan.[7] It is evident both in the north and south of the country, characterized by larger sites located in caves or on river banks, longer periods of occupation, a continued expansion of technology, and a steady increase in the use of plant substances (Yan 2005, 28). Several sites dating from 9000-7000 show this development.

Thus, Bianbiandong 扁扁洞 near Yiyuan 沂源 (Shandong) is a cave containing four ash pits, used either as human burial sites or hearths. Ceramics come in two forms, bowls (*bo* 钵) and cauldrons (*fu* 釜), matching the Houli 后李 Neolithic culture and indicating the transitional nature of this group (Liu and Chen 2012, 57). Another cave is Zengpiyuan 甑皮岩 south of Guilin 桂林 (Guangxi). Huge at 240 m^2, it contains four levels of materials. Besides many different stone tools, ceramics included large jars marked with cords that were used for cooking a large variety of both plants and animals, including wild pigs and water buffaloes. Overall, the site reveals a broad-spectrum subsistence economy, including hunting animals and collecting shellfish, tubers, and many plants (Liu and Chen 2012, 60; Higham 1995, 133).

Early riverside settlements of the same period appear at Zhuannian 转年 in Huairou 坏柔 and Donghulin 东胡林 in Mentougou 门头沟, both near Beijing. Several square miles in expansion, they feature the use of oak and walnut as well as larger amounts of wild cereals as time went on. Tools include chipped stones, knives, and axes, while pottery features flat-bottomed basins, jars, and bowls, all created with coiling and slab techniques and fired at low temperatures. Besides deer, pigs, badgers, geese, and freshwater shells, people ate various types of nuts and grass seeds. They practiced formal primary as well as secondary burials, indicating a trend toward permanence in that they would stay close to or come back to their dead (Liu and Chen 2012, 52-55; Shelach-Levi 2015, 54-55).

Further south is Shangshan 上山 near Pujiang 浦江 (Zhejiang). Five acres (2 ha) in size, the site is located on the banks of the Puyang 浦阳江 River, surrounded by mountains and sporting numerous evergreen, deciduous, fruit, and nut trees—often deliberately managed (Liu and Chen 2012, 265; Anderson 2014, 38). Various pits held pottery vessels, while vertical shafts were for food

[7] Mithen 2004, 361. See also Barnes 2015, 89; Higham 1995, 127; 2005, 237; Jiao 2007, 39; Liu 2004, 24; Meacham 1983, 153.

storage and the disposition of waste. The site shows a mixed pattern of occupation, both intermittent residence and extended habitation. Postholes suggest pile-dwelling structures about 6 by 14 yards in size. Pottery is flat basined, grind stones contain remnants of acorns and other starchy foodstuffs.[8]

More sedentary sites with more intensive storage facilities, allowing the preservation of larger quantities and of materials with a longer shelf life (e. g., acorns), appear in Nanzhuangtou 南庄头 near Xushui 徐水 (Hebei) and Lijiagou 李家沟 near Xinmi 新密 on the Chunban River 椿板河 (Henan). Both dating from about 8500-7000, they were quite large and located on plains rather than in caves or on hills. Surrounded by herbaceous plants and leafy trees, the sites had gullies, ditches, ash pits, grinding slabs, and hearths near buildings framed with wooden poles. Basic pottery was tempered with shell fragments or quartz, shaped in simple designs, and marked with cord marks and incised patterns. Animal remains indicate the presence of chickens, wild birds, rabbits, pigs, buffaloes, deer, turtles, fish, and shellfish as well as wolves and dogs, the latter clearly domesticated. They document a clear link between late Pleistocene microlithic traditions and early Neolithic cultures in China.[9]

However, this tendency was not universal. Some groups continued the Epipaleolithic tradition well into the Holocene, relying on hunting, fishing, and gathering for food procurement and remaining dominantly mobile rather than settling down. This holds true especially for arid areas in the north, high altitude places in the northwest and southwest, and tropical regions in the southeast and Taiwan (2012, 73; see also Jiao 2007; Lien 2015). In other words, the transition toward agriculture occurred in more fertile areas with a wider variety of food resources that were also more densely populated.

Plant Domestication

Around 6500, when the climate was rather unstable, the cold peaking around 5800 (Pechenkina et al. 2000, 18), people in China began to congregate in increasingly larger sedentary communities, creating bigger settlements and more complex social organizations, and systematically domesticating a variety of both plant and animal species.[10] The latter occurred in three distinct patterns and areas: dry-land farming in the north, centering on millet; wet farming in the center, with rice as the main staple; and root crops in the south, focusing on tubers—like New Guinea and Southeast Asia, only partially agricultural with 30 to 50 percent of food cultivated.[11] Generally, the first signs of agriculture are an

[8] Liu and Chen 2012, 61-63. Also Barnes 2015, 101; Shelach-Levi 2015, 57; Zhu 2013, 171.
[9] Liu and Chen 2012, 55-56; Chang 1977, 29; Guo and Li 2002, 196-98.
[10] Shelach-Levi 2015, 68. See also Crawford 1992, 13; Jiao 2007, 32, 37; Li 1983, 23; Li 2013, 22; Pechenkina et al. 2000, 18.
[11] Liu and Chen 2012, 165; Barnes 1993, 97; Shao 2005, 90; Yan 2005, 29-30.

increasing nut economy. Since the most productive nut trees—possibly intentionally planted and grafted—grow commonly at the edge of forests and in open areas, and running water is needed for processing acorns, sites are typically located near rivers in low hilly areas (Liu and Chen 2012, 66).

The oldest grain cultivated in China is millet, harvested with stone sickles (Yan 2005, 32; Higham 2005, 238). It comes in two species: foxtail or spiked millet (*Setaria italica*; *su* 粟, *liang* 梁) requiring dry conditions, and broomcorn millet (*Panicum miliaceum*; *shu* 黍, *ji* 稷), more flexible in growth areas and more glutinous in nature.[12] While it was collected in its wild variety as far back as 18,000, its earliest domesticated form appears around 6200 in the Liao river valley in the northeast. In the Neolithic, it made up 15 percent of food intake, increasing to 99 percent during the Bronze Age under the Shang, when it was also fed to dogs and pigs.[13] The centrality of this grain to the Western Zhou, defined by the agricultural nature of their state, is also evident in the importance of the key deity Lord Millet, Houji 后稷 (Ho 1975, 61; Campany 2005, 99).

The main grain in central China is rice (*oryza sativa*). Since it requires 39 inches of rain per year and a temperature above 61 degrees Fahrenheit (16° C), it did not arise until the weather had become warmer and wetter. While some phytoliths appear around 11,000, rice only makes serious inroads after 8000 (Higham 2005, 240, 242). Domestication began with the stabilization of climate to warmer levels in the hilly terrain of the Yangzi valley around 5000.[14]

The domestication of rice transformed a perennial water plant that reproduces from its roots into an annual swamp grower that multiplies from seeds. Unlike wild rice, which is not an efficient source of nutrients—containing only 1.3 easily scattered grains per panicle—domesticated rice is a powerful resource with 82 closely contained grains per stalk.[15] The latter, moreover, developed into two major variants, non-glutinous, long-grain, lowland rice (*geng* 秔/粳) and glutinous, round-grain, upland rice (*xian* 秈).[16] From here, rice cultivation spread throughout Asia, eventually reaching as far as Japan, the Philippines, and Thailand (Higham 1995, 138; Toyama 2002).

---

[12] Ho 1975, 57-57. See also Anderson 2014, 37; Barnes 2015, 116; Chang 1977, 26-27; Chang 1983, 65-66; Fernandez-Armesto 2002, 91; Fogg 1983, 95; Harlan 1977, 379; Ho 1977, 437-39; Li 1983, 29; Liu and Chen 2012, 82-82; Pechenkina et al. 2000, 19; Simoons 1991, 72; Stuart 1976, 40; Underhill 2002, 35; Zhu 2013, 176.

[13] Liu and Chen 2012, 84; Anderson 2014, 38; Pechenkina et al. 2013, 291.

[14] Liu and Chen 2012, 76. See also Anderson 2014, 36; Barnes 2015, 117; Chang 1977, 27; 1981, 179; Chang 1983, 70; Fernandez-Armesto 2002, 91; Fuller et al. 2009; Graeme and Janowski 2011, 9; Hayden 2011, 82; Higham 1995, 135; Lu 1999, 202; Ohnuki-Tierney 1993, 13; Pechenkina et al. 2000, 18; Pei 2002, 172; Simoons 1991, 66; White 1995; Yan 2002, 152; Yasuda 2002b, 130.

[15] Hayden 2011, 81. See also Lu 2006, 140; Sato 2002, 145-46; Simoons 1991, 69.

[16] Ho 1975, 62. See also Chang 1983, 72-73; Li 1983, 42; Stuart 1976, 295-96; Yan 2002, 152.

Wheat, barley, and oats, the main cereals in the Near East, were not locally domesticated in China, but introduced from outside. They do not appear until the 3rd millennium, wheat gradually moving from Gansu to Shandong, barley being found mainly at higher altitudes, and oats grown only in the far northwest.[17]

The oldest domesticated legume in China is soy (*shu* 菽), with early traces around 7000 in the Yinluo 伊洛 Basin in Henan, closely followed by mung, adzuki, velvet, and broad beans.[18] Major tubers include yams (*shanyao* 山药), taro (*yu* 芋), lotus root (*lian'ou* 莲藕), arrowhead (*cigu* 慈姑), and kudzu vine root (*gegen* 葛根). Easy to grow, they were present already in the Paleolithic and dominantly used in the south, where they functioned as a main staple, with grain not being planted until 4000.[19]

Among vegetables, moreover, sites show remnants of buckwheat, burdock, Chinese cabbage, gourd, hemp, hops, mustard, pea, radish, rape, safflower, and water chestnut; fruits included apricot, jujube, melon, peach, pear, persimmon, and plum; and among trees, besides the ubiquitous wormwood (artemisia), oak, and nuts, there were also lacquer and mulberry.[20]

Domestic Animals

The oldest domesticated animal worldwide species is the dog, evidence for which is found in Belgium and Siberia as far back as 20,000 years (Barker 1994, 73; Herre and Röhrs 1977, 261). Chinese dogs are a domesticated version of the Chinese wolf; first clear traces appear around 7000, when some were ritually buried as hunting partners. Later, Neolithic sites contain many dog remains, indicating that they were also consumed as a source of protein and furnished sacrificial offerings.[21]

The second major domesticated animal in China, ubiquitous in Neolithic sites, is the pig. Also popular in other parts of the world, there is no one location for its domestication, which is clearly evident by 7000 (Herre and Röhrs 1977, 259; Pechenkina et al. 2000, 20). Compared to wild hogs, domestic pigs are smaller in size, both in bones and teeth, and killed at a clearly defined age, usually no later than two years old. Many bones are found among plant remains as are skeletons among buried humans, indicating their importance and close-

---

[17] Liu and Chen 2012, 92-93. See also Chang 1983, 77-78; Ho 1975, 73; Yan 2005, 30.
[18] Liu and Chen 2012, 86-88. See also Anderson 2014, 44; Chang 1977, 28; Chang 1983, 80-81; Li 1983, 30; Simoons 1991, 70, 74.
[19] Liu and Chen 2012, 90-91; Simoons 1991, 102-07, 112-15.
[20] Crawford 1992, 9; Chang 1977, 28; Hayden 2011, 82; Ho 1977, 423; Li 1983, 32-36; Yan 2005, 39. For more on Chinese vegetables and fruits, see also Simoons 1991, chs. 5, 7.
[21] Liu and Chen 2012, 96. See also Anderson 2014, 32; Simoons 1991, 310.

ness.[22] A major wealth item (Anderson 2014, 45), pigs have formed an integral part of the agricultural system of China, kept in pens adjacent to farm houses and fed on household garbage. "The use of large amounts of dark green, leafy vegetables for human consumption inevitably generated large quantities of partially decomposed leaves and stems, which made excellent pig food, supplemented with soybeans" (Harris 1985, 151).

Sheep and goats come in multiple distinct domestic lineages for each species. Domesticated several times in different civilization zones, their remains show an eastward spread parallel to that of oats and barley.[23] It, therefore, appears, that some were of Near Eastern origin while others grew locally, but their domestication was an imported skill (Liu and Chen 2012, 105).

Ancient forms of cattle in China include the humpless tauric in the north and the humped zebu in the south. Important domestic animals in the Near East by 7000 (Herre and Röhrs 1977, 261-68), data suggest that in China they were introduced from the north and south along different routes, arriving around 5000 and increasing steadily in numbers until fully domesticated around 2000 (Liu and Chen 2012, 106-07).

There are also two types of water buffalo: the river buffalo found mainly in India, the Near East, and Eastern Europe, plus the swamp buffalo, at home in China, Bangladesh, and Southeast Asia. The two were domesticated independently, beginning in northwest India some time before Harappa (3300-1300), and in Southeast Asia shortly thereafter (Liu and Chen 2012, 108-10). Another imported species is chickens that were probably first domesticated in India on the basis of red jungle fowl. In China, they first appear around 6000. All these various animals were not only kept for meat but also provided secondary products, such as skins, feathers, bones, eggs, milk, and wool, and—especially bovines—served purposes of transport, pulling, and plowing.[24]

Still, cows remained few, and where other cultures used space for grazing ruminants, the Chinese created irrigation terraces for planting. As Marvin Harris points out,

> China was not compelled to raise traction animals in the zones of dense human settlements since China has always had access to animals raised by pastoralists, who inhabited the vast grasslands of the Inner Asian frontier. The Chinese had no reason to keep large numbers of cows to breed oxen

[22] Liu and Chen 2012, 97; Chang 1977, 29; Simoons 1991, 295.

[23] Herre and Röhrs 1977, 255-58; Anderson 2014, 46.

[24] Liu and Chen 2012, 115; Simoons 1991, 297, 305. The earliest bovine-plow complex did not appear in China until the Eastern Zhou period in the Yellow River region. As the *Guoyu* 國語 (Tales of the States) notes, "The animal which was formerly used as a sacrificial offering in ancestral temples is now used as a productive force in the field" (Jinyu 9) (Liu and Chen 2012, 117; Hayden 2011, 79).

> and therefore never were motivated to use milk as a by-product of their use of animals for plowing. Nor did they have an economic obligation to raise sheep or goats for dairy. (1985, 150)

As a result, the Chinese never underwent the genetic mutation for lactose tolerance, and to them milk remained "an ugly-looking, foul-smelling glandular secretion that no self-respecting adult would want to swallow" (Harris 1985, 131). To obtain the calcium and other nutrients it contains, they used various beans, especially soy.[25]

Neolithic Cultures

A variety of cultures located in five major areas of China bear these facts out: 1. the north, including the northeast around Liaoning (NE) and the northwest in Gansu and Shaanxi (NW); 2. the central and lower Yellow River basin in Shanxi and Henan (YR-1), as well as Shandong (YR-2); 3. central China along the Yangzi, i.e., Hubei and the Three Gorges area (C-1) as well as Jiangsu and Zhejiang (C-2); 4. the south, including Hunan (S-1), Guilin and Guangzhou (S-2), as well as the southern islands, such as Hainan (S-3); 5. other southern areas, notably Fujian in the southeast (SE) and Sichuan in the southwest (SW) (Liu 2004, 7; Underhill 2013, 6).

In terms of time, there is a transition from small to larger settled communities, manifest in two major groups of sites: one dating around 7000-5000, known as the early Neolithic or late Mesolithic, the other from 5000 to 3000, i. e., the Neolithic proper or mid-Neolithic (Liu 2004, 25; Yao 2013, 587-88).

The first group, some cultures of which present over a hundred sites, is characterized by relatively small, spread-out villages (Higham 1995, 133). Only two acres were occupied in every 20-35 square miles or containing five settlements per seven acres, and populations hovered around a hundred (Shelach-Levi 2015, 70). They typically show houses and storage facilities (some subterranean) as well as graveyards, indicating some community planning. Graves may be communal or show gender differentiation, tools being buried with men and ornaments with women.[26]

All cultures have a great variety of stone tools and some domestication, mostly of fruits and nuts, plus tubers and millet. However, they are still heavily weighted toward wild plants: soybeans, acorns, walnuts, hazelnuts, jujube, plums, and water caltrops (Liu and Chen 2012, 144; Bettinger et al. 2010). They also have domesticated dogs, pigs, and some cattle, as well as pottery. Their graves are still rather undifferentiated, with collective burials (some secondary),

---

[25] On Chinese lactose intolerance, see Anderson 1977, 341; 2014, 19, 25; Fernandez-Armesto 2002, 71; Goody 1982, 107; Harris 1985, 151; Schmid 2015, 16; Simoons 1991, 458.
[26] Yao 2013, 587; Zhang 2005, 72; Barnes 2015, 149.

but there is as yet no elaboration, ornamentation, or ranking (Shelach-Levi 2015, 81; Pei 2002, 175-76). More specifically, they include:[27]

	Province	Culture	Duration
NE	Liaoning	Xinglongwa 興隆洼[28] Xinle 新樂	6200-5200 5500-4800
NW	Gansu, W. Shaanxi	Dadiwan 大地灣[29]	6000-5000
YR-1	Henan S. Hebei	Peiligang 裴李崗[30] Cishan 磁山	7000-5000 6000-5500
YR-2	Shandong	Houli 后李[31]	6500-5500
C-1	Hubei, Three Gorges	Zaoshi 皂市 Chengbeixi 城北溪	5800-5000 5800-4700
C-2	Zhejiang	Xiaohuangshan 小黄山 Kuahuqiao 跨湖桥[32]	7000-6000 6000-5000
S-1	Hunan	Pengtoushan 彭頭山[33] Bashi dang 八十垱	7000-5200 6000-5200

The second group shows a "dramatic increase in the number of sites" (2012, 171) over much vaster areas, leading to a differentiation within cultures (*wenhua* 文化), described in terms of subcultures or types (*leixing* 类型) (Shelach-Levi 2015, 69; Liu 2004, 8). Thus, for example, the Yangshao 仰韶 culture reaches from Gansu to Shandong and divides into a number of different types, totaling well over 5000 sites.[34] Major cultures include:[35]

	Province	Culture	Duration
NE	Liaoning Inner Mongolia	Hongshan 紅山	4500-3000 5400-4500

[27] Based on Liu and Chen 2012, 129-62. See also Anderson 2014, 37-38; Higham 1995, 135; 2005, 238-43; Maisels 1999, 271-76.

[28] For a presentation and discussion, see Shelach and Teng 2013, 40-45.

[29] Peterson et al. 2016, 206.

[30] For a study of Peligang tools and social structure, see Zhu 2013, 173-81; for more on its Jiahu 賈湖 site, see Zhang and Cui 2013.

[31] For more on Houli, see Wang 2013.

[32] For a detailed description and analysis, see Jiang 2013.

[33] For a comprehensive study, see Pei 2013.

[34] Liu and Chen 2012, 189; Barnes 1993, 98-100; Ho 1977, 433; Pechenkina et al. 2000, 17.

[35] Following Liu and Chen 2012, 169-215. See also Barnes 2015, 135; Higham 2005, 245-50; Ho 1977, 416; Jiao 2013, Li 2013, 29; Maisels 1999, 277-86; Thorp and Vinograd 2001, 25-27.

		Zhaobaogou 赵宝沟	
NW	Gansu, W. Shaanxi	Yangshao: Banpo 半坡 Yangshao: Miaodigou 庙底沟[36]	5000-4000 5000-3000
YR-1	Henan / S. Hebei	Yangshao: Xishan 西山	5000-3500
YR-2	Shandong	Beixin 北辛 Dawenkou 大汶口[37]	5300-4300 4100-2600
C-1	Hubei, Three Gorges	Daxi 大溪	5000-3300
C-2	Zhejiang	Hemudu 河姆渡 Majiabang 馬家浜 Songze 崧澤 Xuejiagang 薛家岗	5500-3500 5000-4000 4000-3000 4000-3300
S-2	Guangdong	Xiantouling 先头领	4000-3000
S-3	Hainan, Jinmen	Keqiutou 壳丘头 Fuguodun 复国墩 Jinguishan 金龟山[38]	4000-2500 4300-3600 4800-2300
SE	Fujian	Keqiutou 渴求头 Dapenkeng 大盆坑[39]	4000-3000 4000-2500

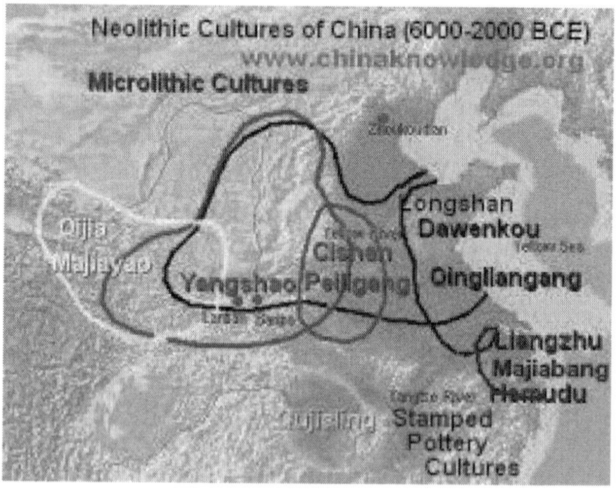

[36] For a description and analysis, see Li X. 2013.
[37] For a comprehensive presentation of Dawenkou, see Luan 2013.
[38] On these southern island sites, see Jiao 2007, 45-57; 2013, 601. For Yue cultures in the south, see Meacham 1983.
[39] For a presentation of these and other southeastern cultures, see Jiao 2013.

Social Change

In the course of the mid-Neolithic, sites became increasingly larger and occupation patterns denser, the result of a steady increase in population, growing into the thousands per location by the end of the period (Liu and Chen 2012, 69; Shelach-Levi 2015, 71). Walled settlements appeared for the first time as well as large public edifices for ritual performances—cairns, altars, temples—requiring a substantial labor force under organized management.[40]

Houses often were still semi-subterranean but increasingly built above ground (Yan 2005, 31)—sizable and more rectangular, gradually replacing the round patterns and curved walls of earlier settlements (McIntosh 2006, 337). The round structures of the Paleolithic remained on a fixed scale and served to enclose, providing an open yet protected space for all in an egalitarian setting. Angular houses, on the contrary, allow expansion and create division into various chambers, corners, and niches, signifying differentiation, segmentation, and specialization (Jones 2007, 140).

In addition, houses at the time were increasingly arranged in organized rows or around a central common or plaza—a prominent example being Jiangzhai 姜寨, a Yangshao site near Banpo (Xi'an), which even features some buildings with multiple rooms and sections, almost like modern apartment blocks.[41] Tools were of higher quality and came in more varieties, including the first leaf-shaped spades as well as rectangular stone knives (Liu and Chen 2012, 173-75). Some pottery sherds even contained incised markings, possibly counters or emblems of social groups, some quite close to later Chinese writing (Cheung 1983, 326 Goepper 1996, 277-78).

Diets moved toward a greater emphasis on grains so that, for example, the Xinglongwa people's diet consisted to 14.7 percent of nuts and tubers, while their successors of the Hongshan culture did not consume them at all, instead eating grain, especially millet (2012, 177; Anderson 2014, 59). Similarly, the percentage of acorns at Tianluoshan 田螺山, a site of the Hemudu culture in Zhejiang, shrank from 50 to 10 percent while rice increased from 8 to 24 percent in the early 5th millennium.[42]

---

[40] Liu and Chen 2012, 182. See also Otterbein 2994, 162; Pearson 1983, 134; Peterson and Lu 2013, 60; Underhill 2002, 32; Yan 2005, 35.

[41] Shelach-Levi 2015, 73-76; Peterson et al. 2016, 207-08. For more details on Jiangzhai, see also Anderson 2014, 42-43; Barnes 1993, 104; 2015, 139; Ho 1977, 419; Liu 2004, 36; Thorp and Vinograd 2001, 29; Underhill 2002, 39; Yan 2005, 37; Zhang 2005, 68. The same also holds true for Hongshan. SeePeterson and Lu 2013, 68; Peterson et al. 2016, 209; Lei 1996, 220-22.

[42] Shelach-Levi 2015, 65. See also Barnes 1993, 93; 2015, 121-22; Hayden 2011, 79; Sun G. 2013, 564; Yan 2005, 29.

Early Yangshao people showed severe masticatory stress due to eating tough food and chewing hides, but they were relatively free from dental caries, iron and vitamin deficiencies, anemia, osteoporosis, systemic infections, and intestinal parasites (Pechenkina et al. 2000, 23-24, 35). The latter may also have to do with the fact that "relatively low population density may still have permitted sufficient access to unpolluted fresh water to ameliorate the adverse effects of close contact with domesticated animals" (Pechenkina et al. 2013, 471).

As diets became more grain based and less diversified, caries and other indicators of dental disease such as crowding increased, showing a clearly discernible pattern that matches the unfolding of complexity in Yangshao from west to east (2013, 316). All cereals are low in protein, amino acids, and vitamins, offering inadequate nutrient content, and millet in particular is the grain with the lowest chemical scores (Pechenkina et al. 2000, 26). As Chinese populations grew to depend on them more fully, they began to suffer widely from low growth, anemia, scurvy, Pellagra, and the like (2000, 26-27; 2013, 468-69).

Impacting the genome, this caused a shortening in people's stature, over time leading to a pattern of continuous decline, with a particular spike in the Eastern Zhou (Pechenkina, Ma, and Fan 2013, 466). It caused shrinkage all the way through the middle ages and did not reverse until the Yuan dynasty (2013, 455). More complex social stratification and greater disparity in gender roles, moreover, resulted in a pervasive increase in sexual dimorphism, i. e., women, close to equal size in the Paleolithic, were becoming increasingly shorter than men (2013, 458-60).

The dominant emphasis on patrilineal descent began at this time, around 4000, predicated by the "fast growth intervals for global male populations" related closely to the establishment of agriculture (Wang et al. 2016, 3). In China, this is clearly evident from separate tombs for lineage branches (*shi* 氏) and clans (*xing* 姓) with elaborate settings and higher numbers of ornate earthenware food vessels and carved jades as grave goods, placed formally on a separate shelf (*ercengtai* 二层台).[43] Thus, society at Hemudu was still rather egalitarian in nature while its successor culture of Songze shows clear social stratification (Liu and Chen 2012, 203; Higham 2005, 247). There is also an increasing hierarchy among settlements, groups of villages congregating around larger sites. However, nothing yet points to pervasive centralized political authority over an entire area (Liu and Chen 2012, 180).

Communication and infrastructure improved and regional exchange economy picked up, raw materials coming from as far as 200 or more miles away. Art work spread—a human figurine in a standing position with arms folded toward the chest found in Hongshan is very close to one discovered in

---

[43] Shelach-Levi 2015, 82. See also Barnes 2015, 138; Maisels 1999, 309; Yao 2013, 588-89; Zhang 2005, 72.

Lingjiatan 凌家滩, 600 miles further south (2012, 180). In some areas, the environment began to show signs of overexploitation such as deforestation, and ecosystems were used to the point of deterioration and desertification.[44]

> Instead of developing technology to improve agriculture, the elites appear to have turned to religion. This situation is clearly reflected by their emphasis on construction of public architecture for rituals and by their obsession with making and using jade ritual objects. . . .
>
> Indicators of civilization, such as increased quantities of monumental architecture and jade artifacts, were in fact desperate measures taken against environmental uncertainties. (Liu and Chen 2012, 183)

This is also borne out by increasing ritual activities related to agriculture as well as enhanced cosmological calculations and the close observation of celestial phenomena (2012, 207).

In addition, population pressure seems to have increased, leading to an expansion even across the ocean. Thus, the southern Dapenkeng culture appears in Taiwan rather abruptly around 2800, complete with millet cultivation, domesticated pigs, and corded pottery ware.[45] Form here, as many scholars agree on both genetic and linguistic grounds, it spread further east and south, spawning Austronesian cultures all over the Pacific—its 1200 languages "spoken as far east as Easter Island and as far west as Madagascar" (Jiao 2007, 82; Anderson 2014, 23).

The Chalcolithic

The agricultural surplus supported the economic foundation of the emergence of social complexity and elite authority as expressed in ritual power and the formation of ideological systems on an interregional scale (Liu and Chen 2012, 251; Barnes 1993, 108). This enhanced civilization, which developed further in the third millennium with the growth of large cities, powerful states, and copper technology in the period known as the late Neolithic or Chalcolithic.[46]

At this time, the first complex societies of chiefdom or beginning state level developed, characterized by extensive "social stratification manifested in mortuary remains, long-distance exchange of elite goods, and hierarchically organized settlement systems."[47] They were the first to experiment with bronze metallurgy and to establish major ritual complexes and systematic flood control systems. Dominant cultures of the time include (Liu and Chen 2012, 216-50):

---

[44] Barnes 1993; 107; Liu and Chen 2012, 171.

[45] Jiao 2007, 91; Chang 1981, 181; Li K. 2013, 614; Meacham 1983, 163.

[46] Liu 2004, 27. See also Maisels 1999, 303; Otterbein 2004, 161; Shao 2005, 90.

[47] Liu and Chen 2003, 34. See also Liu 1996a; 1996b.

	Province	Culture	Duration
NE	Liaoning	Xiaoheyan 小河沿 Xiajiadian 夏家店[48]	3000-2000 2000-1400
NW	Gansu, W. Shaanxi	Majiayao 馬家窯 Machang 馬廠 Qijia 齊家[49]	3300-2650 2350-2050 2200-1700
YR-1	Henan, Shanxi	Central Longshan 中龍山	3000-2000
YR-2 YR-2	Shandong Shandong	Eastern Longshan 東龍山 Yueshi 岳石	3000-2000 1900-1500
C-1	Hubei, Three Gorges	Qujialing 屈家嶺 Shijiahe 石家河[50]	3100-2700 2500-2000
C-2	Zhejiang	Liangzhu 良渚	3400-2250
SE	Fujian	Damaoshan 大帽山 Huanggua shan 黄瓜山[51]	3000-2300 2300-1500
SW	Sichuan	Baodun 寶墩[52]	2700-1750

Some cultures, notably Longshan, had several thousand sites (Sun B. 2013; Zhao 2013) and advanced tool technology (Cunnar 2013, 464), reflecting the rapid population growth of the period (Shao 2005, 91; see also Huber 1983). Towns tended to have walls, populations in the multiple thousands, strong defenses (Yan 2002, 155; Otterbein 2994, 163), and socially stratified and administratively specialized areas. These typically divide into five categories: extraction (mining, farming), manufacturing (ceramics, metal), storage (silos, pits), distribution (merchants, trade), and administration (ritual, palaces) (Barnes 1993, 103).

Thus, for example, Taosi 陶寺 (fl. 2600-2000) was a complex regional Longshan center in the Linfen basin of the Yellow River (Shanxi). Covering 750 acres, it was laid out according to a semi-circular plan and centered on a raised platform 2.5 acres wide, consisting of multilayered rammed earth terraces with square columns, probably used for ritual purposes and astronomical observation.[53] Besides a 6-foot lacquer pole, a gnomon to measure the shadow of

[48] For more details on this late Neolithic culture, see Wang 2013.
[49] For a presentation and discussion, see Chen 2013.
[50] For an examination of these two cultures, see Zhang 2013.
[51] For details on these southern sites, see Jiao 2013, 603-05.
[52] For a presentation and examination of this culture, see Flad 2013, 133-38.
[53] Liu and Chen 2012, 223-24. See also Anderson 2014, 60; Barnes 2015, 166; He 2013, 262-71; Li 2013, 30-33; Rawson 1996a, 40-45; Underhill 2002, 37.

the sun at the equinoxes and solstices, Taosi also produced the earliest metal objects, including a copper bell and an arsenic bronze object attached to jade. Two glyphs in red on a pottery vessel maybe indicate the name of Yao or possibly refer to Wenyi, an early capital of the Xia 夏 dynasty (Liu and Chen 2012, 225-26).

Several hundred graves show a clear social stratification—87 percent being small, 12 percent medium, and 1 percent large and elaborate, given to males with multiple hundreds of grave goods.[54] Well administered and a major center for stone manufacturing and specialized industry, Taosi was the most important economic, political, and religious center of the region at the time, characteristic of early urbanism.[55]

Another major culture was Liangzhu in the Lake Tai area of Zhejiang and southern Jiangsu. The political center of a cluster of smaller cities on the brink between chiefdom and state (Li 2013, 37), the complex was a walled settlement that centered on a raised terrace and supported sacrificial altars on the foot of nearby mountains (Qin 2013, 574). It also contained an extensive burial ground, featuring eleven tombs with over a thousand objects made from locally procured jade, including figurines, tubes (*cong* 琮), and disks (*bi* 璧) (Yang 1996, 226). Here the social hierarchy is evident,[56] both in the organization of the city as a whole and the structure of the graves. In addition, social conflict seems to have increased, as evidenced by the large number of headless and footless corpses and the proliferation of projectile points.

Further south, the Qujialing and Shijiahe cultures along the middle Yangzi near Lake Dongting contained a thousand sites each, with a total of nine large-scale walled cities, located at the juncture between higher mountains and the flat alluvial land near the river or lake. Constructed for flood control, they reveal a great deal of specialization, including areas of workshops for craft production, residential housing complexes, ritual edifices, and cemeteries. Over a hundred tombs yielded thousands of clay figurines, all kinds of animals plus humans holding fish, as well as myriads of cups in red pottery as well as spindle whirls, workshop parts, stone tools, and jade grave goods (Liu and Chen 2012, 242-43).

---

[54] Yao 2013, 589-90; Maisels 1999, 294; Shao 2005, 92-93, 121.

[55] Shelach-Levi 2015, 152-55. See also Chang 2005, 126; Liu et al. 2013, 279.

[56] Liu and Chen 2012, 236-40; 1993, 112-13. See also Barnes 2015, 163; Lei 1996, 223-24; Qin 2013, 579-86; Rawson 1996a, 51-57; Shao 2005, 113-15; Thorp and Vinograd 2001, 34-38; Xu 2013, 310-12.

The Bronze Age

By the beginning of the second millennium, many well-developed complex societies disappeared from the archaeological record. One factor was climatic and environmental change, since the Mid-Holocene climatic optimum was on the wane (Liu and Chen 2012, 251; Keightley 2000, 1). This period also saw frequent devastating floods in many river valleys that destroyed numerous settlements (Barnes 2015, 174-75). It is quite possible that these floods match what the texts describe as the "great flood," controlled by the legendary ruler, Yu the Great (see Lewis 2006b) and that the early Xia site near Dengfeng 登封 in Henan (fl. 2200-1835) was in fact Yangcheng 陽城, Yu's capital (Liu and Chen 2012, 222).

Yu's activities as described in an early Western Zhou bronze inscription (ca. 950-850) indicate the increasing centralization and state formation of the period. It says, "Yu cut off the trees to open land for plantation, taxed the subjugated people, and oversaw virtues. . . . He made himself the partner [of Heaven] and rejoiced in the people, being their father and mother, and gave birth to our kingship" (Li 2013, 50).

The first Bronze Age culture and full-blown state in central China arose at this time: Erlitou 二里頭 in Henan (1900-1600), centered on a site twice the size of Taosi.[57] It contained numerous pits of various functions, indicating social stratification and segmentation as well as massive, ritual bronzes, "vessels of considerably larger size at a much higher degree of technological complexity and sophistication" (Li 2013, 46).

Associated speculatively with the Xia dynasty described in later texts (2013, 51; Chang 1983b, 503), Erlitou established control over an increasingly vast area of the Chinese heartland all the way to the Yangzi by means of military conquest, population migration, colonization, alliance formation, exchange of goods, and marriage (Liu and Chen 2003, 145; Barnes 2015, 187-92). This was necessary because the Yinluo Basin lacked non-agricultural resources, notably timber for constructing palaces and temples, lithic materials for making stone tools, kaolin clay for creating elite (white) ceramics, wood and charcoal as fuel for casting bronzes, and—the most important state monopolies—metals (copper, tin, lead) for making bronzes and salt for cooking and processing food (Liu and Chen 2003, 35).

While copper was mined in southern Shanxi and tin and led came from south of the Yangzi (2003, 39), salt was procured by solar heat drying from the Hedong 河東 Salt Lake near the bend of the Yellow River and the Yuncheng

[57] Li 2013, 43. See also Anderson 2014, 61; Liu 2004, 27, 30; Underhill 2002, 21. Another major Bronze Age site, in the Chengdu basin of Sichuan, is Sanxingdui 三星堆. For its history and characteristics and, see Rawson 1996a, 60-84; Sun H. 2013, 152-59; Zhou 1996.

運城 Basin south of it (2003, 43-46). To establish control over these areas, the Erlitou people colonized Shanxi and established tributary dependencies in other parts of the country (2003, 69, 146). To transport these goods, moreover, they set up several long-distance trade routes, combining waterways with roads, and building major collection and reloading points (2003, 50-56). Still a dominantly a territorial state—as opposed to the city and segmentary states under the Shang (Keightley 2000, 56)—they thus centralized administration, ritual, and technology, laying the foundation for the growth of the Chinese empire.

Another indication of Erlitou's empire building activities is that in its early years, the population had reached 13.5 million (Maisels 1999, 260), of whom 18-30,000 resided in the extensive and highly developed capital city (Chen and Liu 2003, 64). Others lived in as many as 10,000 small states, which the centralized state reduced to 3,000 by the beginning of the Shang in 1554 (Chang 2005, 126; Anderson 2014, 63).

Starting out as a small state and trading partner east of Erlitou (Chang 1983b, 499), the Shang moved their capital five times to sites on rivers (Chao 1982, 17; Yuan 2013, 326, 331), to eventually settle in Yin 殷, modern Anyang 安陽, a hundred miles north of Zhengzhou 鄭州 around 1200 (Keightley 1983, 524). One of its major capitals, Zhengzhou is also the center of the Erligang 而里崗 culture (Li 2013, 56-61). While Zhengzhou itself is hard to excavate, since the site is under a bustling modern metropolis—as are many other sites in China (Murowchick 2013, 25)—Erligang has yielded numerous artifacts. Most important among them are bronzes that served an elaborate ritual structure and pottery with basic written graphs.[58] The culture divides into two major phases, ranging from 1580 to 1450 and from 1450 to 1300, respectively (Chang 1980, 264; Li 2013, 59).

Comparable to Uruk in Mesopotamia, Harappa in northern India (Wang 2014, 69-71), and Naqada in ancient Egypt (Baines 2014, 101), Erligang culture—and thus the early Shang kingdom—was representative of a centralized state with a high level of social complexity, ruled by a militarily backed elite (Wang 2014, 87). Larger than other sites of the same period, including the Near East, it contained temple and palace complexes as well as extensive sacrificial remains, including hundreds of human skulls (Campbell 2014, 122; Chang 2005, 126). Workshops, notably bronze and ceramics but also wood, bone, shell, and more, show a high degree of specialization, while burials reveal a pervasive social hierarchy (Campbell 2014, 123).

Flourishing economically, Erligang—like Erlitou—expanded widely, establishing trade routes complete with military outposts and colonial settlements.

[58] Bagley 2014, 32; Cheung 1983, 370.

Sites range widely all over north and central China,[59] with outposts even south of the Yangzi (McNeal 2014, 173). The best known among them is Panlongcheng 盤龍成 near Wuhan 武汉 in Hubei, a walled site about 300 miles south of Zhengzhou (Yuan 2013, 329). Inhabited by aristocrats, craftsmen, and farmers who most likely moved there from the capital (Wang 2014, 85), it was extensive in size and contains tombs much richer than those discovered to date at Zhengzhou, yielding hundreds of bronzes and thousands of artifacts (Zhang 2014, 51).

The late Shang, with its huge capital complex at Anyang continued this pattern, increasing bronze casting facilities and sizes and for the first time adding inscriptions on bronze vessels (Li 2013, 74-75; Jing et al. 2013, 347). Both lineage and ritual structures became more complex—lineage chiefs being not only military leaders but also key sacrificers (Chang 1983a, 35, 37)—the regional networks intensified (see Li and Hwang 2013), and social stratification and specialization increased, without, however, yet developing into a bureaucratic form of government (Li 2013, 107).

Still, the dynasty established key cultural values, such as the notion that China was "an island of civilization in a sea of barbarous contemporaries" (Chang 1983b, 496) and the idea that governmental "success of failure depended on the rulers' extravagance or temperance" (Chang 1983a, 34)—a major argument in justifying their takeover from the Xia. Rulers, guided by ancestral advice obtained through oracle bones (1983a, 51-54; Li 2013, 92-95), developed strategies and gave commands that organized society, both civil and military.

Personal status and identity rested entirely with the social network, leading to strict obedience structures and a focus on the close cooperation and reciprocity among all different levels and branches of society (Chang 1983a, 37). Status was obtained through control over others as well as through conspicuous consumption and the creation of luscious, intricate art works, art forming a major "path to authority" (Underhill 2002, 48). In ancient Chinese culture, socially defined values such as honor and shame—recognition or rejection—presented central features, leading to feuds among the living and an elevation of the dead, increasingly showing "forefathers as powerful sages and good lords" (Chang 1983a, 41) while enhancing the suppression and impoverization of the peasant masses.

---

[59] Campbell 2014, 128. See also Chao 1982, 93; Fang 2013, 474; Wang 2014, 83; Zheng 1996, 245.

Chapter Four

Fundamental Values

Common folk see differences and are clear-cut.
I alone make no distinctions.
I seem adrift at sea,
Like the wind blowing about,
Apparently without destination.
The multitude all have a purpose.
I alone seem stubborn and rustic. (*Daode jing* 20)

In contrast, Daoists have continued to emphasize the core concerns and key virtues of their golden age, the late Paleo- and Mesolithic. Most important among them are a "sense of reality in its pure and primary form" (Lawlor 1991, 8), i. e., a close connection to nature and the derivation of self-identity, both personal and communal, from the larger environment and the greater universe rather than from social conventions and political power structures.

Closely related to this is the activation of proper cosmic energy flow in space and time, a deep-seated respect for, and honoring of, the earth with its various features, especially mountains, and the heavens with the sun and the moon as the main setters of time. Beyond that, Daoists embrace several key personal values, such as an ease and flow of life in nonaction, social flexibility, individual authenticity, as well as simplicity and sufficiency—knowing who we are in relation to nature and society, what we can and cannot do in any given situation, and when and what it means that there is enough.

Their overall cosmic connection and these personal values make Daoists who they are—both as individual seekers and as members of larger organizations. Creating a form of counter-culture that engenders pristine affluence under all and any conditions, these values make Daoism highly relevant today while pitting its representatives time and again against the dominant culture that surrounds it.

The Cosmic Connection

Like Australian aborigines whose "culture is founded entirely on the remembrance of the origin of life" (Lawlor 1991, 14), Daoists determine their identity and ideal lifestyle in relation to Dao, the power of creation and never-ceasing flow of life that underlies everything. Australian Dreamtime (*tjukurrtjana*) as much as Dao is the "absolute ground of being" and inherent power of all existence (1991, 264). Since it is a continuum beyond ordinary human perception, people can relate to it only by letting go, by transcending common human faculties, by becoming subtler and finer and more potent, more energetically subtle, i. e., more like the ground itself.

In addition, however, this underlying reality also concretely manifests in the give and take of various pairs of complementary opposites, in the natural ebb and flow of things as they rise and fall, come and go, grow and decline, emerge and die. As the *Daode jing* says:

> To contract, first expand; to weaken, first strengthen.
> To destroy, first promote; to grasp, first let go.
> This is the subtle pattern [of life]. (ch. 36)

All things flow in alternating patterns; life is in constant motion. In a continuous flow of becoming, everything always moves in one direction or the other: up or down, toward lightness or heaviness, brightness or darkness, growth or decline, life or death—yin or yang. All that grows must decline; all that declines must transform into new levels of being, and we need to find balance within this dynamic (Lee et al. 2008, 89).

Another way to express the same idea is with the concept of Heaven (*tian* 天) or Heaven and Earth (*tiandi* 天地), more concrete, visible entities that signify the presence of Dao in the world. As the *Zhuangzi* says, "Heaven and Earth are huge, but they are alike in their transformations. . . Pervading Heaven and Earth, that is Dao" (ch. 12; Kohn 2014, 82). Dao or Heaven thus represent the cosmic force par excellence, the core of all existence, what we would call "the universe."

The later religion makes this more explicit. As outlined in the *Chisongzi zhongjie jing* 赤松松子中戒經 (Essential Precepts of Master Redpine, DZ 185[1]), of the 4th-century CE, people consist of the *qi* of Heaven and Earth and their thoughts and actions have a direct impact on the world's functioning.

> Human beings live between Heaven and Earth and are endowed with the two *qi* of yin and yang. Sovereign Heaven, although high, yet has its correspondence down below. Mother Earth, although low, yet has its corre-

[1] Numbers in the Daoist Canon (DZ) refer to Schipper and Verellen 2004.

> spondence far above. Heaven does not speak, yet the four seasons move in order. Earth does not speak, yet the myriad beings come to life.
>
> People reside right between the two. All their licentious intentions and passionate desires, whatever they do or do not do, Heaven and Earth know all about it. For this reason, we say that Heaven has all-round knowledge. (2a; Kohn 2004a, 14)

To make sure they do not interfere with nature's workings, Daoists have instituted numerous rules and precepts, explicitly guiding behavior to activate the direct consonance of the life-giving power of the universe in personal and communal reality. Rather than isolating human conduct in the social sphere, separating it from nature, they embed it fully in the larger context of the cosmic flow. Individual rules, as a result, are not as important as the sense of the codex as a whole. Compliance can be handled flexibly and carries merit primarily if undertaken as an expression of cosmic spirituality. As such, ethical rules and religious precepts are neither foundational nor separate, but constitute a key aspect of practice that affects the nourishing powers of Heaven and Earth and ultimately leads to the transformation of the individual into a cosmic being, one who takes his identity from the universal flow within (Kohn 2004a, 5).

Creating identity by living in relation to the universe is also a clear characteristic of hunter-gatherer communities and primitive cultures. Living "with nature as a given" (Lee 1979, 116), foragers and aborigines appreciate that "all creatures—from stars to humans to insects—share in the consciousness of the primary creative force and each, in its own way, mirrors a form of that consciousness" (Lawlor 1991, 17). Human existence forms a part of the ceaseless cosmic activity of creation—an ongoing movement of consciousness from dream to reality (1991, 37) or, in Daoist terms, of *qi* from spirit to form.

By the same token, cosmic connectivity is a central concern of the new cosmology currently emerging from the scientific community. Also called "scientific cosmology," it is much like Daoism in that it understands the universe less as a "container for everything else" than as a "dynamic evolving being" (Primack and Abrams 2006, 19). Striving to open "patterns that connect humanity to a vaster destiny—a vital participation in earth's unfolding" (Swimme and Tucker 2011, 111), its goal is to make us "know who we are and see from a cosmic perspective" (Abrams and Primack 2011, 37; Kohn 2016, 10).

In light of paleoanthropology, all these can be seen as different expressions of the strife to recover a way of being that came naturally to our Stone Age ancestors. Without the interference of culture and technology, they had no choice but live in close connection to nature. Observing the constellations of the stars and the movements of the planets, following the herds of large mammals, and moving to new areas as plants gave no more fruit and the weather changed, they had to be keenly aware of Heaven and Earth in all their manifestations and adjust to them—not by careful deliberation and rational analysis but by gut reaction, instinct, and intuition.

Space and Time

To supplement this original connection, Daoists consciously enhance their relationship with space and time. Considering "the earth as a sacred vessel" (*Daode jing* 29), they are highly conscious and respectful of their physical environment, placing their practice in the ideal constellation of natural settings and making a conscious effort to connect to the energies of the universe. They also work closely with natural time, being aware of the circadian rhythm of the human body in conjunction with the energetic changes in the course of day and night, summer and winter, and taking care to practice at the right times and with the proper relationship to the spiritual powers (Kohn 2012, 75).

In terms of space, Daoists match hunter-gatherers in their close relationship to the earth. For example, Australian aborigines not only get their sense of personal identity from place (Lawlor 1991, 235), but they understand the relationship of the earth to humanity as "that of a pregnant woman to the child within her: the woman changes both physically and psychologically as the child develops, and the fetus derives all of its capacities to grow from the mother" (1991, 90). They see the earth as a living body and "believe that in the daily act of making camp they again cause the place and surrounding country to come into being" (1991, 235). Appreciating all life as a concert of rhythmic activities, they feel the world consisting of numerous instruments that come together in a musical orchestra to create a symphony (Gleiser 2010, 69), so their Dreamtime consciousness as much as the Daoist understanding of the subtle energy of *qi* moves toward harmonious flow and full entrainment, a completely resonant system, a creative union on all levels and in all dimensions—the fundamental wholeness of the universe (Kohn 2016, 37).

More particularly, Daoists activate the classic Chinese practice of Feng Shui or geomancy, evaluating physical settings in terms of *qi*-flow—acknowledging just like other indigenous people that "the blood of the gods, the subtle magnetic, celestial flow, circulates in the veins of the earth" (Lawlor 1991, 104). In particular, they strive to avoid both excess and deficiency, here called killing *qi* (*shaqi* 殺氣) and dead *qi* (*siqi* 死氣). The former moves too fast, rushing along straight lines and taking health and good fortune away; the latter is deficient or blocked by clutter or heavy objects because it cannot move freely (Kohn 2005, 130). Balancing both Daoists tend to maintain a stark, clutter-free environment, living an example of purity and open energy, placing objects not just for practical use but also to provide a soft undulating motion of *qi* (Kohn 2012, 210).

For best effect, they also prefer to live in a *qi*-rich environment, surrounded by rich vegetation and active wildlife, generally preferring mountains and wilderness to cities and civilization. Mountains play a key role in the Daoist management of space (Hahn 1988, 147). Apart yet essential, they are a feature of the earth that yet connects to the heavens above. Mountains are sacred places that house wondrous plants, animals, and beings who can help the practitioner's quest. They contain grottoes, caverns, caves, underground spaces, hollows, and corridors that possess a number of qualities manmade places lack (Hahn 2000, 693). They are archetypal chambers of reflection and the classical home of the immortals where miraculous phenomena abound.

Mountains form a natural sanctuary, both as holy places dedicated to Dao and as sites of refuge and protection (Schipper 2001, 82). Providing wondrous opportunities to venture into the unknown, they may appear solid, yet are passages of *qi*, allowing smooth air currents and water flows, which reflect the inner workings of the human body. Blood equals water; air equals breath. Spermatic liquids form pools; walls constitute shapes like inner organs or viscera (Hahn 2000, 695). In their self-contained interior, free from the defilements and impacts of the outside world, adepts can perform alchemical and meditative experiments of self-transformation, experience an intimate closeness to Dao.

Just as Daoists place themselves ideally in space, so they also work closely with time, again beginning with common Chinese practices. Thus, they celebrate the Eight Nodes (*bajie* 八節) of the year—the solstices and equinoxes plus seasons' beginnings—and arrange their lives according to twenty-four solar periods of two weeks each, typically named after weather patterns such as "great heat" or "slight snow" (Kohn 2001, 47). As do ancient hunters and modern foragers (Lee 1979, 107), they closely match life to the seasons, adjusting their daily cycles of sleeping and waking, wearing suitable clothes, eating appropriate foods, and generally doing things in proper accord (Liu 1990, 5-10; Kohn 2010, 46-48). They also perform regular ceremonies at major junctions of the year, linking the seasonal transitions with the establishment of cosmic goodness and clarity (Benn 2000, 319).

Beyond seasonal patterns, Daoists also match their activities to the traditional Chinese calendar that uses a cycle of sixty symbolic character pairs applied to years, months, days, and hours. Religious rituals of all Chinese traditions are scheduled according to the auspicious or inauspicious nature of these pairs, and many of the most important Daoist rites occur once every sixty years to mark the renewal of the cosmos (see Saso 1972). In addition, Daoist and other millenarian movements have focused on certain years, such as the first year of the cycle (*jiazi* 甲子), as the starting point of the new world (Kohn 2001, 48; 2012, 76-77). Personal cultivation, too, follows this system, using the character pairs as they designate days and working in periods of sixty (2012, 79-80), allowing Daoists to adjust their activities to the cosmos on all different levels while using universal energies to create a subtler way of being.

The same overall system also applies to daily rhythms. Practically every Daoist text, from antiquity to today, states firmly that, as the 7th -century *Yang-xing yanming lu* 養性延命錄 (Record of Nourishing Inner Nature and Extending Destiny) has it, "From midnight to noon is the time of living *qi*. From noon to midnight is the time of dying *qi*. Always practice during the time of living *qi*" (Kohn 2012, 192). In monastic practice, Daoists match their ritual and meal schedule to the celestial rhythm, chanting every morning and evening and eating to connect to the feeding times of different otherworldly beings (Kohn 2003a, 124-25).

Both in terms of space and time Daoists, therefore, adapt the common understanding and basic patterns of Chinese traditional culture, then add their own specific ways. Both are modes of cosmic manifestation and have to be accepted and activated properly. The relationship to space and time makes all the difference in the positivity of life and the effectiveness of cultivation practices. Key features of the cosmos, they have a strong impact on body, life, and world—always ongoing, never ceasing. Vice versa, their improper use can distort and confuse the cosmic patterns, causing wind and rain to come at the wrong moment, turning day into night and night into day. Keeping with the rhythms and patterns of nature is an important way of enhancing cosmic connectivity.

Self-Being

Closely connected to cosmic forces and their inherent patterns, early humans and contemporary aborigines "foster an encompassing sense of unity with the metaphysical (and physical) world" (Lawlor 1991, 232). They practice what Daoists call *ziran* 自然—self-being, naturalness, or spontaneity—without effort or intention going along with the inherent, self-generating, and self-organizing order of the universe (Wang 2015, 19). In the *Daode jing*, *ziran* functions as an attribute of all beings that are as they are of themselves and move forward of their own accord (2015, 141). As it notes, "Dao models itself on self-being" (ch. 25; 2015, 130); its potency "is not due to some outside command, but rests in constant self-being" (ch. 51).

The *Zhuangzi* uses the term similarly, also applying it to a distinct way of life in prehistory. It says

> The men of old dwelt in the midst of crudity and chaos; side by side with the rest of the world, they attained simplicity and silence there. At that time, yin and yang were harmonious and still, ghosts and spirits worked no mischief, the four seasons kept to their proper order, the myriad beings knew no injury, and living creatures were free from premature death.

> Although human beings had knowledge, they did not use it. This was the state of perfect oneness. At this time, no one did any assertive actions; all rested constantly in self-being. (ch. 15; Wang 2015, 141-42)

In the later religion, the same idea plays out as a pervasive ethical injunction to "act in harmony with self-being," leading to "blessings and good fortune forever resting with your personal body, while bad fortune and harm will eternally stay away from your door" (Kohn 2004a, 175).

In close correlation, Daoists further emphasize different dimensions of self-generation, leading to an entire string of natural or "self" activities: self-transforming, organizing, ordering, stabilizing, clarifying, simplifying, submitting, balancing, flourishing, righting, giving, examining, completing, acting, producing, and so on (Wang 2015, 20; Kohn 2014, 94). These terms show just to what degree Daoists emphasize the spontaneous, natural self-being of things. To them, as to their Stone Age forebears, all beings originally flow through life smoothly and spontaneously, naturally unfolding and instinctively acting in the world, functioning in perfect harmony with their unique needs and specific life situations.

The Daoist project, then, is to recover this state of original oneness and fluidity in life, destroyed after the development of agriculture with the arising of civilization and its discontents. They never cease to find new and creative ways to get people to change their way of being in the world, encouraging them to realize that they are an integral part of universal evolution and at all times energetically connected to the vastness of space and the enormity of cosmic time.

In this, they again match the actions of primitive peoples. "The aborigines did not clear and tear up the earth for agriculture. They did not enslave animals and subjugate plant species for systematic exploitation and slaughter. They did not build homes that cut them off from a natural adaptation to the wonders and ever-changing fluctuations of nature. They did not wrap themselves in clothing to subdue their vitality and sexuality and falsify their identity" (Lawlor 1991, 5-6). Neither do Daoists, and they move beyond concrete actions into more abstract considerations. Matching also the agenda of the new cosmology, they insist that "we are connected to the universe in our bones, our history, our atoms, and our minds" (Abrams and Primack 2011, 78), and that we have to make the active choice to see and experience ourselves in this way.

In practical terms, this means overcoming dichotomous thinking and emotional division. Zhuangzi formulates this in various ways, most poignantly in the notion of freedom from emotions (*wuqing* 無情). He says: "What I mean when I say a person is free from emotions is that he does not allow likes and dislikes entering him and burdening his body, but always goes along with his inherent self-being, never trying to improve on life" (ch. 5; Kohn 2014, 61). He vividly illustrates this in several episodes concerning death and mourning, always showing that life flows on even as individual entities perish. In this, his attitude is close to Paleolithic and foraging ways. As Robert Lawlor notes,

> Death, in the aboriginal view, is not a termination or dislocation from this world to another; rather, it is a shift of the center of one's consciousness to invisible, subjective layers that are substrate to, and involved within, the natural world of mind and matter. (1991, 360)

Pervasive Fluidity

Another area where Daoist values are close to Stone Age living is their emphasis on pervasive fluidity in relation both to the environment and other people. In terms of the environment, this appears in a general reluctance to interfere with natural processes and exploit resources, like hunter-gatherers and prehistoric humans living with nature in organic harmony. Their goal is to work at all times in a stable, homeostatic order that—like a low-maintenance garden—"arises out of spontaneous, mutual adjustment among many elements and forces in a given system" (LaFargue 2001, 52).

Placing priority on situation over agency, they define things not by their "absolute essence" but "correlationally at any given time" (Ames 2001, 269). Each part in the Daoist universe is unique; "each pattern is novel and site-specific" (2001, 277). Interacting with this multilayered and multifaceted world, then, requires the application of *wu* 無 or non-processes, which are non-objectified and encompass all existence, eliminating the need for stratification, control, and the "instrumentalizing aspect of desire" (Hall 2001, 261).

The key Daoist concept in this context is non-interference or nonaction (*wuwei* 無為), i. e., natural action, "nonattached responsiveness" (Burneko 2004, 188), or "perfect congruence" (Jones and Culliney 1999, 645). This is not inaction. "Given that Dao nourishes, sustains, and fulfills, Dao is invariably action-in-itself" (Ip 1983, 340). It is perpetual creativity where there is "nothing that is not done."[2] While this came naturally to ancient hominins, Daoists contend that people at any time and under any social circumstances can be trained to enter and maintain a "steadfast congruence" with the "natural, unconscious, undirected action" of Dao (Jones and Culliney 1999, 645-47). Just as Dao always acts in accordance with its own self-being, so people should follow their own accord and connect to others and the natural world flexibly and fluidly without imposing on them (Ames 1994, 36; Kohn 2014, 251)

Nonaction as non-interference means taking the most appropriate action under any given set of circumstances (Liu 2001, 325, 332). The opposite of

---

[2] The phrase occurs in *Daode jing* 37, 48, and 64. For a discussion of nonaction in Daoist ideals of leadership, see Amaghlobeli and Celepli 2012, 49; Dreher 2000, 223-25; Lee et al. 2008, 94-96.

mastery, control, and conquest—the key values in post-egalitarian societies—it means merging with nature's flow and contributing to a new identity of the system from within (Jones and Culliney 1999, 647). Inevitably active, it means that people remain at the edge of chaos, "functioning at the highest dynamic activity while still maintaining structure and integrity," neither in total randomness nor in a frozen realm, neither frantic nor stoic, neither too yang nor too yin (1999, 649). Resting in the calm center of all life, the pivot of Dao, human beings thus serve as nature's conduit, preserving balance in tension and allowing new dimensions to emerge, revert, and again emerge (1999, 650-51).

In terms of the relationship to other people, later Daoist communities activate the principle of nonaction as an admonition for concrete behavior. In this sense, it appears first in the precepts of the *Xiang'er* 想爾 commentary to the *Daode jing* of the early 2nd century CE, intending that people should act without artifice and in a way that was not contrived or willful. It involved a quiet mind, a laying-to-rest of the passions, and a sense of moving along with Dao (Bokenkamp 1997, 52).

Following these guidelines, Daoists activate continuously changing, pervasively fluid networks that utterly interconnect everything with everything else in different levels of complexity. Even as many as seven billion human beings connect by no more than six steps through the workings of "small worlds," weak ties linking clusters of strongly tied communities into complex webbings (Buchanan 2002, 37). Shown to be true on many different levels of life, this pattern is ubiquitous. "It is not a coincidence that the wiring of the human brain turns out to have the very same small-world structure as our social networks, nor that these patterns turn up again in the Internet, in the way words link together in human language, or in the food webs that underlie the world's exosystems" (2002, 197).

Living in a web of such fluid yet patterned natural and interpersonal networks, Daoists as much as ancient hunter-gatherers are "mobile nodes who form ties of variable commitment, content, and duration" (Gamble 1999, 42). They prefer their networks to remain at a level of low density, emphasizing individual personalities, as opposed to high-density structures that work with a high degree of centralization, incorporate standardized values, and come with greater gender segregation (1999, 43). Daoist communities grow from the bottom up, i. e., through the "succession of interactions between individuals" (1999, 37). Unlike in a top-down society, like Confucian China, which depends on social categories where "individuals are dominantly recognized by their institutional roles such as chief, big man, or priest-king" (1999, 34; Giddens 1984, 376), people here create social life as they go along.

They develop structure through (non)action rather than patterning their actions on established structure. Never trying to fit into a preconceived social ideal, they allow their relationships to unfold through habitual action—within their given resources growing society creatively as they go along (Gamble 1999, 35, 39). Open and negotiable, all interaction patterns including the kinship system are "a reservoir of potential but vague connections, which can form a social focus when required," at all times incorporating the different personalities of individuals (1999, 36-37). Open to choice based on personal preference rather than overarching rules, society here, "rather than being a static straitjacket, is a dynamic keyboard, on which individuals play variations on a theme of options" (1999, 35; Wilmsen 1989, 180).

It is thus no accident that the ideal social connection of Daoists as documented in the *Zhuangzi* is that of friendship, the most equal, balanced, and fluid among the five major relationships codified in Confucianism (Blakeley 2008, 321, 329). Friendship lies between the direct, close reciprocity of kinship and the more complex, indirect reciprocity of acquaintances and strangers, allowing for intimacy without inescapable obligation or the codification of social norms (Henrich and Henrich 2007, 48). Here two individuals engage in a common project of mutual self-realization, respecting each other fully as ends-in-themselves, in mutual recognition and acceptance (Blakeley 2008, 320).

Friends come together on the basis of common convictions and goals, able to "pay no attention to proper behavior, disregard personal appearance and, without so much as changing facial expression, sing in the presence of a corpse" (Galvany 2009, 56). Rather than being defined by social roles and conventional patterns, they are "individuals who, having stopped dwelling on their own bodies and their own lives, are able to dwell *in* them in a more genuine fashion" (2009, 58). "Natural, spontaneous, and irrepressible," their behavior "unabashed and unrehearsed" (2009, 53, 57), they approach life in a non-ego-centered way, in natural fluidity and an overall openness to individual unfolding (Kohn 2014, 242). As the *Zhuangzi* has it,

> The friendship of a gentleman, they say, is insipid as water; that of a petty man, sweet as rich wine. But the insipidity of the gentleman leads to affection, while the sweetness of the petty man leads to revulsion. Those with no particular reason for joining together will for no particular reason part (ch. 20; Watson 1968, 215).

Inner Authenticity

Another way of expressing the notion of easy functioning in the ever changing fluid networks of life and "complete absorption in the natural environment" (Kohn 2014, 37) is with the concept of "wandering" (*you* 遊)—following one's own natural patterns while adapting to the changes of nature and society (Lo 2002, 82; Møllgaard 2005, 13-14). It means that each being with its unique character and abilities does what it does within its own frame of being, following its self-being in nonaction, yet constantly carried by the Dao as the infinite source of universal being (Lee et al. 2008, 89).

You literally means "swim" or "float" (Yang 2003, 112) and "evokes the image of a waving flag" (Robinet 1993, 171). Wandering accordingly means carefree meandering in naturalness (Fox 1996, 60), floating freely and being carried by the swirls and eddies of life (Billeter 2010, 68), taking things as they come and flowing along with Dao. Rather than setting deliberate, conscious goals, one is centered in the transforming processes of Heaven and Earth (2010, 95).

A more subtle analysis of free and easy wandering shows that it has five features: it transcends contingency and is not dependent on circumstances or good fortune; it implies no fixed norms or direction but focuses on adaptation to change; it is grounded in an understanding of the potential range of alternative forms of life; it implies a readiness to transcend limits or boundaries associated with mainstream values and norms; and it is associated with an essentially carefree attitude (Kohn 2014, 18; Fraser 2011b).

In many ways, wandering matches the concept of flow in Western psychology. A deep sense of inner truth, satisfaction, and enjoyment, combined with a feeling of exhilaration, flow is "a state in which people are so deeply involved in an activity that nothing else seems to matter" (Csikszentmihalyi 1990, 4). "Optimal experience," just being who were really are, life in this state is a goal in itself and becomes an "autotelic" experience (1990, 67; Kohn 2014, 19).

Both wandering and flow work by deriving one's identity from Dao or the greater universe, by aligning oneself with the heavenly rather than the human, the cosmic rather than the social (Billeter 2010, 49). This means to "adequately respond to and satisfy the vital injunction that comes to me directly from the immense source of reactivity that lies in the great world process as a whole rather than from the narrow orb of my desires and repulsions" (Billeter 2008, 44). Being true to oneself and at the same time perfect in Dao, one lives from a deep level of personal authenticity, a sense of inner rightness, a way of being inherently at one—a state the *Zhuangzi* describes as *zhen* 真: perfected, true, genuine.

The term indicates the "true state of a thing" as opposed to anything artificial, a way of being in utmost purity and sincerity (Coyle 1998, 197, 199; Kohn 2014, 146). A potent metaphor is the raw piece of jade as opposed to the finely designed ceremonial object or the uncarved block of wood in contrast to the intricately carved masterpiece (Chong 2011a, 324, 327). Being *zhen* means to maintain a pervasive connection to the original, underlying perfection and wholeness of Dao at the root of existence while yet being true to one's particular disposition. Daoists describe this in terms of inner nature or inherent tendencies (*xing* 性), an essential component of personal identity. Like a genetic blueprint, it defines our inborn, genetically determined uniqueness, expressed physically in our fingerprints, retina, hand lines, and all the various physical characteristics that make us who we are. Psychologically it is our predisposition toward certain preferences, behaviors, and skills, i. e., our temperament (Kohn 2014, 102).

The *Daode jing*, too, emphasizes authenticity and the importance of truly being who we are, moving away from established cultural norms and becoming simple and dull even if everyone else strives for sophistication and wisdom (ch. 20). It is better to relax and do nothing than to keep pushing and running after things (ch. 57), realizing that our personal unfolding and physical integrity are more important than reputation, position, and material wealth (ch. 44). It advises us to get away from involvement (ch. 56), discard wisdom, and return to simplicity (chs. 19, 48). People should limit the input of the five senses (ch. 12) and recover the value of emptiness and openness (chs. 11, 45). To be as vital as an infant (ch. 10), they best cultivate weakness and softness (chs. 36, 43), always flowing along with Dao (ch. 64) (see Moeller 2006; Slingerland 2003).

The inner peace and fulfillment ancient Daoists describe closely resembles what Gary Zukav calls "authentic power." He says,

> Authentic power feels good. It is doing what you are supposed to be doing. It is fulfilling. Your life is filled with meaning and purpose. You have no doubts. You have no fears. You are happy to be alive. You have a reason to be alive. Everything you do is joyful. Everything is exciting. You are not worried about doing something wrong, making a mistake, or failing. You do not compare yourself with others. You do not compare what you do with what others do. (2002, 105-06)

Life among foragers lends itself strongly toward this mode of being. Just like Daoists who located their core in the central elixir field and like behavioral kinesiologists who find the mainspring of life energy in the thymus gland (Diamond 1979, 10), they place authenticity into the solar plexus and describe it as the transcendental energy of Dreamtime. "An internalized source of emotive power, this is then directed and modified by the sensitivity to, and knowledge of, one's social and natural surroundings" (Lawlor 1991, 251).

Finely attuned to both their personal center and the world around them, foragers wander about to find and gather food sources, moving for maybe four to five hours a day, always discovering new things as they go along and taking plenty of time to rest, chat, and play (Sahlins 1972, 17). Maintaining a childlike innocence and playfulness in the face of their daily tasks—a key ideal of Daoists (Kohn 2014, 256)—they enjoy what they do and relish what they have. Their economy not being physically demanding, their social organization not being highly stratified, they approach life with relish and enjoy what they do, "their days nothing but pastime" (1972, 29).

They expand their unique skills, gaining expertise without becoming overly specialized or comparing themselves to others. Thus, for example, a craftsman among the Fish Creek group in Arnhem Land who was expert in repairing spears and throwers as well as in making smoking-pipes and drone-tubes also "netted fish most vigorously" and on occasion "went into the bush to get wild bees' nests" (1972, 19). There is, thus, an inherent wholeness to their lives, an authenticity and oneness dearly cherished by Daoists.

Sufficiency

Another aspect of the foraging lifestyle that Daoists embrace with vigor is the value of sufficiency. Sufficiency is a sense of enoughness (*zhizu* 知足), a core focus on relationships with people and living beings rather than the accumulation of artifacts (material possessions) or devotion to abstract concepts (wealth and power) (Gamble 1999, 41). It means a life centered on dynamic process rather than set permanence. It is the innate feeling of flow: material objects and prosperity move through life in a current, constantly coming and going yet always providing just the right amount (Twist 2003, 103). As Lynne Twist says,

> Sufficiency isn't two steps up from poverty or one step short of abundance. It isn't a measure of barely enough or more than enough. Sufficiency isn't an amount at all. It is an experience, a context we generate, a declaration, a knowing that there is enough, and that we are enough. (2003, 74)

The universe being infinitely abundant, there is always enough. It is the foragers' way to consume in a splendid feast whatever they collect today, and to be frugal and patient when there is little. "While there is plenty today, never care about tomorrow" (Sahlins 1972, 30). Having low expectations and a fundamentally simple lifestyle, they enjoy what they have and do not fret about what they do not have—thus reaching pristine affluence. Just like foragers who do not have the means to store and amass, Daoists eschew accumulation and advise moderation in all respects.

Sources on nourishing life from all different periods agree that one should avoid overindulgence in food and drink as well as other sensory and sexual pleasures, observing instead guidelines for healthy living. More specifically, the *Yangsheng yaoji* 養生要集 (Long Life Compendium) by Zhang Zhan 張湛 of the 4th century CE points out that "heavy clothing and thick comforters, spicy foods and heavy meats, sexual attraction and beautiful women, melodious voices and enticing sounds, wild hunting and exciting outings," as well as all strife for success and ambition will inevitably lead to a weakening of the body and thus a reduction in life expectancy (Stein 1999, 178; Kohn 2012, 175).

Along the same lines, the *Baopuzi yangsheng lun* 抱朴子養生論 (Nourishing Life According to the Master Who Embraces Simplicity, DZ 842), associated with the would-be alchemist Ge Hong 葛洪 (283-343), exhorts people "to let go of fame and profit, lessen smells and tastes and moderate wealth and possessions of material goods" (Kohn 2012, 36).

Refraining from wanting more, Daoists reject the "pervasive lie of scarcity," established together with stratification, poverty, and starvation in post-agricultural societies, and its three toxic myths: that there is not enough, that more is better, and that it is just the way it is (Twist 2003, 49-53). Instead, they preempt modern studies that show how little is needed once people have basic security through food and shelter, knowing fully well that "actively wanting money is toxic to happiness."[3]. They insist that we learn to know when it is enough and stop trying to get more of what we don't need.

Relaxed and at ease, yielding and withdrawing, Daoists resting in sufficiency consume only what they need, always knowing what is right for them and never desiring more. As the *Zhuangzi* illustrates it in Yan Hui's answer to Confucius's question, "Why don't you get a job?"

> I don't want a job. I have eight acres of fields outside the city wall, enough for vegetables and grain. I also have an acre and a half of farmland nearby, which gives me enough silk and hemp. Strumming my zither is enough to give me pleasure, studying Dao with you is enough to make me happy. I don't want a job. (ch. 28; Kohn 2014, 73)

Sufficiency is a key factor in self-being and nonaction: it makes us truer to ourselves. The way we manage our goods and spend our money makes a statement of what we value most in life. "It takes courage to direct the flow [of money], but with each choice, we invest in the world as we envision it" (Twist 2003, 131)—according to Daoists, a world of fewer possessions and more happiness (Andrews 2009, 5). People in modern, technological societies tend to be "overfed but undernourished," incomes rising and material goods increasing while happiness is tapering off (Wann 2009, 41). Daoists and modern exponents of simplicity agree that it would be much better to shift from "an emphasis on material wealth to an abundance of time, relationships, and experiences," allowing values of moderation, frugality, and sufficiency to create a high quality of life (2009, 43).

These values, moreover, transform our fundamental outlook in relation to others, seeing them as partners rather than competitors. Virtues such as compassion, empathy, modesty, and respect come to dominate—another characteristic of aboriginal culture, which nurtures a "sympathetic and empathetic sensitivity to the surrounding world" (Lawlor 1991, 246). This signals a major game

---

[3] Biswas-Diener 2008, 315-16; see Maslow 1954, 309.

change. In contrast to traditional games that work with the win-lose principle so that the winner takes all, nothing remains in the pot, and the total sum is zero, this way of interacting in games, life, and business, works with win-win or non-zero sums. That is to say, all participants benefit in one way or another, nobody leaves empty-handed, and there is overall more to go around and great joy and well-being in togetherness (McTaggart 2011, 120; Wright 2000).

In foraging societies, which by definition lack the means to hoard and accumulate since they are constantly on the move, this plays out in a general disdain and detachment from possessions. This may even go so far that some people, such as the Tasmanian aborigines, do not even have a word for the accumulation of goods and let presents from Westerners rot in uncared-for piles (Lawlor 1991, 5, 252).

It also manifests in the two areas of pooling and sharing. Pooling means that everyone contributes to their kinship group and community as they can; it is "socially a *within* relation," the complement of social unity and centricity. Sharing or reciprocity, on the other hand, can take place among various players; it is "a *between* relation," a factor of social duality and symmetry (Sahlins 1972, 188). "Pooling stipulates a social center where goods meet and thence flow outwards" as well as a specific social boundary. "Reciprocity stipulates two sides, two distinct social-economic interests" (1972, 189). Both together allow the continuous flow of goods among group members, making sure that everyone has just enough and is well provided for.

The emphasis on social cooperation, moreover, is also borne out by recent developments in the understanding of evolution. Biology and anthropology still insist that evolution favors the "survival of the fittest." However, the definition of "fittest" no longer includes being the strongest and most aggressive, the alpha-male or the one with the greatest firing power. Rather, the fittest is now the most cooperative, the one who can create the best networks, who garners the most support from the community and furnishes the best living conditions for everyone (Wright 1994). Both ancient foragers and traditional Daoists have understood this all along, developing ways of thinking and being in the world that leave none behind and benefit all.

Chapter Five

The Thinking Mind

> People of old had perfect knowledge. How was it "perfect"? They thought in a way that matched the stage before things existed. Their knowledge was perfect and exhaustive; nothing could possibly be added to it. Next, they saw things as existing things, yet they did not yet make any distinctions among them. Then a stage came when people made distinctions among things, but they had as yet no sense of right and wrong. When right and wrong began to appear in people's minds, Dao was destroyed. The destruction of Dao meant the beginning of personal preference and one-sided love. (*Zhuangzi* 2)

The thinking mind plays a key part in the Daoist project, its understanding matching insights of evolutionary psychologists today. According to this, the thinking mind or discriminating consciousness is a relatively recent phenomenon, the result of a long and varied development. It began with unitary, intuitive sensing and evolved through stages of recognition and objectification to increasingly sophisticated distinctions and delimitations. Eventually the ability to think about a thought and be self-aware in a reflective, analytical manner arose, characterized by selectivity, exclusivity, chaining, and unitarity (Harth 1993, 139). This, moreover, did not happen until after literacy developed and forms "a specifically human ability built upon the basis of the power of language" (Jaynes 2006, 91). In other words, the critically self-aware, dualistically thinking mind is the product of post-agricultural complex societies.

In contrast, Stone Age people still were at a level of mentation characterized by orality—associated with the Human Revolution in the Upper Paleolithic—and a much more immediate form of thinking. They as much as Daoists work more directly with connective consciousness and intuition, the faculty of awareness and perception common to all living organisms and shared widely in the animal world.[1]

Prior to that—reflecting an even more connected way of being also described by Daoists—early hominins relied largely on mimetic skill, "the imaginative enactment of an event" (Bellah 2011, 125). "An extension of conscious

[1] Griffin 1992, 10-11; Shettleworth 2010, 146.

control into the domain of action" using skill, mime, gesture, and imitation, it enabled them to communicate through body language.[2] Transmitted as part of culture and community (Tomasello 1999, 4-5), it brought about the faculty of precise imitation, allowing early man to share particular ways of doing things. This, in turn, led to the growth of skill, the result of "rehearsal, systematic improvement, and the chaining of mimetics into hierarchies" and the evolution of systematic gestures as an explicit act of communication (Bellah 2001, 264-65).

The most elementary and unitary mode of consciousness, what Daoists describe as a state of unknowing, is part of animal life and goes back to the very beginnings of humanity. In the early stages, hominins lived in close harmony with the environment and could feel—and immediately react to—changes as they occurred. That is to say, when the species *homo* first appeared on earth, they were still part of nature and, much like primates, lived purely by instinct and functioned dominantly through perceptual consciousness (Jolly 1999, 274). Paying attention largely to the here and now, they functioned on an energetic level of immediacy (Franks 2010, 25).

Stages of Evolution

The most focused Daoist discussion of the evolution of these different modes of consciousness appears in chapter 2 of the *Zhuangzi* (Kohn 2014, 46-48). It begins by pointing out that "people of old had perfect knowledge." Their minds matching the time before the division of the cosmos into yin and yang, "their knowledge was perfect and exhaustive; nothing could possibly be added to it." Guo Xiang 郭象 (d. 312), the main *Zhuangzi* editor and commentator (Kohn 2014, 89), calls this first stage Chaos Complete (*huncheng* 混成):

> This is the state of complete oblivion of Heaven and Earth, of total abandonment of the myriad beings. On the outside never examining time and space, inside one is never conscious even of the body. Thus, people are boundless and free from all fetters; they go along with beings and are in full accordance with all. (Kohn 2011, 27)

Like embryos in the womb, part of the flow of universal energy, people in this stage have no awareness of external things as separate and "relate to the world as if nothing had yet come into existence" (Coutinho 2004, 167). They are perfect and whole in their perception, their mind at one with all there is.

From here mental awareness evolved to recognizing "beings" (*wu* 物). People at this level perceive things as separate from themselves, yet they make no distinctions between them and do not attach value to one over the other. "There is more now than undifferentiated mush—there is some kind of plurali-

[2] Donald 2001, 269, 283; Trout 2011, 111.

ty of differentiable things, but these things are not grouped into bounded regions" (Coutinho 2004, 166). Guo Xiang describes this as a kind of loss, saying that "oblivion is no longer complete," but gives it a positive tinge in that, despite the fact that "now beings are recognized as existing, there is still the oblivion of distinctions between this and that" (Slingerland 2003, 177). At this time, people were primitive, but they "knew how to live." As the *Zhuangzi* notes,

> In the most ancient of times birds and beasts were numerous while human beings were few. People built nests in trees to avoid them. During the day, they gathered acorns and chestnuts, at night they climbed back up into the top of the trees. For this reason, they are called the people of the nesting clan.
>
> Following this, in high antiquity, people knew nothing about clothes and garments. In the summertime, they would collect great piles of firewood to burn in the winter to keep warm. For this reason, they are called the people who knew how to live. (ch. 29; Kohn 2016, 46-47)

Distinctions such as those of clothes and living quarters appear in the next stage, described as "boundaries" (*feng* 封), a word that has both political and geographical implications (Coutinho 2004, 166). At this stage, as Guo Xiang says, "there is for the first time a distinction between this and that" (*shibi* 是彼). This means, certain objects and phases of life are clearly separate in people's minds, they use them differently and apply categories in life, getting a sense of "destruction and accomplishment," as Guo Xiang puts it. However, they still do not judge things. As the *Zhuangzi* emphasizes, "they had as yet no sense of right and wrong." In other words, they had names and language but merely used it to "pick at things in the world and left it at that, never overstepping its bounds and letting it become reified into rigid concepts and categories" (Slingerland 2003, 177).

That changed with the arising of "right and wrong" (*shifei* 是非), the last stage of the evolution of discriminating consciousness. Here people reach a point where they become slaves to language, establish fixed patterns in their world, and make dichotomous judgments. They mark things in relation to each other and create classifications in terms of values. At this point, "Dao was destroyed," as the *Zhuangzi* has it. Guo Xiang echoes this, again returning to his theme of oblivion:

> If [the distinction between] right and wrong were not there, Dao would still be complete. With the destruction of Dao, emotions begin to be partial and love develops. As long as you cannot forget one-sided love and free yourself from egotism, there is no way you can ever find original oneness in yourself or with others (Kohn 2014, 34).

To sum up, according to the Daoist model, human beings start out in a state of being one with everything, of flowing *acceptance*, then evolve to *objectification*, distinguishing between different things and learning to tell A from B but without evaluating them. Next, they come to *delimitation*, an awareness of things being different and having a particular impact on our lives. Only after that do they move to *judgment*, attaching permanent, intellectually justifiable values to things and setting up firm conceptions of how the world works.

Similar developmental outlines that closely match the Daoist description also appear in two Western studies, Ken Wilber's *The Spectrum of Consciousness* (1993) and Merlin Donald's *A Mind So Rare: The Evolution of Human Consciousness* (2001). They, too, see four stages of increasing complexity and differentiation, characterized quite like the Daoist model: Mind, Existence, Ego, and Shadow according to Wilber; episodic, mimetic, mythic, and theoretic according to Donald (Kohn 2016, 50-52). The main difference is that, while Donald sees the emergence of civilization and the modern mind in a positive light as the "great hominid escape from the nervous system" (2001, 305), Wilber agrees with the Daoists in seeing civilization as a loss of connection and oneness and favors a recovery of more essential modes of awareness.

Critical Consciousness

Daoists describe the critical, self-reflective consciousness of "right and wrong" as the "fixed mind" (*chengxin* 成心), a solidified set of reaction patterns that manifest in rote responses, inflexibility, and stereotypes (Hansen 1992, 276; 2010, 41). In terms of judgment, it means predictability and prejudices; in terms of personality, it means stiffness and set ways (Enzinger 2002, 136; Yearley 2010, 129). The mind here is machine-centered, a "mechanical mind" (*jixin* 機心) that sees the world in terms of personal gain and loss and strives to impose its own preferences on life.

The source of all errors, this mind holds on tight to its set patterns and particularly to established norms, such as the classic Confucian values benevolence and righteousness, loyalty and filial piety. Rather than expressions of spontaneous goodwill and joyful relationships that change over time, they become restrictive, stifling corsets of mind and life (Sommer 2010, 215), expressed physically in the *gong* 躬 body, the ritual, sanctimonious body that occurs frequently in Confucian literature (2010, 213; Kohn 2014, 58).

Later Daoists expand this understanding, integrating the Buddhist notion of mental projections (*jing* 境). Based on language classifications established in the mind, they are mental imaginations that are projected outward to create an apparent reality of "being," contrasted with wisdom (*zhi* 智), a function of clear perception and pure awareness representing "nonbeing" (Robinet 1977, 245; Kohn 2010a, 37). Mental projections, moreover, create agitation and restlessness in the mind, since they continuously demand classification and evaluation, then stimulate an emotional response to them. As the great physician and Daoist Sun Simiao 孫思邈 (581-682) in his *Cunshen lianqi ming* 存神煉氣銘 (Inscription on Visualizing Spirit and Refining Energy, DZ 834; trl. Kohn 2010a, 174-78) notes,

> There is much agitation and little stillness. Thinking is conditioned by myriad different projections, accepting this and rejecting that without any constancy whatsoever. Dreads and worries, plans and calculations keep racing on inside like mad horses. This is the normal [thinking] mind. (1b-2a; Kohn 1989a, 220; 2010, 176)

Daoists have nothing but contempt for this mode of consciousness and insist that it is neither necessary nor useful, an extraneous and superfluous addition to human life. Indeed, rather than a biological given, it is the result of evolutionary and genetic changes that came with the expansion of the higher brain and an increased use and growth of the prefrontal cortex in the newest section of the brain, its so-called neo-mammalian part (Ford and Wortman 2013, 44).

The upper part of the brain, this is the command center, an information-processing system that protects us by rational analysis and classification of information, conscious managing of dangers, and by rejecting ideas that seem impossible or useless. It works with set patterns that create projections of ideal or fearful situations, often distorting actual facts, then sends signals to all other agencies in the bodymind to either excite or inhibit their actions. Yet it also includes the ability to focus intelligently on one issue or the other, enabling us to think clearly and make positive decisions. The locus of ambition, empathy, foresight, and morality, it is the core of our personality, and has been called the "seat of humanity" (Ramachandran 2011, 21; Kohn 2015a, 165).

In terms of the evolution of mind, it is rather late and not as immediate in its experience. Described by Ken Wilber as the Shadow Level (1993, 130-31) and as the "theoretic stage" by Merlin Donald (2001, 139), discriminative consciousness as activated by the prefrontal cortex is evident first around 1200. It is fully manifest in philosophies of about 600, a period of great change that the German thinker Karl Jaspers called the Axial Age, when "man as we know him today came into being" (Jaspers 1953, 1), creating abstractions and sophisticated forms of criticism (Momigliano 1975, 9).

The thinking, discriminative mind is the direct result of literacy, a consequence of the development of writing, originally a secret or even magical power known to a select few that "conferred privileged access to material and spiritual resources" (Keightley 1996, 89). Writing is the visible record of spoken words or logophonic script and thus different from other forms of record keeping of economic and political transactions, such as knotted cords, arranged pebbles, carved ivory bones, or pictographic abstractions (1996, 70, 87; Ong 2002, 85, 92-93). Definitely part of post-agricultural complex societies, its first traces go back to about 3500, when the elites of the great city kingdoms of Babylon and

Sumer developed cuneiform ideographs, soon followed by Egyptian hieroglyphs (2002, 83; Cooper 2004, 80).

Chinese characters appeared about 1500 under the Shang in conjunction with the greater social complexity of the Bronze Age, with some early traces discovered in Chalcolithic remains.[3] Early graphs represented the archaic pronunciation of words and were a phoneticization of early art motives—so that the rounded shape associated with the idea of dragon, for example, came to signify the sound of the word, **kliung* (Keightley 1996, 84-86). Unlike the Greek alphabet of about 800, which was easy to learn and flexible in application, the Chinese character script was a "system that, by its very difficulties, limited access to literacy and conferred great status" (1996, 89; Pankenier 2013, 151)—reflecting the hierarchical and stratified social realities of the agrarian age.

Completely artificial, writing used cortical areas of the brain related to visual input and enhanced prefrontal processing, thus raising consciousness to a new level, and opening the path toward the growth of an inner sense of self (Ong 2002, 81). More specifically, it allowed backward scanning of recorded thoughts, challenging logic, increasing the choice of words, and allowing the reduction of inconsistencies. Writing separated the knower from the known, opening the self to introspection and society to abstract concepts, such as justice and morality (2002, 102-04). For the first time, people became aware of the complexities of their internal motivations and were able to create itemized lists and indexes, gaining a much greater control over the outside world and their inner thinking while being more and more alienated from both.[4]

Emotional Reactions

Prior to this, the mind at the base of reflective discrimination is a form of mentation much preferred by Daoists, although not their ideal. They describe it as *xin* 心, a word that literally indicates the physical organ of the heart and graphically depicts its chambers (Enzinger 2002, 96; Jochim 1998, 50). The seat of both cognitive and affective functions, motivational and emotional patterns (Chong 2011b, 428), it is a structuring force within the person that supervises and manages the senses—the more it leaves them to do their thing, the better they work.

The senses, moreover, provide input described as *qing* 情, "basic tendencies, inclination, disposition, and fundamental qualities" (Puett 2004, 42; Harbsmeier 2004, 71). Chad Hansen understands the term as "reality feedback" (1992, 276) or, more precisely, "reality-induced discrimination or distinction-making reactions" (1995, 196).

---

[3] Keightley 1996, 68; 1989; Boltz 1994, 16-17; Diamond 1998, 330.

[4] Ong 2002, 148-49; Donald 2001, 305-07; Pankenier 2013, 151.

> *Qing* just crop up; we must deal with them. They come like the alternation of day and night; we just don't know where they come from. And it does not matter where they come from. They shape our lives. Without them we would have no notion of 'I' (as distinct from the reality outside us). (1992, 277)

Q*ing* come with distinct likes and dislikes, reactions the *Zhuangzi* describes as being like "music from empty holes" (ch. 2), i. e., pure vital energy (*qi* 氣) flowing from Heaven through the person (Kuriyama 1999, 244). Chinese medical literature places them in the body's organs. As the *Huangdi neijing suwen* 黃帝內經素問 (Yellow Emperor's Inner Classic, Simple Questions) says, "When the *qi* of the liver is too empty, there is fear; when it is too full, there is anger. . . . When the *qi* of the heart is too empty, there is sorrow; when it is too full, there is excessive joy" (ch. 3). *Qing* thus indicates a flow of vital energy in response to sensory experiences in the organs of the body, combined with various mental and affective functions. This flow is felt but not seen, as the *Zhuangzi* says about the true lord in the body (ch. 2). More immediate than critical reflection, emotions provide a system of reaction patterns that allows effective functioning in the world (Kohn 2014, 59).

With all these characteristics, *qing* closely matches the modern neurological and psychological definition of emotions, processed anatomically in the midbrain, which includes the paleo-mammalian brain as well as the subcortical system.[5] It houses several important areas, including the hypothalamus and the thalamus which govern the endocrine hormonal system and manage sensory and affective or emotional processing.

Beyond that, the midbrain also involves the amygdala (lit. almond), the early warning center that alerts us to approaching danger. Critical for the evaluation of all sensory cues in terms of threat, it is particularly the seat of fear and defense. It closely connects to the basal forebrain, which manages levels of anxiety and is in charge of the motivational modulation of attention, especially with regard to reward and pleasure (Wager et al. 2008, 252).

Another important structure in this area, located behind the amygdala, is the hippocampus (lit. sea horse), the seat of long-term memory formation. It coordinates contextual fear, perception, and the processing of emotional stimuli into set response patterns, thus making survival easier. The area is particularly rich in pleasure-inducing neurotransmitters, such as dopamine and endogenous opioids (2008, 253). The perception and reaction patterns established in this midbrain region, make us who we are, determining our relation to the outside world (Kohn 2015a, 164).

Emotions, then, "provide a quick, general assessment of the person's situation that draws on powerful internal and external values," responding to sensory information received by the amygdala and manifesting in aggressive or

---

5 Ratey 2002, 163-64; Ford and Wortman 2013, 43.

defensive, approach or withdrawal modes (Ratey 2002, 171, 174). All emotions have three key components: a felt bodily experience of more or less dominant sensations; a conscious cognition or thought regarding the cause or object of the emotion; and an expressive reaction, a clear behavioral move that can be as subtle as a facial expression and as obvious as an aggressive punch or a loving embrace (Kohn 2016, 60).

The Chinese system allows for this close connection of affect, cognition, and operative relations (Fraser 2011a, 103). The heart-mind as manager moves along with the *qing* throughout the different parts of the body (Ishida 1989, 55), makes sense of the body sensations, creates a narrative around them, keeps a record in memory, and establishes set behavior patterns and conscious judgments (Lee 1998, 459). In doing so, the heart-mind makes clear choices. It can be wide open and flowing everywhere or concentrated in one specific body part and sense organ; it can be easy and relaxed or tight and restrained.

If guided to move smoothly around the body so that it fills more of it, higher states of mental awareness result.[6] This, then, leads to a state where *qing* are experienced as pure cosmic flow, where the person can essentially be free from distinction-making reactions (*wuqing*), "always going along with inherent naturalness, never trying to improve on life" (Kohn 2014, 61). While people in this mode of consciousness, therefore, make distinctions and see boundaries, their reactions remain fairly immediate and are not necessarily predetermined or inescapable.

The same also holds true for the body associated with this mode, *shen* 身. A relational sense of identity, the familial and social persona of the individual (Sommer 2010, 215-16), it can be open and fluid or restricted and controlled, but in all cases depends on the group rather than a sense of unique individuality.

Orality

Ken Wilber calls this mental mode the Ego Level and notes that humanity at this point evolves to "have" a body, separating from organic reality by imagining emotions distinct from physical existence (1993, 118-19). Merlin Donald calls it the "mythic" stage, characterized by human beings here first adding sounds to gestures and developing an oral culture, complete with music, myths, symbols, and internalized or "imprinted" cultural structures that allowed somewhat greater complexity (2001, 285).

Just as writing shapes and characterizes discriminating consciousness, emotional mentation connects to orality. In terms of human evolution, fundamental sounds common to all primates gradually came to signal whether a given danger was near or far, big or small. They might also indicate immediate or delayed action—creating an early form of the imperative. Over thousands of

---

[6] Kohn 2005, 46; Kupperman 1996, 192.

years, these particular calls were standardized within a given group and, through epigenetic transmission and biological evolution, further expanded certain areas of the brain, thus forming part of the fundamental make-up of humanity.[7]

Orality gives expression to object recognition, which is clearly evidenced by the first drawings of animals in caves, such as those in Altamira and Lascaux, dated to around 35,000 and related to the Human Revolution. Associated also with the mutation of the FOXP2 gene in chromosome 7, responsible for speech production, this period is marked by the development of proper nouns, using simple universal phonemes such as *ba* or *pa* and onomatopoeias.[8] This not only enhanced the ability to think about things as separate, but also developed initial forms of memory. "A Middle Pleistocene man would forget what he was doing. But lingual man would have language to remind him," Julian Jaynes says, eerily echoing Guo Xiang's description (1990, 134).

Orally based thought has ten distinct characteristics. Besides relying heavily on auditory memory, in terms of grammatical organization, it is additive rather than subordinative (using "and" more than "while" or "after"), aggregative rather than analytic, i. e., heavily uses proverbs, formulas, epithets, and parallel constructions, as well as redundant or "copious," with repetition and backlooping. In terms of content, it tends to be close to the human lifeworld, homeostatic and present-oriented, "agonistically toned," i. e., deeply engaged with the issues and struggle of the time, as well as focusing on concrete events rather than general patterns. It is overall situational rather than abstract, empathetic rather than detached. Socially, moreover, an oral mindset tends to be conservative or traditionalist, geared toward maintaining the status-quo (Ong 2002, 36-50; Kohn 2016, 60).

Practically demonstrated in fieldwork among illiterate peasants in Uzbekistan and Kirghizia in the 1930s (see Luria 1976), this means that categories of thought are practice and process oriented. For example, when presented with a set of four objects, three of which were tools plus one log of wood, the subjects would class them together since they shared the same use, possibly eliminating one tool as not as practical. When asked whether logically there could be such a thing as white bears, they would take recourse to their own experience. When asked about geometrical shapes, they would answer by pointing to specific objects, and so on (Ong 2002, 50-52). All this shows that in orally-based mentation there are object cognition and acknowledgment of boundaries, but no self-analysis or isolation of the self as a separate entity (2002, 54).

To sum up, orality in human evolution matches the stage of "boundaries" in the *Zhuangzi*, the level of delimitation that allows emotion-based distinctions but still maintains close conscious and social connectivity.

---

[7] Dor and Jablonka 2014, 21; Jaynes 1990, 133; Pagel 2012, 280.

[8] Corballis 2010, 122-23; 2011, 70-72; Ramachandran 2011, 172-73.

Spirit as Mind

A yet more unitary mode of consciousness, much praised by Daoists, goes back even further into prehistory. Matching Zhuangzi's second stage of "beings" or object cognition, Wilber's Existential Level, and Donald's mimetic stage, it works with pure, cosmic spirit (*shen* 神).

Spirit is the core level of the heart-mind, a powerful indwelling agent, as well as a holy force to be held in awe (Roth 1990, 18). The *Zhuangzi* says, "Pure spirit reaches in the four directions, flows now this way, now that: there is no place it does not extend to. Above, it brushes the sky; below, it coils on the earth. It transforms and nurses the myriad things, but no one can make out its form. It is one with Heaven" (*Zhuangzi* 15; Watson 1968, 169).

The active, organizing configurative force and transformative influence in the person, spirit is without limit or judgment and comes before sensory affects and emotional reactions (Lewis 2006a, 22). An integrated whole that is not subject to increase or decrease, it works mainly with precognition and intuition (Roth 1990, 23, 16), open to Heaven and cosmic oneness (Puett 2003, 257). It remains in its lodging place, the body as form (Kuriyama 1999, 167), as long as it stays clear of vexations, predisposed desires, and intentional harnessing (Roth 1990, 17). "Be unseeing and unhearing, guard spirit in stillness," Guangchengzi says (ch. 11). Being whole in spirit means that one uses it to perceive and react instead of the senses, as Cook Ding and Woodworker Qing testify (*Zhuangzi* 3, 19). It also means that one remains unaffected by outer circumstances, as exemplified in the case of the drunken man who falls off a carriage and suffers no injury because "his spirit is whole" (ch. 19; Billeter 2010, 44-45).

The body, moreover, that comes with this is physical form (*xing* 形), "a discrete, visible shape or mass whose edges and outlines stand in contrast to the formless" (Sommer 2010, 218). Not circumscribed by cultural norms or defined through social values, it is part of the natural world, and animals have form as much as human beings. A physical, living entity, it is the lodge or residence of the spirit (*Zhuangzi* 6; Pregadio 2004, 108). The more we keep the spirit whole, retaining innocence and wonder, the more "the form stays whole, so that it can live forever" (ch. 11; Billeter 2010, 63).

By the same token, living through pure spirit and experiencing the body as form people to experience others and themselves as pure beings and find peace with death. "The Great Clod [of creation] has burdened me with form, labored me with life, relaxed me in old age, and is now ready to rest me in death. So, seeing my life as a good thing, I should also see my death as a good thing" (*Zhuangzi* 6; Watson 1968, 85).

Neurologically, spirit manifests within the human brain through the activation of mirror neurons, brain cells of the premotor cortex, particularly clustered in Broca's area (F5), that fire when we see or hear an action someone else performs nearby, mirroring the neuron activity in their brain (Keysers 2009, 18;

Kohn 2016, 56). Beyond merely acknowledging another's action, these neurons make sure that our brain fully shares in them, so that we see, hear, and feel the movements just as if we were doing exactly the same thing (Keysers 2009, 19; 2011, 19).

Present also in primates, mirror neurons rose to the fore in human development due to the increased brain size and capacity of *Homo erectus*, greatly increasing the social intersubjectivity of the species. In addition, they opened a much greater ability to imitate, that is, not only match movements as in mimicry, replicate actions as in mirroring or simulation, act to reach a particular goal as in emulation, but strictly follow the method used. For example, if I pick a fruit hanging above my left side using my right hand rather than the left, which would be closer, strict imitation means using the same hand (Keysers 2011, 35).

Early humans achieved this level of true imitation and created increasingly sophisticated mimetics. The foundation of language, defined as "a complicated system of signs and symbols held together by the logical structure of syntax and grammar,"[9] mimetics are a form of "attention manipulation" that can still be observed among Pygmys today.[10] They involve set mime signals, including basic vocalizations as well as gestures, and require systematic teaching through careful attention, detailed demonstration, and persistent repetition.[11] Meaningful miming, moreover, depends on subtle motor control in coordinated actions and sounds—screams, hoots, barks, grunts, pants, and squeaks (Clay and Zuberbühler 2014, 145)—that match particular objects or situations, key symbols that involve learned associations, and hierarchical structures, i. e., multiple levels and specific orders of actions.[12]

Far from being completely at odds with reality and confused in their environment, Paleolithic humans had thus quite a reservoir of communication skills and practical techniques at their disposal, yet in their thinking and feeling were much closer to nature and less alienated than their later descendants. While they came to identify with their organism and could see "things" outside as separate from themselves, developing a sense of time and space "in the most vividly concrete sense" (Wilber 1993, 116), their perception remained limited and free from thinking. Man at this stage, as Ken Wilber puts it, "prehends his being and his immediate duration, without any extra overlay of abstractions and symbolic interpretations" (1993, 117).

---

[9] Kafatos and Nadeau 1990, 95. See also Corballis 2011, 161-65; Greenspan and Shanker 2004, 163; Power 2014a; Sinha 2014; Wolpert 2007, 177.

[10] Tomasello 1999, 133; see also Lewis 2014.

[11] Dor 2014, 121; Whitehead 2014, 159.

[12] Keysers 2011, 72-73; Gazzaniga 2008, 162-63.

Unknowing

The ultimate overcoming of the thinking mind, the ideal of Daoist mystical attainment, is the state of unknowing, a resting in cosmic oneness, what the *Zhuangzi* calls "complete merging" (Kohn 2014, 64-65). Expanding from individualized existence, Daoists attain a mind that is pure flow of the vast cosmic abyss (*yuan* 淵), opening their body to becoming limitless vacillation of universal energy. A powerful description of this level appears in the story of the Gourd Master who shows all kinds of different dimensions of the bodymind to the shaman, eventually spooking her into escape. At one point, he gets closer to the center of the cosmic patterns.

> What she saw just now was the hub of my vital energy in balance. Where swirling waves come together, there is a deep pool; where still waters come together, there is an abyss; where flowing waters come together, there is an abyss. The abyss [of the cosmic mind] has nine names, and I have shown her three. (*Zhuangzi* 7; Kohn 2011, 71; Puett 2003, 256)

> The nine names are: Whirlpools, still waters, currents, water bubbling up from the ground, water dripping from above, water slanting from the side, water dammed and turned back, water draining away in a marsh, several streams coming from one source, and the all hollowed-out abyss. (*Liezi* 2; Graham 1960, 51; Girardot 2008, 124-25; Kohn 2014, 64)

Each of these stands for a particular state of the cosmic mind that is "both complex and fluid" (Kupperman 1996, 192): from the water that has not yet emerged from the source through the vastness of the primeval ocean and the beginning stages of the world that are without name or substance but already working, to the pattern of Earth—"still and silent, nothing moving, nothing standing up." Unlike the heart-mind and even the spirit, whose activities are written with the "heart" radical, this mind is all water: its activities are running, gurgling, springing, whirling, eddying, and so on (Kohn 2014, 64). The river of life itself, it flows in us and through us, and we merge with it in vastness.

The body that comes with this is "a boundless organism with infinite boundaries" (*ti* 體) (Sommer 2008). Like the body of a plant, all parts of which are interconnected with all others and which can propagate from any of them, so *ti* indicates the limbs and parts of the human body that together form one whole. By extension, it also means the human body as part of a much larger social and cosmic corpus, "consubstantial with the bodies of ancestors and descendants" and "all the people with whom it engages in exchanges of labor and food" (Sommer 2010, 223). The boundless organism of the *ti* body is like an extended network: each individual contains many different *ti* within himself and is outwardly bound in with numerous others. "The largest unit of the *ti* is the cosmos itself, . . a wholeness that can encompass life and death, Heaven and Earth, and all beings" (Sommer 2010, 224).

This is the bodymind of early hominins, who essentially could feel two basic types of disturbances—pain or fatigue and pleasure or delight—processed in brain regions homologous in all mammals and comparable in their localized stimulations (Panksepp 2008, 49). The lowest and oldest part of the brain, sometimes called the reptilian brain, is located in the brainstem, the cerebellum, and next to the limbic system. It has been active since the first vertebrates crawled over the planet. Its nuclei relate to affective processing and generate autonomic output, thereby regulating the body's temperature, its vasculature, and the visceral organs (Ford and Wortman 2013, 43).

The reptilian brain is responsible for basic movement coordination, gait, and posture control as well as the instincts that keep us fed and watered, satisfied and rested (Ramachandran 2011, 18). It also manages the autonomic nervous system in control of the inner organs and of breathing as well as of activity and rest (Ratey 2002, 160-63). It interacts in two directions, communicating with both, the medial prefrontal cortex and the midbrain with the insula and amygdala (Kohn 2015a, 163-64). In other words, the human repertoire of basic reactions, already present in early hominins, functions along a basic axis of like and dislike and consists of instinctual urges that "remain intact even after damage to the neocortex," the thinking part of the brain, and thus work without encoding, conscious processing, or any form of analytical reflection (Panksepp 2008, 50).

Perception in this state of unknowing is completely instinctual. Human beings live in absolute subjectivity or cosmic consciousness, resting in a state of mind only, at one with reality and all things, fully in fusion yet without confusion. Identified with all and at one with the energy of the universe, they live in a reality "without duality but not without relations" (Wilber 1993, 47, 94). They rest in "pure organic consciousness which participates fully in the non-dual awareness of absolute subjectivity. . . The world is given to me only once, not one existing and one perceived. Nothing is reflected. The original and the mirror-image are identical" (1993, 115).

Matching Zhuangzi's "perfect knowledge," people in this state do not actively recognize things outside of themselves or themselves as separate, living instead in a state of complete unity with all. Their behavior is accordingly highly spontaneous and essentially unconscious, free from restraints or recursive evaluations, unfettered by the thinking mind in any form or shape.

Ideal Mentation

Daoists favor any form of mentation that precedes discriminating consciousness as it developed on the basis of literacy in the Agrarian period. Whether functioning through organism, form, or personal body, whether active as deep abyss, spirit, or heart-mind, they see it as nothing firm or stable. Instead, it is the visible expression of the universal flow of energy and spirit (Goldin 2003, 230). A dynamic field of multiple forces and tendencies, the bodymind is a continuous process of materialization, animation, disintegration, and reconstitution. As François Jullien says,

> The "actualized form" is that which arises out of the flows of energy that permeate particular concretions, without any break in the sequence or intrusion from without. In this transition from nonexistence to the existence of an individual person, the Western notion of the body[mind] does not figure—*cannot* figure—because the perspective remains of a homogeneous and continuous process. . . .
>
> Only phenomena of (energetic) individuation and de-individuation truly exist, and this physically oriented process . . . *naturally* retains the (transcendent, animating) "spirit dimension" within itself as it flows from the original energy. (2007, 70)

Actively engaging the spirit dimension, Daoists aim to increase their overall sense of cosmic interconnectedness and enhance their faculty of intuition and state of unknowing. This, however, does not mean that they wish to return to hominin mentation or give up on the thinking mind altogether. Rather, it means that they envision a state where the entire human potential is realized and all inherent faculties are fully activated. These function anyway on the lower level of the brain, but are often stymied and restricted by stereotypes and rote responses instituted by the prefrontal cortex as it is patterned through cultural models.

Attaining this state of complete mental integration is a key feature of Daoist cultivation. It begins with the conscious mind: adepts find an inner, conscious center, like a key spiritual focus or other high value—something like Heaven or life in the *Zhuangzi*—and focus their entire being there. Doing so, they place reality in perspective: the high office becomes a prison compared to relaxing by the riverside (ch. 17). At this point, "you know when your thinking center is really working. You're aware that somehow what you're doing right at that moment is totally worthwhile" (Ford and Wortman 2013, 25). Radically focusing attention switches core concerns from survival to learning and trains the conscious mind to notice alarm signals from the amygdala, then intentionally activate the learning brain and deal with them in focus. Memory remains unimpaired, but the automatization of responses is inhibited (Kohn 2015a, 176).

Once in this mode, people act easily and spontaneously, with strong instincts and intuition. They come to enjoy life as a series of challenges, able to savor quiet times without the need for new stimulation and generally moving in harmony with life, flowing along in free and easy wandering (Ford and Wortman 2013, 36). Activating their optimal brain, they make strong use of all capabilities, unhindered by fear, emotional reactions, and primal thinking. This, moreover, is the root of peak performance, when body, skills, emotions, and thinking all work together as cooperative partners, and all flows intuitively and effortlessly in "skillful spontaneity" (Kohn 2014, 209).

Ideal mentation thus happens not by forgetting the thinking mind but inhibiting it, not by letting go of all conscious evaluations but by learning to control them, not by doing away with the bodymind but by centering it in a spiritual and cosmic dimension (Kohn 2015a, 176). Far from wanting to return to more primitive, prehistoric levels of being, Daoists strive to recover their potential, to activate their benefits, to enhance life with their power. Again, the core issue is one of choice. Once humans developed a prefrontal cortex—after agriculture, statehood, and literacy—they chose to become its slave, mindlessly obeying its classifications, standardizations, and stereotypes (Kohn 2016, 104). Daoists, on the other hand, developed techniques to restrain its dominance and make it work at an optimal level in close integration with the more primitive, intuitive, and spiritual dimensions of consciousness.

Chapter Six

Forms of Community

Let there be a small country with few people.
Let there be ten times, a hundred times as many utensils.
But let them not be used.
Let the people value their lives highly and not migrate far.
Even though there may be boats and carriages, nobody rides them.
Even though there may be weapons and armor, nobody wields them.
Let the people again knot cords and use them.
Let them relish their food, adorn their clothes,
Relax in their homes, and delight in their customs.
Though neighboring communities overlook one another,
And they can hear roosters crowing and dogs barking,
Yet the people there grow old and die
Without ever visiting one another. (*Daode jing* 80)

To fully realize this integration, Daoists developed five major types of community. The earliest, as indicated by the citation above, is the simple, contained sedentary settlement, consisting of small villages where everybody knows everybody and all consumer items are produced locally. The second and third are larger, more formally structured communities as established by the early religious organizations, such as Great Peace and the Celestial Masters. They insist on minimal hierarchies in combination with fluid, open administrative structures. The production of goods centers on households rather than specialists, and the community supports various overarching institutions that benefit all.

Following this, and under the impact of Buddhism, Daoists developed monastic communities with a core focus on spiritual cultivation to aid both, the individual attainment of advanced spiritual states and the enhancement of goodness in the world. With strictly limited possessions and closely circumscribed modes of behavior, they had some specialization and a clear ranking order, yet created inclusive rather than extractive institutions and remained close to the core values of the religion.

Last but not least, Daoists also institutionalized the wandering hermit life, manifest among ancient immortals, medieval alchemists, and later mendicants as well as followers of Complete Perfection (Quanzhen 全真), who had to undergo periods of "wandering like the clouds." Closest to ancient foragers, these communities emphasize minimal possessions, organic and social resources, as well as a close connection to nature.

Each type of community, moreover, can be understood in relation to Paleolithic or Mesolithic models, activating an egalitarian mode of living in steadfast resistance against complexity.

Resisting Complexity

Egalitarian societies as defined in social anthropology are characterized by "fluid group organization, individual freedom of movement and group membership, immediate and relatively easy access to resources, simple division of labor, and relatively direct personal leverage on other individuals" (Cohen 1985, 99-100; see also Woodburn 1982). A form of social organization that is permitted and fostered by the group rather than necessitated by circumstances, it was "the rule throughout the early, and major, part of the archaeological record," i. e., standard among hunter-gatherers of the Paleolithic. Only in later stages, most likely under population and resource pressure, did formalized leadership and delayed consumption appear, marking the way toward sedentism, agriculture, and social complexity (Cohen 1985, 100).

Social complexity has a number of typical characteristics. They include the emergence of chiefs or big men who provide guarantees of support to their followers, in close combination with decision and consumption hierarchies that establish systematic control over storage facilities and mechanisms as well as over the organization of human labor. Social relationships are increasingly formalized in reciprocal patterns, often with the help of ceremony and ritual as well as through the use of luxury goods that symbolize rank and wealth. Prestige becomes an economic commodity, while trade networks expand and the distribution of goods is increasingly regulated as part of a pervasive system of rewards and punishments (Cohen 1985, 105).

Social complexity emerges in response to pressures exerted in larger groups and under circumstances of greater population density. It offsets people's negative response to four key factors: congestion, information overload, loss of control, and lack of privacy. The first two have to do with crowding, both physically and psychologically, while the last two focus on social and personal competence and appropriate action (1985, 106). Control specifically involves the social definition and allotment of manageable tasks and their facilitation as well as the organization and social spacing of the group to provide positive interdependence.

Complex societies address these issues in a variety of ways. First and foremost, they differentiate their membership through (1) segmentation by establishing parallel subgroups, (2) scheduling by creating temporal divisions, (3) specialization by dividing work according to specific tasks and spheres, (4) ranking by giving priority to individuals in certain spheres of action, and (5) stratification by establishing preferred access to resources for elites (Cohen 1985, 109). All these ways of differentiation serve to eliminate certain members from particular areas, reducing competition and conflict. "They accomplish by social separation what can no longer be accomplished by physical separation" (1985, 110; Underhill 2002, 7).

Once stratification is in place, complex societies stereotype their members, reducing people to faceless masses without personal uniqueness, "about whom one need know only their class attributes, from whom one need receive only specific kinds of information, and to whom one need give only automatic, stereotyped responses" (Cohen 1985, 110). To make sure all know to which group everyone else belongs, they establish outward cues through clothing, hairstyles, and accoutrements—notably luxury items—as well as more internal factors, such as posture, gestures, and language or dialects, into which people are systematically socialized. Beyond this, complex societies solidify categories through ascription of status and establishment of permanent leadership, thereby eliminating the need for negotiations and reducing information load (1985, 110). To keep the different groups at peace, they set up proper ways of conflict resolution and authorities that serve to adjudicate disputes, thus improving the efficiency of decision-making. They reinforce group participation by levying taxes and corvee labor—commandeering "every type of household or agricultural commodity" (Sterckx 2011, 125)—as well as organizing public events that everyone has to join. The latter are commonly of a ritual nature, involving repetitive actions at certain times of the year, thus conveying a sense of control and competence (1985, 111).

Seen from this perspective, it is not surprising that Daoists massively resist complexity. Time and again the texts rail against the oppressive structures of mainstream society, bemoaning the ubiquitous presence of stereotypes and categories, both socially and mentally, as well as the pervasive oppression of people by cruel tyrants and ruthless officials. They much favor egalitarian structures that give individuals "the freedom and power to avoid or resist the organizational efforts of the more ambitious of their colleagues" (Cohen 1985, 100) and praise unchartered social organizations, where "one always deals with whole others, with all of their personal complexity and eccentricity" (1985, 110).

Daoists prefer egalitarian social organizations that minimize crowding and information load by being small and fluid. They eliminate privacy issues since all are either kin or friends while offering enough room to withdraw if needed. Resources being easily accessible, all have control and there is little or no specialization. Interaction among members is cooperative rather than imperative, and each individual has the ability to modify the behavior of others through personal influence. "Such societies are largely defined by the absence of formal structuring principles" (Cohen 1985, 109)—they reinvent themselves as they go along, flexibly adjusting workloads, scheduling, leadership, and decision-making in alignment with nature and the greater common good.

The Daoist project, then, is to create an ideal human society based on egalitarian principles and incorporating fundamental cosmic values under conditions of mass population and large-scale organization—remembering, adapting, and developing Stone Age models. On the way toward this overarching goal, then, they developed a variety of specifically Daoist communities, often pockets of sanity in a world gone mad.

Primitivist Simplicity

The earliest formulation of a Daoist community vision appears in the *Daode jing*. Without rejecting leadership or favoring anarchism, it relentlessly slams the various characteristics of complexity, insisting that social leaders, aka the sage, should refrain from all overbearing behavior, never boasting, bragging, showing off, or in any way putting themselves forward (chs. 22, 24, 30). Accumulation of possessions creates problems, any show of superiority is harmful, and "to be proud with honor and wealth causes inevitable downfall" (ch. 9). The text decries any use of force and describes weapons as evil (chs. 29-31). It never tires to admonish its readers to "abandon sageliness and discard wisdom, eliminate humanity and do away with righteousness" (ch. 19). The ideal is to be simple and fluid like water (ch. 8), to behave in close alignment with Heaven and Earth (ch. 5), and to live in non-interference, letting all others and all beings do what comes naturally to them (ch. 64).

The *Daode jing* prefers communities to be small, the size of villages, so that all members can be either closely related or friends. They collect their food and plant their gardens, growing all they need and locally producing their various utensils and necessities. They may have technology and weaponry, but never use them; they may know about the outside world, but never interact with it. Resting peacefully at home, relishing their tasks and their social life, they enjoy their life and pay more attention to living than to rising in a hierarchy or possessing great wealth (ch. 80; Ames 1994, 7).

Keeping their lives simple, they eschew overindulgence in information or sensory stimulation (ch. 12), never, as the *Zhuangzi* supplements, getting "confused by the five notes, bewitched by the six tones, by the sounds of metal and stone, strings and woodwinds" (ch. 8; Watson 1968, 99). Remaining true to themselves, they refuse to strive for anything outside life itself—profit, fame, family, or even the world (1968, 101). Thinking of government leaders as "great thieves" (ch. 10; 1968, 108), they never engage in the "crouchings and bendings of rites and music, the smiles and beaming looks of benevolence and righteousness," markers of complexity that only "destroy naturalness" (ch. 8; 1968, 100). Nor do they interfere with nature, leaving all creatures just as they are. They never break in wild animals to bend them to their use—"singe them, shave them, pare them, brand them, bind them with martingale and crupper, tie them up in stable and stall" (ch. 9; 1968, 102).

Instead, they "stay home with no particular awareness of what they are doing, walk around with no particular awareness of where they are going. Their mouths crammed with food, they are merry; drumming on their bellies, they pass the time" (ch. 9; 1968, 106). Like Paleolithic foragers or Mesolithic collectors, they have plenty of leisure to engage in storytelling, dance, and song.

One known attempt at creating an egalitarian community was undertaken by the Agriculturists (*nongjia*), a group of primitivist proto-Daoists who adopted the Divine Farmer as their hero (Graham 1990a, 81). Around 315, they established a withdrawn community in the state of Teng under the leadership of Chen Xiang (Graham 1990a, 68-69, 101). Consisting largely of farmers and craftsmen, this was self-administered and free from stratification, producing just enough food, clothing, and shelter while eschewing all contact with the outside world (Lee 2007, 600-01). Matching ideas described in the *Daode jing* and *Zhuangzi,* these activists kept their numbers low and strove to align themselves with universal flow (2007, 602).

In many ways, this simple, primitive community matches the Mesolithic reality of prehistoric China, when people were sedentary collectors, living in small villages scattered about the countryside, relying strictly on local resources for subsistence.[1] In terms of social organization, moreover, it reflects a band level of integration, by far the most frequent among hunters and gatherers and the characteristic form of social organization in the Paleolithic (Gamble 1999, 21; Service 1971, 47).

By definition, bands are small social groups autonomous with respect to food supply and vital resources, which they share equally (Woodburn 1982, 441). They espouse some gender division of labor and are often but not necessarily patrilocally centered (Lee 1979, 54-55). Their main social units are based on kinship, each lineage band enjoying maximal autonomy. Not entirely isolated, they form negotiable alliances in a regional framework and work with diverse sets of social relationships of variable level of commitment and duration (Gamble 1999, 22, 25).

Socially they function in several networks—created and maintained by individuals as they routinely travel the same tracks. However, unlike in social complexity, these networks remain fluid, open to change over time, thereby allowing for personal and social developments (1999, 44).

There are four types of networks. Intimate networks consist of three to seven people, most commonly five. Their members—usually but not necessari-

[1] "Local," in terms of prehistory, means within about three miles, as opposed to "regional," which is up to fifteen miles from the village. Beyond that—outside the range of communities until the Neolithic—"distant" refers to areas up to sixty miles away, and everything beyond that is far-reaching or long-distance—areas controlled only by city states after the Bronze Age (Gamble 1999, 88).

ly kin—are very close to each other and serve an essential function in life navigation and personal decision-making. It takes time and effort to create such networks—essential to human social survival—but they are also firm and stable and bring significant rewards in confidence and trust (Gamble 1999, 58). The number five is relevant also in that it signals the limit to any conversational ring: once a sixth person joins the group, it splits into smaller units (1999, 72).

Effective networks, next, are made up of about twenty people, 40 percent of whom are commonly kin. Less stable and multiplex—relevant on a number of different levels of interaction—they are important in daily life, since they provide material and emotional support. A form of social coalition, they may also include relationships with the dead (1999, 58).

Extended networks, third, involve more distant relationships, such as acquaintances, sports buddies, fellow club members, teachers, and coworkers. Either active or passive, these relationships are largely uniplex, i.e., specialized in terms of joint activity. In terms of numbers, they usually consist of several hundred people, ideally ranging around 150—large enough to be interesting yet small enough to allow members to know and relate to each other, easily keeping track of others' reputations and exchanged favors (Kohn 2014, 242). Human beings can only effectively forge a finite number of ties, and studies have shown that any group of about 150 elements tends to form subgroups and create hierarchies.[2] However, extended networks can also involve larger numbers, especially if people are involved in various different jobs or activities, and reach as many as a thousand (Gamble 1999, 60).

Global networks, finally, work with 2,000 and more people, wide-ranging and spread out. They also include strangers—customers, clients, voters, allies, and the like (1999, 61).

As seen among hunter-gatherers, bands typically have an immediate family consisting of five people; a local group or lineage of twenty-five; and a breaking unit of 150 to 200. The maximum tribe size, combining various bands into a confederation, is about 5000. Historically, the same numbers apply to Stone Age populations. While Paleolithic hunters established so-called gatherings, i. e., enduring locales for single or multiple visits, Mesolithic collectors resided in villages, from where they sent out groups for hunting and resource procurement—each allowing space for about 150 people (Gamble 1999, 71). Settlement structures varied: groups in a dry, arid climate were rather self-sufficient and lived in more distant settlements, while those residing in warmer or tropical areas tended to be highly cooperative and lived closer together (1999, 71).

This pattern and these "magic numbers of Paleolithic societies" (Gamble 1999, 63) are entirely applicable to primitivist proto-Daoist communities, ex-

---

[2] Gamble 1999, 59; 2007, 214. This number, as demonstrated by anthropologist Robin Dunbar, has to do with the cognitive limit to the number of people, with whom one can maintain stable social relationships. It has been successfully applied in modern business organization (see Gladwell 2002, 177-81).

cept that they would eschew the larger networks, preferring to remain within easily manageable and personally known environments, in a more organic, natural way of human congregation. Free from imposed social rules and contrived moral reasoning, they pursued the fulfillment of simplicity, self-being, and intrinsic harmony with all.

Peace and Fluidity

The same goals also applied to the first organized religious Daoist communities that emerged in the Later Han dynasty (6-220 CE). Plagued by disastrous circumstances—a succession of floods, droughts, locust plagues, famines, epidemics, and corrupt government—the time saw an overall reduction in China's population from 60 million in the beginning of the dynasty to 7.7 million at its end. It only gradually increased after that, reaching 16 million during the Western Jin, 46 million in the Sui, and again 60 million under the Yuan and Ming (Maisels 1999, 260).

While the dimensions of the disaster are hard to imagine, the process is fairly well known. As crops failed, people could no longer support themselves and were forced to give up their land and thus lost their livelihood. Local governments attempted to alleviate the situation by distributing food from public granaries, promising tax relief and lifting restrictions on hunting, fishing, and the use of government forests (Hendrischke 2006, 16). However, before long "the landless became too numerous for public support and there were frequent violent uprisings" (2006, 17). Local shamans got involved, either as advisers to rebel leaders or as messengers from the gods, creating revolutionary and visionary movements in the process. Beginning in the 1st century CE, they picked up momentum in the 2nd, many insurrections arising especially after 140, "pointing to a weakening of the authority and legitimacy of the ruling dynasty" (2006, 19; Mansvelt Beck 1986, 337).

Some of these movements were more identifiably Daoist than others. Among them, two major organizations stand out: Great Peace (Taiping 太平) and the Celestial Masters (Tianshi 天師), also known as the Way of Orthodox Unity (Zhengyi dao 正一道). The two had much in common, but were located in different regions—in the east (Shandong) and in the southwest (Sichuan), respectively—and each saw its role differently. Great Peace followers believed that they should replace the ruling dynasty and, in 184, rose in rebellion, were defeated, and became extinct as a Daoist school, their main work, the *Taiping jing* 太平經, being reconstituted in the 6th century CE (Hendrischke 2006, 37-38; Mansvelt-Beck 1980). The Celestial Masters saw themselves as advisers to whatever new ruler would arise, submitted to a local warlord, spread throughout China, and became a leading school of the religion (Seidel 1984, 170; Hendrischke 2000, 134).

Working with large peasant populations, deeply steeped in agricultural production, they both strove to create utopia, an ideal society on earth. As Rosabeth Kanter defines it, utopia is the realization of an "imaginary society in which humankind's deepest yearnings, noblest dreams, and highest aspirations come to fulfillment, where all physical, social, and spiritual forces work together in harmony, to permit the attainment of everything people find necessary and desirable" (1972, 1).

Early Daoists describe this in terms of Great Peace. An idea that goes back to the 3rd century BCE, it indicated a realm of total happiness and freedom, where justice prevailed and all cosmic and social energies circulated in a continuous, smooth rhythm. A state of perfect order, Great Peace was effected by good government that satisfied not only the common people but also the forces of Heaven and Earth, thus leading to a state of blissful harmony that would find the natural forces always beneficent and never destructive and human community in perfect concord (Kaltenmark 1979, 23; Kleeman 2016, 13).

More specifically, Great Peace as described in the *Taiping jing* incorporates the fundamental values of ancient Daoists as well as Stone Age community patterns. Closely connected to Heaven and Earth—everybody's father and mother—the people each obtain the place that suits them perfectly to live in full accordance with self-being and work with ease in nonaction, i.e., by allowing the universal flow to move with and through them (Kaltenmark 1979, 22, 30; Hendrischke 2006, 14, 70).

While the text, in accordance with its Huang-Lao 黃老 heritage,[3] sees this flow mediated through a variety of cosmological structures—starry constellations, numerological calculations, and *Yijing* hexagrams (2006, 28, 49, 182, 244-48)—it yet understands the individual as a direct agent of the cosmos, entitled to receive necessities in food, education, and health care but in no way permitted to waste, hoard, slacken, or indulge in resentments and drunkenness (2006, 49, 53; Kaltenmark 1979, 33-34).

It divides people into nine categories, reaching from "divine men without shape endowed with *qi*" through various perfected and wise men, who govern yin and yang and the five phases, to the farming population in general and merchants and slaves at the bottom.[4] Yet it also insists on equality in the sense that all wealth had to be shared and each member, no matter of what status, had to fulfill a particular role for the greater good to prevent "deficiency, want, and worry in any one part of society that would certainly have an impact on the whole" (Hendrischke 2006, 14).

---

[3] Huang-Lao 黃老 is a school of Daoism that began in the late Warring States and flourished under the Han. Utilitarian and political in nature, it uses cosmological systems to define rules and regulations. For studies, see Ames 1994; Yates 1997; Wang 2015.

[4] Campany 2005, 108; Hendrischke 2006, 52, 207; Kaltenmark 1979, 31.

The key value in the *Taiping jing* is "flow" or "circulation" (*tong* 通), its opposite being "blockage" or "disruption" (*jue* 絕) (2006, 14-15). "On all levels—spiritual, material, economic, and physiological—things have to circulate: this is what Dao and life consist of" (Kaltenmark 1979, 35). To ensure an active togetherness of people and the open interchange of information, all members were encouraged to write down observations of strange or calamitous phenomena that might indicate a disharmony of Heaven or Earth in "good texts" (*shanshu* 善書) and drop them into a "hut of kindness" (*shanhao zhai* 善好宅), essentially an oversized letter-box to be erected on the main roads to the capital (1979, 28). They should also present any ideas for improvement of social or production procedures to their elders, allowing sages to deliberate together about their practicality and adoption, thus creating an open forum of flow for the ultimate benefit of all (1979, 27).

This ideal, however hard it may be to realize in large-scale organizations, matches ancient and foraging structures. Among hunter-gatherers, decision-making is based on the interconnection of all possible factors, not just rationally focusing on one, primary consideration nor centered on the authority of a single, powerful leader. Decisions are taken in the doing, by connecting to the cosmic flow—there is no step or pause between theory and practice. Rather than through rational planning, they work with intuition and sensitivity, remaining highly flexible (Gamble 1999, 421). "The hunter, alive to constant movements of nature, spirits, and human moods, maintains a way of doing things that repudiates a firm plan and any precise or specified understanding with others of what he is going to do" (Brody 1981, 37)—in other words, creating open flow while resting in self-being and nonaction.

Essential for both hunter-gatherers and the Great Peace movement, continuous circulation takes place in time and space, constantly reinvented and reenacted through the rhythms of social performance, which in turn depend on those of the body—walking, treading, digesting, sleeping, and producing. Rhythms create particular patterns of temporality in human action as well as spatial organization that allows people to connect or withdraw as needed (Gamble 1999, 80). More specifically, they bring forth paths and tracks, linked through nodal points where people interact with each other or with nature—crossing those of their prey or encountering a plant resource. Paths mark the home territory and create socially constructed landscapes, dynamic itineraries that manifest a yet different dimension of circulation and relate to an ambulatory mode of perception (1999, 85).

Another concept relevant in this context is the notion of the operational sequence (Leroi-Gourhan 1993), a combination of rhythm and tracks that fuses social and technical activity. While the unbounded inventiveness of cultures, a feature Great Peace movers would like to activate among their members, is limited by inescapable physical laws, there is much room for technological choice. That, however, relates closely to social structures and the specific ways of doing things as they grow from the rhythms of the collective tradition—the so-called taskscape, an array of related activities, of practical skills learned in a social context specific to the particular group— just as landscape is an array of related features (Ingold 1993, 157-58). Personal style, social identity, and communal function, therefore, arise from a combination of natural limitations, technological inventiveness, symbolic projections, social training, and personal vision (Gamble 1999, 82-83; Wightman 2015, 165).

With each technical advance that places more of our operational sequences outside the body, the individual gradually disappears into the collective world, moving more and more from natural to artificial patterns, from the corporeal rhythms of the forager to the symbolic rhythms of the city dweller (1999, 84). Daoists reject this tendency, the *Taiping jing* most obviously emphasizing the need for openness, flexibility, and innovation. Just as foragers make things as they go along and work with material objects as part of the body, so communal Daoists encourage creativity within their operative structures, enhancing communication and the smooth flow of ideas and information. Despite the difficulties posed by group size and the organizational needs of agricultural production, they endeavor to bring the egalitarianism and openness of early Stone Age societies into personal and communal living.

Egalitarian Sufficiency

The Celestial Masters, too, pursued this goal, but their activities are much better known from historical sources, since they survived the disastrous Later Han and in due course grew into a major organized religion (see Hendrischke 2000, 141). Their community stands out for its emphasis on equality: members came from all walks of life and included many non-Chinese—notably Ba and Banshun Man—and women were highly valued and could attain leadership positions.[5] It also stressed open communication and easy transit, sponsoring a wide-ranging network of roads and maintaining so-called charity lodges (*yishe* 義舍) where travelers—both local and foreign—could stay on their journeys (Kleeman 2016, 56; Stein 1963, 56).

Like the Great Peace movement, they defined both the individual and the community in close relation to Heaven: the physical health of the person as much as the functioning of the group depended on purity and proper behavior. If someone fell sick, it was because he had blocked his connection to Heaven through moral failure and thus opened himself to a demonic attack; the remedy was confession and petition to the supernatural administration.[6]

---

[5] Kleeman 1998, 74; 2002, 27; 2016, 312. See also Bumbacher 2012, 85; Kohn 1998b; 2003a, 33.

[6] On healing and petitions among early Daoists, see Kleeman 1998, 70-71; 2016, 353; Bumbacher 2012, 115; Kobayashi 1992, 22-25; Lai 2010; Levy 1956, 217-18; Schipper 1984, 206; Tsuchiya 2002.

By the same token, social harmony required the bodily activation of yin and yang, not only by making sure all members married and procreated, but through an initiatory practice known as the "harmonization of *qi*" (*heqi* 合氣). Formally choreographed intercourse between selected partners not married to each other, this was an elaborate ritual that also served as the main initiation rite into higher ritual—and thus administrative—ranks of the organization.[7]

While the group was extensive, with followers numbering in the thousands, the Celestial Masters activated the Daoist ideal of egalitarianism—smallness and fluidity, personal involvement and access to resources. Each community member occupied a particular rank in the overall system. The so-called libationers (*jijiu* 祭酒), administrators of the twenty-four districts or parishes (*zhi* 治), led by a direct representative of the Celestial Master, constituted the leadership. The bulk of the organization consisted of the so-called register disciples (*lusheng* 籙生), devotees in ritual training who received consecutively longer lists of spirit generals, complete with divine troops and supernatural clerks, for protection against demons.[8] These so-called registers (*lu* 籙) documented their otherworldly standing. Although the register spirits actually existed within the body of the bearer, he or she had to wear the written list in a piece of silk at the waist constantly, removing it only temporarily.[9]

Divided into households, all members or "people of Dao" (*daomin* 道民) paid "five pecks of rice" (*wudou mi* 五斗米) or its equivalent in silk, paper, brushes, ceramics, or handicrafts as a tax to the community. Assigned and collected on three major festival days in the 1st, 7th, and 10th months, its exact amount varied according to the number of productive members in each family, allowing maximum flexibility in material production and consumption.[10] Community members, moreover, in accordance with the fundamental principles of sufficiency and integrity, strove to be parsimonious and conscientious in their dealings with resources, striving to fulfill a number of idealized virtues (Kleeman 2016, 308).

As outlined in the 4th-century code of community rules, the *Laojun shuo yibai bashi jie* 老君說一百八十戒 (180 Precepts Spoken by Lord Lao, in DZ 786), members should abstain from killing, including blood sacrifices,[11] theft,

[7] On these practices, see Kleeman 2016, 158-74; Kobayashi 1992, 27-31; Stein 1963, 57-68; Raz 2008.

[8] On community organization, see Kleeman 1998, 68-69; 2016, 5. See also Bumbacher 2012, 107-08; Lai 2002, 253; Levy 1956, 121; Stein 1963, 50-55.

[9] Kleeman 2016, 276-81, 303. See also Bumbacher 2012, 107; Kleeman 1998, 72; Kohn 1998b, 37; Kohn in Pregadio 2008, 18; Lai 2002, 262; Schipper 1985; 1994, 60-71. For their contemporary activation in ceremonial paintings among the Yao, see Höllmann and Friedrich 1999.

[10] On these and other community events, see Kleeman 1998, 72; 2016, 251-56; Stein 1963, 70-71; Schipper 1984, 206.

[11] Kleeman 1994, 201; 2016, 96-97.

adultery, abortion, intoxication, destruction of natural resources, and waste of food, while behaving properly toward community members and outsiders. The text prohibits fraternization with brigands and soldiers, punishes cruelty to slaves and animals, and insists on polite distance when encountering outsiders and officials. It also regulates various details of daily life, discouraging pettiness and rudeness as much as the accumulation of personal wealth. [12]

Occupying the fertile valleys of Sichuan and the plains of Hanzhong, the Celestial Masters established their own state, unimpeded by imperial or local control, which had largely broken down (Kleeman 2016, 52-53). Aside from promising health and healing, they guaranteed safety from violent conflict and opened economic security by creating inclusive institutions and setting low but attainable standards of living, so that nobody would grow rich but all had enough to survive and flourish. In other words, they forged a fundamentally affluent society (Sahlins 1972, 37).

Their main unit of organization and center of production was the household, each working according to its abilities and resources, producing food or other necessities of daily living that were taxed flexibly without extortion. Matching Stone Age economics, their way of being can best be described as the domestic mode of production. A concept developed by Marshall Sahlins, this indicates a *petite* economy centered on the household or family that by its very nature "combines the two essential social elements of production," i. e., the normal work activities of the adult man and woman (1972, 79). Atomized and small scale, it opens maximum autonomy to both household and individual within any given technology. Resources being easily accessible, there is little specialization and no alienation. Implements are homespun and productive processes are unitary, yet at the same time there is room for development, creative invention, and artistic expression (1972, 80).

Every single member has to be an expert, wielding (as well as repairing or even making) specific tools competently and efficiently. Such skill level is essential for human growth and satisfaction, but becomes increasingly unnecessary in post-agricultural societies. As Sahlins points out, "Only an industrial system could survive on the proportion of unskilled workers as it now exists; in a similar case, the Paleolithic perishes" (1972, 81). By choosing the domestic mode of production, Daoists yet again resist mainstream society and its stratification.

In addition, it promotes an overall value system geared toward life benefits as opposed to profits. In other words, the value of goods created is measured in terms of their practical value in actual livelihood and not as a means toward wealth accumulation. They do not primarily serve a high return through investment, trade, and commerce. People here work according to the formula C→M→C, that is, having commodities, they use money to exchange them for

---

[12] For studies and translations of this text, see Hendrischke and Penny 1998, 22; Penny 1996; Kohn 2004a, 73-74, 137-44; Schipper 2001.

other commodities that make life more pleasurable. In contrast, in more specialized and capitalist economies, people follow the pattern M→C→M, i. e., having money and investing it in commodities to make more money (Sahlins 1972, 83).

The big difference is that the former, a commodity-centered economy, is finite, contained by usefulness, especially in societies that emphasize sufficiency and limit accumulation and hoarding. The latter, a system focused on money, in contrast has no limit—wealth becomes an overarching goal in itself, a bottomless bucket that can never be filled. By extension, as long as the focus is on commodities, the human being and his quality of life is the objective of economic activity, while a dominant concern with money turns humans into slaves as "wealth becomes the sole objective of production" (Sahlins 1972, 84).

In other words, the domestic mode produces use values. It "entertains limited economic goals, qualitatively defined in the terms of a way of living rather than quantitatively as an abstract wealth. Work is accordingly not intensive and susceptible to all manner of interruption by cultural alternatives and impediments, ranging from heavy ritual to light rainfall. Economics is only a part-time activity of society," where elsewhere it is "an activity of only part of the society" (1972, 86).

A form of "communism in living" (Sahlins 1972, 94) that relies on egalitarian structures, the domestic mode of production has a tendency toward underachievement, never requiring "maximum effort of a maximum number of people" (1972, 53). Foragers and collectors—as much as communal Daoists—could easily produce more, but leave things well alone once they have enough; they could work longer hours, but rest and relax once sufficient effort has been made; and they could push all members to work hard but typically do not resent or punish individuals (often youths) or households (often seniors) who do not fully participate (1972, 49, 51, 54; Lee 1979, 263). As social harmony takes precedence over material dominance, and oneness with Dao is more important than personal accomplishment, egalitarian sufficiency is realized, leading to integrated living in pristine affluence.

Embodied Spirituality

The same also holds true for monastic communities, although here the mode of production is not so much domestic as external—material needs being met by donors, such as local believers, aristocrats, and the state in exchange for spiritual services such as prayers, rituals, fortune-telling, and healing. Within this framework, however, monastics closely model Stone Age living, consciously and intentionally connecting to the greater universe and actively creating space for personal and ritual cultivation.

The first known Daoist monastery was Louguan 樓觀, the "lookout tower" in the foothills of the Zhongnan range, established around 460 CE. Here the customs officer Yin Xi 尹喜 supposedly spotted the celestial signs of Laozi's emigration and convinced him to transmit the *Daode jing* (Kohn 1997). The institution grew in the wake of the Daoist theocracy under the Toba-Wei, when the state sponsored the New Celestial Masters under Kou Qianzhi 寇謙之 (365-448) to administer the empire, establishing Daoist centers and ritual activities throughout, while demanding—under Buddhist influence—that the central officers lived in a celibate community in the capital (see Mather 1979; Kohn 2000).

In the wake of Louguan, many important institutions developed that not only trained Daoist priests and leaders but also became major centers of learning and economic and political power, notably under the Tang (see Kohn 2004b). Monasticism declined in the late middle ages to be revived again under the auspices of Chan Buddhism in the Southern Song, notably in the Daoist school of Complete Perfection, whose institutions still dominate Daoist monastic life today.[13]

Just like Stone Age bands, Daoist monastics live in fundamental equality. Both monks and nuns do the same work, fulfill the same functions, and equally perform rituals (Herrou 2013, 64), but women wear more elaborate headdresses and officiate in twos rather than alone, matching the cosmic distinction of yin and yang (Kohn 2003a, 81). All limit possessions and keep free from accumulation. They typically own only two sets of clothing—for daily life and ceremonial occasions (Herrou 2013, 44)—have a set of personal dishes for food, and keep cell furnishings to a minimum (Kohn 2003a, 94), conscientiously practicing the Daoist principle of sufficiency.

Their life is centered on Heaven, realizing self-being and nonaction. Matching their overall goal of ascension to the immortals, both through physical longevity practices and spiritual meditations that activate more basic levels of consciousness, their physical setting is designed to create a celestial space on earth. Monasteries, commonly located on mountainsides or surrounded by parks if in cities, form a home for the immortals, where celestials come to sojourn and practitioners can be as immortal as possible within the confines of this world. "Humans imitate the structures found in the high heavens to set up numinous monasteries over here, creating auspicious places and residences fit for immortals" (Kohn 2003a, 91).

Their institutions are inclusive, geared to benefit all; everyone receives according to his need and contributes according to his abilities. There is specialization, since some are more adapt at certain skills—be they scripture studies, ritual performance, herbal remedies, alchemical elixirs, or meditative trance (see Goullart 1961). Training is flexible and the lifestyle fluid. "Monastics are free to do their readings and self-cultivation practices as they want" (Herrou

[13] See Yao 2000; Yoshioka 1979; Herrou 2013.

2013, 68). They can travel to study with masters at other institutions and even leave the organization to return to lay life if they so desire (2013, 142).

While in residence, though, all work equally in the maintenance of community life (Yoshioka 1979, 241). Like Paleolithic hunter-gatherers, Daoist monastics spend only a few hours a day to keep their facility in good shape and care for basic physical needs. The vast majority of their time they practice self-cultivation and interact with the community—including fellow monastics, lay followers, and visitors (Herrou 2013, 31). Also, in imitation of Stone Age living, their daily schedule closely matches the rising and setting of the sun and changes with the seasons—even today they eschew the use of artificial light (Yoshioka 1979, 242).

Their food is simple and vegetarian, but presented formally and—especially at the noon meal—accompanied by ritual: incantations, prayers, bows, and stylized movements (Kohn 2003a, 126; Schipper 1984, 214). Physical behavior in general is highly formalized to the point where "the whole of the cenobitic life is choreographed by the rules of the order," every detail being prescribed so that the "heightened consciousness about the motions and thoughts of everyday life becomes itself a transforming mental discipline" (Weckman 1987, 38). Physical activity then becomes a form of "diffuse prayer" (Hillery 1992, 157), which raises bodily necessities to a higher, more cosmic level. This is most obvious in the chants monastics recite as they undertake ordinary daily tasks, such as washing their face, cleaning their teeth, and donning their vestments—in each case offering prayers for all humanity and connecting to Heaven and Earth (Kohn 2003a, 116-18).

The conscious, structured modification of what Marcel Mauss described as "body techniques," i. e., "ordered, authorized, tested actions" (1979, 102), can be seen as an expansion of the paths and tracks that form operational sequences and lie at the root of both Stone Age and Daoist community life. Shaping the reality and identity of community members, they range from body movements (walking, squatting) through ways of caring for the body (washing, grooming) and modes of consumption to mental attitudes and ways of perception (1979, 98-100, 117-18). Mauss calls this the *habitus* and distinguishes it from mere '*habitude*,' i.e., the customs of the individual, as involving the "techniques and work of collective and individual practical reason" (1979, 101).

The notion asserts that one "cannot take the body for granted as a natural, fixed, and historically universal datum of human societies" (Turner 1997, 17). Pierre Bourdieu further characterizes *habitus* as "systems of durable, transposable dispositions, structured structures predisposed to function as structuring structures" (1990, 53). The various body techniques, therefore, learned and habituated in a culturally determined and structured manner, create a specific set of feelings, conceptions, and expressions that both reflect the culture and society that instilled them and gives them enduring structure.

In other words, in a setting intentionally designed to invite otherworldly powers and activate cosmic cycles, Daoist monastics incorporate the religion's fundamental principles into the very ways of moving and living in the body, instilling "bodily knowledge," i. e., a body of knowledge realized through active embodiment in the physical reality of the individual self and transmitted through bodily experience (Sullivan 1990, 86-87). Daoists like Stone Age humans live as part of the larger universe, their bodies and actions immediately relating to the entirety of things around them. A hub of purity, simplicity, and order in an otherwise disordered world, they engender a life of affluence and positivity.

Flowing Freedom

A yet different form of Daoist community emerges in the more specialized pursuit of individual seekers who leave society altogether to experience personal and spiritual freedom. They wander about, resting in nature, communing with divine forces, concocting elixirs, or exploring the teachings of various masters. Their life is closest to the Paleolithic, as immortals generally—and most obviously in the rejection of grain in their diet—tend to recover prehistoric patterns. Without a settled abode, these Daoists are mendicants or mountain dwellers; begging or foraging in the woods, they rely entirely on their surroundings for survival. Intimately connecting to nature, they are exposed to the elements and open to cosmic flow; independent of cultural and social constraints, they find equality, freedom, and fulfillment.

Chinese culture has long embraced this ideal in the figure of the hermit or recluse (*yinshi* 隐士), who leaves society to espouse solitary isolation in the wilderness where wild beasts and indigenous tribes roam, to follow simpler, even animal ways of life (Goh 2011, 118; Wang 2014, 202). Striving to maintain moral integrity, hermits were moral heroes, sage figures in the Confucian tradition (Vervoorn 1990, 27; 1984, 250; Berkowitz 1989, 44-48; 2010, 298).

The earliest known examples are Boyi 伯夷 and Shuqi 叔齊, who opposed the Zhou conquest and their father's inheritance decision and starved themselves to death rather than give in to moral depravity.[14] Others were more fortunate and blossomed in the clean living of the mountains. Thus Shan Bao 單豹 "lived among the cliffs, drank only water, and didn't go after gain like other people. He went along like that for seventy years and still had the complexion of a young child" (*Zhuangzi* 19; Watson 1968, 201). Choosing a life outside of society for personal rather than moral reasons, they also included longevity masters along the lines of the long-lived Pengzu 彭祖 (ch. 15; Kohn 2014, 50).

---

[14] For details, see Vervoorn 1983; 1984, 266; 1990, 35-37; Berkowitz 1989, 83; Graham 1990a, 86-90; Wang 2014, 198-202.

Later Daoists expanded this ideal and connected it with the goal of immortality. Like hermits living in the wilderness and longevity masters cultivating health and spiritual enhancement, immortals fast by living on pure *qi*, eat raw food they find in the woods, and make themselves garments of leaves or deer skins (Kaltenmark 1953; Eskildsen 1998, 20-21). The very word for "immortal," *xian* 仙, consists of a graph that shows a man next to a mountain. It associates them with the untamed and threatening parts of the natural world that civilized men stay away from (Berkowitz 1989, 123). Pure men of spirit, they are immune to human needs, increasingly associated with birds in the lightness of their bodies and their ability to fly (Kaltenmark 1953, 10-15).

In medieval Daoism, practitioners living in the wilderness tended to be alchemists, striving to concoct an elixir (*dan* 丹) to gain ascension into the Heaven of Great Clarity (Taiqing 太清)—also the name of their Daoist school (see Pregadio 2006). Working in small groups, often only consisting of a master with several acolytes, alchemists needed to have exactly the right ingredients, often found only after extensive wanderings through many parts of the country. Concoction itself had to be completely secluded, because the slightest contact with a nonbeliever could ruin the entire process (Kohn 2001, 85).

Complete Perfection Daoism continued the ancient hermit tradition in yet another way in that it required novices to spend time moving about the countryside "wandering like the clouds" (*yunyou* 雲遊). As the founder, Wang Chongyang 王重陽, describes it in his *Lijiao shiwu lun* 立教十五論 (Fifteen Articles on Establishing the Teaching; DZ 1233), this is "to pursue inner nature and destiny in search of mystery and wonder [Dao]. One who wanders like this climbs into high mountains over dangerous passes and visits enlightened teachers without tiring. He crosses distant streams with turbulent waters and inquires for Dao without slackening" (Kohn 2001, 160). Practitioners moved about in small groups, always at least having one companion who would help out in emergencies, but avoided getting deeply attached to each other. They would beg for their food or forage in the mountains, also collecting herbs to enhance their *qi* (see Eskildsen 2004; Komjathy 2007).

Their possessions were strictly limited. As the 17th-century manual *Guiju xuzhi* 規矩須知 (Rules to Know) says that monks should have:

1. a rush mat, to keep free from demons on the outside;
2. a quilted robe, to cover heart and inner nature;
3. a single calabash, to contain the food and drink of the wise;
4. a palm-leaf hat, to keep off wind and rain, frost and snow;
5. a palm-leaf fan, to brush off dust from things;
6. a pure satchel, to carry and hold the sacred scriptures;
7. a flat staff, to point to great Dao, pure wind, and bright moon.

(Kohn 2001, 160; 2003b)

This enforced simplicity and exposure to nature, besides activating Paleolithic hunter-gatherer modes of living, serves to strengthen the inner resolve and positive connection to nature within the practitioner. As Mihalyi Csikszentmihalyi points out, "many individuals who have suffered harshly end up not only surviving but do so thoroughly enjoying their lives" (1990, 193). The psychological mechanism is not complex: the physical hardship creates new challenges, sets clear goals, and reduces inessentials. It also enhances "courage, or what in earlier times was known simply as 'virtue'—a term derived from the Latin word *vir*, or man" that closely matches the Daoist ideal of authentic inner potency (*de* 德), linked to ideals of "resilience, perseverance, mature defense, and transformational coping" (Csikszentmihalyi 1990, 200, 202)—all core characteristics of hunter-gatherers and advanced spiritual seekers.

Still today, people intentionally separate from society and eschew material comfort to find their own inner truth as hermits, vagrants, prophets, or wanderers. An example is Reyad, an Egyptian who decided to walk to Western Europe and has continued his wandering for over twenty years. His reflections echo Daoist asceticism as much as the forager's life of pristine affluence:

> During my journey I have seen hunger, war, death, and poverty. Now through prayer I have begun to hear myself, I have returned toward my center, I have achieved concentration, and I have understood that the world has no value. . . . If I am to live like a free man who does not depend on anyone, I can afford to go slowly; if I don't earn anything today, it does not matter. It means that this happens to be my destiny. (1990, 196-97)

No matter what happens, inner potency is strong and he can cope, resting in "unselfconscious self-assurance" and finding sufficient resources for his simple needs. Flowing freedom happens "when a person no longer sees himself in opposition to the environment, as an individual who insists that *his* goals, *his* intention, take precedent over everything else. Instead, he feels a part of whatever goes on around him" (Csikszentmihalyi 1990, 204). Part of personal and universal self-realization, Daoist communities in whatever form, therefore, enhance the greater cosmic dimension of Dao as realized in practical living.

Chapter Seven

Leadership and Violence

> It will not do to have files of marching soldiers filling the whole area within your fortress towers, or ranks of cavalry drawn up before the Palace of the Black Altar. Do not store in your heart what is contrary to your interests. Do not try to outdo others in skill. Do not try to overcome others by stratagems. Do not try to conquer others in battle. If you kill the officials and people of another ruler and annex his lands, using them to nourish your personal desires and your spirit, then I cannot say which contender is the better fighter, and to which the real victory belongs! (*Zhuangzi* 24)

However much Daoists advise that we live in cosmic harmony and communal equality, differences in individual ability, conflict and competition as well as a distinction between leaders and followers always form part of life (Chagnon 1990, 80). Access to resources being a biological need to survival, unless there is always plenty to go around and people stick together in an overarching attitude of humility and contentment, conflict is unavoidable. As Kevin Avruch says, "Conflict is a struggle over values and claims to scarce status, power, and resources, a struggle in which the aims of opponents are to neutralize, injure, or eliminate rivals" (1998, 24).[1]

Most species of social animals show a tendency to seek status, establish dominance with aggression, and defend already secured resources—thus living in a state of competition.[2] This situation always results in forms of leadership, the "process whereby an individual influences a group to achieve a common goal" (Amaghlobeli and Celepli 2012, 47). A transactional event, leadership occurs in groups, involves influence over others, and is directed toward a specific goal (Northouse 2001, 3).

Established leadership, moreover, leads to power, the ability "to frame and define the reality and conduct of others."[3] Always involving a principal and subaltern(s), it is a capacity to control, channel, or restrict "the choice that sub-

[1] See also Coser 1956, 8; Rubin et al. 1994, 5.

[2] Lorenz 1966, 45; Levy and Thompson 2011, 26; McCauley 1990, 17.

[3] Amaghlobeli and Celepli 2012, 47; Scott 2001, 1.

alterns are able to make: the greater this restriction, the greater is the power of the principal" (2001, 3; Wrong 1995, 2, 6). The desire to establish and enhance power, then, comes with various elementary forms of execution, such as "manipulation, signification, and legitimation" (Scott 2001, 15). Setting up a self-perpetuating and self-justifying cycle of control and fear (Johnson 1997, 51), it creates command structure and lines of authority, both enhanced by and in turn enhancing the dominant social and political hierarchy. As Hannah Arendt says,

> The authoritarian relation between the one who commands and the one who obeys rests neither on common reason nor on the power of the one who commands: what they have in common is the hierarchy itself, whose rightness and legitimacy both recognize and where both have their predetermined stable place. (1970, 45; Wrong 1995, 40)

In addition, the execution of power, if and when authority and manipulation are "unsuccessful in cowing others into compliance" (Wrong 1995, 41), may well lead to violence, i. e., controlling, dominating, subduing, coercing, or even killing another by direct assault with brute force (1995, 24; Scott 2001, 18). In post-agricultural states, moreover, it further led to war, defined as "sustained, coordinated violence between political organizations" (Levy and Thompson 2011, 3).

Daoists oppose all of the above. Not only do they prefer a life before agriculture, but they also tend to eschew violence and aggressive or domineering leadership—time and again extolling the humility and withdrawing nature of the sage. Their communities being egalitarian and harmony-centered, they work hard to keep leaders humble and altruistic, to avoid competition and fighting, recovering prehistoric patterns. In addition, they abhor all forms of sanctioned violence and social dominance, developing ideals of freedom and personal realization that again define the individual more in terms of universal connection and personal ability than through social and political status. War in this context—very much a post-agricultural phenomenon—is to be avoided or at least minimized.

Aggression

Aggression is a built-in part of human and animal behavior, an "endogenous, instinctive energy" (Klama 1988, 107) or "crude genotypic tendency" (Hunt 1973, 35). Activated in competition for resources essential for survival, forcing one competitor to leave and/or surrender access (Sunday 1991, 58).

Resources, moreover, come in three forms: physical sustenance, reproductive opportunity, and social support or status. These match the three dominant emotional operating systems in the brain—emotions being a way "for the brain to represent biological survival values to the evolutionarily emergent cognitive deliberation," facilitating rapid decision-making and empathy plus group-sharing and cohesion (Panksepp 2008, 59-60). Emotions, then, manifest in three approach and three withdrawal reactions, i.e., seeking (desire), lust (sexuality), and play (joy), plus anger (aggression), fear (anxiety), and panic (grief). A seventh, variable attitude is caring (nurturing, worry), particularly related to maternal devotion (Panksepp 1998; Kohn 2016, 98).

When resources are plentiful, approach reactions dominate. However, when there is not enough to go around or when there is preference for particular items, withdrawal reactions emerge, leading to aggressive competition for materials, fearful cowering for self-preservation, and a turning-inward in sadness at times of loss. Aggression in particular leads to fights within the same species. It is clearly distinct from the hunger that causes predators to attack and consume members of other species as prey—careful never to kill excessively lest they exterminate their food source (Lorenz 1966, ix, 23). It tends to be territorial, sex-related, and irritable, and occurs most frequently among males, females tending more toward maternal and fear-induced emotions.[4] The three dominant functions of aggression, moreover, are balanced population distribution, selection of the strongest, and defense of the young (Lorenz 1966, 43).

Ubiquitous in nature, aggressive fighting is an "ever-present process", leading to particular evolutionary tendencies.[5] For example, territorial marking occurs with various sensory means—using coloration in fish, song variations in birds, and olfactory signals in mammals (Lorenz 1966, 34). Aggression serves the survival of specific genes in the individual as well as the species, a sociobiological phenomenon known as "the selfish gene" (Dawkin 1976). Leading to either the departure or starvation of certain members of the group, it causes a reduction in numbers and thinning out of the population (Lorenz 1966, 31)—including also the wide-spread practice of infanticide (as many as 25 percent of newborns) among different species.[6]

While aggression is a biological given, it is not, as Konrad Lorenz portrayed it in his psychohydraulic model (1966), "an endogenous, instinctive energy that increases steadily with time and must sooner or later be released" (Klama 1988, 107). Rather, its mechanism is more like a thermostat, with a neurophysiological set point as the preferred state. The brain with its multiple systems carefully monitors all sensory inputs and "initiates corrective action whenever they indicate a significant departure from the set point."[7]

This also means that aggression is by no means as inescapable as was assumed by ethologists in the 1960s (e.g., Ardrey 1966; Morris 1967), but is very much learned and culturally determined in its management, activation, and ex-

---

[4] Sunday 1991, 52-53; 28. See also Lorenz 1966, 24; Moyer 1974; Muller et al. 2009a, 5-7.

[5] Lorenz 1966, 23; Otterbein 2004, 22.

[6] Wrangham and Peterson 1996, 158-59. See also Clarke et al. 2009, 43; McCauley 1990, 3; Pettit 2011, 15.

[7] Klama 1988, 111; Pribram and Melges 1969.

pression.[8] Generally, rather than being biologically given, so-called instinctive behavior develops from "crude genotypic tendencies as they are modified, perfected, and pieced together by experiences gained from the environment" (Hunt 1973, 35). All animals, and especially higher primates, need extensive "schooling" for adult life "through direct imitation and trial-and-error learning" (Klava 1988, 83). Behavior, in other words, can be modified and transformed; it is subject to a constant process of evolutionary adaptation (Ridley 1997, 6).

As a result, there is a wide variety in the level of aggression in all known species (Wrangham and Peterson 1996, 175). Some, such as nomadically wandering animals (deer, antelope) or hunter-gatherers in well-provided areas (!Kung San), show minimal aggression, with conflicts limited to social factors—leadership for group defense or issues of food distribution and gift exchange.[9] At the other extreme are certain predators (hyenas) and warrior tribes (Yanomamo). For them violence is a way of life, and they regularly engage in raids to purposefully hurt, suppress, and kill others.[10]

Most cultures, then, have developed socially supported ways to resolve conflicts, creating habituated pathways and evolutionary models (Lorenz 1966, 68) as well as sanctioned strategies to end socially visible or public episodes of conflict (Avruch 1998, 25). In addition to the classic modes of resolution—retreat, submission, or fight—they often also work toward cooperative solutions especially when faced with frequent interaction and/or an equal ability to do harm.[11] These solutions typically involve negotiations to share resources or adjust perceptions as well as the intervention or judgment by an authoritative third party who stipulates a solution (1998, 26; Kelly 2000, 27).

In the animal kingdom, fights most commonly occur between two contestants in semi-ritual affairs that are formally staged and executed (Lorenz 1966, 58), beginning with shouts and grunts and ending with the wounding and rapid departure of the loser (Wrangham and Peterson 1996, 6). Similarly, among foragers and primitive peoples, hostilities tend to occur either in short outbursts, specially constructed settings, or formally enacted sequences.[12] Medieval jousts and sports events today are the continuation of this inherent biological tendency: they provide an opportunity for the demonstration of prowess, allow the acting out of competition, and establish rank.[13] Only in post-agricultural states with their stratified, complex societies does violence become socially institutionalized or sanctioned, serving particular purposes and enabling elites to establish and maintain rigid power structures as well as conquer and suppress neighboring countries through acts of war (Gregor 1990, 107).

---

[8] McCauley 1990, 2-3. See also Casey 1991; Klama 1988; Montague 1973; Rapoport 1995.
[9] Lorenz 1966, 39; Lee 1979, 372; Kelly 2000, 25.
[10] Wrangham and Peterson 1996, 69, 160; Levy and Thompson 2011, 30.
[11] Axelrod 1984, 20; Chagnon 1990, 80; Ridley 1997, 6.
[12] Lee 1979, 376; Lawlor 1991, 253; Harris 1977, 35.
[13] Fabbro 1978, 71; Kelly 2000, 17; Otterbein 1970, 32.

Non-Competition

Daoists counter the natural tendency toward aggression by resetting the internal thermostat toward the virtues of simplicity, humility, and altruism (Lee et al. 2008, 89; Dreher 2000, 79). Matching hunter-gatherer lifestyle, simplicity is the absence of luxury, pretentiousness, and extraneous ornaments combined with a freedom from deceit and guile, the practice of plainness and clarity (Andrews 2009, 4). Concomitantly, humility involves an accurate assessment of one's own characteristics and abilities, admitting limitations without downplaying oneself and relishing the ability to just be—a way of self-definition that is internally centered and based on a connection to the universe rather than socially determined status. It means being open-minded to new ideas and advice, tentative of one's own beliefs, free from self-focus or self-preoccupation, and generally non-competitive (Kohn 2016, 211; Tangney 2009).

Altruism, moreover, is "the willingness to act in consideration of the interests of other persons, without the need of ulterior motives" (Nagel 1970, 79; Alward 2001, 262). It, too, involves a way of looking at the world that echoes prehistoric patterns, regarding oneself as an integral part of a group, a member among others, and finding identity as part of a larger whole (Munroe 1996, 6). Reflecting the smaller communities of early humanity, it means seeing others as fellow travelers instead of as strangers or potential threats. As a result, altruists typically state that their unselfish actions are entirely natural and that they do not have a choice over whether or not to help someone. They have a strong will to give and a vivid sense of social interconnectedness.[14]

These virtues can be intentionally developed. To this end, positive psychologists today use an ongoing process of "broaden and build" to facilitate approach behavior and motivate exchanges with the environment, encouraging people to be playful, flexible, creative, and generally open to new information and different ways of doing things (Fredrickson 2006, 81). Again, it is a matter of choice: competition is by no means inevitable. As Konrad Lorenz puts it,

> The rushed existence into which industrialized, commercialized man has precipitated himself is a good example of an inexpedient development caused entirely by competition between members of the same species. Human beings of today are attacked by so-called manager diseases, high blood pressure, renal atrophy, gastric ulcers, and torturing neuroses; they succumb to barbarism because they have no time for cultural interests. And all this is unnecessary, for they could easily agree to take things more easily. (1966, 41-42)

Daoists agree fervently with this sentiment, expressing their preference for ease of life and their concern for health and harmony in numerous different ways. Thus, they emphasize nonaction as a way of being (*Daode jing*, ch. 43),

---

[14] Munroe 1996, 9-14, 197-216; Nagel 1970, 82-83; Kohn 2016, 210; Winterhalder 2001, 282.

prefer "feminine" qualities of tranquility and steadiness (ch. 61), discard "the extreme, the extravagant, and the excessive" (ch. 29), and in general place peace above possessions. They particularly value the three treasures of caring or fundamental kindness (*ci* 慈), thriftiness or frugality (*jian* 儉), and "not daring to be ahead of the world" (*bugan wei tianxia xian* 不敢爲天下先) (ch. 67)—interpreted to reflect a fundamental principle, a basic attitude, and way of being (He 2016, 481). The three, moreover, clearly link material simplicity with altruism in contrast to stratification and competition. The text further notes,

> Do not exalt the worthy, and the people will not compete.
> Do not value rare goods, and the people will not steal.
> Do not display desirable objects,
> and the people's hearts will not be troubled.
> (ch. 3; see also chs. 44, 46, 53, 59)

"Not daring to be ahead of the world," then, means embracing a stance of non-competition (*buzheng* 不爭) even in the face of social inequality and authoritarian hierarchies (Autry and Mitchell 1998, 131), placing oneself below and behind others (chs. 22, 66), never allowing to be in a state of strife with the world (ch. 68), and remaining entirely free from all "desire to display one's excellence" (ch. 77). The overall attitude is one of withdrawing, of being useful to the group and true to oneself without boast or brag, ambition or competition (ch. 8). These values, moreover, have continued to play a key role in the religion, and later leaders and community rules never tire to emphasize the importance of caring and remaining free from competition (He 2016, 481-84).

Daoists, therefore, understand that while "there is always competition, its forms vary, and there is no need to develop competitive temperaments" (Wrangham and Peterson 1996, 172). They propose a life in accordance with the fundamental principles of pristine affluence, like hunter-gatherers largely eschewing competition (Lawlor 1991, 173). Like them, they honor Heaven and Earth, decrying both the aggressive acquisition of land and the destructive subjugation of others (Lawlor 1991, 55). Sharing resources rather than hoarding them, Daoists value all beings equally and consistently honor expertise over rank. It is thus no accident that the figures with the greatest knack, the most admired characters of great accomplishment in the *Zhuangzi* and later Daoism are not of high social rank. Doing quite ordinary things with extraordinary skill, they are low-class: woodcarver, cicada catcher, ferryman, butcher, and so on (Kohn 2014, 209; Graham 1981, 135-42).

Leadership

Along the same lines, leaders in Daoism are not necessarily aristocrats or specially trained agents but sages who embody Dao and best serve their communities. As the *Daode jing* has it, "The best person is like water; water is good: it benefits all beings and does not compete" (ch. 8; Heider 1985, 15). Like water, which is invisible and only takes form through its container, the leader is imbued with altruism, humility, flexibility, transparency, honesty, and gentle persistence (Lee et al. 2008, 91-93). Living in fulfillment of the virtues of non-competition, kindness, faithfulness, order, timeliness, and competence (ch. 8), the sage "places himself in the background, puts himself away, and has no personal interests" (ch. 7).

A good leader never engages in self-justification or struts in the limelight, remaining consistently without pride, possessiveness, and personal acclaim (ch. 22; Heider 1984, 43). He or she may act in the world, but "withdraws as soon as the work is done" (ch. 9), "managing affairs without action and spreading relevant teachings without words" (ch. 2). In other words, recognizing the underlying spiritual dimension of reality and respecting all beings for what they are, the sage lives simply and humbly and consistently rejects the trappings of rank and status (Lee et al. 2008, 91).

Possessing the relevant knowledge, skills, and expertise for his tasks, the Daoist leader has a clear mission yet remains free from personal desires and never takes interfering action (Ames 1994, 101). Without exerting force or control, he inspires people to do their best, closely matching nature and the continuously changing circumstances of life (*shi* 勢) (Ferruggia 2016). The "particular configuration," tendency, or "propensity" of reality, circumstances change continuously in an inherently dynamic process (Jullien 1995, 12, 221). As much as life is "a fluid configuration" or "a field of flux," leadership is "a set of experientially located and responsive relational skills-in-process.[15] As a result, the leader works with efficacy rather than for effect, blending energies as he serves as "facilitator, communicator, and team builder."[16]

Exerting only a minimal influence on the lives of his followers and employing "soft tactics, such as persuasion, empowerment, modeling, collaboration, and service"—never resorting to force or violence—he or she encourages followers to take ownership of and responsibility for their tasks. Demonstrating creativity and flexibility, he promotes harmony with nature and others, living a life of service rather than rulership (Johnson 1999; Lee et al. 2008, 90).

In modern business terms, the Daoist leader possesses various key traits and characteristics, including vision, insight, responsibility, adjustment, initiative, tolerance, competence, and integrity (Northouse 2001, 18; Williams 2012,

---

[15] Ames 1983, 67; Eno 1996, 139; Amaghlobeli and Celepli 2012, 49.

[16] Autry and Mitchell 1998, 57, 79; Dreher 1996, 3; Davis 2004.

29). He or she also has a high degree of "leadership agility" (Joiner and Josephs 2007), the ability to deal with management issues flexibly, increasingly "dissolving her small self and living in the awareness of his true self" and the greater good of all (Josephs 2013, 81). This manifests in the three highest forms of leadership: Catalyst, Co-Creator, and Synergist. Catalysts are open to others' viewpoints, able to zoom attention in or out as needed, and constantly self-reflecting even in tight situations. No longer equating the exercise of power with self-interest, they empower everyone around them and stimulate things to evolve in new ways. Co-Creators go even farther, plugging more into the larger social, even global context, always "intent on developing organizations animated by shared purpose," and able "to remain with difficult feelings for longer periods" (Joiner and Josephs 2007, 111-15, 127).

Synergists, finally, have present-centered awareness, expansive, and even universal vision, and a purpose that reaches far beyond the self to the greater good of humanity (2007, 181-82). Like Daoist sages, they take a playful approach to life and are highly agile, creative, and imaginative. Purposeful without being rigid, they stay connected to the present and work with their intuition, allowing Dao to flow. Synergists truly synchronize energies in ever widening circles—moving more and more from "I" to "us" (Amaghlobeli and Celepli 2012, 50). Fully human yet also fully cosmic, they are inspired and deeply empowered people who bring benefits wherever they go (Kohn 2015b, 151).

Types of Leaders

In terms of leadership types, Daoist leaders are democratic as opposed to autocratic, laissez-faire as opposed to coercive, service-oriented as opposed to domineering, and charismatic as opposed to bureaucratic (Amaghlobeli and Celepli 2012, 47). They represent the highest type of leaders as defined in the *Daode jing*:

> The highest—you don't even know they're there.
> The next—you love and praise them.
> The next—you fear them.
> The lowest—you despise them. (ch. 17)

One interpretation of this passage reads it to be a generic discussion of different modes of leadership.[17] Another connects it specifically with Daoist, Confucian, Legalist, and tyrannical forms of government during the Warring States.[18] Yet another sees it as referring to stages in human history, reading "highest" to mean "highest antiquity" (Legge 1962).

Following this line, the four types can indeed be related to Stone Age modes, matching the social evolution from band through tribe and chiefdom to

---

[17] Amaghlobeli and Celepli 2012, 49; Dreher 1996, 1.
[18] Fan and Zhu 2003, 117; Lee et al. 2008, 97.

state. Bands—the dominant form of social organization in the Paleolithic—are egalitarian. Their leadership is consensual and highly fluid; it focuses on the well-being of the entire group (Keeley 1996, 26; Haas 2001a). Leaders—competent, intelligent, strong, and healthy—receive deference and make decisions (Otterbein 2004, 80) yet remain in the background, so that "the people say they did it all themselves," as the *Daode jing* has it (ch. 17). Without force or coercion, they have authority, i. e., recognized and accepted capabilities to which followers respond with willing obedience, and thereby "sustain the smooth operation of their society."[19]

Abraham Maslow calls this "Being-leadership," reflecting a way of life that focuses on being rather than deficiency, on the present rather than the future, the well-being of all rather than the might of a few (1965). He observed it in action among Native Americans:

> The Blackfoot Indians tended not to have general leaders with general power but . . . different leaders for different functions. . . Another aspect of Being-leadership in the Blackfoot was that the leader had absolutely no power whatsoever that wasn't deliberately and voluntarily given to him *ad hoc* by the particular people in the particular situation. That is to say, he didn't really influence anyone or order anyone about. (Maslow 1965, 123-24; Lee et al. 2008, 101-02)

In contrast, all other types of leaders are focused on deficiency, always striving for more, higher, better. Rather than authority, they have power, that is, they exercise forceful mastery over others whose compliance is commonly unwilling (Earle 1997, 3). Chiefs derive it socially from kinship and community networks, economically from "control over production and exchange of subsistence," and militarily from "coercing compliance" with superior strength (1997, 7; 1991a, 4). Rulers or kings, finally, the leaders of full-blown states as they emerged in the late Neolithic, in addition have control. This indicates "the ability to restrain access to resources" at the root of power, mediated by a hierarchy of feudal followers and a tightly structured bureaucracy (Earle 1997, 4; Kristiansen 1991, 18). Before long, moreover, they evolved into tyrants, the fourth Daoist category, who ruled with brute force, deriving political authority from blood sacrifices, systematic warfare, and other forms of sanctioned violence (Lewis 1990, 17).

---

[19] Earle 1997, 3; Otterbein 1970, 18; Wrong 1995, 35.

Violence

Violence, defined as "an act of physical hurt deemed legitimate by the performer and illegitimate by (some) witness" (Riches 1986, 8; Perez 2012, 13), means forcefully subduing, controlling, or even killing another, commonly involving injuries and leading to radical dominance or even extinction. An extreme form of aggression and documented from the earliest times of prehistory, it is the result of a particular line of evolution, linked closely with social and institutional structures,[20] and comes in two major forms: within the group by and against individuals (rape), and outside the group by and against gangs (raids).

Rape is "a copulation where the victim resists to the best of her (or his) ability,", most commonly involving a male aggressor subduing and battering an unwilling female.[21] It is "routine among only two species of nonhuman mammals: orangutans and elephant seals," and occasionally occurs in three other mammalian species, i.e., chimpanzees, gorillas, and howler monkeys—four out of five being closely related to humans.[22] It also appears to happen among scorpion flies and some species of ducks (Wrangham and Peterson 1996, 139). While rape clearly serves to increase the potential of fertilization and thus enhances the genetic survival of the aggressor, its immediate purpose is domination and control, establishing fear and submissiveness in the victim (1996, 141).

Raids are intentional excursions of a small, select group into neighboring territory with the object of killing one or two victims and, over time, exterminating the entire band. Known from primitive human tribes (Lawlor 1991, 255) and observed among chimpanzees in the wild (Stanford 2001; Wrangham and Peterson 1996, 12-18), they are similar to attacks among spotted hyenas, lions, and wolves on individual animals that have wandered into a pride's territory, that is, persistent, deliberate, and ruthless (1996, 160-61). Lethal raiding typically occurs among animals "in societies that are xenophobic" and given to "wandering in small parties and fighting with neighbors" (1996, 165). Not gender-specific—chimpanzees are strongly patriarchal, yet among hyenas all dominance and fighting are done by females—it typically results in a net gain in territory that potentially benefits the survival of the entire group (1996, 166; Otterbein 2004, 48).

There are certain general rules about the arising and use of violence. For one, most creatures "will engage in battle (or rape) only when they discover a massive imbalance of power," making sure that the risk of defeat on the side of the aggressor is low (Wrangham and Peterson 1996, 164).

For another, as cost-of-grouping theory points out, party sizes vary in accordance with environmental restraints, and the larger and more cohesive the

---

[20] Harrod et al. 2012, 63; Wrangham and Peterson 1996, 151.

[21] Wrangham and Peterson 1996, 138; Muller et al. 2009a, 17; Thompson 2009, 346.

[22] Wrangham and Peterson 1996, 138. For specific studies, see Connor and Vollmer 2009; Knott 2009; Muller et al. 2009b; Robbins 2009.

group the less likely it is to either engage in, or be subject to, violence. That is to say, if there is sufficient sustenance, the entire band will travel together; if there is not quite enough to sustain the group, they will split into smaller segments or "party-gangs," growing more likely to commit violence. "Party-gang species, for ecological reasons, cannot afford to live in permanent troops year-round." They also typically are competitive and selective in their food choices, "their lifestyles centered on eating high-quality but sometimes hard-to-find foods" (1996, 169).

A third factor in the presence of violence is the degree of community cohesion and togetherness. As Richard Wrangham and Dale Peterson point out, "males can't rape if society prevents them . . . A sufficient mob of supporting kin or others could stop a rapist" (1996, 142). While orangutans live and travel alone, subject to rape—making up a third to half of all copulations—gorillas live in troops, their females protected by their bond with a chosen mate—and there is no rape (1996, 142). Expressed differently, the degree of violence increases with the level of group segmentation. Unsegmented groups, mobile and with vague group identity, form a "transitory collectivity," with little to fight about, either materially or conceptually. Segmentation creates separate identity and values as well as a hierarchy of units—more ground for competition and aggression (Levy and Thompson 2011, 30; Kelly 2000, 131).

Still, even segmented groups can live violence-free. An example of how such a lifestyle emerges and is biologically cemented is found in the split of the bonobos from the chimpanzees about 2.5 million years ago (Otterbein 2004, 42). Their home ground on the banks of the Zaire River underwent a 10,000-year drought, causing the forests to recede to the mountains. Since there were no mountains on the southern, left bank of the river, the gorillas who depend most strongly on forest herbs (Schoeninger et al 2001, 180), migrated north, leaving the chimpanzees to survive by eating fruit. "When the drought ended, they would have found themselves in a new world," i. e., in lush forests without any gorillas. "Now the southern chimpanzees could exploit the plentiful herbs that gorillas had monopolized as a food source" (Wrangham and Peterson 1996, 226).

As a result, they could travel in large troops without competing for resources and in due course set out on "a threefold path to peace," reducing violence between the sexes, among males, and between communities (1996, 204-05). Over the years, they developed into one of the most harmonious societies and peaceful personalities on the planet (Levy and Thompson 2011, 25)—becoming bonobos, only recognized as a separate species in 1924. Bonobos look very much like chimpanzees but are slightly smaller and infinitely gentler (Schoeninger et al 2001, 181-82). As also among another monkey species, the muriquis of southeastern Brazil (Wrangham and Peterson 1996, 174), the sexes here are codominant, equal in rights and power, with ranks that "depend on who you are, not what sex you are" (1996, 205). Sons are close to their mothers, and females cooperate with each other in ways males do not, engaging in close, often sexual, relationships (1996, 209-10; McGrew 1996, 51). This leads to a level of "female power" that may well be "the secret of male gentleness among bonobos."[23] It may also account for the fact that they, among all primates, utterly lack sexual dimorphism (Hart and Sussman 2005, 120).

Chimpanzees, in contrast, continued to live with the gorillas and had no access to forest herbs, requiring more extensive efforts of food procurement that led to the growth of party-gangs, male dominance, and violent interactions. Over generations these features became part of their genetic make-up, so that their "males are demonic at unconscious and irrational levels." A chimpanzee attacks and fights "simply to dominate his peers. Unconscious of the evolutionary rationale that placed this prideful feat in his temperament, he devises strategies to achieve it that can be complex, original, and maybe conscious" (1996, 199).

War

Around the same time as these two primate species split, "one line of woodland apes was evolving into humans," "a funny little group that chose a strange little path."[24] Moving from the woodlands into the savannas, they soon grew bigger brains and smaller teeth while developing bipedal locomotion (Schoeninger et al 2001, 182). But they did not have the ease of the bonobos. "A diet of meat and fruits and nuts and honey and roots would demand constant splitting up to find the best patches" (Wrangham and Peterson 1996, 229). As a result, they lived in party-gangs that experienced imbalances of power and developed patterns of male aggression that females could not restrain, forever forging "powerful, unpredictable, status-driven, and manipulative coalitions" (1996, 233) and eventually unleashing variant forms of both interpersonal and group violence. Thus, life in the Paleolithic was peppered with warlike activities, even the earliest burials showing evidence of violent death, and Australian and other aborigines were "inveterate raiders".[25]

Over time, different groups developed their own unique forms of violence "as a complex expression of cultural performance" (Perez 2012, 14), a "meaningful action that communicates a message between perpetrators, victims, and witnesses" (Hatch 2012, 202, 218). They formalized and sanctioned it to create warrior ideologies of glory and heroism (Otterbein 2004, 6), often combined with repressive social structures—a phenomenon called "structural violence" (Klaus 2012, 31). A "feature that only a rigidly hierarchical society can achieve," it institutionalizes systems of social inequality, expressed among oth-

---

[23] Wrangham and Peterson 1996, 206-07. See also Huber 2007, 48; Jones 2007, 37; Paoli 2009 411-12.

[24] Wrangham and Peterson 1996, 227, 232. See also Otterbein 2004, 43.

[25] Keeley 1996, 37, 29; Haas 1990, 177.

ers in elitism, sexism, and poverty (2012, 32, 35), and includes "the politicization of the dead" as well as "torture and terror as ritualized art forms" (Perez 2012, 23, 18; Taussig 1987, 133).

Creating particular social and cultural norms, violent patterns of behavior and conceptualizations of reality eventually led to war, the pinnacle of human aggression and the largest-scale expression of the basic male defense of the community. War is "the sustained, coordinated violence between political organizations."[26] Entailing "the deployment of violence in accordance with a distinctive logic" (Kelly 2000, 21), it requires "planning, organization, and specialized weaponry and warriors" (Wrangham and Peterson 1996, 33). Minimally present in the animal kingdom—such as among honeypot ants that practice it to gain slaves, additional food supplies, and the extinction of rivals (1996, 163)—it is closely associated with the social complexity that came after the development of agriculture. Thus beginning with the Neolithic, weapons technology underwent a vast increase and the first walled settlements appeared.[27]

"Primitive hunter-gatherer lifestyle does not include the activity of warfare as we know it."[28] Rather, it grew out of hunting and was limited to raids and formally staged contests. "Not until after agriculture began did human societies begin to unveil their habits clearly" (Wrangham and Peterson 1996, 171). "As more information has become available, the starting point for war has been slowly brought closer and closer to the present" (Otterbein 2004, 30). First wars are evident in the battles of Jericho around 7000, but even then, as long as people lived in isolated villages, had little to fight about, and room to move on, "warfare remained sporadic and limited" (Keeley 1996, 18). Only when arable land became scarce and need arose for distant resources, when elites insisted on higher output and greater accumulation, "the incentives to take territory away from neighboring settlements increased," leading to war, which escalated with control over multiple villages and the accompanying rise in power.[29]

This in turn led to the extensive militarization of entire sections of the population, the massive control of resources by elite players, the creation of an entire technology of destruction, as well as systematically funneled aggression against other humans.[30] Studies have clearly shown that more efficient military practice is closely related to political centralization. "In order to have a professional military organization," there must be "the social, economic, and political development to support it" (Otterbein 1970, 20).

Beginning with Neolithic states, then, war—along with political organization—has continued to grow both in scope and complexity, leading to the full-

---

[26] Levy and Thompson 2011, 3. See also Chagnon 1990, 80; Ferguson 1990, 26; Gregor 1990, 106; McCauley 1990, 1-2; Otterbein 1970, 3; 2004, 9; Worne et al. 2012, 141.

[27] Schmookler 1995, 79; Cauvin 2000, 125; Levy and Thompson 2011, 29.

[28] Lawlor 1991, 55; Ferguson 1990, 33; Otterbein 2004, 26.

[29] Levy and Thompson 2011, 34-35; Otterbein 2004, 13.

[30] Levy and Thompson 2011, 14. See also Casey 1991, 1; Ferguson 1990, 47; Lewis 1990, 64.

fledged conquest of other states and the creation of empires, typical of post-agricultural societies (Levy and Thompson 2011, 36, 40, 65).

> When an invading people conquers another culture with similar fundamental structures, the existing culture is not destroyed. The conquerors are usually able to maintain their dominance by setting up institutions within the existing structures. Some taxes and goods are commandeered for the benefit of the conquerors, but the fundamental way of life is permitted to continue. The aggressors often refrain from interrupting the social fabric and the customs and lives of the people. . . . This type of invasion, referred to as military or political imperialism, developed as an accepted, if undesirable, way of life among city-based agricultural settlements. (Lawlor 1991, 54)

In the course of history, moreover, war underwent three major phases of acceleration, each "predicated on the spiraling warfare among competitive states": in Mesopotamia around 3000; in the eastern Mediterranean and China in the late first millennium BCE, and in Europe between 1500 and 1945 CE (Levy and Thompson 2011, 15). In addition, there is a certain logic to the escalation of violence in general and the changing nature of war in particular. As Richard Lee says,

> As human societies have evolved from bands to tribes and chiefdoms, each step up in the level of sociocultural integration has reduced the problems of violence at the previous level of integration, *but has opened up new forms of violence at the new level*. . . . At each new level of integration, the scale on which violence is practiced becomes greater in terms of the numbers involved, the degree of organization, the length and intensity of the conflict, and the technological sophistication. (1979, 399; see also Otterbein 1970, 82-85)

Generally, the higher the level of political centralization, the more complex, powerful, technologically advanced, and efficient the military becomes (Otterbein 1970, 71). Vice versa, the high degree of subordination and pervasive authoritarian command structure within the military exerts an influence on civil society, increasing social stratification and elite dominance (1970, 25, 27). War and its concomitants, therefore, impact various other, non-military coevolutionary factors, such as economic production, political organization, and social conditions or threat environment, moving in an ongoing and often escalating spiral, so that changes in each modify the functioning of the whole (Levy and Thompson 2011, 56-57).

Ancient China

Early Daoists lived in an extremely violent society, where killing, warfare, and blood sacrifices were the order of the day, constituting "a cornerstone of religious life" (Stercks 2011, 123). Laozi, the earliest thinker—contrary to allegations that make him largely a legendary figure (see Graham 1990b)—according to recent scholarship did indeed live around the time of Confucius (551-479). Born in the southern area of Chu around 570, he later served as a minor official in the Eastern Zhou capital of Luoyang (Chen 2015, 2). His lifetime, the 6th century, saw the transition from the Spring and Autumn period (770-481) to the Warring States (480-221). It signaled major shifts in society and culture.

The Western Zhou inherited the social stratification and warrior culture of the Shang, where the king was a valiant fighter as well as the chief sacrificer and where as many as 30,000 human victims were offered at ancestral tombs.[31] As documented in oracle bones, bronze inscriptions, and textual sources such as the *Zuozhuan* 左傳 (Transmissions of Mr. Zuo),[32] the state "was dominated by a warrior aristocracy whose privileged status was marked by its monopoly of ritually directed violence. Sanctioned killing in the forms of sacrifice, warfare, and hunting"—which also served as military exercise and formed part of the king's seasonal inspection tour[33]—"constituted the central rites of the cults of the ancestors and the state altars, and the performance of these rites set the aristocracy apart from the common people."[34]

Not just in China, but equally also in ancient Greece, India, and Israel (Kleeman 1994, 189), hunting, war, and sacrifice were "symbolically interchangeable" (Lewis 1990, 18; Sterckx 2011, 141). They went on year round, the former two producing spoils (*huo* 獲) to be used as offerings at the latter, the "great services" (*dashi* 大事). Rulers and lineage leaders took an active part in all three and performed the killing of the sacrificial victim in person (1990, 21). Violence as a key expression of power being at the root of the social system, "the noble was, therefore, above all a warrior and sacrificer, a man who took life in order to feed the spirits who gave him power" (1990, 17, 20; Kleeman 1994, 187).

Living in a state of constant warfare, aristocrats defended their honor and avenged every potential cause of shame, however slight (1990, 36-38). As Mark Edward Lewis puts it,

> [Spring and Autumn China was] a world in which the casual social intercourse of the nobles provided a fertile ground for quarrels, any perceived

---

[31] Li 2013, 71, 74. See also Chang 2005, 126; Chao 1982, 11; Wang 2000, 41; Yuan 2013, 339.

[32] For sources on the period, see Li 2013, 118, 135, 166; Falkenhausen 1994, 2; Kleeman 1994, 186; Lewis 1990, 16. For detailed studies of statecraft and history, see Li 2005; 2007.

[33] Chao 1982, 59-60; Falkenhausen 1994, 4; Puett 2002, 61.

[34] Lewis 1990, 15. See also Chao 1982, 8; Falkenhausen 1994, 4. Sterckx 2011, 26-27.

> slight was answered with force, the segmentation of authority turned appeals to force into wars, and the probability and the severity of reprisals placed great pressure on anyone involved in a quarrel to strike first with full military force in order to avoid falling victim himself to an adversary's assault. It was a world where men showed that they treasured honor by fighting to the death of a single insulting word, and where elaborate social rituals were gradually erected to minimize the possibility of misunderstandings. (1990, 40)

Concomitantly, while the common people worked to keep the aristocracy clothed and fed, their modes of production unchanged from the Neolithic, all more advanced technology, especially metal, served military purposes. Bronze was used almost entirely for "the manufacture of weapons, ritual paraphernalia associated with sacrifice, and carpenters' tools necessary for the construction of chariots" (Lewis 1990, 19; Chang 1983, 108).

The nobility, moreover, was organized through a close network of kinship ties, consisting of clans (*xing* 姓), septs (*zong* 宗), lineages (*zu* 族), and branches (*shi* 氏), constituting a systematic group hierarchy inherited from the Shang (Chao 1982, 27-33). Each lineage, then, had its own capital, temple, and military force—made up of family members who trained systematically to become valiant, courageous, and strong-minded soldiers. In the late Spring and Autumn period, this family-based pattern disintegrated as lineages split into various branches of unequal status (Falkenhausen 1994, 4). As a result, interlineage conflicts and interstate wars increased. The aristocracy, needing ever more fighters, added comrades-in-arms by means of blood covenants (*meng* 盟), instituted in formal rites and sealed "through the collective drinking of blood of a sacrificial victim" and the shared consumption of meat.[35] Establishing interpersonal ties for those not linked through "sacrificial duties to common ancestors," covenants also secured alliances between increasingly independent states, fighting constantly for honor and supremacy or hegemony (*ba* 霸).

Beginning with Guan Zhong 管仲 (ca. 720-645), adviser to Duke Huan of Qi (r. 685-643), states began to tighten their organization, progressively extending military service to create universal conscription and make every adult male into a soldier (Lewis 1990, 54-55). Establishing the integrated squad of five men as the lowest independent tactical unit, he unified the army into a single body. Pervasive military training changed "to turn previously autonomous fighting men into standardized, predictable, functionally differentiated members of a coordinated whole," reducing troops to passive objects of manipulation. Since commanders were entirely responsible for the performance of their armies, the new military "reduced soldiers to the status of natural objects, children, or animals" and replaced the ideal of courage and strength with obedi-

[35] Lewis 1990, 44; Li 2013, 174-78. See also Kleeman 1994, 185; Kohn 2003c, 381.

ence and compliance, "systematically criticizing and punishing any attempts at individual initiative or heroism" (Lewis 1990, 104).

This in turn affected civil society in the Warring States, creating a brutally repressive system of sanctioned violence by organizing the entire population into units of military service as the primary means of civil control (Lewis 1990, 63). It brought force a totalitarian and tyrannical regime that wielded "extensive, comprehensive, and intensive power" (Wrong 1995, 19). Its main engineer was Shang Yang 商鞅 (390-338), the prime minister of Qin (Falkenhausen 1994, 8). As the *Shiji* 史記 (Record of the Historian) describes it:

> He commanded that the people be divided into tens and fives and that they supervise each other and be mutually liable. Anyone who failed to report a criminal activity would be chopped in two at the waist, while those who reported it received the same award as that for obtaining the head of an enemy. . . .
>
> Those who devoted themselves to the fundamental enterprises and through their farming and weaving contributed much grain and cloth would be remitted [from tax and corvee]. Those who worked for peripheral profits [in trade and crafts] and those who were idle and poor would be confiscated as slaves. (68.2230; Lewis 1990, 61-62)

War duly became an inescapable fact of life for everyone, the entire population conscripted into its service, farming in spring and summer and campaigning in fall and winter (Lewis 1990, 65). People essentially devoted all their efforts to never ceasing sacrificial and military activities (Sterckx 2011, 125). Equipped with new weaponry, such as the cross-bow and the iron sword, and supported by mounted cavalry that replaced the war chariots of old,[36] large infantry armies of up to 600,000 men—ten times the size of Spring and Autumn forces—fought each other to the death, creating destruction and devastation everywhere (1990, 60).

The Daoist Response

Given the brutality of life at the time, it is not surprising that Daoists reject violence and deplore war. Generally, the execution of power always involves resistance. This can be isolated and localized, manifesting as "resentment, hostility, or withdrawal," or it can be fully developed, "when resources and communities are mobilized for the pursuit of shared goals and interests and put to use in struggles against the established leadership" (Scott 2001, 25-26).

---

[36] Horse taming, herding, and riding goes back to western Asia and probably began around 4000, as evidenced from the Ukrainian site of Dereivka, where large numbers of horse remains were found. The earliest wheeled chariots go back to the Yamnaya culture on the Dniepr, dated to 2900 (DiCosmo 2002, 25-27).

Both the *Daode jing* and the *Zhuangzi* tend toward the former, proposing a withdrawing attitude, ways of quiet living, and avoidance of official involvement. "Violent and fierce people," the *Daode jing* says, "do not die a natural death" (ch. 42), and adds, "He who is brave in daring will be killed" (ch. 72). It also notes,

> The use of force usually brings requital.
> Wherever armies are stationed, briers and thorns grow.
> Great wars are followed by great famines. (ch. 30)
>
> Fine weapons are an instrument of evil.
> They are hated by men.
> Therefore, those who possess Dao turn away from them. (ch. 31)
>
> When Dao prevails in the world,
> Galloping horses are turned back to fertilize the fields.
> When Dao does not prevail in the world,
> War horses thrive in the suburbs. (ch. 46)

At the same time, war was so much part of life that the text notes how "the people are not afraid of death" (ch. 74), either being killed in battle or starving "because the ruler eats too much tax grain" (ch. 75). Then, however, it gives suggestions on how best to succeed in military action—proposing an attitude of non-competition and withdrawal (ch. 68), followed by strategic advice. For example,

> A good general achieves his purpose and stops. (ch. 30).
> A skillful leader of troops is not oppressive with his military strength. (ch. 68)
> A small state can take over a big state if it places itself below. (ch. 61)
> Operate the army with surprise tactics. (ch. 57)
> Take the defensive; retreat a foot. (ch. 69)

The *Zhuangzi*, too, deplores war and violence. "In the world today, the victims of the death penalty lie heaped together, the bearers of cangues tread on each other's heels, the sufferers of punishments are never out of each other's sight" (ch. 11; Watson 1968, 118). "For Zhuangzi, the realm of man is totally dominated by power," leaving the people "mutilated, punished, and intimidated" (Møllgaard 2003, 359, 354). He never tires to point out the dangers of social and political domination, the "unmitigated power exercised by those in command" (Lee 2007, 608). Political power in the *Zhuangzi* is a burden on self and society that presents a danger to integrity and self-realization. Those who carry it are either corrupted by it or find a way to free themselves from it.[37]

---

[37] Billeter 2008, 57; Møllgaard 2003, 358-59; Wang 2014, 35.

Working close to political power is like dealing with a tiger. A skillful trainer "doesn't dare to give the tiger any living thing to eat for fear it will learn the taste of fury by killing it. He doesn't dare to give it any whole thing to eat for fear it will learn the taste of fury by tearing it apart. He gauges the state of the tiger's appetite and thoroughly understands its fierce disposition" (ch. 4). The trainer does all he can to avoid arousing the tiger's ferocity. Always maintaining an attitude of accommodation, he can coexist with the beast, but the moment he goes against the tiger's nature, he dies. The person in power is like a tiger: never arouse his fury but go along with what he wants and avoid all confrontation or criticism (Wang 2014, 40).

The primary solution Zhuangzi offers is avoidance or escape, time and again telling of people who refuse to serve or remain beyond normalcy, for example, by being crippled (see Moeller 2015). However, he also recognizes that, no matter how far you run, as long as you live on this earth, you cannot possibly escape the two fundamental relationships with kin and ruler. He resolves this by suggesting that one go into "inner emigration," live as a recluse within society, doing some basic work to provide for oneself while staying clear of political and military structures (Wang 2014, 203).

Unlike this, Daoist communities, from the early primitivists to the organized movements of the Later Han, can be seen as expressing fully developed resistance to dominant power structures. As social movements, they are "challenger groups organized for counteraction" (Scott 2001, 27), intentionally creating an alternative, an inherently peaceful society.

Peaceful Societies

Although far and few between—only 13 percent of societies studied by anthropologists engage in warfare rarely or never, and only seven out of hundreds of groups are truly harmonious—peaceful societies do exist.[38] Their overall characteristic is—quite independent of ecological, economic, and population patterns yet closely matching Daoist contentions—that they made the choice to honor and nurture qualities of cooperation and harmony and condemn all forms of violence and aggressive behavior (Robarchek 1990, 62). They typically establish a deep sense of community obligation and caring within their members, have no special roles for warriors but reward prestige to those who avoid conflict, and—like the Celestial Masters and other Daoist communities—believe in an otherworld that punishes anti-social actions with divine sanctions, such as bad luck, disease, or early death.[39] They do not use collective violence

[38] They tend to be small groups, often but not necessarily mobile hunter-gathers, settled people living in isolation, or tribes protected by warrior neighbors. See Keeley 1996, 28; Gregor 1990, 106; Kelly 2000, 14; Otterbein 1970, 20; 2004, 81.

[39] Robarchek 1990, 65. Also Fabbro 1978, 69; Gregor 1990, 106; McCauley 1990, 21.

within their society and resolve interpersonal situations with peaceful means (Gregor 1990, 106).

Thus, for example, the Swazi in southeastern Africa place harmony first, defining it in terms of social solidarity and cultural integrity, at all times emphasizing the key values of "unity, consensus, cooperation, compliance, passivity, and docility" (Nader 1991, 47). In cases of conflict, they activate a process of reconciliation and egalitarianism, aiming at positive outcomes and working with a legal system geared toward solutions acceptable to all. "In the traditional African community, there was no polarization of needs, of taste, or of values, and once the facts were established, the same solutions will appeal to all and ways to achieve them will seem obvious. The feeling of "balance will be something spontaneous and self-evident" (1991, 46).

Similarly, the Dou Donggo, an Indonesian people of about 20,000, living on the island of Sumbawa near Java, culturally incorporate their "strong feeling that disputes, conflicts, and misbehavior are matters for the community to deal with internally" (Just 1991, 108). As a result, they do not call in the police or file a lawsuit to resolve conflicts, never relinquishing control to outsiders whom they see as not sensitive to local needs. Community solidarity being their primary motivation, they resolve all conflicts by mediation through village elders (1991, 109).

Just as the Dou Donggo have created a legal system and moral economy that reflect their underlying cultural assumptions and social order (1991, 113), so the Semai Senoi in western Malaysia are pervasively non-aggressive and avoid all conflict, both within and without. Staying close to home, like early Daoist communities they see life on the outside as highly dangerous, full of wild animals and uncouth strangers (Robarchek 1990, 66). While "pettiness, jealousy, theft, and disagreement" still occur (1990, 57), they resolve those peacefully and with debate rather than violently by fighting. Their debates, moreover, rather than formal law suits or court hearings, tend to be friendly, social events, where everyone joins together, eats and drinks, and has their say. Eventually the group as a whole finds "a solution agreeable to all," warning and stigmatizing wrongdoers but never imprisoning or punishing them with force (1990, 58-61). Rather than obedient chattels or mindless pawns, here "people are conceived of as active participants in their own destinies, goal-directed decision-makers in pursuit of particular goals and objectives" (1990, 63).

All these groups, thus, make intentional choices for harmony, culturally determine what forms of behavior are unacceptable, and orient the motivation of the entire group toward peaceful living (Robarchek 1990, 69). In other words, closely matching the Daoist agenda, however different their environment, people are still free to choose peace rather than violence. "No accounting of the material correlates of these people's actions can truly explain them unless it addresses their specific decisions and the intentions and motivations" (1990, 63).

Harmonious Living

Another case in point is the Xinguano tribe in central Brazil. Free from any traditions of violence, its members define goodness as being peaceful and responsive to the feelings of others, see killing as wrong and blood as defiling (Gregor 1990, 110, 115)—another feature common among medieval Daoists, who, in sharp contrast to mainstream society, "saw the performance of blood sacrifice as a crime punishable by the heavenly tribunal" (Kleeman 1994, 201; 2016). Like Daoists, the Xinguano believe in supernatural sanctions that inhibit the expression of aggression and award prestige to empathetic people (Gregor 1990, 106). Like the Daoist sage, their chief embodies key virtues of "generosity, hard work, lawfulness, and peacefulness," and serves as an idealized father who takes good care of others as one would of children. He guides by example and has minimal functional authority. "One word from the chief, and everyone does whatever they want" (1990, 113-14)—a poignant way of expressing nonaction.

Unlike other peaceful societies, the Xinguano are sedentary and reside in permanent villages. Echoing the history of the early Celestial Masters, they arrived in their native basin as refugees from more aggressive tribes and there made the decision to live differently and with greater emphasis on harmony (Gregor 1990, 107). Different from the Celestial Masters whose precepts warn against outside contact and the Semai Senoi who live in isolation, the Xinguano engage in outside interaction, establishing "enduring relationships while preserving their individual autonomy" (1990, 109). They trade frequently in specialized goods with a number of neighboring tribes, each respecting a particular monopoly, such as salt, ceramics, shell belts, necklaces, and more. Although they possess the technology and expertise to make these things themselves, they trade for them to maintain harmonious relationships—any breach potentially causing anger, shame, or divine sanctions (1990, 111).

In addition, if subject to unprovoked aggression from neighboring tribes, the Xinguano engage in defensive raiding. Since they think of aggressive people as wild animals—"wild Indians are not people"—after returning from battle all warriors have to be decompressed and decontaminated. "They have to consume medicines to rid themselves of the enemy's defiling blood" and are not allowed back into the village unless they have fully recovered a peaceful mindset (Gregor 1990, 117).

Another aspect of a conflict situation, which echoes Celestial Masters' practice, is that the Xinguano will adopt their defeated enemies or other strangers into their own circle, leading to a case of "native acculturation." Generally open to tribes from four different language groups, they freely share their clothing, body ornamentation, cuisine, and other ways and happily teach them their ritual and music. In this manner, they make enemies into members and overall create "a remarkably homogeneous Xingu culture" (1990, 108).

A yet different peaceful society is the Buid, a highland group in Mindoro, Philippines. For them, "aggression" connotes all that has a negative value, from boasting and egotistic desires through the uncontrolled expression of emotion to violence and murder (Gibson 1990, 130). Their language has no word for "courage" or other warrior-like attributes, but abounds in terms for "fear," "flight," and "escape," to them the only rational response to danger (1990, 131). Their young learn to love poetry instead of weaponry, and prestige comes through the knowledge of verse, usually full of gentle and loving imagery.

Highly independent as individuals, each with his or her own spirit familiar, the Buid do not rely on social ties and have no priests or sacred texts to communicate with the supernatural. Although personal relationships tend to remain fluid, the community as a whole is stable, and—similar to Daoist communities—all have to share their goods and services with the entire group (1990, 132). All are equal, no matter what their expertise or success. Feasting, in many societies used to establish superiority, tends to happen only at times of severe illness or death; it signals misfortune and evokes sympathy rather than admiration (1990, 132). Like the Celestial Masters, the Buid believe that moral failure or quarreling with others makes them vulnerable to supernatural attacks and that contact with outsiders is dangerous and defiling. They accordingly maintain detached relationships that express their personal independence while gaining cultural and social identity from the group as a whole (1990, 133).

The core factor, therefore, in the creation of peaceful societies is the centrality of peaceful values, enhanced by both, a social structure that keeps aggressive impulses in check and a conceptual superstructure that provides supernatural sanctions for infringements. Redirecting the biological tendency toward resource competition and status recognition toward positive values and expressions of social harmony, these societies utilize inherent human impulses as a key mechanism of translating values into behavior (McCauley 1990, 22). They literally *learn* to live peacefully and award prestige to moral values.

To sum up, "moral cognition, like many other competences, is acquired through the interaction of individual cognitive adaptations with an informationally organized learning environment. . . The acquisition of norms is biologically prepared, but the crucial adaptations are perceptual and motivational" (Stevelny 2012, 164). Societies can engender the absence of structural violence, promote equality and social justice, and thereby live in peace (Kelly 2000, 16). In other words, the Daoist contention again prevails that anyone at any time and under any economic, social, and cultural circumstances can choose—and learn—to live in peace and harmony.

Chapter Eight

The Role and Position of Women

> The spirit of the valley never dies.
> It is called the Mysterious Female.
> The gate of the subtle and profound female
> Is the root of Heaven and Earth.
> It is continuous, and seems to be always existing.
> Use it and you never wear it out. (*Daode jing* 6)

Another dimension of peace and harmony is the relationship between the sexes that, especially in post-egalitarian societies, tends to be characterized by male dominance and the suppression of women. Going far beyond the biological differences between male and female, this meant the development of gender roles and stereotypes—socially determined and systematically learned "ways of being masculine or feminine according to the norms of a particular culture" (Nelson 1997, 15). Gender is a process that creates social and symbolic metaphors for the particular complementarity between variously sexed people necessary for the functioning of a given society (Gilchrist 1999, xv, 8). Rather than a fact or an essence, it consists of a systematically reinforced set of acts, a process of repeat performances or mode of social *habitus* that produces stereotyped patterns and thus structures culture from within (Eller 2000, 75).[1]

Daoists have always lived in a highly gendered society, Chinese mainstream culture codifying life in terms of yin and yang and thus placing females in a position of weakness and inferiority. They have worked with this in three different ways: counterbalancing gender values, promoting gender neutrality, and ungendering practitioners.

First, the *Daode jing* counterbalances male-centered culture by extolling yin-type values and forms of behavior. It lauds the "mysterious female" and places it at the core of creation; it compares Dao to the mother and calls it the womb of the universe; it emphasizes the feminine as a positive value, praising

[1] For more definitions of gender, see Butler 1990, 32; 1993, 12-16, 230; Conant 1982, 27; Costin 1996, 113; Eller 2000, 75; Hutson et al. 2013, 50; Johnson 1997, 56; Joyce 1996, 168; 2008, 43-44, 99; Mercer and Durham 1994, 177; Milcinski 1996, 196; Miller 1993, 4-5; Sørensen 2000, 7, 42; Wallman 1978, 22; Weglian 2001, 137.

virtues of weakness, stillness, passivity, humility, and emptiness (Chen 1969, 393)—not entirely surprisingly, since such characteristics tend to facilitate religious and mystical experiences (Mercer and Durham 1994, 180). However, by doing so, the text does nothing to reverse or overcome established stereotypes but works within the fundamental dichotomy of mainstream culture, keeping particular activities and values linked to the female. Its views, in other words, leave women firmly in their traditional place within the greater cosmological scheme, modifying and balancing but "not significantly disrupting the public, patriarchal world and its policies" (Eller 2000, 65).

In contrast, Daoist communities do away with stereotypes and actively promote gender neutrality. They recover prehistoric patterns by again leveling the playing field between the sexes, classifying people on the basis of personal skill and social contribution (Joyce 2008, 7). Thus, unlike mainstream society, the Celestial Masters supported women to work as much as men in the domestic mode of production. They received the same number of protective deities in their registers and participated as equal partners in the key rituals, attaining leadership positions and deification as individually merited (Despeux and Kohn 2003, 12; Kleeman 2016, 312).

Daoist monastics and immortals go even further and actively ungender practitioners. Thus, every rule in the medieval codes begins with the words, "all Daoists whether male or female" (Despeux and Kohn 2003, 121), and additional precepts just for women did not appear until the late Qing (Kohn 2004a, 63; Herrou 2013, 153). More than that, all monastics wore—and still wear—the same hairdo and the same vestments, the one exception being that women during ritual functions don a more elaborate headdress, the "capeline [*guan* 冠], an uncommon word for a type of woman's headgear."[2] All participate equally in the different tasks of the institution, living together and addressing each other in an intentionally ungendered way by using male relationship terms, such as "brother" and "uncle" (Herrou 2013, 214-15). In other words, Daoists, whether in thought or in social practice, strive to consciously overcome the gender dichotomy of mainstream Chinese culture, variously recovering Stone Age models.

Male Dominance

There are two biological causes for the tendency of males to create patriarchal domination in post-egalitarian societies: neurological and genetic. Neurologically, human beings retain highly primitive patterns in the lowest and oldest part of the brain, the so-called reptilian brain. Located in the brainstem, the cerebellum, and next to the limbic system, this is the seat of instinct and basic physical functioning. Its nuclei relate to affective processing and generate autonomic

---

[2] Schafer 1978, 11. See also Kohn 2003a, 152; 2004a, 91; 2004c, 150.

output, thereby regulating the body's temperature, vasculature, hormonal output, and visceral organs (Wager et al. 2008, 250; Ford and Wortman 2013, 43). It is responsible for basic movement coordination, gait, and posture control as well as the urges that keep us fed and watered, satisfied and rested (Ramachandran 2011, 18). In addition, it manages the autonomic nervous system that controls the inner organs, the breathing apparatus, as well as all cycles of activity and rest (Ratey 2002, 160-63).

This part of the brain is present among all creatures as basic organismic being. In humans, it continues to activate fundamental reptilian structures, including their "social behavior as based on repressive dominance and submission. Even their 'courtship' behavior is derived from intimidation display, with females assuming submissive postures to express their readiness to copulate" (Eibl-Eibesfeldt 1996, 33). At the next level of evolution, offspring came to learn who their parents were and underwent an imprinting-like process that led to carc-taking and bonding. "Thus the reptilian heritage was overlaid by new structures in the brain responsible for prosocial behaviors" (1996, 33). Nurturant courtship activities such as grooming, kiss-feeding, licking, and the like replaced the old dominance-submission patterns to a significant degree (1996, 34).

However, reptilian hard-wiring has remained at the very foundation of human behavior and key hormones still function on its basis. Thus anyone establishing superiority or winning over another experiences a spike in testosterone (Fine 2010, 36). Since men carry more testosterone and are more subject to its imbalance than women (2010, 101; Zillmann 1984, 88), they tend to compete, contest, and dominate more (Huber 2007, 120; Wright 1993, 37). As Irenaeus Eibl-Eibesfeldt has it, "The remaining link between male sexuality and repressive dominance is demonstrated by the fact that the achievement of dominance in all forms, e. g., winning a tennis match, is accompanied by a rise of blood testosterone in the winner and a corresponding drop in the loser" (Eibl-Eibesfeldt 1996, 33). This, moreover, comes with a deep-seated fear of losing, leading men to strive for control over nature and other men—and women—at all cost.[3]

This biologically based pattern, however, is not an irreversible sentence. "Just because control and oppression became possible, it did not follow that they had to take over social life" (Johnson 1997, 48). Cultures can enhance or limit the degree, to which its members express competition and dominance versus modes of cooperation, compromise, and sharing. They can also determine modes of expression—fisticuffs versus poetry, for example. Brains, moreover, have a high degree of plasticity. "The circuits of the brain are quite literally a product or our physical, social, and cultural environment, as well as of our behavior and thoughts. What we experience and do creates neural activity

---

[3] Johnson 1997, 31. See also Fisher 1979; French 1985, 47; Hopkins 2013, 81.

that can alter the brain, either directly or through changes in gene expression" (Fine 2010, 236; see also Eller 2000, 70).

Men in post-agricultural, patriarchal cultures have tended to enhance patterns of dominance and aggression, increasing sexual dimorphism and programming women to be smaller, weaker, and less competent. They were able to do so genetically because of sheer numbers. Mitochondrial DNA analysis in worldwide populations to uncover geographical lineages, each sample based on a run of 30 million generations, shows that the sexes were about evenly distributed in most of the Paleolithic. After the Last Glacial Maximum around 20,000 years ago and well before the first appearance of agriculture, many places show major maternal lineage expansions (Wang et al. 2016, 2). This coincides with the population increase that eventually led to the Pleistocene extinction and the beginning of sedentism.

A study of globally distributed whole Y chromosome and mitochondrial genomes of 526 male samples from the Genome Project, moreover, shows that most major paternal lineage expansions coalesced in the Neolithic. "The estimated effective population sizes through time revealed strong evidence for a 10- to 100-fold increase in population growth of males with the advent of agriculture" (Wang et al. 2016, 1). A more stable food supply led to more births and increased infant survival. It also kept males away from dangerous hunting, causing more to live longer (Cohen and Bennett 1993, 287) and leading to a "sex-biased Neolithic expansion" (Wang et al. 2016, 3). In other words, males given to testosterone-driven dominance behavior vastly increasing in numbers soon established segmented and stratified social complexity, creating patriarchal structures—male-dominated, male-identified, and male-centered (Johnson 1997, 5)—complete with organized war and the massive suppression and comprehensive lowering of women.

Matriarchy

Many cultures possess a subtle memory of the transition from maternal to paternal lineage expansion, postulating "a time before written records when society was centered on women. Women were revered for their mysterious life-giving powers, honored as incarnations and priestesses of the great goddess. They reared their children to carry on their line, created both art and technology, and made important decisions for their communities" (Eller 2000, 3).[4]

Formulated in ancient Greek myth as well as described in Chinese sources—"In the age of the Divine Farmer, the people lay down peaceful and easy, woke up wide-eyed and blank. They knew their mothers but not their

[4] For more on women's seemingly magical powers of reproduction and nurturing as a source of power and awe, see also Eisler 1987, 47; 1995, 25; Gimbutas 1974, 38; Joyce 2008, 52; Markale 1999, 5, 8.

fathers, and lived side by side with the elk and the deer" (*Zhuangzi*, ch. 29)[5]—the myth of matriarchy came to indicate a golden age when human societies provided "peace, prosperity, harmony with nature, appropriate use of technology, sexual freedom, and just and equitable roles for men and women." Not coincidentally, the height of this delightful state is dated to the Mesolithic, the precise time to which Daoists project their ideal society (Eller 2000, 40-41).

In the modern West, the idea of matriarchy first appeared in *Das Mutterrecht* (The Mother Right) by Johann Jakob Backofen (1861) where he postulated a primitive and simplistic age before the arrival of civilized patriarchy on the basis of Greek mythology. In his wake, Lewis Henry Morgan, in *Ancient Civilization* (1877), proposed social and technological evolution in three less evaluative stages: savagery, barbarism, and civilization, roughly matching foraging, agriculture, and statehood (Eller 2000, 31). He also connected matrilocal living with Native American reality as found among the Seneca Iroquois tribe, setting the stage for the projection of ethnographic findings into the remote past.

The narrative changed with Friedrich Engels who, in *The Origin of the Family, Private Property, and the State* (1884), saw matriarchy as a form of primitive communism, describing the "overthrow of the mother right" at the beginning of agriculture as the "world-historic defeat of the female sex." In his wake, Will Durant, in the first volume of *The Story of Civilization* (1935), credited women with the invention of practically everything, from agriculture through pottery to trade and woodworking (Eller 2000, 33; Eisler 1987, 45). Feminists in the late 20th century followed this, seeing women at the core of life and reading matriarchy as "a myth of regress, of paradise lost" (Eller 2000, 34).

To them, life under female rule was—and can again be—perfect, "without class stratification, centralized government, taxation, technology, warfare, or slavery" (Noble 1991, 227). Free from the divisive distinction of public and private, people pool and share their resources, freely giving and caring for all (Eller 2000, 42). Women serve as priestesses, healers, and wise women, creating a "culture that functions so smoothly that there is no need for socially appointed leaders" (2000, 44). Any guidance is done lovingly and a form of mothering, resting on greater experience, knowledge, and ability, the "intention of her 'rule' being to free the child, to make it independent" (French 1985, 27). Aided by senior women, eventually all attain the full virtue of "the cultured norm of femininity" (Bulger and Joyce 2013, 76), living for "connectedness, social cohesion, union, and communion" (Eller 2000, 60), realizing "nature in the process of naturing" (Markale 1999, 19).

Ancient Daoists in many ways support this vision, emphasizing feminine values as defined by mainstream culture, unquestioningly seeing the female

[5] Similar sentiments are also expressed in other pre-Han sources, notably the *Huainanzi* and the *Lüshi chunqiu* 呂氏春秋 (Spring and Autumn Annals of Mr. Lü; trl. Knoblock and Riegel 2000), later to be happily picked up by Marxist archaeologists (Shelach 2004, 13-14).

with softer, gentler characteristics, secondary to the outgoing, active male. As the *Zhuangzi* notes,

> The ruler precedes, the minister follows; the father precedes, the son follows; the older brother precedes, the younger brother follows; the senior precedes, the junior follows; the man precedes, the woman follows; the husband precedes, the wife follows. Honor and lowliness, precedence and following are part of the workings of Heaven and Earth, and from them the sage draws his model. (ch. 13)

Understood to be natural and inescapable (Linduff and Rubinson 2013, 352), the yin-yang dichotomy associates action, movement, transformation, and expansion with yang, and structure, quietude, stability, and contraction with yin. By extension, yang signifies Heaven, summer, day, ruler, father, nobility, military, and superiority in general, while yin—and therefore women—relate to Earth, winter, night, subject, mother, lower classes, laborers, and overall inferiority. In terms of values, yang equals valor, courage, hardness, initiative, and the giving of orders, while yin finds expression in humility, letting go, softness, submissiveness, and obedience.[6]

Working within this framework, the *Daode jing* represents Dao as the great mother, the essential element of water that nurtures all, possessed of feminine qualities such as softness and weakness (Despeux and Kohn 2003, 6; Milcinski 1997, 201). Dao as mother is where all beings come from and to which they all return, the invisible, deep, dark, and mysterious (female) source of the universe, the all-embracing and nurturing core at the root of all. The womb of the cosmos that brings forth and nurtures all, it is a single, integrated organism (Chen 1974, 57). People who attain Dao consequently have total trust in it as their universal mother. They allow all changes and transformations—even death—to happen naturally and place themselves in the mother's position at the mysterious center, where, as Ellen Marie Chen points out, "things at the same time emerge into the activities of life and return to the quietude of death" (1973, 235; Despeux and Kohn 2003, 7).

Besides the strong emphasis on motherhood, the *Daode jing* also links Dao with female animals (chs. 6, 10, 28, 61) and uses various symbols that indicate containing and latency—such as the empty vessel (ch. 4), the bellows (ch. 5), the dark unborn (ch. 1), water (chs. 6, 78), and the valley (chs. 6, 28, 32) (Chen 1974, 53). It also emphasizes that Dao embraces all (chs. 27, 32), evenly spreads its goodness (ch. 32), and cherishes all beings with motherly love (ch. 67). It notes that the female overcomes the male by its quality of stillness (ch. 61) and that in order to attain union with Dao one should abide by the female (ch. 28),

---

[6] Kohn 2005, 21-22. See also Eller 2000, 62; Eisler 1987, xix; Johnson 1997, 61-62; Milcinski 1997, 198-99; Wang 2012; Zhou 2003, 8, 22.

cultivating the qualities of weakness and softness (Chen 1974, 51; Milcinski 1997, 203).

In addition to giving and nurturing, Dao is yin in that it manifests as stillness, passivity, darkness, emptiness, and withdrawal (Zhou 2003, 9). The *Daode jing* exalts this shadowy, submissive side of the female as a way to overcome and balance the dominant yang mode of the world. At the same time, it suffers from the same fallacy as the myth of matriarchy, never going beyond the dominant link of the feminine with values of chastity, modesty, and meekness that make women inferior and easy to control. Creating "a straightjacket that denies the inherent complexity" of human beings (Johnson 1997, 73), "a strong conception of femininity not only encourages sexism, it also encourages racism and classism" (Eller 2000, 68).

Patriarchal Patterns

The alternative—just as lop-sided—vision of prehistoric life is the essentialist, sociobiologist hypothesis known as "Man the Hunter," developed by Raymond Dart in the 1950s and popularized in the following decades (Hart and Sussman 2005, 26). It says that males, biologically predetermined to be active and outgoing, created the hunting way of life. "It involves divisions of labor between male and female, sharing according to custom, cooperation among males, planning, knowledge of many species and large areas, and technical skills" (Washburn and Lancaster 1968, 296). Naturally bigger and equipped with greater strength, males were the sole creators of all new developments from bipedalism to agriculture. Females, on the other hand, bound by reproductive and nurturing functions, did light work close to home, being overall passive and reclusive, unable to hunt and fashion, let alone invent, a stone or other kind of tool.[7]

Limited biologically, women did work compatible with child care, that is, dull and repetitive, easily interrupted, close to home, and free from potential danger (Barber 1994, 29; Joyce 2008, 92). They thus came to be in charge of simple domestic tasks—low on the social scale and removed from all innovation and decision-making (Gilchrist 1999, 38). They focused their activity on sewing, spinning, weaving, and gardening as well as, toward the later Paleolithic, pottery making (Barber 1994, 43, 85, 95). Waiting patiently for the men to bring home the bacon, they would barter sexual favors for meat and generally grovel before their masters (Eller 2000, 108), serving as "passive handmaidens or compliant harem girls" (Hart and Sussman 2005, 216).

Reality is significantly different. For one, primate and hominid behavior shows a large percentage of female or equal dominance—40 percent among all

---

[7] Gilchrist 1999, 20-21. For more, see also Ardrey 1976, 8; Barber 1994, 84; 2007, 175; Bentley 1996, 24; Bolger 2013b, 161-62; Brown 1970, 1074; Conant 1982, 26; Costin 2013, 189; Finlay 2013, 145-46; Huber 2007, 21; Johnson 1997, 24-25; Joyce 2008, 42, 72; Sørensen 2000, 185, 188; Wilson 1975, 194.

200 species of primates, especially among strictly seasonal breeders. 60 percent of activities among all species take place in a reciprocal, cooperative, family-centered manner, with little or no division of labor and minimal sexual dimorphism.[8] In addition, females always play an important role in structuring societies, often serving as the repositories of group knowledge, while the most successful males are also the most cooperative (Hart and Sussman 2005, 216, 244). Only where "the males are much larger than the females" do females rarely dominate (Silk 1993, 215). "Not so coincidentally, these are also the only primate species that most sociobiologists know about" (Hart and Sussman 2005, 197). Some primate sexual dimorphism we see today, moreover, is the result of genetic adaptation. Thus, unlike the chimpanzees, among the bonobos, whose societies evolved egalitarian, females are the same size as males (2005, 120).

There is little evidence for sexual dimorphism among early hominins, since "there is no reliable method to assign sex and size to early bone fragments" (Zihlman 1993, 46-47). It is quite clear, however, that in the Upper Paleolithic women were close in size to men and only grew shorter through genetic modification over the millennia.[9] There is no reason to assume that they were subservient. Among primates, females commonly are aggressive, competitive, and promiscuous, asserting their rights and positions (Wright 1993, 128). Nor were they weak. The "assumption that strenuous physical activity and training develops 'masculine traits'" is simplistic and unfounded (Conant 1982, 31). There is "no sexual difference in trainability" of fitness and working capacity in males and females. Rather, the "sedentarization of girls at puberty or before affects their later working capacity, as well as size, build, body composition, and performance" (Conant 1982, 31; Eller 2000, 71).

While women biologically need more fat to be reproductive, that does not mean they cannot be fit; nor is their working capacity impaired by pregnancy or lactation (Conant 1982, 33). In addition, there was no "domestic" sphere in contrast to "outside" work in the past. Homes being essentially units of production (Gilchrist 1999, 34; Joyce 2008, 23), all had to work equally to maintain and support life. As Dianna Ducette says,

> It is not feasible to assume that women waited for men to bring home the meat, or that they waited for men to make them a stone tool. . . .
>
> If men were the primary hunters and went off on prolonged hunting trips leaving the women and children behind, it seems unlikely that the women sat idly by during more than a million years of male hunting activities. The value placed on men and men's work has masked not only the value of what women did (and do), but also has tended to rule out the possibility that women could have performed the same basic tasks as men.

---

[8] Wright 1993, 127-29, 138. See also Johnson 1997, 46; Silk 1993, 215, 224; Zihlman 1993, 34.

[9] Pechenkina, Ma, and Fan 2013, 460; Cohen and Bennett 1993, 282.

> The next question to be asked is: Could men have performed some of the same tasks as women? Other than childbirth and breast feeding—obviously yes. It wasn't those things that kept women from small-game hunting or extensive foraging. (2001, 170, 172; Nelson 1997, 125-26)[10]

Looking closely at the activities of contemporary hunter-gatherers, moreover, it is obvious that women are not always pregnant or breast feeding—typically spacing births over four or five years (Bentley 1996, 31-33). In addition, they remain active throughout, doing as much physical labor as men. Even in the last months of pregnancy, they commonly carry as much as sixty pounds of provisions using a sling that also serves for towing small children.[11]

While women among hunter-gatherers tend to work more on gathering food, providing 80 percent of subsistence (Zihlman 1993, 33; 1997, 91), they also participate in hunting and are often good at throwing spears and atlatls, projectiles that deliver a high degree of accuracy over short to moderate distances with a minimum of body motion (Ducette 2001, 171). To sum up, "the male potential for greater strength is not the ultimate determinant of the division of labor between men and women" (Conant 1982, 45). Also, technology is adaptable: if felling a tree with an ax using physical strength is not feasible, one can ring and burn the trunk, then chip at it until it gives way (1982, 46), making women just as competent as men.

Archaeological Evidence

Archaeological data, too, provide no firm evidence for pervasive gender-based social distinctions (Eller 2000, 81). A key source is mortuary analysis, which focuses on specific attributes in archaeological sites to obtain information about the status and social complexity of prehistoric people. These include the biological conditions of human remains, the configuration of cemeteries, the presence of primary and secondary burials, the energy expended on the grave and its components, as well as the value and significance of grave goods.[12]

The only readily sexed data are adult skeletal remains—those of infants and children requiring DNA analysis—and visual depictions of human figures with clear sexual markings.[13] Despite the fact that skeletal and clothing remains from the Paleolithic show "no obvious differentiations along lines of sex" (Joyce 2008, 15) and that there is "no particular association of male or female

---

[10] In fact, in many societies as well as among primates, males take care of infants, especially when there is paternal certainty (Wright 1993, 139).

[11] Conant 1982, 43. See also Ducette 2001, 172; Gilchrist 1999, 35; Hrdy 1999, 198.

[12] Ducette 2001, 160. See also Cohen and Bennett 1993, 277; Costin 1996, 119.

[13] On sexing skeletons, see Milner and Boldsen 2012, 276; Keightley 1999, 55. For DNA analysis, see Bramanti 2013, 100, 106-14; Lewis 2007, 54; Roberts 2013, 85. For sexual marking on figurines, see Bailey 2013, 247. Two thirds of all human representations in the Paleolithic are sexually indeterminate (Clottes and Courtin 1996, 155).

skeletons with beads" and other grave goods (Conneller 2013, 350), traditional androcentric archaeologists have tended to apply inherently modern ideas of gender differentiation to excavated data, often using ethnographic analogies in the so-called direct-historical approach and projecting the present into the past.[14] In other words, archaeologists, themselves mostly male and subject to modern cultural prejudices, have tended to interpret the evidence on the basis of preconceived notions of what gender roles should be (Decette 2001, 161). Thus, the different-sized footprints near the discovery of Lucy are immediately translated into a larger male followed by a tiny female (Hart and Sussman 2005, 17). Similarly, finding a cluster of spindle whorls among house foundations, the "natural" assumption is that the area was the women's quarters—when in fact there is no telling who exactly used the whorls and what the interior set-up was (Joyce 2008, 39-40; Nelson 1997, 62).

While burial patterns, moreover, often arrange males and females in specific ways, there are always also abnormalities: an old man buried like a female, a young woman buried like a male, grave goods of body ornaments, tools, or weapons next to members of both sexes, and the like.[15] There are plenty of examples of women warriors all over the world (Joyce 2008, 61, 75), including China (Chao 1982, 3) and Korea (Nelson 1993, 298), as well as cases of men doing domestic work. Rather than projecting a gender-based social division, it is, therefore, more reasonable to assume social distinctions according to other categories, such as civil and military, young and old, artistic or productive.[16]

"Variations between individuals of the same sex being invariably greater than categorical differences between the two sexes" (Eller 2000, 69), archaeologists now tend to assume that prehistoric people afforded status more on the basis of specific personal qualities and acquired skills than biological factors (Nelson 1997, 55). As Rosemary Joyce says,

> A specific woman would have been someone's parent, child, and sibling, the teacher of another person, the make of textiles, the artist who painted the wall in a cave, the hunter who shared a kill. None of these roles necessarily required specific biological characteristics, although individual physical traits might have helped a person distinguish herself at some of them . . . Within a small group known intimately to each other, individual distinction is more likely to have been pertinent as a basis for planning and action than abstract identities. (2008, 65)

---

[14] Eller 2000, 82. See also Arnold 1985, 100; Binford 1968; Bolger 2013a, 4; 2013b, 163; Freeman 1968; Huber 2007, 37; Joyce 2008, 8; Sørensen 2000, 3. Contemporary hunter-gatherer societies used as models include Australian aborigines (Pilling 1968; Yengoyan 1968), the Birhor of India (Williams 1968), the Hazda of Tanzania (Woodburn 1968a; 1968b), as well as various indigenous groups of northwest America (Suttles 1968).

[15] Eller 2000, 88; Joyce 2008, 49, 75; Weglian 2001, 141-46.

[16] Bolger 2013a, 13; Joyce 2008, 50; Sørensen 2000, 186; Weglian 2001, 149.

By the same token, there is now evidence that women used, made, and even invented numerous tools in prehistoric society (Hart and Sussman 2005, 215). Besides wood, bones, and plant fibers, they also worked with "all kinds of stone tools, in all kinds of lithic materials, for a variety of uses and contexts" (Finlay 2013, 146; Gero 1991, 176). More sophisticated microwear examination in combination with DNA analysis of blood residues (Finlay 2013, 150) and practical replication studies have shown not only a wide variety in expertise, strength, and coordination during stone knapping, but also revealed that numerous specimen were fashioned by children, i. e., "kid-knapped" (2013, 155; Wightman 2015,164). Rather than the prerogative of only one portion of the population—much like among contemporary hunter-gatherers and people working in the domestic mode of production, the fashioning, and by extension development and invention, of tools formed an integral part of everybody's life (Gero 1991, 192). Those more skilled, better trained, or more creative would be afforded higher status, quite independent of biological sex.

The same neutrality toward gender also plays out in the understanding of ancient infanticide, commonly thought to target mainly females.[17] Based on contemporary patterns in patriarchal societies such as India and China, the assumption is that prehistoric men killed their unwanted female offspring. Contrary to this "simplistic cross-cultural model," evidence suggests that while infanticide was widespread in the past, its "causes, effects, and meanings varied culturally." [18] Boys and girls were killed equally by both mothers and fathers, who saw them as unfit for life and returned them to a limbo state where they would await birth at a more auspicious time.

To sum up, the most likely scenario is that prehistoric societies were flexible, cooperative, and egalitarian, without any specific kinship organization or lineage pattern (Steward 1968, 332). Women as much as men cared for the young, procured sustenance, provided group stability, transmitted knowledge, enhanced techniques, and spread innovations (Hart and Sussman 215, 243).

The Chinese Case

In early China, too, "the distribution of tools in graves used to reconstruct social division of labor is not conclusive," the underlying assumptions being recognized as highly problematic "that a social division of labor along sex lines exist and that the distribution pattern of tools in burials reflects it" (Sun and Yang 2004, 31; Keightley 1999, 6). Over the last few decades, archaeologists have become increasingly aware of potential fallacies and revised the Marxist orthodoxy that proposed a linear progression from matriarchy to patriarchy,

---

[17] Lewis 2007, 94; Washburn and Lancaster 1968, 302.

[18] Scott 2001, 18. Thus, for example, in ancient China, children who resembled dangerous animals and were thus "not fully human" or who appeared too adult, such as being born with eyes open, "must not be reared" (Lewis 2006b, 86-88).

seeing a slave-holder society in the making as men increasingly gained control over the means of production (Pearson 1988, 1, 24; Shelach 2004, 13). They are now aware that contiguous burials do not necessarily mean clan or family relationships and that larger or more elaborate grave sites may indicate a compensatory honoring after death as much as high social status during life (Pearson 1988, 5).

While later tombs in patriarchal cultures tend to have males in positions of honor, surrounded by multiple females, the fact that the sex ratio in Neolithic Chinese cemeteries, especially among secondary burials, is "biased in favor of males" is no longer understood as inevitably pointing to matrilineal societies. Rather, there could be various other reasons, such as female infanticide, a higher mortality rate for young women, fewer formal burials for women, or faults in sexing the skeletons (Keightley 1999, 8; Shelach 2004, 18). Similarly, the various positions of skeletons may have different reasons, a prone, supine laying-out not necessarily indicating superiority nor a flexed, bent posture meaning subservience (Pearson 1988, 7).

Local diversity is another area of more careful differentiation. "Statistical analysis shows that different communities held very different attitudes toward sex and gender in mortuary ritual" (Sun and Yang 2004, 33; Keightley 1999, 6). Developmental sequences are often not simply chronological, but different patterns appear at different periods, even within the same area. Mortuary ritual seems to create a gender-neutral environment at many cemeteries, while at others it establishes social divisions along other, not necessarily gendered lines (2004, 37).

Grave goods, too, have undergone a shift in evaluation, many scholars realizing that it is often hard to attribute them correctly, especially in collective graves, and difficult to tell whether they reflect the living reality of the deceased or post-mortem projections of survivors (Jiang 2001, 123-24; Pearson 1988, 17). The bottom line, then, is that "we cannot really reconstruct social reality from grave patterns" (1988, 15) and "because different kinds of decisions concerning age, sex, and vertical and horizontal status create cross-cutting groups, it is unlikely that descent groups are clearly represented" (1988, 21; Shelach 2004, 24). Nonetheless, there is clear evidence for certain overarching developmental tendencies—notably an increase in the roles and status of males over the course of the Neolithic (Pearson 1988, 20).

More specifically, the oldest studied cemetery, at the Jiahu site of the Peiligang culture in Henan (7000-5000), contains collective burials, both primary and secondary. There is some differentiation in grave goods: tools such as axes, projectiles, and choppers are placed closer to males while vegetation rollers and ornaments are located near females. In addition, certain degenerative bone formations due to repetitive tasks indicate a gender-specific work culture.[19] Tombs from the later phase of Peiligang, around 5000, moreover, reveal clear status distinctions: males are buried with richer goods and ritual paraphernalia, while women's bones show iron deficiency, indicating a difference in access to food resources (Yao 2013, 588).

Further west, on the other hand, the early Yangshao Banpo site of Yuanjunmiao 元君廟 in western Shaanxi indicates a society "characterized by the principle of equality," where all shared resources and participated in common customs (Zhang 1985, 21). Living in small villages of 50 to 100 households, i. e., 200-300 inhabitants, people practiced incipient agriculture and joined together in communal meeting places, indicated by foundations of larger structures—as opposed to single houses of 200-300 square feet (Zhang 1987, 11-12).

The cemetery contains fifty-one graves in a planned and orderly arrangement, for the most part on a north-south axis. Tombs divide into two sections, possibly of one tribe with two clans and various lineages (1987, 7; Zhang 1985, 19-21). Burials are for the most part secondary, and 92 percent of skeletons were placed in collective tombs of 4 to 26 people of both sexes and all ages, the oldest being around 30 years old.[20] Secondary burial indicates an active memory and care for the dead, possibly an incipient ancestral cult (Keightley 1999, 10). Overall more men were found than women, but the same tools were placed with both (Jiao 2001, 54), and all graves contained women. In addition, two girls were buried with particularly rich goods, including adult ornaments (Zhang 1985, 30-31).

This, together with the fact that more women received primary burials, has led to the speculation that women were particularly honored and the society was matriarchal.[21] On the other hand, the evidence is not conclusive, and it is most likely that—matching early finds in other parts of the world and the classical vision of Mesolithic living—the society was household centered and largely egalitarian, men and women being partners with equal rights and duties and no clear division of labor (Jiao 2001, 55; Zhang 1987, 16).

The Goddess

Another potentially matriarchal culture is Hongshan in western Liaoning, dated to 4500-3000. Its main site at Dongshanzui 東山嘴 and the ceremonial complex at Niuheliang 牛河梁, with temples and raised stone circle tombs but no houses or storage pits, revealed numerous fragments of predominantly female figures.

---

[19] Keightley 1999, 19-20; Yao 2013, 587; Zhang 2005, 64.

[20] Zhang 1985, 24. See also Jiao 2001, 55; Keightley 1999, 11.

[21] Jiao 2001, 54; Keightley 1999, 11. See also Pearson 1988, 4; Thorp and Vinograd 2001, 29; Yao 2013, 586; Zhang 1985, 30; Zhang 2005, 44.

> Conspicuous female features can be observed in the breasts, arms, and shoulders. The life-sized human head is very striking. It has a plump face, long and smoothly contoured ears, and a slightly raised nose. It was painted red, and the eyeballs were represented by inlaid pieces of round jade. (Jiao 2001, 59)

Original icons were quite varied. Several were life-sized, others two or three times as large. They differed in age and status, forming a group of figures arranged according to a hierarchical system, potentially indicative of a complex pantheon or social representation. Matching traditional interpretations, the complex is generally understood as connected to fertility and beginning agriculture. It is also thought to reflect an early, matrilocal stage of social evolution, when women enjoyed high status and were honored as givers of life and primordial ancestors.[22]

Hongshan is one of numerous finds of female statues, the earliest of which go back to the Upper Paleolithic, including the famous Venus of Willendorf, Germany (30-25,000), numerous clay images from Dolní Věstonice, Czech Republic (26,000), as well as various figures from France (23,000).[23]

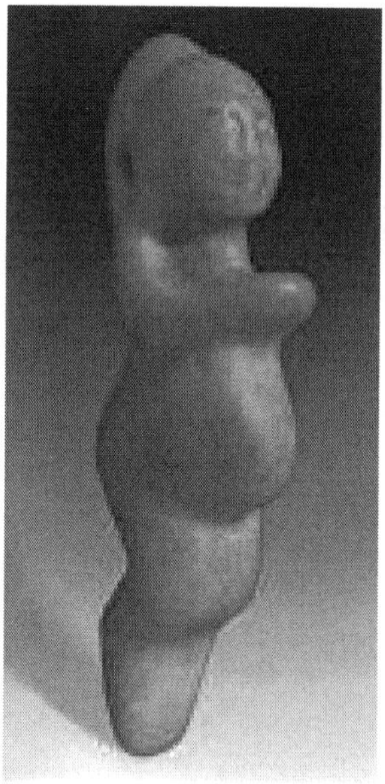

Hongshan Goddess

Venus of Willendorf

[22] Jiao 2001, 58, 60. See also Hutson et al. 2013, 47; Keightley 1999, 25-26; Nelson 1991; Nelson and Rosen-Avalon 2002, 65.

[23] Eller 2000, 135; Jarzombek 2013, 53-57; Rawson 1996a, 440; Sørensen 2000, 193.

Thousands of fragments have survived, over 200 figurines providing a three-dimensional but miniature similarity to the human body. Divergent in size and degree of naturalism, production materials, and fashioning techniques,

> They have in common that they represent naked or almost naked human bodies with some parts of the body enhanced or emphasized and others only sketched. The parts commonly emphasized (and even exaggerated) are the breasts, abdomen, and thighs, and in this emphasis the figurines are made to appear as female bodies. Typically, the hands and feet are merely suggested, and facial features are usually vague, although there are indications of hair and plaits. (Sørensen 2000, 198; see also Bailey 2013, 249; Eller 2000, 136)

Succeeded by more frequent examples from the Neolithic, including significant images found in Catalhöyük in Turkey (7500-5700), Malta (3600-3000), and Minoan Crete (1600),[24] these figurines, are often "monstrously exuberant and overabundant, with pendulous breasts, broad hips, rotund buttocks, and excessive corpulency" (Eller 2000, 135). Although they "rarely show signs of pregnancy, childbirth, or lactation" (2000, 134, 138), and are in fact in the minority among early art works (Bailey 2013, 245), they have been taken to signify the existence of a worldwide goddess complex, an overarching "matristic consciousness" in human prehistory.[25]

By extension, since most early figures, carvings, and murals represent animals as well as geometric shapes, these have been interpreted as symbolic representations of female power. For example, a snake or spiral stands for rising life energy, while crescents (including the half moon), caterpillars, and horns (including bull's heads) indicate the active process of creation. Crosses represent the four corners of the cosmos, while straight lines, waves, meanders, or zigzags show water and rain, the vitality of life, and any oval or triangle shape symbolizes a vulva.[26]

Not only is this rather far-fetched, but art in general is not a direct reflection of reality. As Cynthia Eller notes,

> European heraldry is full of lions and eagles, though in the ordinary run of their lives, Europeans were vastly more likely to encounter cows and pigs. Likewise, if women's magazines were my sole record of American culture, I might conclude that there were no fat people in 21st-century America. (2000, 116-17)

---

24 Eller 2000, 143-55. See also Cauvin 2000, 28-29; Eisler 1987, 25, 29; Johnson 1997, 45.

25 Eller 2000, 119; Bailey 2013, 246; Goodison and Morris 2013, 267.

26 Gimbutas 1974, 98-94, 124. For further discussions, see Eller 2000, 119, 128; Eisler 1987, 27; Chapman and Palincas 2013, 415; Goodison and Morris 2013, 265, 269; Markale 1999, 52; Marshack 1991, ch. 13; Nelson 1997, 161.

By the same token, figurines like language are representations, providing an interpretation of reality and opening conceptualizations of body and life (Bailey 2013, 245, 252; Hays-Gilpin 2013, 126). Involving touch as well as sight, they offer ways of identity formation and shape people's conceptions of being. "No figurine fully depicts the biology of the human body; the creative process of selection and abstraction is present everywhere" (2013, 249).

Symbolizing more the general fact of life than depicting a certain person or deity, their practical function may well be more important than their looks. Quite possibly figurines formed an essential part of households, serving as charms or talismans with ritual, healing, or protective functions (Eller 2000, 138; Brumfiel 1996, 148). Having to be made new for each occasion, moreover, would explain the seamless continuum between rough, unfinished pieces and more polished ones and "why so many figurines are found in garbage middens" (Eller 2000, 139).

This understanding is further substantiated by careful analysis of clay fragments from Dolní Věstonice. Here breakage was intentional, probably resulting from possibly ceremonial throwing of wet clay objects into a fire, causing them to explode. In other words, potters did not even try to make complete figurines, but experimented with fire-related properties (Bolger 2013b, 168). Similarly, the Hongshan figures may have served particular ritual and communal functions, expressing an increasingly hierarchical but not necessarily matriarchal social structure.

Growing Complexity

Beginning around the year 4000, the trend toward social complexity is also evident in other parts of China. Although villages were still small, as mortuary evidence from Shijia 世嘉, Shaanxi, shows, women would migrate to marry while men stayed home, indicating increasing exogamy and patrilocality (Keightley 1999, 16).

More intricate social stratification, moreover, becomes first obvious in the Dawenkou culture of Shandong (4100-2600), described as the Chinese "threshold to civilization" (Yao 2013, 588). More fully agricultural than previous cultures, it shows a growing reliance on domestic crops as evidenced by greater storage facilities. In addition, there is an increasing differentiation in the scale and construction of tombs, complete with more elaborate funerary displays. Mixed sex burials are rare, giving way to socially ranked graves, large tombs housing only a single person, who is provided with ample food offerings in special vessels (Jiao 2001, 56; Keightley 1999, 23). The tomb's occupancy is not gender specific, but tends to reflect residential or kin affiliation. Females often have more pottery vessels, indicative of some specialization in ceramic production and jade working (Zhang 2005, 72). There are also more grave gifts from other places, revealing a wider circulation of long-distance goods (Yao 2013, 588).

By 3000, many sites show graves "that contain two skeletons—one of a male and one of a female—providing signs for the transition to monogamous families and the beginning of male dominance" (Shelach 2004, 19). Notably the Majiayao culture of western Shaanxi and Gansu (3300-2650), together with its successors at Machang (2350-2050) and Qijia (2200-1700), demonstrates the gradual unfolding of patriarchal patterns (Keightley 1999, 9, 24-25; Rawson 1996a, 37). In its early documented stage, the Banshan 半山 period (2650-2350), there is no significant association between tools and sex. Tomb structure, furniture, and location do not present any patterned differences among men and women, which means that "sex and gender differences have been either similarly expressed or equally depressed" (Sun and Yang 2004, 38).

Both during Machang and Qijia, on the other hand, certain types of tools are exclusively associated with one sex (Jiao 2001, 57). Chisels, awls, adzes, axes, and knives made of stone and animal bones are placed with males, while stone and ceramic spindle whorls characterize females (Sun and Yang 2004, 33; Zhang 2005, 66). In the latter, moreover, in about ten percent of graves, males are placed supine and extended, while females lie flexed on side facing the male, indicative possibly of an increasing discrimination against women and maybe even of human sacrifice (Keightley 1999, 15). In some cases, females are even placed outside the coffin, like burial offerings (Sun and Yang 2004, 39-40). Society is clearly becoming more hierarchical and gendered. The later phase of the culture, moreover, as documented in the Zhangjiatai 張家台 cemetery, leaves most males with tools and no objects with females, not even one spindle whorl (Sun and Yang 2004, 35).[27]

It is significant that the widespread connection of women with textiles, and to a lesser degree with pottery (Nelson 2013, 335), begins in close conjunction with growing social complexity. "Linked to the use of symbols as part of the process of institutionalization" (Conroy 1993, 153), it is not naturally part of early life or due to any biologically based division of labor.[28] While the earliest fibers and sewing utensils go back to 15,000, found in the caves at Lascaux (McIntosh 2006, 340), even during early agriculture both males and females contributed to textile processing in various functions, by "herding, shearing, growing, harvesting, preparing, spinning, plying, dyeing, weaving, sewing, embroidering, and finishing" (Costin 1996, 124).

This changed after agriculture and civilization arose, when cloth transformed into a status symbol, appeared in "public displays and important ceremonies," and came to serve as a means of social exchange and wealth accumu-

---

[27] The same also holds true for finds at Tugutai 土谷台 in Gansu, dated to the 3rd millennium. Here men are clearly given priority while women are buried in secondary positions together with children (Keightley 1999, 12).

[28] Costin 2014, 188; Joyce 2008, 56; Sørensen 2000, 200.

lation, gaining "social, political, economic, and religious functions" (Wright 1996, 85). As clearly documented in ancient Mesopotamia, this gave rise to a "gender ideology linking weaving with women" (1996, 99). Similarly and more recently, in the Inca empire (1400-1533 CE), textiles were originally part of basic survival and only became women's work after their economic value rose in the wake of the Spanish conquest (Costin 1996, 124). That is to say, gendering of labor is part of growing complexity and patriarchal dominance, linking women with textiles for just the reasons usually given: the work is flexible enough to allow child care and keeps women close to the house (Barber 2007, 175; Costin 2013, 189). However, rather than a nature-based development, the division reflects intentional, cultural discrimination.

Gender division by culture is also borne out by other historical examples where gender may have been understood in a less dichotomous fashion. Thus, the ancient Greeks understood all humans to be part of a single sex, "from which adult males develop due to a greater level of heat," making women the same as young boys (Joyce 2008, 19; Johnson 1997, 17). As a result, "'free' women in classical Greece"—not unlike aristocratic ladies in China—were lifelong legal minors who were mostly forbidden to leave their homes and who were not even their husbands' preferred sexual partners" (Eller 2000, 106). Zuni Indians, on the other hand, were all understood to be born male, developing either into that identity or changing gender as they went through life (Joyce 2008, 57).

Gendered Culture

In China, the highly gendered society of later dynasties continued to grow throughout the Neolithic. Thus, the Longshan culture (2600-2000), with larger sites and stronger stratification in the heartland and on the eastern seaboard, clearly indicates an escalation of social differentiation, with males attaining increasingly higher rank. Highly elaborate graves, making up only one percent of the total, are solely occupied by men (Yao 2013, 589-90; Pearson 1981, 1086). At Taosi (2200-1700), moreover, hundreds of objects are buried in graves, but exclusively with males, showing "marked disparities in wealth and status" (Keightley 1999, 27).

Even the Chinese periphery underwent the same developments, as documented by the Dadianzi 大甸子 cemetery in Inner Mongolia, dated to 1735-1463. Here goods placed in the coffin chamber seem to be associated with the personal life and skills of the deceased, while those found in niches in the outer chamber are more about general social status and funerary actions (Jiang 2001, 124; Wu 2004, 51). Among its about 800 graves, males were buried with dogs, tools, and weapons (2004, 79), while females have spindle whorls, ceramic vessels, and ornaments—in larger quantities if the deceased is more senior (2004, 67-68). Buried in family clusters, women seem to have received their status through men, who also were buried with much larger numbers of cowrie shells, the active currency at the time, thus showing that they accumulated more wealth than women (2004, 76).

By the Shang dynasty, gendered culture was firmly in place. Women were chiefly considered as nourishing mothers, and the early pictograph for "woman" shows a kneeling and submissive figure.[29] Rulers had large numbers of consorts, commonly called "lady" (*fu* 婦) in conjunction with their place of origin. Many of them came from vassal states (*fang* 方) and brought troops and wealth to the capital. [30]

King Wuding (1250-1192), for example, had ninety consorts, three of whom were posthumously worshiped as queens (Chao 1982, 1; Keightley 1999, 30). Best known among them are Fu Jing 婦姘 and Fu Hao 婦好, who both enjoyed high status and great influence, even leading armies into battle. Fu Hao in particular, besides having three children, served as top military leader and commanded key generals (Zheng 1996, 240). Her tomb was discovered undisturbed in Anyang in 1976. It contained sixteen sacrificial victims, six dogs, 440 bronzes, 800 jade and bone objects, large numbers of pottery objects, numerous weapons, as well as 7000 cowrie shells.[31] Still these warrior ladies were the exception. Both the overall numbers and physical tombs of women were much smaller than those of men (Keightley 1999, 43-44), and oracle bones repeatedly note the birth of a daughter as being "not good" (1999, 34).

Under the Western Zhou, women still had a fair amount of freedom, but were no longer associated with war or charioteering (Chao 1982, 4; Jiang 2001, 133). The massive suppression of women, for which traditional China is justly notorious, fully took off in the Eastern Zhou, not coincidentally the period of a major spike in the continuous decline of women's health and height (Pechenkina, Ma, and Fan 2013, 466). The *Shujing* 書經 (Book of History) expresses it most pertinently: "The hen does not announce the morning. The crowing of a hen in the morning indicates the subversion of the family" (Legge 1969, 302). By the same token, many early sources tend to demonize women, holding them responsible for excessive lascivious behavior of male rulers that causes the downfall of dynasties (Chao 1982, 4; Linduff and Rubinson 2013, 356).

---

29 Gulik 1961, 5; Ho 1975, 249; Keightley 1999, 3.

30 Chao 1982, 1; Keightley 1999, 29, 33; Wang 200 4, 99.

31 Chao 1982, 2; Keightley 1999, 40-41. See also Rawson 1996a, 90-111; Wang 2004, 100; Wu 2004, 104; Yao 2013, 591-92; Zheng 1996, 242-44.

Daoist Women

Counteracting this overarching cultural trait, Daoist communities from their very inception recovered early Stone Age patterns and created a gender-neutral environment for their practitioners. Thus, among the early Celestial Masters, all members, independent of sex, from early childhood on underwent formal initiations at regular intervals, receiving registers of spirit generals for protection against demons—reaching 75 for an unmarried person and 150 for a married couple.[32]

Among adults, moreover, some of these initiations took the form of the "harmonization of *qi*," involving formally choreographed intercourse between selected non-married partners in an elaborate ritual that enacted the cosmic matching of yin and yang and thus contributed to greater universal harmony. Each partner performed a particular role, none less important or active than the other. The complex ceremony joined male (yellow) and female (red) sexual energy in accord with cosmic forces. Held in the oratory (*jingshi* 靜室), it consisted of slow, formal movements accompanied by meditations to establish harmony both in bodies and universe.[33]

In ordinary life, too, women functioned as equal partners. They were valued as important members of the community and carried their fair share of responsibility and benefits, active in the domestic mode of production. They had access to all leadership positions up to the rank of libationer, and also functioned as "female masters" (*nüshi* 女師) in charge of teaching and ritual supervision.[34] For example, as Tao Hongjing 陶弘景 (456-536) notes in his *Dengzhen yinjue* 登真隱訣 (Secret Instructions on the Ascent to Perfection, DZ 421), when the later libationer Wei Huacun 魏華存 (252-334) received the formulas of Zhang Wei 張瑋, adepts entered the quiet chamber and formally greeted the three masters present: the celestial master, the female master, and the personal master. Unlike in the later organized religion, the text adds, the female master in the early communities was an independent agent and not the leading master's wife (3.8a; Despeux and Kohn 2003, 105).

Women would also perfect their personal cultivation. Thus, Wei Huacun was originally the daughter of a high official and an adept of the Celestial Masters (Reed 1987, 167). Married to a leading religious officer and the mother of two sons, she retired to a separate part of the family compound and devoted herself to self-cultivation. In 299, she had visions of several perfected beings

---

[32] Despeux and Kohn 2003, 106. See also Bumbacher 1998, 689; Kleeman 2016, 277-81; Overmyer 1991, 97; Schipper 1994, 87.

[33] Despeux and Kohn 2003, 11-12, 106-07; Bumbacher 2012, 86-88; Kleeman 2016, 158-74; Raz 2008; Schipper 1984, 203.

[34] Kleeman 2016, 284; see also Bumbacher 2012, 98; Jia 2017.

who presented her with sacred scriptures and oral instruction and became a libationer with ritual powers and administrative duties.

During the war that led to the rise of the Eastern Jin in 317, her family fled to Jiankang 建康 (modern Nanjing), after which she spent much of her life in seclusion, receiving further visits from celestial perfected of high rank (Despeux 2000, 388). Eventually she attained Dao on the holy mountain of the south (Mount Heng 衡山) in Hunan, which at the time was an active center of both Buddhist and Daoist practices (see Robson 2009). She was accordingly called Nanyue furen 南岳夫人 (Lady of the Southern Peak) and after her ascension to Heaven became a key revealing deity of the Highest Clarity (Shangqing 上清) school.[35]

To the present day, Daoism propagates cultivation techniques that are gender neutral and includes many female deities in its pantheon, even among generals and other supernatural warriors. Although priests officiating at rituals are commonly male, members of both sexes follow the same rules and rise through the same ritual ranks (Reed 1987, 176; Saso 1978, 156-60).

Daoist communities then and now provide an alternative living environment in the form of fluid and liminal *communitas* (Turner 1974, 273-87), expanding chances of self-realization for women in an otherwise radically gendered society. From unmarried youngsters through married women joining their husbands to widows and divorcees (Despeux and Kohn 2003, 112), they all get the chance to receive religious instruction, work in social harmony, and attain spiritual salvation. Communities succeed in this endeavor partly by maintaining a distant yet respectful relationship to the society around them. But most importantly, they succeed because they place gender second in their daily and ritual activities, opening a social context that changes personal identity patterns away from gendered roles.

That is to say, gender is essentially an emergent property (Hutson et al. 2013, 55), a continuously learned cultural construct of primed representations that individuals absorb into their identity as "bodily memories accumulate through shared experiences" (Bulger and Joyce 2013, 80).

> The gender inequality you see is *in* your mind. So are the cultural beliefs about gender that are so familiar to us all. They are in that messy tangle of mental associations that interact with the social context. Out of this interaction emerges your self-perception, your interests, your values, your behavior, yes, even your abilities. (Fine 2010, 235)

Being a learned pattern, however, gendered self-perception can also be unlearned—and relatively quickly. Many experiments have shown, that "when

---

[35] Despeux and Kohn 2003, 19; Bumbacher 1998, 690-91. For more on Lady Wei, see Despeux 1990, 56-60; Schafer 1977b; Strickmann 1981, 142.

we are not thinking of ourselves as 'male' or 'female,' our judgments are the same" (Fine 2010, 25), as are our skills, abilities, concerns, and cares.

The way we function in any given task depends on our cultural priming and socially determined self-evaluation—in terms of gender, status, social role, and skills (Fine 2010, 28). "Everything we do, we do with a mind that is exquisitely sensitive to the social environment around it" (2010, 39). Changing the social structuring, the threat level, and thus the dominant identity patterns in any given situation can have an immediate and tangible effect on ability (2010, 30). That is to say, the fewer self-doubts and anxieties we have, the better we become at fulfilling our tasks, the easier it is to succeed (2010, 33; Csikszentmihalyi 1990, 49). As Malcolm Gladwell puts it, "We can alter the way we thin-slice [i.e., react spontaneously] by changing the experiences that comprise our impressions," taking active steps to "manage and control priming conditions" (2005, 97).

Daoists were well aware of the impact of conditions on thinking and of thinking on performance, as the *Zhuangzi* demonstrates, speaking of archery:

> If you join a contest and shoot to win a nice brick, you will be skillful. If you shoot for a fancy buckle, you will be nervous. If you shoot for a gold bar, you will be a wreck.
>
> Your shooting skill is the same in all cases, but if there is something you want badly, your focus will be outside. And the more your focus is outside, the more you get clumsy on the inside. (ch. 19; Kohn 2014, 210)

By the same token, if women learn that being female means lesser competence or greater weakness, as long as gender roles are central to their identity and social interaction, they will act incompetent and weak. "Both descriptive and prescriptive elements of gender stereotyping create problems for women" (Fine 2010, 56), growing brain patterns from even before birth that set up characteristic structures of behavior and expectation (2010, 192). "The social phenomenon of gender comes into the brain and becomes part of our cerebral biology" (2010, 236). On the other hand, the brain possessing enormous plasticity, people's mental and physical abilities are greatly malleable: they can be enhanced and even transformed by training—especially in a gender-neutral setting, where skills and personality count for more than any biological factor. Daoist communities, thus, counteract mainstream culture and empower women by creating such a setting, reactivating patterns from the distant past, their golden age of pristine affluence.

Intentional Ungendering

They continue and intensify this process in their monastic institutions. Going beyond gender neutrality, here Daoists engage in an active program of ungendering, creating a new level of androgynous living, actively "liberating the individual from the confines of the appropriate" (Heilbrun 1973, x; Zhou 2003, 4).

Overcoming sexed identity, Daoist monastics no longer think of themselves as men and women and instead call themselves "Heaven Dao" (*qiandao* 乾道) and "Earth Dao" (*kundao* 坤道), adopting terms from the *Yijing* (Herrou 2013, 66). In their community living, they make no difference among male and female ranks, status, activities, or clothing (Cahill 1990, 36; 2006, 10; Kleeman 2016, 233). Both historically and today, men and women pursue the same goals, undergo the same training and ordination, participate equally in community tasks, and attain the same ranks (Herrou 2013, 180).

Thus, once the family agrees to the move, the future monastic sets up his or her hermitage near a master or lives with a teacher, avoiding contact with ordinary people and undergoing basic instruction. After another training period at a larger institution, she undergoes several levels of ordination, then either sets up her own convent or rises in an existing institution (Strickmann 1978, 470; Kohn 2003a, 82). "There is no need to choose a master of the same sex: in the master-disciple relationship, one does not distinguish between men and women" (Herrou 2013, 148).

To ungender personal perception, moreover, monastics work with the methods of internal alchemy (*neidan* 内丹) (Skar and Pregadio 2000). They merge yin and yang internally in self-cultivation and invert the process of cosmic unfolding. To refine their sexual essences such as seminal fluid and menstrual blood, they begin with sex-specific techniques, then equally circulating the purified energy throughout the body to sublimate it into pure spirit. Eventually they store this in the lower elixir field beneath the navel and there grow their spiritual alter ego, the immortal embryo. In the process, due to hormonal modifications, sexual characteristics diminish. Women stop menstruating and their breasts shrink while men experience a retraction of the penis or a shrinking of testicles (Herrou 2013, 236; Réquéna 2012, 144).

Becoming physically more alike, all Daoists wear their hair tied up in a topknot and don the same vestments: a dark-blue robe (*daopao* 道袍) of thick fabric crossed in front, combined with loose pants, held below the knee by while puttees (*wa* 袜). The feet are clad in black cloth shoes (*buxie* 布鞋), also known as "cloud shoes" (*yunlü* 云履) (Yoshioka 1979, 237; Herrou 2013, 43).

> Not differentiated in garb or status, or even in the lines of teaching, they all receive the same monthly stipend and do the same jobs. Nor are there special quarters for either of them: monks and nuns live in individual cells scattered throughout the temple territory. Having single rooms avoids

problems possibly caused by too much closeness and facilitates ascetic practice. The administrators assign rooms as they become available, to no particular scheme or layout. (Herrou 2013, 231).

Daoist garb: I. long robe; II-III. midi robe; IV. short habit (Herrou 2013, 44)

Both monks and nuns take on domestic and community chores, each working according to their skill and expertise. Unlike in mainstream society, monks frequently clean vegetables, cook, or wash linens, while nuns carry heavy loads, push transport carts, or work in construction. In ritual activities, too, Daoists pursue ungendering: all serve in the same roles, all officiate at various ceremonies—funerary, healing, celebratory, or inaugurational—and all work in administration, when needed even taking on the post of honorary abbot (*fangzhang* 方丈) (2013, 232).

In all these various ways of ungendering, monastic Daoists fulfill an androgynous ideal already expressed in the *Daode jing*, which understands the realization of the sage in the world as lying in the reconciliation of all opposites and the attainment of life as a consummate person who is neither feminine nor masculine (Ames 1981, 43; Hall and Ames 1998, 19). They also follow the age-old ideal of immortals, already in Han tomb reliefs depicted as androgynous beings (Wallace 2012, 79). Androgyny, moreover, plays a role in other religions that see the recovery of gender oneness as a reunion with the primordial and a recovery of godlike being (Eliade 1978, ch. 12; Milcinski 1997, 197). Thus, in early Christianity "the unification of opposites, and especially of opposite sexes, served as a prime symbol of salvation."[36] Christian baptism as much as Daoist sagehood conferred a state of lived androgyny, a recapturing of the "primal,

[36] Welch 1996, 71. See also Hopkins 2013, 79, 83; MacDonald 1987, 5; Meeks 1974, 165-66.

undifferentiated unity" of humankind's original state (Brown 1988, 50). The transcendence of all divisions (1988, 115), it was a recovery of a more original way of being, a consciousness before the awareness of sexual identity, a restoration of the person to the divine image of original man (Meeks 1974, 189)

Beyond religion, androgyny has risen to prominence also in modern psychology. Here it refers to two different modes of being, either working within or going beyond gendered frameworks. Working within established concepts, it reflects the ideal of the person as embracing the full range of human character traits (Zhou 2003, 4) by establishing a balance of standard characteristics, becoming fluid in gender role behavior, and allowing various new properties to emerge.[37] As such, androgyny manifests in various traditional cultures that offered the potential "transformation of gender identity" (Gilchrist 1999, 60; Bolger 2013a, 13), including the Indian *hijra*, the Byzantine eunuch, and the Native American "two-spirit" (*berdache*).[38] It also appears in late imperial China, where "flourishing commerce, a surplus of wealth, widespread education, a booming printing industry, rising individualism, prevailing hedonism, and the cult of *qing* [feelings]" (Zhou 2003, 15) diluted traditional gender roles. As a result, women came to function increasingly as religious leaders, martial arts masters, and warriors, while men underwent a feminization as homosexual prostitutes or eunuchs (2003, 16-45).

Going beyond cultural limitations, androgyny as understood in psychology serves to create a completely new level of being "fully human" (Olds 1981), an identity that surpasses all established gender characteristics, goes beyond situational flexibility, transcends sex roles, and renders cultural patterns irrelevant in favor of "fluid, integrated wholeness."[39] Involving the deconstruction of all binary opposites in combination with new ways of processing cognitive data, the free expression of unique personality traits, and the activation of an unchartered repertoire of social behavior (Cook 1985, 24-25), it is both the primal and ultimate stage of human development. Ungendering as much as gender neutrality, therefore, represent yet another choice Daoists make to recover, enhance, and transform prehistoric modalities toward attaining a more complete and harmonious state of being human and to live in pristine affluence.

---

[37] This understanding matches various "cojoint models": modulating or balancing, additive or enhancing, and interactive or multiplicative (Cook 1985, 22). Among psychologists, Carl Jung was the first to emphasize the integration of male and female archetypes (1941; 1959). See also Singer 2000.

[38] See Gilchrist 1999, 59-62; Nanda 1994; Ringrose 1994; Roscoe 1994. Androgyny relates to but is not the same as economic or sexual emancipation, the absence of role differentiation, and physical hermaphroditism or bisexuality (Cook 1985, 19).

[39] This reflects the developmental and transcendence models of psychological androgyny (Cook 1985, 23). See also Heilbrun 1981; Kaplan and Bean 1976; Singer 2000. Various scales and questionnaires have been developed to assess the degree of androgyny within people's psyche (Cook 1985, 40-46).

Chapter Nine

Foodways

> This is what the world honors: wealth, eminence, long life, a good name. This is what the world finds happiness in: a life of ease, rich food, fine clothes, beautiful sights, sweet sounds. This is what it looks down on: poverty, meanness, early death, a bad name. This is what it finds bitter: a life that knows no rest, a mouth that gets no rich food, no fine clothes for the body, no beautiful sights for the eye, no sweet sounds for the ear. (*Zhuangzi* 18)

The preference for prehistoric modalities also holds true for the Daoist way of dealing with food. "Food is a many-splendored thing, central to biological and social life" (Counihan 1999, 6). Satisfying both physical and emotional hungers, it determines how we live and interact with others and the environment.[1] What we eat and how we prepare and consume our food is what makes us human. "In every culture, foodways constitute an organized system, a language that—through its structure and components—conveys meaning and contributes to the organization of the natural and social world" (Counihan 1999, 19).

Food plays a major role in the Daoist life, used differently according to the level and social setting of the practitioner, but in all cases recovering prehistoric structures and attitudes within a post-agricultural environment. Most Daoists are lay followers, living ordinary lives in the greater Chinese society. They follow the same fundamental principles—cooking their food thoroughly and making sure to eat appropriately of all the five flavors. In addition, however, more than ordinary people, Daoists tend to pay close attention to local origins and seasonal availability of the food, eat a wide variety of items, focus consciously on the way food supports their body, and supplement it with herbal remedies.

Daoists committed to communities work closely within the organized framework. Thus, the early Celestial Masters as part of their social and ethical system observed a number of food taboos, including vegetarianism, combined with major community celebrations at certain key points of the year (Kleeman 2016). More than just using food to take care of the body, they followed ancient precedents and activated it as a social medium, a symbolic form of the

[1] Johnson 1982, 19; Ohnuki-Tierney 1993, 1; Ungar and Teaford 2002, 1.

exchange of goods, a way of reinforcing their commitment to the organization and each other.

Monastic Daoists, then and now, follow the same pattern, holding so-called vegetarian feasts on a daily basis as part of their regular noon meal. Sharing food here is representative for the communion not only among members, but also with donors and supplicants and, reaching even farther, with all beings, divine and demonic. Food serves as a major medium to enhance a particular vision of the world and way of life, providing harmony and integration as well as nourishment.

A fourth and final way Daoists use food is the practice of extensive fasting as part of the transformation to immortality. Originally a thorough abstinence from any form of grain or beans, it also involves a systematic process of food reduction, leading to living on pure *qi*—on occasion for prolonged periods—and its accompanying physical changes. Here food is again a major representative of culture and lifestyle, the refusal to partake showing the rejection of entire aspects of civilization.

The idealization of the Paleolithic and recovery of pre-agricultural living is most obvious in this last dimension, but even within Daoist communities foodways focus on sharing rather than dominance or display, and lay followers' conscientious use of local and seasonal food items recalls the care foragers take with their resources.

Cooking

The most fundamental way in which human eating differs from any other species is cooking. "Cooking defines the human essence" (Wrangham 2009, 13). Already the structuralist Claude Lévi-Strauss (1969) had the insight that cooking is a defining feature of humanity, but he tended to see it more as a metaphor, focusing on primitive mind, perception, and mythology (Counihan 1999, 21). Now we understand that the Australopithecines, the prehistoric precursors of humanity, ate raw food with high fiber content, utilizing bush fruits, fresh greens, raw meat, insects, and other natural products as efficiently as apes do.[2] Their successors, the habilines, were one step closer to humans and walked upright, but they but were still apelike, raw-food eaters of small size with big chewing teeth (Wrangham 2009, 97). In contrast, early hominins such as *Homo ergaster*, the maker of the Acheulean stone tools who lived 1.8 million years ago, had some control over fire and cooked his food,[3] even while still scavenging and before organized hunting (Outram 2007, 40-41). As Eugene Anderson says,

---

[2] Conklin-Brittain et al. 2002, 61-62; Eaton et al. 2002, 8; McGrew 2001, 163; Milton 2002, 120; Rodman 2002, 79-81, Schmid 2015, 18; Schoeninger et al 2001, 189; Sept 2001, 85; Wrangham 2009, 37, 45.

[3] Counihan 2009, 96; Conklin-Brittain et al. 2002, 67; O'Connell et al. 2002, 59.

> The average human of one million years ago probably lived largely on tender young plant material, got at least 10-20 percent of calories from meat from hunting and scavenging, ate many insects and loved them, dug up roots and tubers during bad times, and gorged on anything and everything edible when a good patch was found. . . .
>
> 500,000 years later, more hunted game and fewer small animals would have been in the picture, and by then cooking was important, rendering available a vast range of roots, tubers, and seeds such as beans. 50,000 years ago, when modern *Homo sapiens* was established throughout most of the Old World, hunting was even more important. . . and carrion, coarse shoots and leaves, small seeds, and the tougher insects were falling out of the picture. (2005, 18; see also McGrew 2001, 168-71)

In fact, human survival depended on cooking. Although some groups claim that humans are made to be vegetarian and that eating raw food greatly enhances energy, boosts lymphocyte production, empowers the immune system, and contains enzymes that aid digestion (see Kenton and Kenton 1984), the Giessen study in the early 2000s that made people eat raw food for several years and clearly revealed its shortcomings. While there were some initial positive health effects, such as a sense of well-being, a reduction in pain, and more emotional stability, over time people typically lost too much weight and had no energy. Unable to sustain the high physical activity that would be needed in the Paleolithic, women also tended to stop menstruating and lacked the fat necessary to produce offspring—meaning that early man would never have survived, let alone flourished, on a purely raw diet (Wrangham 2009, 16-21).

In terms of chemistry, cooking changes the water content of the food and reduces the concentration of vitamins while leaving the density of calories unchanged (2009, 56). It also gelatinizes starch and denatures protein by weakening its internal bonds, causing the molecules to open up. As a result, the protein loses its original three-dimensional structure and therefore its natural biological function. It becomes more digestible because its open structure exposes it to the action of digestive enzymes. This holds true not only for processing through heat via cooking but also through acidity (pickling), sodium chloride (salting), and drying (smoking) (2009, 65).

Opening proteins and softening fibers, cooking substantially increases the amount of energy the organism can obtain from food (Wrangham 2009, 60; Jones 2007, 80). It enhances especially the first part of digestion via mouth, stomach, and small intestine (ileum), which alone delivers full energy to the person. The second part, fermentation by over 400 species of bacteria in the large intestine (colon), only delivers a fraction of useful energy and offers no proteins at all (2009, 58). In other words, cooking assists the bodily system, rendering mastication easy and allowing a much faster and more efficient production of internal energy (2009, 71).

After early humans began to cook their food, they developed new dimensions of taste and gradually underwent various genetic mutations (Outram 2007, 42-43). Their jaws, teeth, and lips grew smaller, they developed greater hand coordination, and their digestive tract shrank, becoming inefficient for processing raw meat (Wrangham 2009, 42-43; O'Connell et al. 2002, 50). "Cooking makes for a smaller gut, yet opens the way toward a bigger brain" (2009, 114).

The earliest form of cooking was grilling meat over an open fire, followed by the roasting of nuts by placing them on hot rocks (Fernandez-Armesto 2002, 12-13). In addition, people marinated, dried, buried, or fermented food to make it more digestible (2002, 4). Only later did cooking pits and earth ovens develop: the latter consist of two chambers, with fire in one and the food in the other (Goody 1982, 100). Boiling, stewing, and steaming depended on the use of containers, initially leaves or shells, then clay basins and pots—found first about 20,000 years ago.[4]

While cooking applied to all sorts of foods, also making numerous plants more palatable, its dominant effect was a major increase in the degree of meat consumption, still up to 90 percent of the diet of some hunter-gatherers today.[5] Meat is a better source of energy than most plant foods, consisting to a higher percentage of protein (40 vs. 10 percent), which the body uses most efficiently to promote and regulate tissue (Gedgaudas 2009, 8).

All the body's thousands of different proteins are built from twenty-two amino acids. We can synthesize twelve of these directly from food, but have to get the other ten, the so-called essential amino acids, in already integrated form by eating a plant or animal that has the ability to synthesize them or that has eaten them for us. Without these, the body uses stored materials until the acid in shortest supply is used up. Once this happens, the assembly of amino acids into proteins ceases completely, regardless of how many others may still remain. If these acids, moreover, are not used for protein assembly, they are converted into energy and either burned or deposited as fat (Harris 1985, 31-32; Perlmutter 2013, 182).

Beyond providing essential amino acids, meat, fish, fowl, and dairy products are a concentrated source of vitamins (A, B, D, E, B12, K) and contain a healthy amount of fat necessary for survival.[6] Especially the latter is often overlooked, and few people realize that persistent lack of fat results in a phenomenon called rabbit starvation. As described by the Arctic explorer Vilhjalmur Stefansson,

---

[4] Wrangham 2009, 122-23 See also Fernandez-Armesto 2002, 15-16; Jones 2007, 7.

[5] Lee 1979, 205. See also Conklin-Brittain et al. 2002, 67; McIntosh 2006, 345; O'Connell et al. 2002, 51; Ridley 1997, 89; Ungar and Teaford 2002.

[6] Harris 1985, 35, 41. See also Conklin-Brittain et al. 2002, 70; Gedgaudas 2009, 10; Hart and Sussman 2005, 228; Outram 2007, 42; Perlmutter 2013, 27; Price 1989, 230; Yudkin 1969, 548.

> If you are transferred suddenly from a diet normal in fat to one consisting wholly of rabbit (lean meat), you eat bigger and bigger meals for the first few days until, after about a week, you are eating in pounds three or four times as much as you were at the beginning. By that time, you are showing both signs of starvation and of protein poisoning. You eat numerous meals; you feel hungry at the end of each; you are in discomfort through distention of the stomach with much food and you begin to feel a vague restlessness. Diarrhea will start in from a week to ten days, and will not be relieved until you secure fat. Death will result after several weeks. (Harris 1985, 42; Wrangham 2009, 48)[7]

Cuisines

It is thus no surprise that humans prefer meat over plant food and traditionally considered fatty meat a particular delicacy.[8] How much of that they could obtain depended on the natural environment. "The most carnivorous cuisines are associated with relative low population densities and lands not needed or unsuitable for planting crops. In contrast, the most herbivorous cuisines are associated with dense populations whose habitat and food production technology cannot support the production of animals for meat without reducing the amount of proteins and calories available for humans" (Harris 1985, 16). This, in turn, has an impact on culture so that, for example, in India "the ecological impracticality of meat production so far outweighs the nutritional benefits of carnivory that meat is avoided: bad to eat and therefore bad to think" (1985, 16).

While the environment has a strong impact on the development of cuisines, defined as particular systems of producing, distributing, and consuming food that requires multiple ingredients and a large variety of recipes,[9] socially, cuisines come in high and low, elite and peasant forms, closely associated with class structures and hierarchies, i.e., post-agricultural life (Goody 1982, 191). In the early Stone Age and among hunter-gatherers, on the other hand, people still maintained an intimate, responsive relationship to nature, coexisting with multiple other predators and collecting food close to home (Jones 2007, 170, 202).

The so-called Paleo diet, increasingly fashionable these days, accordingly consists exclusively of naturally based products, whether animal or plant. Low in salt and heavy in fiber, it is particularly rich in vitamins, minerals, as well as fatty and amino acids, often to much higher levels than mainstream food.[10] Wild, lean animal products provide a high protein intake, while carbohydrates

---

[7] Similar experiences are also documented for early American explorers, such as Lewis and Clark as well as Captain Randolph. See Outram 2007, 45.

[8] Harris 1985, 26. See also Eaton et al. 2002, 9; Foley 2001, 309.

[9] Goody 1982, 98; Counihan 1999, 19; Wiessner 1996a, 6.

[10] Fernandez-Armesto 2002, 62. See also Gedgaudas 2009, 10, 18; Nelson 2013, 50; Pechenkina, Ma, and Fan 2013, 445; Price 1989, 247; Schmid 2015, 23, 65-70.

come largely from nonstarchy fruits and vegetables, Fats are healthful, monounsaturated, polyunsaturated, and omega-3. Dairy is excluded, few cereal grains and are, and sweetener would be in the form of wild honey (Gedgaugas 2009).

In contrast, civilizations ever since the Neolithic have exercised control over nature, emphasizing grains as a main staple while increasingly importing luxury items and thus widening the gap between rich and poor.[11] They would allocate specific foods to specific roles, offices, or classes, opening a wide gulf between the frugal diet of the peasantry who often suffered from malnutrition and the elaborate tables of the ruling classes who commonly indulged in excess (Goody 1982, 99). The elite, moreover, catered to "a sizable corps of adventurous eaters" and encouraged "attitudes toward food that made its consumption a pleasure beyond necessity," thus creating the typical features of local and national cuisines (1982, 98).

Cuisines divide vertically according to regions and horizontally according to social classes. Thus, Chinese cooking typically is regionally divided according to north, central, south, southeast, and Sichuan cuisines.[12] Overall, It tends to be grain-based and emphasize cooked over raw consumption. As K. C. Chang notes, "A Chinese by definition ate grain and cooked his meat" (1977, 42).[13] Generally the Chinese like to eat animal products, supplemented with a variety of vegetable dishes, with grain an afterthought among the upper classes and a main staple in the lower. They typically insist on using very fresh items, often selecting a fish or fowl while still alive, which also means they prefer local, seasonal, and whole foods. Preparation immediately precedes a meal, and pickled or preserved items make up only a minor portion. Everything is cooked, and even the fresh cucumbers common on menus today are not strictly speaking raw but heavily soaked in garlic, vinegar, and soy sauce.

Ingredients vary widely, ranging from wild animals, plants, and fungi through various domesticated species to all sorts of odd items. For example, until very recently, the Chinese consumed insects of various sorts, eating "silkworm pupae, cicadas, crickets, giant water beetles, stinkbugs, cockroaches, scorpions, grasshoppers, and fly maggots."[14] While traditionally used by the poor who had no other source of food, some are making inroads into gourmet circles today, showing up on banquet tables and at night markets. Their delicacy status is enhanced by the fact that they are highly inefficient in terms of the rate of caloric return for the time spent obtaining them, i. e., finding, gathering, and processing—which means they rank low among hunters and collectors (Harris 1985, 165; Ridley 1997, 113).

The vast variety of food stuffs goes back far into antiquity, when major vegetables included mallow, melon, gourd, turnip, leeks, lettuce, cattail, worm-

---

[11] Chang 1977, 15; Earle 1982, 66.

[12] Anderson 1977, 354; Freeman 1977, 168; Goody 1982, 106.

[13] See also Campany 2005, 98; Fernandez-Armesto 2002, 6; Huang 2000, 28.

[14] Harris 1985, 157-58; Simoons 1991, 121-26.

wood grasses, lotus root, as well as cabbage, garlic, scallions, water chestnuts, and bamboo shoots—representing many classic ingredients of Chinese dishes.[15] Meats in prehistoric China came both from domesticated and wild species, such as pigs, dogs, and cattle, as well as the common deer and rabbit and the less frequently hunted wild boar, fox, panther, and tiger. Fowls included chicken, pullet, goose, quail, partridge, pheasant, sparrow, curlew, and others; fish was mainly carp and mullet, supplemented by various kinds of shellfish (Chang 1977, 29-30; Huang 2000, 55-66). Chinese culture thus presented a rich dietetic environment that allowed the creative combination of many different kinds of food (Anderson 1988, 23).

Daoist Eating

Lay Daoists typically match the overall patterns of Chinese cuisine, but tend to be more aware of the health impact of food, like medical and longevity practitioners classifying foodstuffs according to their warming or cooling, rising or sinking, expanding or contracting, calming or stimulating effect on the *qi*-flow of the body (Kohn 2010b, 17; Engelhardt 2001). They also emphasize the balanced consumption of the five flavors: spicy, sweet, sour, bitter, and salty, matching the key inner organs of lungs, spleen, liver, heart, and kidneys, respectively.[16]

In addition, Daoists are more keenly aware of the seasonal and local dimensions of foods, like ancient hunter-gatherers connecting closely to the natural cycles. Thus, Sun Simiao dedicates an entire treatise to guidelines for monthly eating. His *Sheyang lun* 慑養論 (On Preserving and Nourishing [Life], DZ 841) presents both the overall pattern and specific dietary recommendations (Kohn 2010b, 47-49). He says categorically, "Many diseases in the body can be traced back to an excessive consumption of cold food in spring and summer. Also, many dishes containing raw meat and cold foods do harm to people in a variety of ways. Thus one should avoid them" (Engelhardt and Nögel 2009, 30).

Another avoidance many texts warn against is the consumption of stale or old food, items that have been exposed to the elements or chewed by animals (Lo 2005, 180). Unlike mainstream cookbooks yet matching the freshness common in prehistory, Daoist documents warn against things that have been preserved by drying, pickling, or fermenting and note certain signs that provide clear warnings. They include vegetables that are discolored, rabbits with their eyes shut, sheep's liver with holes, fruit or meat that has been on the ground, peaches and apricots with a double kernel, and any foodstuff shunned by animals (Despeux 2007, 25).

---

[15] Chang 1977, 28. See also Anderson 1988, 10; Sterckx 2011, 17.

[16] Kohn 2010b, 23. See also Huang 2000, 14-16; Lo 2005, 164, 167.

More specifically, the *Laozi shuo Fashi jinjie jing* 老子說法食禁戒經 (Prohibitions and Precepts on Ceremonial Food as Revealed by Laozi), a Tang-dynasty manual of Daoist food rules found among Dunhuang manuscripts (P. 2447), prohibits the consumption of any food left behind by birds, beasts, worms, or fish; left over from offerings to spirits and demons at altars, shrines, or temples; as well as any rice or wheat cakes that are unclean or rotten, have moldy or damaged spots, are broken or burnt, were returned by children, or dirtied by flying birds (Kohn 2004b, 126-27; 2010b, 75).

Unlike mainstream society, moreover, Daoists respect natural resources to a high degree, avoiding conspicuous consumption as much as food waste and insisting on pervasive moderation in all matters (Campany 2005, 109). They recommend to limit consumption of anything and particularly avoid cold, canned, frozen, and irradiated foods as well as those preserved, sprayed, or chemically treated. Matching prehistoric patterns, moreover, ever since medieval times, Daoists have eschewed materials imported from far-away places, emphasizing local and organic quality over exotic exclusivity (Kohn 2010b, 74). While there is such a thing as Daoist cuisine, therefore, it tends to be inclusive and centered on respect and sharing rather than hierarchical and demonstrative of dominance patterns.

The respect for nature further manifests in the great emphasis Daoists place on the proper treatment and careful preparation of food (Saso 1994, xvii). Kitchens should be light and airy, comfortable rooms that create a happy work environment. The design should match the rules of traditional Feng Shui and apportion light, water, and fire in the proper manner (Miles 1998, 35). All base materials and utensils, moreover, should match the requirements of naturalness and clarity, so that Daoist cooks preferably using unglazed pottery or earthenware, wooden spatulas and strainers (Kohn 2010b, 75). In addition, they stress that the mind of the cook is essential, and cultivate a calm, meditative, and cosmically aware attitude at all stages of the food process.

The Shared Meal

This process, then, has five distinct components, beginning with *procurement*, how to select and collect food stuffs. This largely depends on ecological and technological factors, but is not completely devoid of cultural modification such as taboos, i. e., prohibitions and restrictions on the use of certain foods. Second is *preparation*, beginning with the decision whether to modify the food or maintain it in its natural state, running the entire gamut from raw to cooked and including the nature of the kitchen, its set-up, utensils, and workers.

Following this is *distribution*, the way the food moves from its place of preparation to that of consumption and who exactly is involved to what degree as host, guest, server, or else. Fourth is *consumption*, including the physical setting, participants' garb, and variety of utensils as well as all the rules of etiquette, i.e., the various customs governing what, with whom, when, and where one eats. The final part of the process is *disposal*, the end of the food event related to issues of why and/or how people deal with quantities—whether all should be consumed or whether there may or even must be left-overs, and if the latter, what happens to them.[17]

All these different dimensions, moreover, are social events that center on integrated effort and focus particularly on the shared meal, a major punctuating factor in all human life (Fernandez-Armesto 2002, 5). Animals generally eat alone and rarely share food. If they do, it is commonly not on an equal basis, but as a nurturing from mother to infant (McGree 1996, 59; Ross 2001, 151) or a reluctant parceling out by a dominant male.[18] Among them "direct eye-contact is typically hostile, as is the opening of mouths and the exposure of teeth. Combine these with the placing of food, midway between a group of individuals other than parent and child, and we have clear recipe for conflict and violence. At some point our ancestors turned those danger signals around and transformed them into the very essence of conviviality that defines humanity" (Jones 2007, 1-2).

It is more than likely that this turning point had to do with the natural need to band together when hunting larger game—one man alone might be able to gather plant stuff, scavenge a carcass, or hunt small animals, but anything of significant size required cooperation. Humans share with primates the basic use of tools, a deep instinctive knowledge of nature, and various ways of food acquisition. However, they are unique in that they hunt larger beasts and cooperate as a community, also mutually taking care of babies and establishing patterns of labor distribution and cycles of eating.[19]

The earliest evidence of a shared meal is found in England at a site near Boxgrove, dated to 500,000 years ago, which contains the remains of an organized horse slaughter, including a variety of tools and weapons that indicate community action.[20] One way of describing the evolutionary process at the base of this is Steven Mithen's metaphor of the mind as a cathedral: unlike the archaic mind which is fragmented into numerous chapels, the modern mind is largely interconnected, easily matching information based on ecological, technical, and social intelligence. That is to say, while primates may know which plants to use and how to trap animals, have dexterous hands and the ability to shape inanimate materials, as well as recognition of their own species through direct interaction, they do not integrate these levels, functioning within a particular niche at any given moment. Sharing communally in the process of procuring, preparing, and consuming food, on the other hand, requires a great deal

---

[17] Powers and Powers 1984, 45-46; Fernandez-Armesto 2002, 119.
[18] Eibl-Eibesfeldt 1996, 34; Ridley 1997, 88-89; Wiessner 1996a, 7.
[19] Jones 2007, 41-42. Also Fernandez-Armesto 2002, 11; Hawkes 2001; Ridley 1997, 105-06.
[20] Jones 2007, 45. See also Gamble 2007, 237-39; Hayden 2001, 42.

of cross-referencing between the different sections of the mental cathedral, leading to increasing brain and social evolution.[21]

Food, then, is a central factor in social organization. "Eating together lies at the heart of social relations; at meals we create family and friendships by sharing food, tastes, values, and ourselves" (Counihan 1999, 6). Just as "food conveys a sense of belonging" (Douglas 1984, 31), "the shared meal is a prime way to put the world in order, reaffirm relationships, narratives, and ranks" (Jones 2007, 8). Not only do foodways influence the shaping of community, personality, and family, but food itself is a product and mirror of the organization of society on both the broadest and most intimate levels. When we come right down to it, "food was, and continues to be, power in a most basic, tangible, and inescapable form" (Arnold 1988, 3; Counihan 1999, 7).

By extension, "manners and habits of eating are crucial to the very definition of community, the relationships between people, interactions between humans and their gods, and communication between the living and the dead" (Counihan 1999, 13). Already Sigmund Freud notes that "to eat and drink with someone was at the same time a symbol and a confirmation of social community and of the assumption of mutual obligations" (1918, 174). This also means that food is the prime gift in a pervasive and increasingly complex system of exchange "that keeps individuals constantly indebted to each other and continuously engaged in positive interaction through giving and receiving."[22] As Marshal Sahlins puts it, "Food is an extremely important component of reciprocal exchanges, more so than any other object or substance, and is subject to strong prescriptions of sharing across most cultures" (1972, 215; Alvard 2001, 264).

As societies became more complex—once accumulation was possible through sedentism and storage facilities, and transportation networks allowed the import of luxury items (Meighan 1982, 91)—food became the classic and most essential good of consumption, a widely visible flag of social life alignments whose patterned flow reveals "a map of social integration" and whose consumption allows people "to say something about themselves" (Douglas and Isherwood 1979, xxii, xxiv, 45). Beyond satisfying real needs, physical and spiritual, it developed into "a marker in a temporal and spatial frame, a medium for discriminating values—and the more numerous the discriminated ranks, the more varieties of food will be needed" (1979, 44).

As a result, in post-agricultural and transegalitarian societies, "class, caste, race, and gender hierarchies are maintained, in part, through differential control over and access to food" (Counihan 1999, 8). "The hierarchy between ranks and classes takes a culinary form" (Goody 1982, 113), and one's place in the social system is revealed by what, how much, and with whom one eats. A classic recent example is sugar, which was at first only a food of the rich, but

---

[21] Jones 2007, 60. See also Chase 1989, 325-26; Gibson 2007, 69; Mithen 1996; Ridley 1997, 87, 96.

[22] Counihan 1999, 14, 95. See also Jones 2007, 139; Mauss 1967; Ridley 1997, 119.

whose consumption soon came to convey "the complex idea that one could become *different* by consuming *differently*" (Mintz 1985, 185).

Food, in other words, is at the core of human cultural self-definition. Physical, psychological, and social, its consumption always carries meaning and affects both body and mind (Douglas and Isherwood 1979, 49; Douglas 1984, 5). As a commodity, its specific forms and activations are endowed with value by the agreement of fellow consumers. It is a prime means for creating a particular world, "constructed from commodities that are chosen for their fitness to mark events in an appropriately graded scale" (1979, 51). Its consumption forms "part of an information system operating between rather than within households, where the consumer's main objective is to gain or keep control of the sources of information so that his own rational interpretations are secure" (1979, 53). More than other goods, food is both a prime necessity and a composite commodity at the root of personal, cultural, and social power, attained specifically through control over material resources and the actions of others—a facet most visible and tangible in its most organized, often conspicuous consumption, i.e., the feast.

The Feast

A feast is a ritual activity that involves the communal consumption of food and drink (Dietler 2001, 65; 1996, 89). More specifically, it consists of any sharing between two or more people of special foods that are not generally served at daily meals in a meal for a particular purpose or occasion, often involving highly ritualized components (Hayden 2001, 27; Anderson 2005, 127). It differs from the shared meal in two major respects: by the often excessive amounts consumed and by the fact that it serves a purpose beyond feeding and community cohesion (Wiessner 2001, 216). In fact, feasting forms "part of commensal politics" and is "a domain of political action," whose symbolism infuses social norms and categories with emotion (Turner 1967, 29; Outram 2007, 50). It constitutes a way of transforming "friendly nurturant acts into strategies by which nurturant dominance is achieved" (Eibl-Eibesfeldt 1996, 37).

Food and drink, being a highly perishable form of good, contain major politico-symbolic potential realized in the drama of public-consumption events. A form of gift exchange where the main object given is destroyed and also embodied, i.e., physically made one with the recipient, feasting engenders complex social debts and establishes dominance patterns. By allowing a demonstration of confidence and managerial skills, it is a way of reciprocally converting surplus food into symbolic capital, of translating material goods into political wealth (Dietler 2001, 73-74; Ridley 1997, 115).

Important worldwide, feasting can be documented in archaeology to go back to the Human Revolution in the Upper Paleolithic.[23] However, in prehistoric times as much as among hunter-gatherers today, it would depend on spontaneous rather than accumulated surpluses. "The relation between production and consumption is immediate" and foodstuffs are used within forty-eight hours of collection.[24]

Also, its main purpose is "real alliance and solidarity" (Hayden 2001, 42) rather than dominance and separation (Anderson 2005, 125), status being established more through "activities that benefit the group in some way," such as superior knowledge, expertise, abilities in planning, mediation, and the like, rather than the control of resources (Wiessner 1996b, 174). As Robert Lee notes about the !Kung San, "Food is never consumed alone by a family; it is always (actually or potentially) shared out with members of a living group or band up to thirty or more members. Every member receives an equitable share—although only few able-bodied members go out to hunt or forage. The hunting band or camp is a unit of sharing, and if sharing breaks down, it ceases to be a camp" (1979, 118).[25] Not even possessing individual utensils, all participants share by eating from the same bowl (Lee 1979, 155), documenting a sense of enlarged social and cosmic identity through relatedness to everyone (Lawlor 1991, 168, 172).

After agriculture made surpluses possible and infrastructure allowed the import of delicacies and accumulation of luxury goods, feasts became more complex and formed part of competitive giving, enhancing not only social ties but also hierarchies among the participants.[26] While "hosts may aim to enhance their prestige by displaying their ability to amass and give away large quantities of costly foods," obtained and prepared through the extensive control of human labor, they would demonstrate both their virtue by showing their blessings from Heaven (Sterckx 2011 34) and their power by signaling exclusion to uninvited guests (Underhill 2002, 11).

Beyond food, hosts would also provide vast quantities of alcohol usually in the form of ale (*jiu* 酒) and exhibit their wealth and power by presenting the food in costly dishes.[27] Thus, in Neolithic and Bronze Age China, "ceramic and bronze vessels, especially those for the consumption of food in ritualized contexts, were valued goods for displaying and negotiating power relations. The containers displayed status, wealth, and honor for individual households as well as descent groups that managed economic resources such as land" (Underhill

---

23 Dietler 2001, 66; Hayden 1996, 127, 137; 2001, 25, 47; Outram 2007, 50.

24 Lee 1979, 118; Hayden 1996, 128; Wiessner 1996b, 172; Woodburn 1982.

25 See also Lawlor 1991, 247; Ridley 1997, 101; Schmid 2015, 22-23; Winterhalder 2001, 292;

26 Dietler 1996, 92. See also Anderson 2005, 104; Fernandez-Armesto 2002, 86; Hayden 1996, 134; Underhill 2002, 3.

27 Dietler 1996, 89-90; Hayden 1996, 138; McIntosh 2006, 346; Wiessner 1996a, 12. On the nature and role of ale, see Sterckx 2011 89.

2002, 2; Fung 2000). Music and dance, as well as other forms of entertainment, might complete the banquet, as documented in relief art work as well as early writings from cities of the ancient Near East.[28]

The most widespread and fundamental form of feasting, a universal feature in agrarian societies where communities depend on the organization of large voluntary work projects, is the so-called work feast, a way to mobilize collective labor. A local leader convenes a group of people to work on a specific project and in return plies them with food and/or drink—not only getting the work done but also enhancing his power and prestige.[29] A work feast may be voluntary or obligatory. Whether a small labor exchange of fifteen or twenty people or a wide social even of well over a hundred, in all cases creates precise and explicitly defined mutual obligations (Dietler and Herbich 2001, 243-44).

Its most elaborate version is the redistribution feast, which "seeks to bond (or control) labor (people) to organizers on a more permanent basis."[30] That is to say, as societies become more stratified and segmented, status competition causes significant changes in craft specialization (Goldman 1970, 495). Elites consolidate their power by controlling the production of prestige goods, managing the procurement of raw materials, setting up workshops near palaces, households, or temples, and feasting their workers to establish a permanent sponsorship of craft specialization (Underhill 2002, 5). This, moreover, tends to be easier to achieve if the technology employed is more complicated—Chinese bronzes being a classical case in point (2002, 48; Earle 1997).

The other major form of feasting is competitive, serving an increase in the donor's status as well as three major practical purposes: "(1) direct material gains in the form of 'gifts' or return on investment; (2) indirect benefits such as increase in power or control within communities; and (3) less obvious benefits of attracting highly skilled or industrious labor" (Hayden 1996, 130; Counihan 1999, 14). A subcategory here is the "diacritical feast," designed "to create exclusive elite circles that exclude lower classes, display status and belonging of the participants, and engage in rank competition within the group" (Hauden 1996, 128; Dietler 1996, 98-99).

Feasting in China

Food is central to Chinese life, serving as a "social lubricant, stimulus, and marker" (Anderson 1988, 245; Sterckx 2011, 11). Banquets—then as now serving food in the order wine, stew, meat, fish, vegetables, and grain (Yu 1977, 69)—form a mainstay of the establishment and maintenance of social relations, both among the living and with the dead, affirming both the ritual and the po-

[28] Schmandt-Besserat 2001, 391-92; Damerow 1996, 151; Fernandez-Armesto 2002, 104.
[29] Dietler and Herbich 2001, 240-41; Dietler 1996, 93-97; 1996, 128-29; Hayden 2001, 39.
[30] Hayden 1996, 129; Counihan 1999, 14; Fernandez-Armesto 2002, 111.

litical order.[31] Just as generally "sharing food and drink enhances powerful social ties among participants," so "feasts were important components of strategies for negotiating power relations in ancient China" (Underhill 2002, 11, 12). Chinese society has been characterized by a "close link between food, containers, mortuary rituals, and the development of social stratification" (2002, 242). Clearly visible in the archaeological record, the types and designs of vessels signal changes in the nature of communal eating and feasting, indicating increase in degree of social inequality over time and even serving as "weapons of exclusion" to those who cannot afford them.[32]

Typically, low social inequality and widespread access to food surpluses as common in pre-agricultural societies manifest in small-scale feasting, geared toward sharing and community integration. On the other hand, marked competition and social mobility, characteristic of transegalitarian states, leads to fewer, larger feasts, geared toward prestige and the accumulation of power (Underhill 2002, 242). In other words, after sedentism and agriculture, just as food became a kind of wealth item, accumulated and invested in various ways to maintain or increase status, so containers, and especially labor-intensive vessels, began to mark social rank (2002, 243). In addition, the more competition there was, the less general access people had to high-level food and containers, which elites used increasingly to form and enhance ties with other elite members and their supporters.

The archaeological record clearly shows a "strong trend toward increasing nucleation of population and production of labor-intensive craft goods" in the Longshan period, beginning around 2600.[33] At this time, in the late Neolithic, there is also more emphasis on sustaining the dead in the afterlife (Anderson 1988, 245). Reflecting an increase in social inequality, many areas began to show "considerable differentiation among burials with respect to quality and quantity of craft goods" (Underhill 2002, 48). By the early Bronze Age, societies grew into states with marked social segmentation and stratification. The highly intricate and difficult-to-produce bronze vessels typical for the Xia and Shang dynasties, then, were the "prestige good of choice," used particularly in sacrifices for royal ancestors and reflecting the degree to which the acquisition, preparation, and presentation of offerings was a major concern to elites at the time (2002, 48, 82; Rawson 1996b, 248).

Not only in sacrifices, food, drink—notably alcoholic, fermented ale made from millet, some specially for ancestors[34]—and containers also became central as a means for social competition, commonly undertaken by giving food to

[31] Freeman 1977, 163. See also Campany 2005, 102; Cook 2005, 9; Mote 1977, 218; Schafer 1977a, 133; Simoons 1991, 13, 15; Sterckx 2011, 107-10; Underhill 2002, 71.

[32] Underhill 2002, 71. See also Goody 1982; Keightley 1988.

[33] Underhill 2002, 47. See also Liu 1996; Rawson 1996a, 12; 1996b, 251.

[34] Chang 1977, 30; 1983, 55; Sterckx 2005, 35; Underhill 2002, 83.

others in the form of feasts.[35] As shown in oracle bone records and from bone fragments, "the Shang already had an abundance of food sources and paid particular attention to color, gender, and type of animal in their ancestral sacrifices" (Cook 2005, 16). Over time, moreover, as documented in more complex, ornate vessels, feasting grew more intense and more competitive. There was a greater variety of prestige goods to display status, with obvious "differences in quality, labor input, foreign origins, decoration, and exotic nature" (Underhill 2002, 61). At the same time, highly valued, special foods were increasingly restricted, and the gulf between high and low cuisines widened.

An early literary documentation of a feast's richness appears in the Zhaohun" 招魂 (Summoning the Soul) section of the *Chuci* 楚辭 (Songs of Chu). The shaman entices the soul of the deceased to return home by laying out all sorts of special foods:

> Ribs of the fatted ox, tender and succulent;
> Sour and bitter blended in the soup of Wu;
> Stewed turtle and roast kid, served up with yam sauce;
> Geese cooked in sour sauce, casseroled duck, fried crane;
> Braised chicken, seethed terrapin, highly seasoned;
> Fried honey-cakes of rice flower and malt-sugar sweetmeats.
> Jade-like wine, honey flavored, fills the winged cups;
> Ice-cooled liquor, strained of impurities;
> Clear wine, cool and refreshing.[36]

A very similar array was also typical of the mortuary feast, "in which the dead and living participants shared food in ritual space" (Cook 2005, 11; Underhill 2002, 74) and in effect transformed ghosts into ancestors (Puett 2005, 93). As documented in bronze inscriptions from the Shang and Western Zhou, feasts marked both the departure of the deceased and his or her arrival in heaven as well as the ongoing relationship with the living. Often part of lineage competition, they served to reaffirm social identity and hierarchy—size and opulence reflecting directly on the prestige and power of the host (2005, 11-12; Sterckx 2005, 34).

The Mawangdui tomb of the early Han similarly contained bronze tripods for meat stews, rare lacquer dishes, and different size wine cups together with a long list of the various foods provided for the dead, which closely matches that found in the *Liji* 禮記 (Book of Rites).[37] The banquet mural at Hongmen, dated to 206, similarly shows large numbers of revelers relishing different kinds of food, including beef, dog, bear paw, panther's breast, suckling pig, deer, lamb,

---

[35] Chao 1982, 62; Underhill 2002, 82.
[36] Hawkes 1985, 227-28; see also Anderson 2014, 87; Sterckx 2005, 48.
[37] Legge 1967, 397-99. See Underhill 2002, 73.

as well as owl, duck, sparrow, goose, chicken, crane, carp, perch, and turtle (Yu 1977, 63, 67; Poo 2005, 128).

Reflecting a continuous increase in social stratification that caused greater varieties and quantities of food to become an exclusive right of the upper class (Anderson 1988, 56), the Han imperial court invested tremendous resources in feeding family members and officials. At one point, it employed a staff of 57,546 people, many of whom dealt exclusively with food.[38] Not only royalty, but elite families in general were compelled to acknowledge the support of their ancestors by making numerous food sacrifices in temples. As population increased and agriculture intensified, the strain on resources became so great that ritual responsibilities for elites had to be simplified, alleviating some of the social, economic, and environmental pressure.[39]

Daoist Communal Meals

Daoists, too, engage in feasting, however, in contrast—and probably conscious opposition—to the material excesses and social dominance patterns of mainstream society, they reverted to pre-Neolithic models and developed forms of food-sharing to build and enhance community, not only with people, living and dead, but also with nature and the gods.

Thus, the early Celestial Masters, as documented in their code of 180 precepts, the *Laojun shuo Yibai bashi jie*, in an effort to keep the group harmonious prohibits eating the five strong vegetables (*wuxin* 五辛), various kinds of onions and garlic of the genus *Allium,* believed to increase aggressive yang energy (no. 10; Kohn 2010b, 85-86). It also honors the life-giving powers of food by warning against wasting it by throwing into the fire (no. 7) and evaluating it according to good or bad (no. 90; 151). Members should show respect for their food and avoid touching it with bare hands, even if left over (no. 131).

Matching Paleo- and Mesolithic models, they should always eat fresh food of a known origin (no. 174, 175). Content with what is offered, they should abstain from selectively picking out rare items (no. 131), or "discussing the good or bad qualities of what others eat and drink" (no. 133). Along similar lines, they must not claim higher status over others by using gold and silver for eating utensils (no. 15), echoing the practice among hunter-gatherers to eat from same bowl (Lee 1979, 155). Again like early humans, they should share all food and never eat alone (no. 26), always honoring their fellow members by taking their proper turn (no. 151) and eating "sparingly like a deer" (no. 142). When visiting someone, they should not expect to be fed (no. 160), however, if food is given, they should receive it graciously, offering good wishes to the donor (no. 154).

---

[38] Anderson 1988, 53; Sterckx 2005, 37; Underhill 2002, 73.

[39] Anderson 1988, 53; Sterckx 2011, 148.

In addition, the text prohibits the raising of pigs and sheep (no. 8) and discourages the eating of the six domestic animals (no. 176), not only going back to pre-agricultural patterns but also demonstrating an opposition to mainstream civilization as it depended to a large extent on blood sacrifices.[40] Rejecting the elite tendency to drink heavily and competitively, it prohibits the consumption of alcohol (no. 24). In opposition to mainstream status seeking through the serving of meat, moreover, it also prohibits eating the flesh of wild animals specially killed for eating (no. 172, 173), while encouraging members to live largely on vegetables (no. 176). The latter, moreover, in a conscious effort to increase the connection to nature and the greater universe, should be harvested locally and at the correct time, matching the starry constellations above (no. 177).

Large quantities, and even excess, of food would only appear at special occasions (no. 155), such as the festivals of the Three Primes (*sanyuan* 三元). These were times of general assemblies and tax management: in the first month, the tax was set according to the number of people in the household; in the seventh and tenth months, it was collected as the harvest was brought in (see Kleeman 2016, 256). Daoists celebrated them by holding the so-called kitchen-feasts (*chu* 廚), described in some detail in the 4th-century *Yunzhong yinsong xinke jiejing* 雲中音誦新科戒經 (Precepts of the New Code, Recited in the Clouds, DZ 785), the main code of the Daoist theocracy under Kou Qianzhi (Mather 1979; Ware 1933, 233).

To prepare for a feast—also called "fortunate feeding" (*fushi* 福食) or "rice for the wise" (*fanxian* 飯賢; Mollier 2000, 46)—whether grand, medium, or lesser, members had to purify themselves by abstaining from meat and the five strong vegetables as well as from sexual relations and contact with impure substances (no. 11). A typical banquet, then, consisted of three courses—a vegetarian meal, wine, and rice—but those who could not afford all three could resort to having just wine, up to a maximum of five pints (no. 12). The ritual activity during feasts (no. 20) as well as during daily services and ancestral worship (no. 23) involved a series of bows and prostrations, burning of incense, and offering of a prayer or petition (no. 19; Mather 1979, 113).

The kitchen-feasts continued even after the various Daoist schools integrated into one organizational and doctrinal structure in the early Tang dynasty, as the *Yaoxiu keyi* 要修科儀 (Essential Rules and Observances, DZ 463) documents. It too recognizes three levels of feasts and distinguishes various types, such as seasonal (Three Primes), situational (birth, sickness, death), and occasional (repentance, liberation) (Kleeman 2005, 152; 2016, 251). Part of organized religion rather than performed in a closed millenarian group, the feasts would be arranged by sponsor or donor and run by professionals. They included most importantly the "kitchen supervisor" (*jianchu* 監廚) who examined the

---

[40] Campany 2005, 116; Kleeman 1994; Sterckx 2011, 125.

food, balanced raw and cooked materials, managed flavors, and decided on the order of dishes; and the "group regulator" (*jiezhong* 節眾) who checked the time, sounded the chimes for each new phase, and in general kept people in line (Kleeman 2005, 154).

The feast would be joined by local people who served as secondary participants and appreciative audience. They would receive the distribution of leftovers, particularly grain, after the event (9.11b), a practice much like the sharing of offerings after rituals of universal deliverance (*pudu* 普渡), requiem services (*gongde* 功德), and other ceremonies today (see Dean 2000). The entire emphasis of the feast was on sustaining community and creating cosmic harmony—in close similarity to prehistoric practice and sharp contrast to the competitive or power-mongering practices of post-agricultural mainstream society (Kohn 2010b, 104-08).

The same holds also true for the monastic meal held at noon and known as a "purgation" or "fast" (*zhai* 齋). As described in the Tang manual *Shishi weiyi* 十事威儀 (Ten Items of Dignified Observances, DZ 792), it typically involved four phases:

(1) preparation: donning vestments, cleaning hands and face, picking up dishes, and entering the refectory;

(2) initial formalities: rites to the Dao and dedication of the food to gods, ancestors, and all beings;

(3) the actual meal: rice plus various vegetarian dishes, announced and handed around by serving monks to the chanting of ritual verses;

(4) concluding formalities: repentance of all rule violations during the meal, obeisance to Dao, divine law, and community, stacking of bowls, and exiting the hall (9b-12a).[41]

While this represents a highly stylized and formalized affair, the items served remain simple and there is little excess—all left-overs being carefully treated and used to support local indigents. As food is shared, incantations and inner visualizations activate group cohesion, linking the taking of each item with merit for everyone who engages in its donation and connecting ritually to the celestials and all beings. Recovering early human equality and intimate connection to the cosmos, the purpose of the feast is not to establish power patterns and dominance structures. Rather, it serves to ensure the widest possible spread of merit and to reaffirm integration and harmony throughout the universe, among humans, animals, nature, and the cosmic realms.

[41] A Similar account also appears in the early Tang manual *Fengdao kejie* 奉道科戒 (Rules and Precepts for Worshiping the Dao, DZ 1125). For more detailed descriptions and discussions of medieval monastic meal practices, see Kohn 2003a, 123-32; 2004c, 157-62; 2010b, 108-12.

Immortals' Diet

In contrast to the integrative role of food among Daoist communities, among immortality seekers it becomes a means to reject mainstream values, both in time and space. In terms of time, they go back to the time before the domestication of grains and animals, consciously recovering a more primitive and more primordial state (Lévi 1983). In terms of space, they move into mountains or the fringes of society, rejecting the hallmarks of civilization and proper Chineseness as found in cooking (Campany 2005).

Food refusal is a meaningful statement in all cultures, a way to signify rupture of connection, an active denial of relationship as commonly expressed in the reciprocal circulation of gifts that involves obligation through giving, receiving, and repaying (Counihan 1999, 95; Mauss 1967). More than other material goods, "food is life-giving, urgent, ordinary symbolic of hearth and home, if not of mother. By comparison with other stuff, food is more readily, or more necessarily, shared. . . Food dealings are a delicate barometer, a ritual statement as it were, of social relations, and food is thus employed instrumentally as a starting, a sustaining, or a destroying mechanism of sociability" (Sahlins 1972, 215-16).

In Daoist immortality, as much as in Christian medieval fasting (Bynum 1987) and forms of holy anorexia (Bell 1985), food no longer serves primarily to connect adepts to others but rather "enables them to transcend their mundane and earthly selves in the quest for piety or perfection" (Counihan 1999, 99). As Mary Douglas notes, "The human body is always treated as an image of society," so that the passage of food in and out of the body can stand for social boundaries as well as their transgression (1973, 70). Adepts accordingly use fasting and ecstasy not only to escape their social roles (Bynum 1987, 221), but also to establish a deep-seated control over physical reality and their own bodies as manifest in "the life-sustaining mechanisms of appetite" (Bell 1985, 1).

It is thus not surprising that "the ultimate and most advanced level of Daoist dietetics is the complete avoidance of ordinary food while living on pure *qi*, being upheld by spirit and transforming into an immortal" (Kohn 2010b, 117). Daoists not only went back to before agriculture and civilization by recovering a diet of uncultivated plants collected from the wild, already described in the ancient philosopher Mozi 磨子 as "plain eating" (*sushi* 素食) (Campany 2005, 107). This centered on non-grain substances such as plant parts, herbs, and fungi as well as naturally found minerals and trace metals (2005, 113). Many immortals described in early Daoist literature, such as the *Liexian zhuan* 列仙傳 (Immortals' Biographies; trl. Kaltenmark 1953) and historical sources, such as the *Shiji*, focused their food intake on these substances (Campany 2005, 110-11; 2002, 25). Often they would be rare or exotic, found only far away from the agricultural heartland, either in the mountains or on the distant fringes (2005, 114), requiring a clear physical distance to the agricultural mainstream.

Going beyond this, immortals also strove to eliminate food completely and live on breath alone. They thought of breath as heavenly (round) *qi*, much superior to grains, i.e., an earthly (square) form of vital energy (Campany 2005, 106, 115; 2002, 26). Mentioned briefly in the *Zhuangzi* (Watson 1968, 33; Graham 1981, 46), the "Neiye" 內業 (Inward Training) chapter of the *Guanzi* 管子 (Roth 1999, 46; Campany 2005, 101), and the "Yuanyou" 遠遊 (Far-off Journey) of the *Chuci* (Hawkes 1985, 195), the move from grain to breath is first spelled out in the *Quegu shiqi* 卻穀食氣 (Giving Up Grain and Eating Qi), unearthed at Mawangdui. The text outlines scheduled procedures of reducing food, placing strong emphasis on replacing it first with herbs, notably *Pyrossia*, then with *qi* alone.[42] It is further supplemented by the *Shiwen* 十問 (Ten Questions), another Mawangdui manuscript that also mentions sexual control in addition to fasting and breathing practices (Harper 1998, 392-96; Campany 2005, 107).

By the middle ages, this had developed into a formal system known as *bigu* 辟穀, literally "avoiding grain," which involved a multiplicity of practices: dietary changes, herbal formulas, breath control, *qi* guiding, embryo respiration, and visualization (see Arthur 2006; 2009, 2013). Rejecting the very foundation of Chinese civilization, the practice aimed at replacing ordinary food with *qi* while maintaining the digestive system (*shiqi* 食氣) as well as transforming all nutrition toward pure *qi* and thereby reverting toward a primordial level of being (*fuqi* 服氣) (Jackowicz 2006, 89).

Grains, representing ordinary food and mainstream society and thus "good to oppose" (Campany 2005, 116), in this understanding are literally the food of the devil. Medieval Daoists saw the human body inhabited by a plethora of deities, mostly of celestial origin who gave spirit and power to the person.[43] Among them, however, were the so-called Three Worms (*sanchong* 三蟲) or Three Corpses (*sanshi* 三尸)—a term that uses the word "corpse" in a causative way and thus means agents that bring about death, i.e., Deathbringers.

Originally mere leeches gnawing on human intestines, by the 4th century CE, as described in Ge Hong's *Baopuzi* 抱朴子 (Book of the Master Who Embraces Simplicity, DZ 1185; 6.4b; Ware 1966, 115-16), they had become officials of the celestial hierarchy, placed in the body to monitor human behavior and punish sins and transgressions by afflicting it with disease, misfortune, and death.[44] More than that, their prime nourishment was grain, and fasting—or at least eating pure vegetables during worm-related vigils—served as a prime way of elimination. Vice versa, as Sun Simiao notes in his *Qianjin fang* 千金方 (Reci-

---

[42] On the text, its translation and discussion, see Harper 1998, 305-09; Arthur 2006, 94; Campany 2005, 106; Engelhardt 2000, 86; Jackowicz 2006, 69.

[43] See Andersen 1980; Huang 2010; Kohn 1991; 2006; Kroll 1996; Schipper 1978.

[44] Arthur 2006, 102; 2009, 142; 2013, 115, 125; Campany 2005, 113; Kohn 2010b, 123-27; 2015c.

pes Worth a Thousand Pieces of Gold), the very first step toward dietary refinement was the removal of the Three Worms using various medicinal recipes (Kohn 2010b, 125).

To do so, practitioners had to separate from ordinary society, give up on family and lineage, and leave civilization and its trappings behind (Campany 2005, 117)—in a very practical way moving back to more primitive and primordial settings. "A Daoist adept distances and cuts himself off from human traces and lives quietly in the mountains. He practices a perpetual retreat and lives along in a desolate valley. He no longer selects a master of the teaching [as his preceptor] but simply makes his mind converse with his mouth" (Eskildsen 1998, 115; Kohn 2010b, 128). Rather than seeking human guidance, again echoing Paleolithic patterns, adepts would closely communicate with nature and the stars, matching cosmic phases, observing calendar rules, following daily prohibitions, and controlling spirits and lesser gods (Campany 2005, 116).

The literature outlines various regimens to follow, but typically adepts would begin by taking simple, grain-based food to harmonize spleen-*qi* and activate the saliva, such as rice porridge, boiled wheat dumplings, or cooked barley, often supplemented with dried meat and peppercorns. After a few weeks of breathing practice and this simple diet, they would skip one or two meals, then increasingly replace grains with steamed, lightly seasoned vegetables, enhanced with medicinal formulas (Poo 2005, 135). This cleansed the colon and weaned the body from its need for grains. After another week, adepts could do away with the vegetables and only take their juice. Three days later, food intake is given up completely, but liquids—such as boiled water, wine, ginger soup, or vegetable juice—are taken until such time when reliance on primordial *qi* is complete.[45]

While the initial response of the body to this change in diet is weakening and detoxification, over a period of several months—as also documented in recent experiments—adepts not only can cease eating altogether, but will actually start to become stronger.[46] They may maintain this state and live vigorously without food for however long they desire, but they can also return to ordinary food, gradually reintroducing cooked items and grains. Overall, they become healthy and vigorous, look youthful and radiant, enjoy good hearing and eyesight, and live for an extended period (Poo 2005, 134). In their very bodies returning to Palaeolithic wholeness, free from food and all the trappings of civilization, they have become beings of spirit, deeply at home in nature and in close communication with the heavens (Campany 2005, 108).

---

[45] Huang and Wurmbrand 1987, 60; Kohn 2010b, 129-30.
[46] Arthur 2006, 113-14; Eskildsen 1998, 52; Kohn 2010b, 131.

Chapter Ten

Ritual and Self-Cultivation

> For him who understands heavenly joy, life is the working of Heaven; death is the transformation of things. In stillness, he and the yin share a single power; in motion, he and the yang share a single flow. Thus he who understands heavenly joy incurs no wrath from Heaven, no opposition from man, no entanglement from things, no blame from the spirits. So it is said, his movement is of Heaven, his stillness of earth. With his single mind in repose, he is king of the world: the spirits do not afflict him, his soul knows no weariness. (*Zhuangzi* 13)

Close communication with the heavens is also at the center of much of Daoist ritual and self-cultivation practices. While many specific techniques developed in the middle ages under the influence of imperial rites, popular religion, Chinese medicine, and Buddhism, certain key features again take recourse to Stone Age patterns and stand in contrast to post-agricultural, mainstream structures.

The Daoist connection to the stars, unlike imperial and popular culture, is direct and free from mediation, activating the heavenly bodies as protectors and guides in meditation and ritual. While the mainstream, post-egalitarian management of space imposes human artifice and favors rectangular structures and straight lines, Daoists generally—with the notable exception of temple buildings that follow dominant architectural models—prefer spatial fluidity as manifest in curved shapes, circles, and roundness. Several ritual and self-cultivation patterns, moreover, can be linked with prehistoric patterns of shamanism, the immediate connection to the otherworld that includes both ecstatic soul journeys as well as the activation of celestial powers on earth.

The intimate link with the supernatural is further borne out in the Daoist relationship to death, seen as a transformation and journey to a different but not separate dimension. Echoing Paleolithic and hunter-gatherer models, and in stark contrast to the elaborate burial practices and mourning prescriptions of mainstream Chinese culture, Daoist thinkers see death as an entirely natural phenomenon, while priests opt for simplicity and emphasize the positive encouragement of the departing soul over and above vivid expressions of grief. Last but not least, Daoists continue prehistoric patterns in their strong emphasis on, and application of, the reddish mineral cinnabar, whose use as pigment and life-enhancing substance goes back to the Neolithic, inheriting the widespread Paleolithic application of red ochre.

Activating the Stars

The stars loomed large over early humanity. Unlike today, where the night sky is shrouded by reflected artificial light, in the Stone Age it was a tapestry of starry radiance, creating intricate ever-shifting patterns (Belmonte 2010, 2052; Marshack 1991, 126). It is not clear how people in prehistory understood the celestial spheres, but the fact that they had some significance is evident from reproductions of starry constellations in paintings and drawings, probably serving purposes of time keeping, as mnemonic devices, or maps.[1]

Thus, for example, a carved baboon fibula from the Kwazulu Border Cave in South Africa, dated to 35,000, shows twenty-nine notches, interpreted to signify the phases of moon in the course of a month (Bahn and Vertut 1997, 31). An ivory tablet, found in Weiler, Germany, and dated to 32,500, presents a pattern very close to the constellation Orion. Its 88 notches match the number of days in three lunar cycles and those of the visible appearance of Betelgeuse, the brightest star in Orion (Gamble 2007).

A red ochre cross, moreover, painted over the entry to the Chauvet Cave in southern France, dated to about 30,000, might signify the solstices and equinoxes. More obviously, the Venus of Laussel, from the same period and also painted in red ochre, holds a horn in her right hand, whose shape and thirteen vertical lines have been interpreted to signify the crescent moon and number of annual lunar cycles.[2] An engraved bone plate from Abri Blanchard in the Dordogne as well as a number of marked antlers, batons, bones, ribs, ivory pieces, and stones, dating to 35-10,000, similarly contain series of dots and lines that may well connect to the positions of the moon and serve as time-keeping devices (Marshack 1991, 28). Similar objects among Australian aborigines, moreover, function as message sticks, detailing the length and distance of a journey (1991, 136-37).

One of the richest Paleolithic star documentations appears at Lascaux, [3] a complex of caves near the village of Montignac, also in the Dordogne. Dated to 15,000, the caves are covered in wall paintings of large animals such as horses, bulls, bison, and deer, some of which may be symbolic representations of lunar phases. In addition, in several places the caves show sets of painted dots, interpreted to depict starry constellations, such as the Pleiades, Hyades, and Taurus, as well as the so-called "Summer Triangle," made up of Vega, Deneb and Altair.

---

[1] Petzinger 2016, 237; Pfeiffer 1982, 124, 161.

[2] Bahn 1998, 74-75; Belmonte 2010, 2052; Joseph 2003; Marshack 1991, 334-35.

[3] Taylor 2012, 200-03. For more on Lascaux, see Bataille 1955; Belmonte 2010, 2053; Brown 1976; Davenport and Jochim 1988; Jarzombek 2013, 68; Jèguez-Wolkiewiez 2011; 2015; Joseph 2003; Marshack 1991, 219-31; Petzinger 2016, 230; Pfeiffer 1982, 29-30.

Sets of painted dots among animal images in Lascaux

Functioning as an observatory, moreover, the main cave was oriented toward the solar cycle, allowing the setting sun on the summer solstice to illuminate the entire rotunda. A similar phenomenon holds also true for well over a hundred other Paleolithic cave sites in southern France, all connecting to sunrise or sunset on the solstices or equinoxes (see Jègues-Wolkiewiez 2015). Such observatories not only allowed prehistoric people to keep track of the changing seasons, but also to predict migratory patterns of large mammals.

The archaeological record changed after the transition to agriculture and post-egalitarian societies. Observatories then appeared as large, megalithic structures, with complex orientations and multiple functions—calendrical, administrative, and ritual. Examples include the famous stone rings at Stonehenge, Newgrange, Carnac, and more, as well as the megalithic temples of Malta, the ziggurats of Sumer and Babylon, and the extensive temple complex at Karnak in Egypt (Taylor 2012). They all have in common that they date to around 3000 and represent artifacts that could only be constructed by large numbers of people working in close cooperation, i. e., under the supervision of an organized leadership.

They also indicate the increased importance of calendar determination, since the success or failure of agriculture depends closely on the correct time of sowing and harvesting. Unlike among Paleolithic hunter-gatherers, the stars in the Neolithic had become a political factor, their knowledge controlled by the ruling class. It is no accident, furthermore, that months were divided into clearly structured weeks of a set number of days around 2500: seven in Mesopotamia, begun under the Gutian dynasty of Sumer, and ten in Egypt and China, under the First and Shang dynasties, respectively.[4]

[4] Belmonte 2010, 2054, 2058; See also Parker 1950; Needham 1958.

Neolithic monuments, moreover, echoing Paleolithic caves, were not easily accessed. While their layout is diverse, they all "possess a narrow and restricted passage that leads from the outside world to a rather more spacious internal chamber."[5] Not only controlling and intimidating in nature, the inner chamber was set up in such a way as to filter, distort, and intensify any sounds—creating a powerful and awe-inspiring setting. Hearing being the more dominant sense in the ancient world, the monuments were "places within which the propagation of sound was artificially bounded and controlled to a greater extent than had ever been possible before" (Watson 2001, 181). Voices and musical instruments would generate a level of sound unlike anything in the natural world, while senses were heightened by the surrounding darkness, imposing megaliths, and texture of stone (2001, 188). All this again enhanced the control of leaders, who alone had the power to activate the stars.

The Chinese Take

In China, too, with the inception of early state formation, astronomy began to play an important social role, soon reaching "a point where ritually and politically important structures were uniformly quadrilateral in shape and cardinally oriented, with the longitudinal axis aligned with varying precision in a north-south direction" (Pankenier 2004, 211; Wheatley 1971, 423).

The earliest Chinese equivalent to the megaliths of Europe and temples of the Near East are altar structures discovered as part of the Liangzhu culture in Zhejiang, at several sites near Yaoshan 瑤山. Dated to the early third millennium and located a few kilometers apart, they consisted of three terraces reaching over 60 feet in height and constructed of contrasting layers of differently colored soils. Sharing the same concentric configuration as the Chinese character *hui* 回 and oriented toward the solstices, they were positioned to afford a clear view of the horizon, probably functioning as horizon calendars using solar observations (Pankenier 2013, 29-31).

The first extensive astronomical and ritual center in China was found at Taosi, an important economic, political, and religious walled city, covering 750 acres in the Linfen basin of the Yellow River that flourished in the Chalcolithic, 2600-2000 (Liu and Chen 2012, 222). The complex covered an area of about 2.5 acres and similarly consisted of a three-level altar, made of stacked rammed earth terraces. The top level was a semicircular platform with a curved pounded-earth wall facing south-southeast. Surviving traces of its base are still perforated by twelve regularly spaced grooves, about five feet apart and ten inches wide. The apertures match the arc traced by the sun between the solstices, allowing solar observations as well as other astronomical functions (Pankenier 2013, 20-21).

---

[5] Watson 2001, 180; Pfeiffer 1982, 127, 143.

In its midst, moreover, was a lacquer pole about 6 feet (180 cm) high, serving as a gnomon, i. e., a shadow-casting device used to measure the solar range and thereby determine the exact date of the equinoxes and solstices, an essential feature to set the parameters for the agricultural year (Liu and Chen 2012, 223). The site has yielded hundreds of objects, including the earliest metal artifacts, such as a copper bell, an arsenic bronze object attached to a jade, as well as fragments of a rim of a basin. Two glyphs in red on a pottery vessel may indicate the name of Yao, placing the observatory into the golden age of Confucianism.[6] In addition, the cemeteries at Taosi, located close to the complex, provide clear evidence of social stratification and strong leadership, a society run under the "central authority of a king."[7]

The most prominent later development of the astronomical-ritual complex is the Hall of Light (*mingtang* 明堂), best known from both textual and archaeological sources of the Han dynasty. It appeared first under this name after the Zhou conquest, continuing a Shang institution known as the Multistoried Chamber (*chongwu* 重屋). A central ritual structure, oriented on a north-south axis in alignment with the sun—as were the key palaces ever since the Xia dynasty (Pankenier 2004, 216)—it imitated the Great Square of Pegasus in the sky and consisted of twelve palaces, representing the twelve months of the year as well as the central time-keeping constellations (chronograms, *chen* 辰) in the sky. Surrounded by water on four sides, showing the Four Seas, it was the central point in a world consisting of concentric squares, a microcosm of the greater universe, and served as a key site for the assembly of all vassals, imperial ancestral sacrifice, and many other ceremonial events.[8]

The tendency to establish political power in the universal center and create a replica of the cosmos, complete with ritual enactments, is common among early states worldwide. As Mircea Eliade points out, it expresses the key notion that reality is a function of the imitation of a celestial archetype, achieved solely through participation in the symbolism of the center. This center, properly marked as sacred space and aligned exactly with the cardinal directions, links the fundamentally parallel worlds of the macrocosm and the microcosm and is activated through specific ritual ceremonies, undertaken in exactly the right manner at the right time and in the right space.[9]

Not only would the Chinese ruler, as mediator between Heaven and Earth, enact the proper rituals in the proper space to activate the Monthly Commandments (*yueling* 月令) (Lewis 2006, 264),[10] thereby keeping the world in order, but he also represented the most potent divine power of the center,

[6] Liu and Chen 2012, 225-26. Also Keightley 1999, 27; Liu 2004, 172; Maisels 1999, 291-94.
[7] Shao 2005, 121; Shelach-Levy 2015, 155.
[8] Pankenier 2010, 2030-31. See also Lewis 2006, 261-69; Soothill 1952.
[9] Eliade 1981, 6. See also Pankenier 2004, 224; Wheatley 1981, 418.
[10] The Monthly Commandments are spelled out in *Liji* 6 (trl. Legge 1967), *Lüshi chunqiu* 1-12 (trl. Knoblock and Riegel 2000), and *Huainanzi* 5 (trl. Major 1993).

matching the central star or constellation in the heavens. The heavenly pivot or celestial pole, the true north and ultimate geographical center of the universe, this is known as North Culmen (Beiji 北極) or Palace of Purple Tenuity (Ziwei gong 紫薇宮), the residence of the Great One (Taiyi 太一) (Pankenier 2004, 213). The power that controls everything, this central location, however, is not stable but migrates over the millennia and is thus not represented by any particular star or constellation, although certain stars such as Thuban and Kochab came close in the late Neolithic (2004, 226; Needham 1958, 261).

Having no "obvious physical presence," the starry residence of the Great One represents "the marvel of an efficacious 'nothing' at the center of the rotating dome of the sky" (Pankenier 2013, 92; 2004, 218). A giant hole at the galactic center, it is the core of cosmic emptiness, the symbol of the spontaneous power of non-doing in the center of all.[11] As such its deity has enormous powers, including control of the Northern Dipper (Beidou 北斗), ruler of fates and central ordering power of the universe. As the *Shiji* notes,

> The Dipper is the carriage of the emperor; it is placed in the center, . . . governs the four cardinal points, separates yin and yang, and determines the four seasons. It balances the five phases, arranges the divisions [of time] and the levels [of space], and sets the various measures. (Robinet 1989, 178; 1993, 212)

Under the Shang, moreover, the celestial pivot was identified with the High God, Shangdi—the very word for *di* possibly representing an astronomical measuring device to locate true north (Pankenier 2004, 233; 2013, 105-07). Pole Star, Lord of the Sky, and First Ancestor, he was the "symbolic center, from which royal charisma radiated," in control of wind, rain, sun, and moon, the guarantor of good harvests and protector against calamities.[12] Not part of regular ancestral worship, he was beyond direct approach, far from humanity and its efforts (Allan 2007, 14; Li 2013, 99)—as much as all astronomical calculations and calendar determinations were managed by a growing hierarchy of aristocratic and appointed officials and the original calendar was increasing overlaid by numerology, cosmology, and philosophy (Lewis 2006, 267).

Daoist Practice

In contrast to this bureaucratic separation from the stars and their essential power in mainstream Chinese culture, medieval Daoists recovered prehistoric patterns by aligning themselves closely with them. Not only believing that each human being receives a personal star at birth, which shines or dims in accord-

---

[11] Li 1995, 32; Pankenier 2004, 219; Rees 2000, 36.

[12] Allan 2007, 2, 7. See also Keightley 2000, 21; Li 2013, 99; Pankenier 2004, 225; Puett 2002, 40; Wang 2000, 30.

ance with his or her moral stature, earthly actions, and celestial standing (Kohn 2004a, 17), they would visualize starry constellation and divine palaces in their very bodies, seeing themselves as a microcosmic replica of the universe.

Thus, the celestial headquarters within are located in the head and match the immortals' paradise of Mount Kunlun, often depicted as a large, luscious mountain surrounded by a wide lake. Between the eyes, which are the sun and the moon, there is the Hall of Light, one of nine palaces in the head. Best reached by passing through the deep, dark valley of the nose, it is guarded by the two high towers of the ears. Underneath the valley of the nose is a small lake, i. e., the mouth, which regulates the water level of the upper lake in the head (Kohn 2006, 9).

Crossing the mouth-lake over its bridge (tongue) and moving further down, one reaches the twelve-storied tower of the throat, then comes to the Scarlet Palace (heart), the Yellow Court (spleen), the Imperial Granary (stomach), the Purple Chamber (gall), and various other starry palaces transposed into the body's depth. Going ever deeper, another cosmic region is reached, with another sun and moon located in the kidneys, the center of human vitality. Beneath them, the Ocean of *Qi*, the cosmic vastness, extends with another Mount Kunlun in its midst. All sorts of starry deities, moreover, reside in the body, creating vitality and providing spiritual resources (Kohn 2006, 10).

To begin the activation of this celestial landscape, medieval Daoists would center themselves in the comically aligned oratory, then invoke the deities of the Dipper to hover over them for protection (Robinet 1989, 180). Next, they would place themselves in the very center of the cosmos and surround themselves with the most potent guardians of the universe: the four heraldic animals (*siling* 四靈), massive constellations in the four cardinal directions of the night sky that comprise a number of stars not unlike Western zodiac images.[13]

Consisting of vermilion red bird and the snake-and-turtle (dark warrior) in the south and north as well as of the green dragon and white tiger in the east and west, they appear first as mussel shell mosaics in a Yangshao tomb of the late fourth millennium, then feature in a Shang oracle-bone inscription (Pankenier 2013, 212, 337). Later, essential to Han cosmology and calendrics, the four heraldic animals with their changing positions in the course of the year provided celestial guidance of when to sow and plant in agriculture and when to advance and retreat in warfare. Literally guiding the ancients in their most essential undertakings, they were responsible for the survival and prosperity of nations (Pankenier 2013, 294-95). Daoists, unfazed by this might, used them as personal guardians, not only obtaining a unique celestial level of protection and establishing themselves in the center of the cosmos, but also exchanging vital energy with the stars and commandeering an extensive retinue of protective forces.

---

[13] Pankenier 2013, 4. For more on these four, see also Chao 2011, 15-20; Csikszentmihalyi in Pregadio 2008, 908-111; Karetzky 2015, 72-73; Major 1986; Staal 1984.

As the *Daode zhenjing xujue* 道德真經序訣 (Introductory Explanation to the Perfect Scripture of the Dao and Its Virtue), an instruction manual for the ritual application of the *Daode jing* discovered at Dunhuang and dated to the a 5th-century CE, says,

> Visualize the green dragon to your left, the white tiger to your right, the vermilion bird in front of you, and the dark warrior at your back.
>
> Your feet stand between the eight trigrams, the divine turtle and the thirty-six masters bow to you. In front of you, you see the seventeen stars of the central universe, your five inner organs give forth vibrant *qi* in five colors, and a network pattern streams across your body.
>
> On three sides you are joined by an attendant, each having a retinue of a thousand carriages and ten thousand horsemen. Eight thousand jade maidens and jade lads of Heaven and Earth stand guard for you. (Part 4; Kohn 1998a, 72)

Thus equipped, Daoist practitioners would go on extensive ecstatic excursions, following the routes of the sun and the moon, and traveling to the stars. They reached out to visit the higher spheres of the planets and superior heavens, eventually approaching the ruling power of the Dipper in a practice known as "pacing the void" (*buxu* 步虛).[14] From here, they transcended to the empty pivot, the Palace of Purple Tenuity, the home of the Great One and the quiet center of Dao, thus becoming one with the root of creation. On their way, moreover, they typically encountered numerous gods and immortals, from whom they learned cosmic secrets and received instructions for further attainment. By ecstatically traveling through far-off reaches, Daoists increasingly became denizens of the otherworld, completely at home in expansive nature and at one with the stars, light and airy, radiant and bright, fluid and flowing.

Geometric Patterns

This fluidity, moreover, is expressed variously in Daoism in geometrical forms that favor circles, waves, curves, twists, turns, and figures of eight. Their temples sport round shapes in canopies, prayer cushions, thrones, calligraphy, talismans, and Taiji symbols; their art work is full of cloudy swirls, billowing robes, and winding dragons; their ritual movements proceed in undulating, circular, winding patterns; and their compounds are pervaded by meandering paths and planted richly with trees and shrubberies.[15]

---

14 See Andersen 1990; Robinet 1998; Schafer 1977c.

15 On symbols and calligraphy, see Legeza 1975. For studies of art, see Huang 2012 135; Wallace 2012, 82. On ritual movements, such as the Pace of Yu, see Dean 200. On monastic compounds, see Kohn 2003a, 91.

Activating the curving fluidity of *qi* as it flows through nature and the human body—often understood as a complex system of waterways (Kohn 2005, 11)—Daoists create spaces filled with "curlicue patterns of waves" that undulate in and out of each other, reflecting fractals, "branching, self-similar patterns that occur repeatedly at increasingly smaller scales, found throughout nature, not only in trees but also in waves, snowflakes, seashells, and flowers . . . as well as in mountain ranges, coastlines, the veins of leaves, and the cells of the human body" (Sternberg 2004, 34).

Best known from Japanese woodblock prints and Zen gardens, these fractals "are intrinsically satisfying to the human mind," allowing it to "move inward and outward, up or down at will, freed from rigid boundaries of scale" (2004, 35). Flowing, wavelike designs and round shapes, "squiggly lines oscillating around the horizontal, in what appears to be a chaotic pattern," moreover, reflect the complexity of human heart-rate variability and are an indicator of health. "The more complex and variable a system, the healthier it is." In contrast, "the condition, in which there is the least variability in heart rate is death. In death, there are no rhythms at all—the body generates only straight lines" (Sternberg 2004, 71-72).

Straight lines generally are not part of living nature in any of its vibrant, growing, energy-infused structures, as vividly pointed out by Buckminster Fuller, the father of the geodesic dome and proponent of the "energy event,"[16] nor do they form part of human architecture in the Paleolithic or among hunter-gatherers today. After living in trees and converging in caves, when early humans began to construct living spaces, they worked in close alignment with nature, so that the original house was round or oval, typically partly subterranean, a pit dug into the soil and covered with straw or shrubbery.[17]

The earliest remnants of such houses go back to 36,000, located at Kostenki, Russia, on the northern shores of the Black Sea. They were longish, oval domes over a series of fire places, housing several families in "separate living zones, separated by means of hide partitions" (Jarzombek 2013, 22). Known in modern times from Native American tribes and today still used among the Dayak in Borneo, such "longhouses produced strong social bonds" (2013, 24). Another early communal structure is the ritual center or "dance house," typically consisting of a round dome supported by a set of pillars and a smoke hole over a fire pit in the center (2013, 42-43). Both the hunters at Dolní Věstonice (Pfeiffer 1982, 58), and the sedentary Natufians in the Levant produced round living structures, building sets of smaller huts for individual families, often set in a circular pattern around a central common space (Cauvin 2000, 128-29; Jarzombek 2013, 94). The same pattern still holds true among aborigines and hunter-gathers today, from the !Kung in Botswana to the aborigines of Australia (2013, 92-101).

---

[16] Aasang 1986, 44; Edmonson 1987, 8. See also Fuller 1992.

[17] Aurenche 1981, 185; Cauvin 2000, 128; Pfeiffer 1982, 57.

In other cultures, however, this changed after the development of agriculture and stratified societies. The transition away from small, limited domes is first obvious in the construction of megalithic tombs and ritual complexes in the mid-Neolithic. "Fitting together disparate elements selected from the natural world," their construction required active planning and careful measurements, "restructuring building materials to conform to preordained designs" (Bradley 1998, 229). Involving "a considerable amount of carefully coordinate labor" (1998, 239), they show social stratification and beginning patterns of land-ownership. Highly visible, the megalithic tombs were "defining features of the surrounding space," monuments of the dead expressing a particular social action that "marked the territory of the living" (Wright 2013, 407, 414).

Around the same time, houses came to be built increasingly above ground. They were more rectangular, gradually replacing the round patterns and curved walls of earlier settlements.[18] Thus, in China, by the fifth millennium, tombs and dwellings were mostly square or rectangular, "already oriented with particular attention to the cardinal directions and the seasonal variations of the sun's location" (Pankenier 2013, 83). For example, the entrances to the early Yangshao dwellings at Banpo were oriented toward the location of the mid-afternoon sun, "when at its warmest a month or so after the solstice."[19]

The construction of such buildings "supposes that people knew how to make a free-standing rectangular wall and how to fit walls together at right angles," technology that possibly developed from the construction of vertical walls dividing round houses with wooden frameworks (Cauvin 2000, 129). While it is obvious that angular houses made expansion of space easier and allowed clearer division into various chambers, corners, and niches, signifying differentiation, segmentation, and specialization (Jones 2007, 140), round cells could just as easily be juxtaposed with some shared walls. In addition, to the present day there are numerous rectangular houses consisting only of one room (Auvenche 1981, 192; Cauvin 2000, 129).

The transition, moreover, is not ubiquitous. Beyond hunter-gatherers who still use dominantly circular structures, quite a few cultures in the eastern Mediterranean during the 7th and 6th millennia "deliberately retained round plans"—although the technology was available and "their builders were fully competent" (Cauvin 2000, 130). This means that the move toward straight lines and rectangular patterns, like the adoption of agriculture, is more than mere technological advancement. It is an expression of an organizational and cultural choice, a momentous change in cosmology and dominant thinking, an orientation toward a different way of living. As Mircea Eliade notes, "The cosmic symbolism of the house is attested in numerous primitive societies. In a more or less clear manner, the home is considered as an *imago mundi*" (1978, 55).

---

[18] McIntosh 2006, 337; Wang 2000, 50; Yan 2005, 31.

[19] Pankenier 2013, 84. See also Barnes 1993, 104-05; Keightley 1998, 794; Liu 2007, 129, 37; Wheatley 1971, ch. 5.

That is to say, the circle, dome, or sphere represents "cosmic totality." It "signifies that which transcends man and remains beyond his reach, but also covers and includes him." In contrast, the rectangular requires human initiative: "Stone is not cubic or rectangular unless it is so fashioned" (Cauvin 2000, 152). The straight line, the right angle, the square structure—including the "four quarters" (*sifang* 四方) of the Shang cosmos (Wang 2000, 26)—are visible expressions of control over nature, of the manifest over the unseen. They represent the human power to impose new, artificial, and preconceived forms on natural patterns, "an affirmation of a culturally expressed separate self" (Cauvin 2000, 152). While humanity after agriculture went full-speed ahead in developing ever stronger expressions of this separation, extending its control over nature, Daoists, although housed in rectangular structures, in their expressions, ornamentations, designs, and ritual movements chose to remain true to an older, saner, more integrated cosmology with circular and swirling forms.

Shamanism

A similar pattern also applies to ritual and spiritual access to the universe and the otherworld, characterized by shamanism, "archaic techniques of ecstasy" (Eliade 1964). Commonly pervaded by animistic, polytheistic, and religiously pluralistic worldviews, shamanic cultures generally assert that nature is a living force, where all entities are imbued with life energy and jointly participate in the greater cosmos.[20] Reality is fluid, manifest in constant change, consisting of a complex set of multiple layers that are interdependent and permeable and allow open-ended yet always mysterious transformations, so that "whatever happens in our world is caused or influenced by supernatural powers" (Cottes 2013, 9). All life being a closely interconnected web, moreover, human beings have the ability to interact with all other levels to enhance the common good as well as the duty to maintain cosmic functioning by performing appropriate rituals.[21]

Shamans as mediators to the divine go into trance with the help of psychedelic drugs, music, chanting, drumming, dancing, fasting, austerities, and more—techniques possibly arising from mimetic performances imitating and magically transforming the power of predators (Trout 2011, 108)—then travel in their souls to the otherworld to connect to spirit beings and collect information.[22] They guide the dead to their proper level and ensure that all agents are in harmony and at peace. In some traditions, they also open themselves to the presence of divine entities, housing the spirits in states of possession

---

[20] Jarzombek 2013, 31, 33; Dowson and Porr 2001, 172; Winkelman 2002, 75. They are also often associated with totemism, the identification of clans through animals. See Dowson and Porr 2001, 172; Sauvet et al. 2009, 320, 333; Winkelman 2002, 75.

[21] Clottes 2013, 10; Price 2001, 6; Ryan 2011, 182; Whitley and Keyser 2003, 387.

[22] Winkelman 2002, 72-73. See also Pfeiffer 1982, 163; Price 2001, 3; Sauvet et al. 2009, 320. For more on shamanism, see further Ryan 1999; Smith 1992; Walsh 2007.

(Walsh 2007). In addition, they typically gain assistance from natural forces, mountains, trees, and in particular from strong, powerful animals (Chang 2005, 129). "Shamanic processes construct social and personal consciousness through conceptualizations of 'others' as embodied in the spirit world (animism), the socialization of self through internalizing 'sacred others,' and the construction and diversification of self as exemplified by the guardian-spirit complex" (Winkelman 2002, 74).

Neurologically, moreover, shamanic states reflect an integrative mode of consciousness, a balanced organic functioning and fundamental homeostatic dynamic of the nervous system. This involves "production of interhemispheric synchronization in the prefrontal cortex by high-voltage slow-wave EEG activity, which in turn originates in the circuits linking the brain stem and the hippocampal-septal area of the limbic system. These high-voltage slow-wave limbic discharges intensify connections between the limbic brain and brain stem and impose synchronous slow-wave patterns on the frontal lobes, leading to integration across the neuraxis and thus the synthesis of emotion, thought, and behavior (Winkelman 2002, 73).

Present among hunter-gatherer populations today [23] and documented widely in historical records in cultures all over the world, shamanism is generally assumed to represent the fundamental religious system of prehistoric humanity, going back at least as far as the Human Revolution. "Invocation, dancing, singing, music, masked mime, and sorcerers' tricks—the paraphernalia of modern shamanism—all existed in ice-age magic" (Maringer 1960, 142-43).

Some archaeological evidence for this appears in art, both portable and parietal—"objects that negotiated the individual's intimate and powerful relationships to the otherworld" (Dowson and Porr 2001, 174). Among portable objects are musical instruments, such as bone flutes, stone drums, turtle rattles, as well as statuettes, ivory carvings, thaumatropes, and personal ornaments or charms.[24] Parietal art includes all works *in situ*, such as depictions of masked or half-human "sorcerers" in caves[25] as well as a variety of geometric designs—

---

[23] Dowson and Porr 2001, 172; Whitley and Keyser 2003, 388; Winkelman 2002, 78. Commonly cited examples include the Hazda (Jarzombek 2013, 38), the San (Lewis-Williams and Pearce 2004), Australian aborigines (Sauvet et al. 2009, 322), as well as fnative Americans and indigenous Indo-Chinese (Marshack 1991, 136-47)

[24] Abadia and Morales 2013, 272. On flutes in European caves, see Maringer 1960, 143; Pfeiffer 1982, 181-82; Winkelman 2002, 76. For drums and rattles, see Jarzombek 2013, 35. On statuettes, see Dowson and Porr 2001, 165, 173. A thaumatrope is a disk made from bone, ivory, stone, or wood, with a hole in the center and drawings on both sides. As the disk spins, the image seems to move—as much as many cave paintings see to illustrate movement (Azéma and Rivère 2012, 320-21; see also Marshack 1991, 182; Pfeiffer 1982, 133; Welker 2016, 40).

[25] For such sorcerers, see Azéma and Rivère 2012, 318; Cottes and Coutin 1996, 153; Marshack 1991, 272, 279; Palacio-Pérez and Redondo 2014, 261; Pfeiffer 1982, 177; Price 2001, 171; Winkelman 2002, 77. In contrast to primitive rock art world wide, where human figures

triangles, circles, squares, pentagons, arrows, crosses and more (Clottes and Courvin 1996, 63, 143). It also includes paintings of various types of animals of land, sea, and air (1996, 127). Typically depicted in motion or in threatening postures (Dowson and Porr 2001, 168-69), they divide in various categories—"impossible to identify, spirited, docile, horned, jumpers, felines, and robust bison" (Bahn 2001, 344).

Discovered in the late 19th century, the cave paintings of southern Europe were first understood to reflect primitive hunting magic—painting the beast providing power over it—then seen in a structuralist manner as symbolic representations of myths (Clottes 2013, 7). Other interpretations include purely artistic ornamentation, signs of good luck, or entertainment during the long cold winters (Sauvet et al. 2009, 320). More recently, as more paintings have come to light from other parts of the world—including one of a pig in Pettakere Cave in Sulawesi, Indonesia, dating to 33,000—scholars have adduced neurophysiology and linked the paintings to a state of "enhanced creativity," predicated by mental disorders, such as autistic, bipolar, Asperger's, or schizophrenic syndromes.[26] The most popular, although not universally accepted, hypothesis today is that geometric designs in caves are due to entoptic (inner-eye) visions while paintings of animals go back hallucinations experienced during shamanic trance or ritual.[27] Another supporting fact for the shamanic hypothesis is that, in analogy to contemporary hunter-gatherers, unusual grave goods appear first in the tombs of ritual specialists rather than social leaders (Conneller 2013, 349).

---

are very common, often depicted in ritual or hunting activities (Watson 2012, 3), they constitute "a marginal phenomenon" among Paleolithic cave paintings. Since they are usually drawn in a "schematic, caricature, distorted, or partial manner" (Fuentes 2013, 987, 991; also Pfeiffer 1982, 140; Price 2001, 169), the sorcerer figures are that much more unusual.

[26] See Bullen 2011; Whitley 2009. This understanding presupposes the same brain structure and mentation in the Paleolithic as today, which contradicts genetic developments and the fact that modern self-aware consciousness with its particular disorders does not appear until after the development of literacy (Bednavik 2013, 71-74; Helveston 2015, 85). On the arising of modern consciousness, see Jaynes 1990, 208; 2006, 91; Kohn 2016, 65; Ong 1982, 77.

[27] This is presented notably by J. D. Lewis-Williams (2002; and Dowson 1988; and Pearce 2004; 2005), Thomas A. Dowson (and Porr 2001), and supported by Jean Clottes (2013; and Courtin 1996, 153) and others (e.g., Palacio-Pérez and Redondo 2014, 363-64; Price 2001, 8).

In opposition, Paul G. Bahn (2010), Patricia A. Helveston (2015), and Maria Cruz Berrocal (2011) maintain that there is no firm empirical evidence to support shamanic activities and/or states as fact beyond theory; that altered states of consciousness come in more than three stages; and that modern experiences under the influence of psychedelic drugs or due to sensory deprivation are not necessarily the same as Paleolithic trances. Also, hallucinations do not commonly produce realistic images of animals (Helveston 2015, 87), geometrical designs are not necessarily due to entoptic visions, nor do the latter occur only in altered states of consciousness (Berrocal 2011, 15; Layton 2000, 174). Derek Hodgson (2000; 2006), too, finds that shamanism is not a viable explanation and instead proposes a neurovisual theory that accounts for repeating patterns (fractals) and stick figures.

Chinese Developments

The earliest evidence for shamanism in China goes back to the Peiligang site at Jiahu, dated to 6500. While various tombs contained musical instruments, they were particularly found in the grave of a male skeleton with no skull. He was buried with eight turtle carapaces containing pebbles and possibly used as rattles, two 7-hole bone flutes, a fork-shaped bone tool, as well as a turtle plastrum with strings (Zhang and Cui 2013, 208). In addition, turtle shells were also found at the foot of house pillars, possibly indicating sacrifices, and dog bones appeared near graves, potentially serving as afterlife guardians (2013, 207).

In total, the site yielded ninety turtle shells and twenty-three complete flutes of different sizes, ranging from five to eight holes (Zhang and Lee 2005, 43). One of them, nine inches long and made from the ulna of a large bird's wing, is very smooth and can still be played, as demonstrated by the folk music scholar Xiao Xinghua and the flautist Ning Baosheng.[28] Others were decorated with images and symbols, including a curled snake and potential precursors of writing (Zhang and Cui 2013, 210). The understanding is that these finds are indicative of shamanistic practices and particular respect given to ritual specialists (Anderson 2014, 40-41).

Bone flutes, stone drums, and an ocarina made from pottery were also recovered from the Lower Yangzi culture at Hemudu, dated to 5500-3300. It also sported houses raised on poles as well as pottery with cord impressions, ivory carvings showing a sun with two birds, and daggers with the image of a long-tailed bird—again interpreted in the light of shamanic practice.[29] The clearest indication comes from a Yangshao tomb at Xishuipo 西水坡 in Puyang, Henan, dated to around 3500. An over 6-foot tall man was found buried with shell mosaics showing a dragon to the east, a tiger the west, and the Dipper constellation to the north. Accompanied by three young children, placed outside the constellations, he is widely understood to have been a shaman, protected by the stars and able to communicate with the supernatural.[30]

Further shamanic tools in the form of polished alligator bones appear in burials at Dawenkou (4300-2600), while alligator skin drums were found at Taosi (2600-2000). Some 350 miles from their customary range, "they attest to the presence of that creature in the eastern Yellow River drainage, and to the alligator's importance in elite ritual and trade" (Pankenier 2013, 62; Barnes 1993, 100). No longer present in north China today, the alligator may well be the source of widespread Chinese dragon worship. "Throughout Chinese history, drumming was an essential feature of rites intended to induce the dragon spirit to deliver rain and may have simulated the alligator's 'thunderous' bellowing during the mating season" (Pankenier 2013, 62; Chang 2005, 94).

---

[28] Zhang and Cui 2013, 209; Zhang et al. 2005, 775.

[29] Yan 2005, 39-41. See also Barnes 1993, 93; Higham 1995, 137; Liu and Chen 2012, 200.

[30] Liu and Chen 2012, 194. See also Chang 2005, 129; Pankenier 2013, 337.

The various shamanic indicators developed over time. Thus, in the early stages, they were scattered in many tombs, indicating a wide spread of abilities and ritual competence among the population. Here, as among hunter-gatherers and presumably prehistoric peoples, shamans were guides rather than leaders (Jarzombek 2013, 33) and large portions of the population held some shamanic skills—as many as 40 percent among the !Kung San (Petzinger 2016, 248). Already in late Yangshao, however, as society grew more segmented and stratified, specialization is evident, paraphernalia becoming more and more concentrated, leading eventually, by the Three Dynasties, to the monopolization of shamanic potency by the state (Chang 2005, 130). Under the Shang, the right to communicate with Heaven and Earth was clearly reserved for the ruler and his elite, and all "magical techniques like divination and writing—and others associated with shamanism and otherworldly powers—were completely under the control of the ruling class" (2005, 131).

Animal and spirit-type imagery continued to be strong, transitioning from bones through ceramics into bronzes (2005, 136). Transforming their shamanic heritage, Shang ruling clans used animals for their names—bear, monkey, elephant, horse, deer, tiger, sparrow, dragon (Keightley 2000, 110)—and increasingly reoriented the role of shamans. Whether or not the Shang king went into trance himself, "the transition to state authority involved a routinization and bureaucratic control of shamanistic practices" (Keightley 1998, 816-17; Puett 2002, 37). As much as "the Shang ancestral cult represented an attempt to forge nature spirits and the ghosts of deceased humans into a single, unified system" (2002, 53), the king became the key communicator with the hierarchy of the dead, using "rigorously scheduled sacrifices and ordered groups of rituals, highly formalized techniques of pyromantic divination, and specially commissioned inscriptions" (Keightley 1998, 813). This tendency continued to dominate later imperial China, marking the government's ongoing effort to control and subdue shamanic cults and trance tendencies among the people (Keightley 1978b, 211-12).

Daoists, too, transformed the shamanic heritage of old, but remained closer to its original patterns, receiving key scriptures and instructions in revelations from the gods, using dance-type movements closely associated with animals in their healing exercises (and still today in qigong), instituting formal training for ecstatic soul travel, establishing themselves as officials in the otherworld, and actively cultivating supersensory powers (Ryan 2011, 183-84; Kohn 2016, 189).

Immortals, moreover, as already found in Eastern Han tom reliefs, were spiritually empowered figures that served as soul guides to paradise and mediators to Heaven (Wallace 2012, 73, 89). Androgynous and often part-bird or part-serpent—with feathers, snake-like legs, or dragon haunches—they tend to look unkempt and wild, barbarian and big-eared, strange and distorted (2012, 75-78). Like the sages of ancient Chinese myth and Lord Lao in medieval Daoism, who often had animal paternity, four faces or eyes, multiple rows of teeth, small horns on their forehead, and other odd features or deformities (Lewis 2006b, 71; Kohn 1996), they represented the epitome of being foreign, barbarian, primitive, and superhuman, with close links to the natural world and customs contrary to Chinese norms (Wallace 2012, 81). Both calling upon shamanic agents and making shamanic skills widely available to practitioners, Daoists maintained an openness to otherworldly connections and altered states of consciousness in clear opposition to mainstream dictates. Again, they made the choice of living as part of the cosmos rather than in control over it, of empowering individuals rather than submitting to official command structures.

Otherworld Transitions

The same also holds true for the Daoist relationship to death and dying, seen as a smooth and fluid transition to an otherworld that is neither hostile nor alien. Thus, like the Hazda and !Kung San who are rather informal in their relationship to death and simply place the dead person in a thatched hut and then burn it (Jarzombek 2013, 31), Daoists accept death as part of the natural flow of life. Zhuangzi states that "seeing my life as a good thing, I should also see my death as a good thing" (ch. 6) and refuses "to whine about either" (ch. 22). To him, death is "a return to perfection," a recovery of his "true home," a natural transformation in the ongoing flow of existence (Kohn 2014, 148; Down 2000, 3). He says,

> "I will have Heaven and Earth for my coffin and coffin shell, the sun and moon for my pair of jade discs, the stars and constellations for my pearls and beads, and the ten thousand things for my parting gifts. The furnishings for my funeral are already prepared—what is there to add?"
>
> "But," his disciples said, "we're afraid the crows and kites will eat you, Master!"
>
> "Above ground I'll be eaten by crows and kites, below ground I'll be eaten by mole crickets and ants. Wouldn't it be rather bigoted to deprive one group in order to supply the other?" (ch. 32; Watson 1968, 361)

Matching this attitude, Zhuangzi refuses to participate in the elaborate funerary rites and mourning practices of mainstream society with its need to reconstitute community and reestablish social identity through burial rites, gifts, and mourning (Conneller 2013, 352). Commonly in post-egalitarian cultures, the opulence of the gathering as well as the quantity and types of grave goods signal wealth and social standing and—like elaborate feasts—serve to enhance status, power, and inequality.[31] Zhuangzi rejects all this. For example, while sad

[31] Conneller 2013, 348; Stutz and Tarlow 2013, 7. See also Binford 1971; Brown 1971; Hayden 2009; O'Shea 1984; Saxe 1970.

at the loss of his wife, "his grief being unexceptional and its origin obvious," he expresses it by drumming and singing, showing that there is no need for "sorrow of greater duration" (Olberding 2007, 342). Other figures in the text, when confronted with death, go even further, claiming to feel not even a sense of loss and grief and instead having come fully to terms with death as a natural part of the flow of life.[32]

In a similar manner, medieval Daoist monastics carefully planned the transition to the otherworld, moving dying members into the Transformation Building in the northwest corner of the monastery. Here a statue of the Heavenly Worthy, with his left hand pointing skyward, was the focal point they should face, ideally sitting up in a meditative posture to consciously experience their passing (Kohn 2003a, 191). Understanding the ultimate identity of the practitioner as eternally part of Dao and thus beyond destruction, for Daoists death is a step either toward ascension to the immortals or, if the person's merit is not quite complete, a passage to yet another round on the lower levels of life (2003a, 192).

Funerals were accordingly simple and mourning nonexistent. As medieval documents record, Daoists made sure the body was bathed and combed, dressed in formal vestments and headdress, and laid out on his back so as to face Heaven. He or she would be placed between his personal staff, talismans, and writing tablets on the left and a divine sword on the right—potentially replacing the corpse for bodily ascension (Campany 2002, 70-72). Overall, the goal of the treatment was to speed the journey and send the deceased along with good wishes rather than hold him back. The texts clearly discourage crying or other expressions of grief near the dead, instead admonishing people to be positive and emphasize how the deceased had successfully fulfilled his destiny. Eventually a pit was dug in the monastery's graveyard or on a suitable mountain side, the corpse was wrapped in a shroud, and a formal burial was held, with commemorative services to follow at regular intervals to further aide his otherworldly journey (Kohn 2003a, 192).

Both the matter-of-fact acceptance of the transition and the simplicity of the rites echo practices that go back into prehistory. Funerary ranking structures and burials with large numbers of grave goods, including human and animal sacrifices, do not appear until the mid-Neolithic, well after social stratification brought about by agriculture.[33] Cemeteries as formal locations for the dead are a phenomenon that goes back to the Mesolithic and is associated with sedentism (Pettit 2011, 251). Prior to that, the norm in the Upper Paleolithic, after the Human Revolution, was "simple inhumation in shallow graves," sometimes

---

[32] Kohn 2014, 61. See also Galvany 2012, 36; Olberding 2007, 344-45.

[33] Stutz and Tarlow 2013, 7; Pettit 2011, 269.

with a few grave goods, such as pieces of ochre, seashells, animal bones, or stone tools, with some indication of social perception of diversity.[34]

"Fully symbolically structured mortuary activity" (Pettit 2011, 269), in turn, is a development from funerary caching, i. e., placing the body in various postures in caves or natural hollows, with the occasional inclusion of objects, sporadic indications of ritual activities, and some grave markers. Not requiring complex communication or symbolic thought, this was common among Cro Magnon man during the Middle Paleolithic, 100-60,000, and is also found to a limited degree among the Neanderthals.[35] In some places, the dead—typically isolated individuals—were covered with mammoth scapulae, pinned down with wood, tightly bound, partially burned, or weighed with stones, indicating a tendency toward ritual containment that eventually led to more systematic inhumations (Pettit 2011, 213).

Prior to that, the earliest finds indicate a tendency toward abandonment combined with mortuary defleshing or flensing and the curation of crania and/or other bones. That is to say, some bones show clear signs of intentional stripping, indicating that hominins, like chimpanzees, would poke at the corpse and take off some flesh, partly to investigate the status of the deceased, partly as an expression of emotional turbulence, and partly as a form of cannibalism if and when nutritionally necessary. Some sites, furthermore, such as the Bone Cave or Sima de los Huisos in Atapuerca, Spain, which dates back to the Lower Paleolithic at 500-400,000, contain a cache of bones, indicating the intentional collection of remains in a certain location (Pettit 2011, 15-17, 53; Wightman 2015, 181, 183).

Still, the dominant way of disposing the dead among hominins was simple abandonment, leaving them to decompose and be scavenged (Pettit 2011, 212). This reflects an early tendency toward "open consignment, a gesture of outwardness, extroversion, transcendence, and submission, willing the body to become part of something larger and external." It stands in contrast to burial practices, which signal "closed consignment, a gesture of introversion and intimacy, hiding, protecting, cherishing, and controlling, keeping the body tied to the particular" (Wightman 2015, 187). In other words, the entire history of man's treatment of his dead—echoing also the transition from round to square living quarters—can be described as an ongoing separation from the cosmos and increased focus on human centeredness—a tendency Daoists intentionally strive to reverse.

---

[34] Pettit 2011, 76, 140, 268-69; Wightman 2015, 192. See also Richard 2013, 28; Chapman 2013, 50; Formicola et al. 2001, 378; Giacobini 2007, 19; Harrod 1980, 198; Trinkaus et al 2014, ch. 3.

[35] Pettit 2011, 55-68; Wightman 2015, 188-90. See also Hovers et al. 2003, 507.

Cinnabar

In a yet different dimension of the same overall tendency, medieval Daoists used the mineral cinnabar (*dan* 丹) as the basis of their most potent elixir of immortality. Cinnabar is a mercury sulfite (HgS) that dissolves into its parts when heated, then reconstitutes itself back into cinnabar (i. e., "reverted cinnabar"). Combining it with a variety of other ingredients—pine needles, pine resin, mushrooms, persimmons, apricot kernels, deer antlers, mother-of-pearl, mica, aconite, realgar, sulfur, mercury, arsenic, silver, and gold—Daoists would prepare their elixirs, also called *dan*, in secrecy over extended periods of time, and with proper ritual and spiritual preparations.

Thus, as described in the *Baopuzi,* alchemists had to set up their furnace in a secluded spot with the right kind of *qi*, then time their work according to a cosmic schedule, observing the right times of firing and cooling, stirring and burying, to properly imitate the growth of gold in the earth on a microcosmic scale. If and when the elixir had been created successfully, alchemists had to perform a thanksgiving sacrifice and give away large portions of the newly created "gold." They could then take varying doses of the elixir, a gray-brown mud that was ingested either rolled into a pill or dissolved in liquid. Depending on the dose, they could attain magical powers, gain divine protection, find lightness and radiance in body and mind, and have the choice of either extending life on Earth indefinitely or ascend to the immortals.[36]

The life-giving, magical power of cinnabar has to do with its strong, brilliant red color, commonly called vermilion and covering the range from bright orange-red to a more somber bluish tinge. Chemically the powdered ore of mercury, it was highly toxic and had to be carefully mined in a process that was difficult, expensive, and dangerous (Madhihassan 1986, 65)—and undertaken only after the development of agriculture. Thus, its earliest traces appear in the Neolithic village of Catalhöyük in Turkey (7500-5700), in a mural showing aurochs, deer, and humans.

In ancient Rome cinnabar was the most expensive red pigment and served to create the bright vermilion murals in the Villa of Mysteries in Pompeii (Neiman et al. 2015; Sheldon 2014). In Mesoamerica, it was popular among the Olmecs (1500), used in royal burial chambers among the Maya—notably in the Tomb of the Red Queen in Palenque (600-700 CE), widely covered with bright red powder made from cinnabar—and widely applied among the Incas (see Cooke et al. 2009). In India, it is known as *sindoor*, marking the partition of women's hair as a sign of fertility and matrimony, a practice that has been traced back as far as the ancient Indus Valley city of Harappa and is mentioned in the *Mahābhārata.*

[36] Kohn 2005, 158. See also Needham, Ho, and Lu 1976; Pregadio 2006.

In China, cinnabar appears in the mid-Yangshao period (4000-3500), applied in the plastering of building walls, mortuary practice, and in symbols on painted pottery at Banpo.[37] In its wake, a considerable number of late Shang oracle bones bear traces of red and black pigments—the red being cinnabar while the black is a carbon compound (Tsien 1985, 238). Red, moreover, was the dominant royal color in the late Shang and early Zhou, applied to robes, vestments, carriages, palace buildings, banners, and all kinds of other objects (Needham, Ho, and Lu 1976, 5), while cinnabar ink was used in some sacred inscriptions on Zhou bones for divination.[38]

Functioning as a "strong magic of resurrection" (1976, 3), cinnabar under the Zhou was also used to color "amulets of jade, beads, or cicadas placed in the mouth of the dead." By the same token, "tombs of the 6th century have been found to contain masses of cinnabar and vermilion paint on the remains and the bones" of the deceased, soon leading to the development of a synthetic compound (1976, 3). Over the centuries, mainstream culture moved away from this magic and came to use cinnabar or its equivalent as vermilion pigment—known as Chinese Red—for artistic purposes, coloring lacquerware, walls, columns, and the like. Daoists, in contrast, held on to its magical and life-giving qualities, in their quest maintaining its original symbolism as already manifest in prehistory.

"Red was the color of blood and its ceaseless movement, so it was a natural piece of sympathetic magic to use red pigments in symbolic revivification of the entombed dead" and other life-enhancing activities.[39] Preceding the mining of cinnabar, red ochre was the key substance to symbolize the power of life, the essence of blood, "the soul concentrate, the drug of longevity,", as well as "the sun, blood, and the energy that permeates all things."[40] Much less poisonous, it is an anhydrous iron oxide (Fe2O3) and also known as red earth. Containing hematite, dehydrated iron, or iron hydroxide, it is easily mined and processed—notably through grinding, scoring, and rubbing.[41]

Common worldwide,[42] red ochre was used variously as a preservative and adhesive agent as well as a means toward healing and longevity, insect repellent,

[37] Liu and Chen 2012, 192; Tsien 1985, 237; Liu 2005, 71.

[38] Tsien 1985, 25. During the Qin, lacquer and cinnabar—heat-stable if not fire-proof (Madhihassan 1986, 66)—were used to write names of official units on government tools, armor, and weapons, i. e., on surfaces that would not lend themselves to incisions yet that needed to be permanently marked (Tsien 1985, 239). Continuing this tradition, medieval Daoists wrote their charms and talismans on painted paper smeared with cinnabar (1985, 109).

[39] Needham, Ho, and Lu 1976, 3. See also Durkheim 1961, 159; Watts 2009, 66. The symbolic power of red may also be responsible for the importance of peaches in Daoism, since their pits tend to be blood red at the core (Madhihassan 1986, 64).

[40] Christian 2008, 97; Jarzombek 2013, 9; Madhihassan 196, 64 McIntosh 2006, 272.

[41] Hodgskiss 2014, 409; Watts 2009, 63.

[42] Duarte 2014, 561. See also Petzinger 2016, 32; Needham, Ho, and Lu, 1976, 3.

sun screen, neutralizer of smells, disinfectant, and blood coagulant.[43] More pertinently, there is also evidence that—very much like later cinnabar—it played a role in body painting for ornamental and ceremonial uses as well as in the visual arts and mortuary practices for symbolic purposes (Domingo 2012, 868; Watts 2009, 90). The earliest evidence goes back to Wonderwork Cave in South Africa around 500,000, followed by Zambia and Kenya (Olorgesailie) around 300,000.[44] Ubiquitous in Africa by 170,000, the regular use of red ochre signals an increase in "habitual collective ritual across vast landscapes" as well as the growing establishment of a "symbolic culture" (Watts 2014, 222-25). This also hold true for Layer 4 of the Peking Man site at Zhoukoudian, where ornamental stone beads were found painted with hematite, surrounded further by large quantities of red powder (Needham, Ho, and Lu 1976, 3).

A major find, moreover, appears in the Blombos Cave in South Africa, dated to about 100,000, where a full paint kit and processing set were found together with over 1500 pigment pieces, some with geometric engravings.[45] Within mortuary ritual, the earliest use of red ochre use is evident in the Qafzeh cave near Nazareth, Israel, dated to 90,000. Here seven adults and three children were found intentionally placed, together with ochre-stained marine shells and lumps of the mineral.[46] The Sibudu Cave in South Africa, dating to 70-50,000, as well as finds among Neanderthals (ca. 60,000), lend additional support to a widening variety of red ochre applications and processing methods, further enhanced by numerous finds from the Upper Paleolithic, after the arrival of modern humans when it became ubiquitous (Pettit 2011, 68).[47]

The mineral, moreover, is still actively used among hunter-gatherers (Jarzombek 2013, 10), who generally practice some form of body marking (Watts 2009, 82). Thus, for example, "the Tasmanian Aborigines applied red ochre mixed with the fat of wallabies and possums in wavy, energy-field patterns on their arms and torsos and through their matted, curly hair. They painted their bodies with the ochre on an everyday rather than ritual basis, even though red ochre is in very limited supply in Tasmania. This fact suggests that they represented an older or at least a more orthodox form of Aboriginal spirituality" (Lawlor 1991, 104; Ryan 1981, 11-14). More particularly, after female initiation, in some areas the girl's body was painted with red ochre, the crescent moon symbolizing that she was empowered with menstrual blood (Lawlor 1991, 206).

Similarly, Native American lore suggests an explanation of the importance of red body painting. "Ochre, when rubbed on the body, allows the spiritual force trapped within us to flow outward." As a result, they "paint themselves for all journeys into the otherworld as well as for tuning the body into the

---

43 Petzinger 2016, 32. Madhihassan 1986, 64; Rifkin 2011; Tributsch 2016; Watts 2009, 72.

44 Jarzombek 2013, 9; Watts 2014, 217; Watts et al. 2016, 297.

45 Abadia and Morales 2013, 286. Henshilwood 2011; Petzinger 2016, 58; Watts 2009, 82-86.

46 Petzinger 2016, 46. See also Hovers et al. 2003, 57; Mayer et al. 2009, 308; Watts 2009, 70.

47 Watts 209, 79. See also Hodgskiss 2014; Roebroeks et al. 2012; Villa et al. 2015.

magnetic flows of the natural world in order to hunt" (1991, 104). The Indian application of *sindoor* as well as the use of henna—also containing the haemo pigments—in ancient Egypt and the modern Arab and Indian worlds may well relate to similar beliefs. The latter in particular is applied to fingertips to increase sensitivity in food selection, to the soles of feet to enhance a sense of mission and direction on earth, as well as, among the dead, "to aid them in finding their way through the intermediate worlds" (1991, 104).

In other words, cinnabar and its precursor red ochre were powerful agents for enhancing direct contact with the otherworld, opening links to cosmic energies and supernatural powers while creating passageways to longevity and immortality. Unlike in mainstream Chinese culture, where the use of cinnabar was preempted by the ruling classes and diminished in life-enhancing power to appear mostly symbolically in artistic expression, in Daoism it retained its full potency and continued to express its original importance. This, then, is yet another example—like the close connection to the stars, the preference for round shapes and curvy lines, the personal interaction with the otherworld, and the eschewing of elaborate death rituals and prolonged grieving processes—where Daoists made the choice to preserve pristine affluence by developing and enhancing prehistoric models in contrast, and even resistance, to post-egalitarian structures.

Conclusion

Lynne Twist, in *The Soul of Money*, speaks of "scarcity" as a "great lie," (2003, 43). She defines scarcity as "the lack of food, water, shelter, freedom, or opportunity" and notes that it applies equally to people living in abject poverty and those who "have bounty way beyond their needs." In each case, people's thinking and acting is dominated by "what they don't have and what they want to get."

She then moves on to define scarcity in terms of three toxic myths. The first is that "there is not enough," which means that "the total of our life energy, everything we think, everything we say, and everything we do becomes an expression of an effort to overcome this sense of lack and the fear of losing to others and being left out" (2003, 49). This, in turn, leads to distrust, competition, status seeking, and segregation, the pursuit of outside goals that leave us ever more dissatisfied. Running after things, "actively wanting money is toxic to happiness" (Biswas-Diener 2008, 315-16; Maslow 1954, 309).

The second toxic myth is that "more is better," which creates a stressful, rushed, and overwhelmed existence. "The rush for more distances us from experiencing the deeper value of what we acquire or already have;" it "is a chase with no end and a race without winners" (2003, 51). In addition, as the *Zhuangzi* already points out, people end up with "more stuff piled up than they could ever use, keep on grasping for more than they could ever hold; their minds full of care and close to exhaustion, yet they still keep going after projects and things, not knowing when to stop" (ch. 29; Kohn 2011, 11). This, moreover, is "the driving force for much of the violence and war, corruption and exploitation on earth" (Twist 2003, 52).

Next, and even more detrimental, is the third myth, "that's just the way it is." It fosters the belief that scarcity is inevitable, that "it's a hopeless, helpless, unequal, unfair world, where you can never get out of this trap" (2003, 53). This myth is the one with the most grip, since it builds on centuries, even millennia, of tradition and social structures, cloaking it in the guise of naturalness, of something that was always there and will always remain. Not only leading to resignation and hopelessness, it also "justifies greed, prejudice, and inaction" and protects "institutionalized racism, sex discrimination, and social and economic discrimination against ethnic and religious minorities" (2003, 54).

Many of the themes Lynne Twist addresses in her discussion of scarcity are also the focus of this work on Daoist roots in the Stone Age. Looking at the history of humanity, and especially its transition from a hunter-gatherer lifestyle in the Paleolithic to agriculture, civilization, and statehood in the Neolithic, it becomes very clear that a life of poverty, scarcity, and misery for the vast majority of human beings is by no means intrinsic to the human condition, but was "systematically instituted by the market-industrial system" (Sahlins 1972, 4). That is to say, all the various features of life that we deplore but tend to think of as natural and permanent, inevitable and unchangeable, are in fact the result of particular choices made at the dawn of civilization, due to a variety of circumstances, that have then, over time, led to genetic and social changes that now appear set in stone.

While the Malthusian trap that mired people in poverty and scarcity throughout the Agrarian period could have been avoided by the systematic control of population growth, time and again people have chosen quantity over quality, accumulation over happiness, population growth over higher standards of living, increase of power over spiritual and cultural advances. This is why Jared Diamond has called the Neolithic Revolution "the worst mistake in the history of the human race," arguing that when "forced to choose between limiting population or trying to increase food production, we chose the latter and ended up with starvation, warfare, and tyranny" (1987, 66).

The Daoist Alternative

Uniquely in human history, Daoists have recognized this fact and strongly affirmed that not only was this choice for scarcity avoidable historically but that there is an alternative and that the choice can be avoided or reversed at any time by anyone in any social situation. "We are all capable of repudiating the distorting influences of civilization and recovering our original nature" (Ames 1994, 8). Emphasizing the primordial or original (*yuan* 元) quality of life in body, mind, and spirit, Daoists have developed a large range of methods on all different levels—philosophical, communal, and self-cultivation—to aid in this process of becoming truer to ourselves, more appreciative of what we already have, more joyful in living, and more harmonious in social interaction.

Thus, there are philosophical documents expounding key values, including a sense of reality in its primary form, a close connection to nature, and an identity derived from Heaven rather than humanity, the universe rather than social convention. They also encourage a deep respect for the earth and propound key personal values, such as living in so-being by recognizing one's personal strengths and inclinations, finding an ease and flow of life in nonaction, and embracing individual authenticity, social flexibility, as well as simplicity and sufficiency.

The texts also discuss the ideal mode of consciousness, the way the mind works most powerfully and to our best advantage, describing time and again how sages or perfected act with ease and in spontaneity, using deep-rooted instincts and relying on clear intuition. Recovering the "unknowing" state of being merged with cosmic oneness, experiencing themselves as pure beings of spirit, allowing emotions to flow freely, and yet able to use the discriminating, rational mind to function in the world and explain all this in words, ideal Daoists activate their optimal brain and make strong use of all their capabilities. Doing so, they make a choice for peak performance, when body, skills, emotions, and thinking all work together as cooperative partners, and all flows intuitively and effortlessly in skillful spontaneity, providing a model of how one can live in the world enthusiastically, positively, and harmoniously.

More than just writing about it, though, Daoists also put their ideas into practice, creating communities that make different choices than mainstream culture by activating an egalitarian mode of living in steadfast resistance against complexity, keeping numbers small, relationships honest, and economic activity simple. This holds true for primitivist villages in antiquity, religious organizations of Great Peace and the Celestial Masters, as well as the monastic institutions since the middle ages with their core focus on spiritual cultivation. Leadership in these various communities, moreover, takes the form of guidance rather than governance, embracing virtues of non-competition, kindness, faithfulness, order, timeliness, and competence. As the *Daode jing* has it, "The sage places himself in the background, puts himself away, and has no personal interests" (ch. 7).

Another dimension of the same positive community structuring is the Daoist emphasis on equality and focus on nurturing individual qualities above and beyond social status or gender roles. They thus counterbalance male-centered culture philosophically by extolling yin-type values and forms of behavior, lauding the "mysterious female," comparing Dao to the mother, and generally emphasizing the feminine as a positive value. In community life, they do away with stereotypes and actively promote gender neutrality, classifying people on the basis of personal skill and social contribution, and affording equal rank and status to women. Monastics and immortals, finally, actively ungender practitioners, making no distinctions in garb, tasks, roles, and living quarters, thus providing a viable alternative to the gender dichotomy of mainstream culture.

By the same token, Daoists support egalitarian community by holding vegetarian feasts, which do not engage in excess or demonstrate rank and status but serve to share food as a sign of communion not only among members but also with donors and supplicants and, reaching even farther, with all beings, divine and demonic. Food, honored as part of nature and a great gift from Heaven, not only provides nourishment and life energy, but is also a major medium to enhance harmony and integration. Other religious activities, too, be they to connect to the stars, ecstatically journey to the otherworld, honor the passage of the deceased, or activate the magic of potent minerals, celebrate the fullness of life, the flowing openness of all different spheres, and the ultimate realization of wholeness on every level—individual, community, world, and the greater universe.

Pristine Affluence

In all these different dimensions, Daoists strive for a state Marshall Sahlins, in *Stone Age Economics*, has called "pristine affluence" or the "Zen road to predicated affluence" (1972, 29, 37). What he means by this is that, while people in prehistory or hunter-gatherers today have few possessions and maintain a low standard of living, they are certainly not poor or deprived. Rather, secure in a deep "trust in the abundance of nature's resources," they have few needs and minimal goods, giving them little to worry about and instead offering lots of space and time to enjoy life. With plenty of food to go around, adequate shelter to keep out the elements, and a harmonious community to live in, workdays are short and interspersed with breaks and fun, people are tall and healthy, enjoying rather than enduring life.

Affluence in this context, rather than being another word for wealth or riches, is used in its literal sense—*ad-fluere*—that is, "to flow in." It means allowing goods, services, and relationships to flow into our lives as they arise, open to receive and grateful for what is. It becomes pristine when it evolves into a flowing way of life, easily functioning in the ever changing networks of the world while being completely absorbed in what we love to do and do best, our very own skillful spontaneity. Being affluent in this sense means living in a deep connection to the universe and other beings, allowing life to happen in an essentially carefree attitude, always ready to adapt to change and transcend limitations or boundaries associated with mainstream values and norms. Pristine affluence is an inner sense of richness—personal truth, satisfaction, and enjoyment of life—combined with a feeling of exhilaration and enthusiasm, what Mihalyi Csikszentmihalyi calls the optimal or autotelic experience (1990, 67).

The key value that leads to this state is sufficiency, a sense of enoughness, what Swedes call *lagom*, literally being "connected to a team" (AtKisson 2009, 101), the innate feeling how things and people move through our lives in a current, constantly coming and going yet always being there when needed and in just the right amount (Twist 2003, 103). As the *Daode jing* has it, "Who knows when it is enough is truly rich" (ch. 33). This has nothing to do with amounts and everything with attitude, an attitude, moreover, we are free to choose at any moment. As Lynne Twist puts it,

> We each have the choice in any setting to step back and let go of the mindset of scarcity. Once we let go of scarcity, we discover the surprising truth of sufficiency. By sufficiency, I don't mean a quantity of anything. Sufficiency isn't two steps up from poverty or one step short of abundance. It isn't a measure of barely enough or more than enough. Sufficiency isn't an amount at all. It is an experience, a context we generate, a declaration, a knowing that there is enough, and that we are enough. (2003, 74)

Sufficiency makes us truer to ourselves, moving from a material to an ethical value. "The question of what you want to own is actually the question of how you want to live your life," Marie Kondo says (2014, 182). The way we spend our time, energy, and money makes a statement of what we value most. Our job is not to gain, hoard, and accumulate, it is only to direct the flow. As David R. Hawkins notes, "Everything in the human domain is temporary, transient, evolutionary. All belongs to God, nothing can be really owned, and all ownerships and relationships are stewardships only." He accordingly recommends that we "focus on alignment rather than attachment or involvement, cling to principles rather than people, objects, conditions, or situations, and resolve to live with courage and dignity, summoning forth unseen power" in close connection to the universe (2006, 100-01).

This, in turn, leads to deep wisdom and a great sense of personal integrity, the power to make choices, to shift from an emphasis on material wealth to an abundance of time, relationships, and experiences, creating a high quality of life. In all these dimensions, Daoists draw on Paleolithic and Mesolithic models in affirming the possibility of an alternative way of being in the world. To be sure, they never simply want to return to a prehistoric lifestyle, unknowing mentation, or primitive existence. Rather, their point is that all these aspects, which once dominated the human experience, are still accessible to us and that we have a choice to activate them in the here and now.

We as individuals have the power to limit procreation, reduce accumulation, refrain from exercising power, and refuse to give in to economic, political, and social pressure. We can live in pristine affluence even in an agricultural or industrial setting, even under the auspices of statehood, even within a stratified society. We can practice peaceful coexistence, cultivate ourselves to perfect health, eat a simple and nutritious diet, and live in sufficiency, peace, and moral integrity, spending our time in cultural and spiritual pursuits. We can create communities that embrace these values and develop a form of life on earth that is as close to perfection as imaginable at this level of human development.

Bibliography

Aaseng, Nathan. 1986. *More with Less: The Future World of Buckminster Fuller.* Minneapolis: Lerner Publications.

Abadia, Oscar Moro, and Manuel R. Gonzales Morales. 2013. "Paleolithic Art: A Cultural History." *Journal of Archaeological Research* 21:269-306.

Abrams, Nancy Ellen, and Joel R. Primack. 2011. *The New Universe and the Human Future: How a Shared Cosmology Could Transform the World.* New Haven, Conn.: Yale University Press.

Acemoglu, Daron, and James A. Robinson. 2012. *Why Nations Fail: The Origins of Power, Prosperity, and Poverty.* New York: Crown Publishers.

Aikens, C. Melvin. 1995. "First in the World: The Jōmon Pottery of Early Japan." In *The Emergence of Pottery: Technology and Innovation in Ancient Societies*, edited by William K. Barnett and John W. Hooper, 11-21. Washington, D. C.: Smithsonian Institution Press.

Allan, Sarah. 1991. *The Shape of the Turtle: Myth, Art, and Cosmos in Early China.* Albany: State University of New York Press.

_____. 2007. "On the Identity of Shang Di and the Origin of Concept of a Celestial Mandate." *Early China* 31:1-46.

Alvard, Michael S. 2001. "Mutualistic Hunting." In *Meat Eating and Human Evolution*, edited by Craig B. Stanford and Henry T. Bunn, 261-78. New York: Oxford University Press.

Amaghlobeli, Givi, and Miray Celepli. 2012. "Understanding Taoist Leadership from a Western Perspective." *Journal of Business* 1.2:47-52.

Ames, Roger T. 1981. "Taoism and the Androgynous Ideal." In *Women in China: Current Directions in Historical Scholarship*, edited by Richard W. Guisso and Stanley Johannesen, 21-45. Lewiston, NY: Edwin Mellen Press.

_____. 1994. *The Art of Rulership: A Study of Ancient Chinese Political Thought.* Honolulu: University of Hawaii Press.

_____. 2001. "The Local and the Focal in Realizing a Daoist World." In *Daoism and Ecology: Ways within a Cosmic Landscape*, edited by Norman Girardot, James Miller, and Liu Xiaogan, 265-82. Cambridge, Mass.: Harvard University Press, Center for the Study of World Religions.

Andersen, Poul. 1980. *The Method of Holding the Three Ones.* London: Curzon Press.

_____. 1990. "The Practice of *Bugang*." *Cahiers d'Extrême-Asie* 5:15-53.

Anderson, Edgar. 1952. *Plants, Man, and Life.* Boston: Little & Brown.

Anderson, Eugene N. 1988. *The Food of China.* New Haven: Yale University Press.

_____. 2005. *Everyone Eats: Understanding Food and Culture.* New York: New York University Press.

———. 2014. *Food and Environment in Early and Medieval China.* Philadelphia: University of Pennsylvania Press.

Andrews, Cecile. 2009. "Introduction." In *Less Is More: Embracing Simplicity for a Healthy Planet, a Caring Economy, and Lasting Happiness*, edited by Cecile Andrews and Wanda Urbanska, 1-7. Gabriola Island: New Society Publishers.

Anton, Susan C. 2013. "*Homo Erectus* and Related Taxa." In *A Companion to Paleoanthropology*, edited by David R. Begun, 497-516. Malden, Mass.: Wiley-Blackwell.

Ardila, Alfredo. 2009. "Origins of the Language: Correlation between Brain Evolution and Language Development." In *Foundations in Evolutionary Cognitive Neuroscience*, edited by Steven M. Platek and Todd K. Shackelford, 153-74. Cambridge: Cambridge University Press.

Ardrey, Robert. 1966. *The Territorial Imperative: A Personal Inquiry into the Animal Origins of Property and Nations.* New York: Atheneum.

———. 1976. *The Hunting Hypothesis: A Personal Conclusion Concerning the Evolutionary Nature of Man.* New York: Atheneum.

Arendt, Hannah. 1970. *On Violence.* New York: Harcourt, Brace, and World.

Arnold, David. 1988. *Famine: Social Crisis and Historical Change.* New York: Basil Blackwell.

Arnold, Dean. 1985. *Ceramic Theory and Cultural Process.* Cambridge: Cambridge University Press.

Arthur, Shawn. 2006. "Life without Grains: *Bigu* and the Daoist Body." In *Daoist Body Cultivation*, edited by Livia Kohn, 91-122. Magdalena, NM: Three Pines Press.

———. 2009. "Eating Your Way to Immortality: Early Daoist Self-Cultivation Diets." *Journal of Daoist Studies* 2:32-63.

———. 2013. *Early Daoist Dietary Practices: Examining Ways to Health and Longevity.* New York: Lexington Books.

Asouti, Eleni, and Dorian Q. Fuller. 2013. "A Contextual Approach to the Emergence of Agriculture in Southwest Asia: Reconstructing Early Neolithic Plant-Food Production." *Current Anthropology* 54.3:299-345.

AtKisson, Alan. 2009. "The *Lagom* Solution." In *Less Is More: Embracing Simplicity for a Healthy Planet, a Caring Economy, and Lasting Happiness*, edited by Cecile Andrews and Wanda Urbanska, 101-06. Gabriola Island: New Society Publishers.

Aurenche, Olivier. 1981. *La maison orientale.* Paris: Geuthner.

Autry, James A., and Stephen Mitchell. 1998. *Real Power: Business Lessons from the Tao Te Ching.* New York: Riverhead Books.

Avruch, Kevin. 1998. *Culture and Conflict Resolution.* Washington, DC: United States Institute of Peace Press.

Axelrod, R. 1984. *The Evolution of Cooperation.* New York: Basic Books.

Azéma, Marc, and Florent Rivère. 2012. "Animation in Paleolithic Art: A Pre-Echo of Cinema." *Antiquity* 86:316-24.

Bagley, Robert. 2014. "Erligang Bronzes and the Discovery of the Erligang Culture." In *Art and Archaeology of the Erligang Civilization*, edited by Kyle Steinke and Dora C. Y. Ching, 19-50. Princeton: Princeton University Press.

Bahn, Paul G. 1998. *The Cambridge Illustrated History of Prehistoric Art.* Cambridge: Cambridge University Pres.

______. 2001. *The Penguin Archaeological Guide.* London: Penguin Books.

______. 2010. *Prehistoric Rock Art: Polemics and Progress.* Cambridge: Cambridge University Press.

______, and Jean Vertut. 1997. *Journey through the Ice Age.* Berkeley: University of California Press.

Bailey, Douglas W. 2013. "Figurines, Corporeality, and the Origins of the Gendered Body." In *A Companion to Gender Prehistory*, edited by Diane Bolger, 244-64. Malden, Mass.: Wiley-Blackwell.

Baines, John. 2014. "Civilization and Empires: A Perspective on Erligang from Early Egypt." In *Art and Archaeology of the Erligang Civilization*, edited by Kyle Steinke and Dora C. Y. Ching, 99-120. Princeton: Princeton University Press.

Ball, Philip. 2016. "How Human Sacrifice Propped Up the Social Order." www.nature.com/news

Bar-Yosef, Ofer. 2002. "The Role of the Younger Dryas in the Origin of Agriculture in West Asia." In *The Origins of Pottery and Agriculture*, edited by Yoshinori Yasuda, 39-54. New Delhi: Roli Books.

______, and Mordechai E. Kislev. 1989. "Early Farming Communities in the Jordan Valley." In *Foraging and Farming: The Evolution of Plant Exploitation*, edited by David R. Harris and Gordon C. Hillman, 632-42. London: Unwin Hyman.

Barber, Elizabeth Wayland. 1994. *Women's Work: The First 20,000 Years—Women, Cloht, and Society in Early Times.* New York: W. W. Norton.

______. 2007. "Weaving the Social Fabric." In *Ancient Textiles: Production, Craft, and Society*, edited by Carole Gillis and Marie-Louise Nosch, 173-79. Oxford: Oxbow.

Barker, Graeme, and Monica Janowski. 2011. "Why Cultivate? Anthropological and Archaeological Approaches to Foraging-Farming Transitions in Southeast Asia." In *Why Cultivate? Anthropological and Archaeological Approaches to Foraging-Farming Transitions in Southeast Asia*, edited by Graeme Barker and Monica Janowski, 1-16. Cambridge: McDonald Institute Monographs.

Barnes, Gina L. 1993. *The Rise of Civilization in East Asia: The Archaeology of China, Korea, and Japan.* London: Thames & Hudson.

______. 2006. *Women in the Nihon Shoki: Mates, Mothers, Mystics, Militarists, Maids, Manufacturers, Monarchs, Messengers, and Managers.* Durham, UK: Durham University Press.

______. 2015. *Archaeology of East Asia: The Rise of Civilization in China, Korea and Japan.* Oxford: Oxbow Press.

Barnicot, N. A. 1969. "Human Nutrition: Evolutionary Perspectives." In *The Domestication and Exploitation of Plants and Animals*, edited by Peter J. Ucko and G. W. Dimbleby, 525-30. Chicago: Aldine.

Barton, Huw, and Tim Denham. 2011. "Prehistoric Vegeculture and Social Life in Island Southeast Asia and Melanesia." In *Why Cultivate? Anthropological and Archaeological Approaches to Foraging-Farming Transitions in Southeast Asia*, edited by Graeme Barker and Monica Janowski, 17-26. Cambridge: McDonald Institute Monographs.

Bataille, Georges. 1955. *Lascaux: The Birth of Prehistoric Painting.* Translated by Austryn Wainhouse. Lausanne: Skira.

Baumer, Christoph. 2012. *The History of Central Asia: The Age of the Steppe Warriors.* New York: I. B. Tauris.

Baumhoff, M. A. 1981. "The Carrying Capacity of Hunter-Gatherers." In *Affluent Foragers: Pacific Coasts East and West*, edited by Shuzo Koyama and David Hurst Thomas, 77-87. Senri: Senri Ethnological Studies.

Bednarik, Robert. 2008. "The Domestication of Humans." *Anthropologie* 40.1:1-17.

______. 2013. "Brain Disorder and Rock Art." *Cambridge Archaeological Journal* 23.1:69-81.

Bell, Rudolph M. 1985. *Holy Anorexia.* Chicago: University of Chicago Press.

Bellah, Robert N. 2011. *Religion in Human Evolution: From the Paleolithic to the Axial Age.* Cambridge, Mass.: Harvard University Press.

Bellwood, Peter S. 2005. *First Farmers: The Origins of Agricultural Societies.* Malden, Mass.: Blackwell.

______, and Colin Renfrew, eds. 2005. *Examining the Farming/Language Dispersal Hypothesis.* Cambridge: McDonald Institute for Archaeology.

Belmonte, Juan Antonio. 2010. "Finding Our Place in the Cosmos: The Role of Astronomy in Ancient Cultures." *Journal of Cosmology* 9:2052-62.

Benn, Charles. 2000. "Daoist Ordination and *Zhai* Rituals." In *Daoism Handbook*, edited by Livia Kohn, 309-38. Leiden: Brill.

Bentley, Gillian R. 1996. "How Did Prehistoric Women Bear 'Man the Hunter'? Reconstructing Fertility from the Archaeological Record." In *Gender and Archaeology*, edited by Rita P. Wright, 23-51. Philadelphia: University of Pennsylvania Press..

Berkowitz, Alan. 1989. "Patterns of Reclusion in Early and Medieval China." Ph.D. Diss., University of Washington, Seattle.

______. 2010. "Social and Cultural Dimensions of Reclusion in Early Medieval China." In *Philosophy and Religion in Early Medieval China*, edited by Alan Chan and Yuet-Keung Lo, 291-318. Albany: State University of New York Press.

Berman, Judith C. 1999. "Bad Hair Days in the Paleolithic: Modern (Re)Constructions of the Cave Man." *American Anthropologist* 101.2:288-304.

Berrocal, Maria Cruz. 2011. "Analogical Evidence and Shamanism in Archaeological Interpretation: African and European Paleolithic Rock Art." *Norwegian Archaeological Review* 44.1:1-20.

Bettinger, Robert, et al. 2010. "The Transition to Agriculture at Dadiwan, People's Republic of China." *Current Anthropology* 51:703-14.

Billeter, Jean François. 2008. *Études sur le Tchouang Tseu.* Paris: Éditions Allia.

_____. 2010. *Leçons sur le Tchouang Tseu.* Paris: Éditions Allia.

Binford, Lewis R. 1968a. "Post Pleistocene Adaptations." In *New Perspectives in Archaeology*, edited by Sally R. Binford and Lewis R. Binford, 313-41. Chicago Aldine.

_____. 1968b. "Methodological Considerations of the Archaeological Use of Ethographic Data." In *Man the Hunter*, edited by Richard B. Lee and Irven DeVore, 268-73. Chicago: Aldine.

_____. 1971. "Mortuary Practices: Their Study and Potential." In *Approaches to the Social Dimensions of Mortuary Practices*, edited by James Brown, 6-29. Washington, DC: Memoirs of he Society for American Archaeology, vol. 25.

_____. 1980. "Willow Smoke and Dog's Tails: Hunter-Gatherer Settlement Systems and Archaeological Site Formation." *American Antiquity* 45:4-20

_____. 1983. *In Pursuit of the Past.* London: Thames & Hudson.

_____, John F. Cherry, and Robin Torrence. 1983. *In Pursuit of the Past: Decoding the Archaeological Record.* London: Thames & Hudson.

Birdsell, Joseph B. 1968. "Some Predictions for the Pleistocene Based on Equilibrium Systems among Recent Hunter-Gatherers." In *Man the Hunter*, edited by Richard B. Lee and Irven DeVore, 229-40. Chicago: Aldine.

Birrell, Anne. 1993. *Chinese Mythology: An Introduction.* Baltimore: Johns Hopkins University Press.

Biswas-Diener, Robert M. 2008. "Material Wealth and Subjective Well-Being." In *The Science of Subjective Well-Being*, edited by Michael Eid and Randy J. Larsen, 307-22. New York: Guilford Press.

Blakeley, Donald N. 2008. "Hearts in Agreement: Zhuangzi on Dao Adept Friendship." *Philosophy East & West* 58.3:318-36.

Bokenkamp, Stephen R. 1997. *Early Daoist Scriptures.* With a contribution by Peter Nickerson. Berkeley: University of California Press.

Bolger, Diane. 2013a. "Introduction: Gender Prehistory – The Story So Far." In *A Companion to Gender Prehistory*, edited by Diane Bolger, 1-19. Malden, Mass.: Wiley-Blackwell.

_____. 2013b. "Gender, Labor, and Pottery Production in Prehistory." In *A Companion to Gender Prehistory*, edited by Diane Bolger, 161-79. Malden, Mass.: Wiley-Blackwell.

Boltz, William G. 1994. *The Origin and Early Development of the Chinese Writing System.* New Haven, Conn.: Yale University Press.

Boroditsky, Lera. 2009. "How Does Our Language Shape the Way We Think?" In *What's Next? Dispatches on the Future of Science*, edited by Max Brockman, 116-29. New York: Vintage Books.

Bourdieu, Pierre. 1990. *The Logic of Practice.* Stanford: Stanford University Press.

Bradley, Richard. 1998. "Architecture, Imagination, and the Neolithic World." In *Creativity in Human Evolution and Prehistory*, edited by Steven Mithen, 227-40. London: Routledge.

Braidwood, Robert J. 1967. *Prehistoric Man*. Glenview: Scott and Foresman.

Bramanti, Barbara. 2013. "The Use of DNA Analysis in the Archaeology of Death and Burial." In *The Oxford Handbook of Archaeology of Death and Burial*, edited by Sarah Tarlow and Liv Nielsson Stutz, 99-122. New York: Oxford University Press.

Brindley, Erica F. 2010. *Individualism in Early China: Human Agency and the Self in Thought and Politics*. Honolulu: University of Hawaii Press.

Brody, Hugh. 1981. *Maps and Dreams*. Vancouver: Douglas and McIntyre.

Bronson, Bennet. 1977. "The Earliest Farming: Demography as Cause and Consequence." In *Origins of Agriculture*, edited by Charles A. Reed, 23-48. The Hague: Mouton.

Brothwell, D. R. 1969. "Dietary Variation and the Biology of Earlier Human Populations." In *The Domestication and Exploitation of Plants and Animals*, edited by Peter J. Ucko and G. W. Dimbleby, 531-46. Chicago: Aldine.

Brown, James. 1971. "The Dimensions of Status in the Burials at Spiro." In *Approaches to the Social Dimensions of Mortuary Practices*, edited by James Brown, 92-112. Washington, DC: Society for American Archaeology.

Brown, Judith K. 1970. "A Note on the Division of Labor by Sex." *American Anthropologist* 72:1073-78.

Brown, Peter Lancaster. 1976. *Megaliths, Myths and Men: An Introduction to Astro-Archaeology*. New York: Taplinger Publications.

Brown, Peter R. L. 1988. *The Body and Society*. New York: Columbia University Press.

Brumfiel, Elizabeth M. 1996. "Figurines of the Aztec State: Testing the Effectiveness of Ideologicla Domination." In *Gender and Archaeology*, edited by Rita P. Wright, 143-66. Philadelphia: University of Pennsylvania Press.

Buchanan, Mark. 2002. *Nexus: Small Worlds and the Groundbreaking Science of Networks*. New York: W. W. Norton.

Bulger, Teresa Dujnic, and Rosemary A. Joyce. 2013. "Archaeology of Embodied Subjectivities." In *A Companion to Gender Prehistory*, edited by Diane Bolger, 68-85. Malden, Mass.: Wiley-Blackwell.

Bullen, Margaret. 2011. "Creativity, Mental Disorder, and Upper Paleolithic Cave Art." *Rock Art Research* 28:117-22.

Bumbacher, Stephan Peter. 1998. "Abschied von Heim und Herd: Die Frau im mittelalterlichen Daoismus und Buddhismus." *Asiatische Studien / Etudes Asiatiques* 52:673-94.

______. 2012. *Empowered Writing: Exorcistic and Apotropaic Rituals in Medieval China*. St. Petersburg, Fla.: Three Pines Press.

Bunn, Henry T. 2001. "Hunting, Power Scavenging, and Butchering by Hazda Foragers and by Plio-Pleistocene *Homo*." In *Meat Eating and Human Evolution*, edited by Craig B. Stanford and Henry T. Bunn, 199-218. New York: Oxford University Press.

Burneko, Guy C. 2004. "Ecohumanism: The Spontaneities of the Earth, *Ziran*, and K=2." *Journal of Chinese Philosophy* 31.2:183-94.

Butler, Judith. 1990. *Gender Trouble: Feminism and the Subversion of Identity*. London: Routledge.

_____. 1993. *Bodies That Matter: On the Discursive Limits of 'Sex'*. London: Routledge.

Bynum, Caroline Walker. 1987. *Holy Feast and Holy Fast: The Religious Significance of Food to Medieval Women*. Berkeley: University of California Press.

Cahill, Suzanne. 1990. "Practice Makes Perfect: Paths to Transcendence for Women in Medieval China." *Taoist Resources* 2.2:23-42.

_____. 2006. *Divine Traces of the Daoist Sisterhood*. Magdalena, NM: Three Pines Press.

Caldwell, Joseph R. 1977. "Cultural Evolution in the Old World and the New, Leading to the Beginnings and Spread of Agriculture." In *Origins of Agriculture*, edited by Charles A. Reed, 77-88. The Hague: Mouton.

Campany, Robert F. 2001. "Ingesting the Marvelous: The Practitioner's Relationship to Nature According to Ge Hong." In *Daoism and Ecology: Ways within a Cosmic Landscape*, edited by Norman Girardot, James Miller, and Liu Xiaogan, 125-48. Cambridge, Mass.: Harvard University Press, Center for the Study of World Religions.

_____. 2002. *To Live As Long As Heaven and Earth: A Translation and Study of Ge Hong's Traditions of Divine Transcendents*. Berkeley: University of California Press.

_____. 2005. "Eating Better than Gods and Ancestors." In *Of Tripod and Palate: Food, Politics and Religion in Traditional China*, edited by Roel Sterckx, 96-122. New York: Palgrave MacMillan.

Campbell, Roderick. 2014. "Erligang: A Tale of Two 'Civilizations'." In *Art and Archaeology of the Erligang Civilization*, edited by Kyle Steinke and Dora C. Y. Ching, 121-36. Princeton: Princeton University Press.

Capra, Fritjof. 1991 [1975]. *The Tao of Physics: An Exploration of the Parallels between Modern Physics and Eastern Mysticism*. Boulder: Shambhala.

Carneiro, Robert L. 1970. "A Theory of the Origin of the State." *Science* 169:733-38.

Carneiro, Robert L. 1981. "The Chiefdom: Precursor of the State."In *The Transition to Statehood in the New World*, edited by Grant D. Jones and Robert Kautz, 37-79. Cambridge: Cambridge University Press.

_____. 1990. "Chiefdom-Level Warfare as Exemplified in Fiji and the Cauca Valley." In *The Anthropology of War*, edited by Jonathan Haas, 190-211. Cambridge: Cambridge University Press.

Carter, George F. 1977. "A Hypothesis Suggesting a Single Origin of Agriculture." In *Origins of Agriculture*, edited by Charles A. Reed, 89-134. The Hague: Mouton.

Casey, Geraldine.1991. "Eleanor Burke Leacock: A Tribute." In *Genes and Gender VI: On Peace, War, and Gender—A Challenge to Genetic Explanation*, edited by Anne E. Hunter, 1-33. New York: City University of New York Press.

Cauvin, Jacques. 2000. *The Birth of the Gods and the Origins of Agriculture*. Translated by Trevor Watkins. Cambridge: Cambridge University Press.

Chagnon, Napoleon. 1990. "Reproductive and Somatic Conflicts of Interest in the Genesis of Violence and Warfare among Tribesmen." In *The Anthropology of War*, edited by Jonathan Haas, 77-104. Cambridge: Cambridge University Press.

Chang, K. C. 1977. "Ancient China." In *Food in Chinese Culture*, edited by K. C. Chang, 23-52. New Haven: Yale University Press.

______. 1980. *Shang Civilization.* New Haven, Conn.: Yale University Press.

______. 1981. "The Affluent Foragers in the Coastal Areas of China: Extrapolation from Evidence on Transition to Agriculture." In *Affluent Foragers: Pacific Coasts East and West*, edited by Shuzo Koyama and David Hurst Thomas, 177-86. Senri: Senri Ethnological Studies.

______. 1983a. *Art, Myth, and Ritual: The Path to Political Authority in Ancient China.* Cambridge, Mass.: Harvard University Press.

______. 1983b. "Sandai Archaeology and the Formation of States in Ancient China: Processual Aspects of the Origins of Chinese Civilization." In *The Origins of Chinese Civilization*, edited by David N. Keightley, 495-521. Berkeley: University of California Press.

______. 1986. *The Archaeology of Ancient China.* New Haven, Conn.: Yale University Press.

______. 2005. "The Rise of Kings and the Formation of City-States." In *The Formation of Chinese Civilization: An Archaeological Perspective*, edited by Sarah Allan, 125-40. New Haven, Conn.: Yale University Press.

Chang, Te-Tzu. 1983. "The Origins and Early Cultures of the Cereal Grains and Food Legumes." In *The Origins of Chinese Civilization*, edited by David N. Keightley, 65-94. Berkeley: University of California Press.

Chanock, Martin. 1987. *Law, Custom, and Social Order: The Colonial Experience in Malawi and Zambia.* Cambridge: Cambridge University Press.

Chao, Lin. 1982. *The Socio-Political Systems of the Shang Dynasty.* Taipei: Academia Sinica.

Chao, Shin-yi. 2011. *Daoist Rituals, State Religion, and Popular Practices: Zhenwu Worship from Song to Ming* (960-1644). London: Routledge.

Chapman, John, and Nona Palincas. 2013. "Gender in Easter European Prehistory." In *A Companion to Gender Prehistory*, edited by Diane Bolger, 413-38. Malden, Mass.: Wiley-Blackwell.

Chapman, Robert. 2013. "Death, Burial, and Social Representation." In *The Oxford Handbook of Archaeology of Death and Burial*, edited by Sarah Tarlow and Liv Nielsson Stutz, 47-58. New York: Oxford University Press.

Chase, Philip G. 1989. "How Different Was Middle Paleolithic Subsistence? A Zooarchaeological Perspective on the Middle to Upper Paleolithic Transition." In *The Human Revolution: Behavioral and Biological Perspectives on the Origins of Modern Humans*, 321-37. Edinburgh: Edinburgh University Press.

Chen, Ellen Marie. 1969. "Nothingness and the Mother Principle in Early Chinese Taoism." *International Philosophical Quarterly* 9.3:391-405.

______. 1973. "Is There a Doctrine of Physical Immortality in the *Tao-te-ching*?" *History of Religions* 12:231-49.

_____. 1974. "Tao as the Great Mother and the Influence of Motherly Love in the Shaping of Chinese Philosophy." *History of Religions* 14.1:51-64.

Chen, Guying. 2015. *Rediscovering the Roots of Chinese Thought: Laozi's Philosophy.* Translated by Paul D'Ambrosio. St. Petersburg, Fla.: Three Pines Press.

Chen, Honghai. 2013. "The Qijia Culture of the Upper Yellow River Valley." In *A Companion to Chinese Archaeology*, edited by Anne P. Underhill, 105-24. Malden, Mass.: Wiley-Blackwell.

Cheung, Kwong-Yue. 1983. "Recent Archaeological Evidence Relating to the Origins of Chinese Characters." In *The Origins of Chinese Civilization*, edited by David N. Keightley, 323-91. Berkeley: University of California Press.

Childe, V. Gordon. 1951. *Man Makes Himself.* New York: Mentor.

_____. 1958. *Prehistory of European Society.* Baltimore: Penguin.

Chong, Kim-chong. 2011a. "The Concept of *Zhen* in the *Zhuangzi*." *Philosophy East & West* 61.2:324-46.

_____. 2011b. "Zhuangzi's *Cheng Xin* and Its Implications for Virtue and Perspective." *Dao* 10.4:427-43.

Christian, David. 2008. *Big History: The Big Bang, Life on Earth, and the Rise of Humanity.* Chantilly, VA: The Teaching Company.

Clark, Gregory. 2007. *A Farewell to Alms: A Brief Economic History of the World.* Princeton: Princeton University Press.

Clarke, Parry, Gauri Pradhan, and Carel van Schaik. 2009."Intersexual Conflict in Primates: Infanticide, Paternity Allocation, and the Role of Coercion." In *Sexual Coercion in Primates and Humans: An Evolutionary Perspective on Male Aggression against Females*, edited by Martin N. Muller and Richard W. Wrangham, 42-77. Cambridge, Mass.: Harvard University Press.

Clay, Zanna, and Klaus Zuberbühler. 2014. "Vocal Communication and Social Awareness in Chimpanzees and Bonobos." In *The Social Origins of Language*, edited by Daniel Dor, Chris Knight, and Jerome Lewis, 141-56. New York: Oxford University Press.

Clottes, Jean. 2013. "Why Did They Draw in Those Caves?" *Time and Mind: The Journal of Archaeology, Consciousness and Culture* 6.1:7-14.

_____, and Jean Courtin. 1996. *The Cave beneath the Sea: Paleolithic Images at Cosquer.* New York: Harry N. Abrams.

_____, and David Lewis-Williams. 1998. *The Shamans of Prehistory: Trance and Magic in the Painted Caves.* New York: Harry Abrams.

Coatsworth, John. 1996. "Welfare." *American Historical Review* 101:1-17.

Cochran, Gregory, and Henry Harpending. 2009. *The 10,000 Year Explosion: How Civilization Accelerated Human Evolution.* New York: Basic Books.

Cochrane, Ethan E., and Andrew Gardner, eds. 2010. *Evolutionary and Interpretive Archaeologies: A Dialogue.* Walnut Creek: Left Coast Press.

Cohen, David Joel. 2002. "New Perspectives on the Transition to Agriculture in China." In *The Origins of Pottery and Agriculture*, edited by Yoshinori Yasuda, 217- 27. New Delhi: Roli Books.

Cohen, Mark Nathan. 1977a *The Food Crisis in Pre-History: Overpopulation and Origins of Agricultures.* New Haven: Yale University Press.

______. 1977b. "Population Pressure and the Origins of Agriculture: An Archaeological Example from the Coast of Peru." In *Origins of Agriculture*, edited by Charles A. Reed, 135-78. The Hague: Mouton.

______. 1981. "The Ecological Basis for New World State Formation: General and Local Model Building."In *The Transition to Statehood in the New World*, edited by Grant D. Jones and Robert Kautz, 105-22. Cambridge: Cambridge University Press.

______. 1985. "Prehistoric Hunter-Gatherers: The Meaning of Social Complexity." In *Prehistoric Hunter-Gatherers: The Emergence of Cultural Complexity*, edited by T. Douglas Price and James A. Brown, 99-119. New York: Academic Press.

______, and Sharon Bennett. 1993. "Skeletal Evidence for Sex Roles and Gender Hierarchies in Prehistory." In *Sex and Gender Hierarchies*, edited by Barbara Diane Miller, 273-96. Cambridge: Cambridge University Press.

Collard, Mark, and Mana Dembo. 2013. "Modern Human Origins." In *A Companion to Paleoanthropology*, edited by David R. Begun, 557-81. Malden, Mass.: Wiley-Blackwell.

Collinder, Björn. 1977. *Fenno-Ugric Vocabulary.* Hamburg.

Conant, Francis Paine. 1982. "Strength, Reproductive Capacity, and the Division of Labor in East Africa." In *Culture and Ecology: Eclectic Perspectives*, edited by John G. Kennedy and Robert B. Edgerton, 26-55. Washington, DC: American Anthropological Association.

Conkey, Margaret W. 2013. "The Future of Gender in Prehistoric Archaeology." In *A Companion to Gender Prehistory*, edited by Diane Bolger, 108-20. Malden, Mass.: Wiley-Blackwell.

Conklin-Brittain, Nancy Lou, Richard W. Wrangham, and Catherine C. Smith. 2002. "A Two-Stage Model of Increased Dietary Quality in Early Hominid Evolution: The Role of Fiber." In *Human Diet: Its Origin and Evolution*, edited by Peter S. Ungar and Mark F. Teaford, 61-76. Westport, Conn.: Bergin & Garvey.

Conneller, Chantal. 2013. "Power and Society: Mesolithic Europe." In *The Oxford Handbook of Archaeology of Death and Burial*, edited by Sarah Tarlow and Liv Nielsson Stutz, 347-58. New York: Oxford University Press.

Connor, Richard C., and Nicole L. Vollmer. 2009. "Sexual Coercion in Dolphin Consortships: A Comparison with Chimpanzees." In *Sexual Coercion in Primates and Humans: An Evolutionary Perspective on Male Aggression against Females*, edited by Martin N. Muller and Richard W. Wrangham, 218-43. Cambridge, Mass.: Harvard University Press.

Conroy, Linda P. 1993. "Female Figurines of the Upper Paleolithic and the Emergence of Gender." In *Women in Archaeology: A Feminist Critique*, edited by Hilary du Cros and Laurajane Smith, 153-60. Canberra: Australian National University Press.

Cook, Constance A. 2005. "Moonshine and Millet: Feasting and Purification Rituals in Ancient China." In *Of Tripod and Palate: Food, Politics and Religion in Traditional China*, edited by Roel Sterckx, 9-33. New York: Palgrave MacMillan.

Cook, Ellen Piel. 1985. *Psychological Androgyny*. New York: Pergamon Press.

Cooke, Colin A., Prentiss H. Balcom, Harald Biester, and Alexander P. Wolfe. 2009. "Over Three Millennia of Mercury Pollution in the Peruvian Andes." *Proceedings of the National Academy of Sciences* 106.22:8830-34.

Cooper, Jerrold S. 2004. "Babylonian Beginnings: The Origin of the Cuneiform Writing System in Comparative Perspective." In *The First Writing: Script Invention as History and Process*, edited by Stephen D. Houston, 71-99. Cambridge: Cambridge University Press.

Corballis, Michael C. 2010. "Did Language Evolve Before Speech?" In *The Evolution of Human Language: Biolinguistic Perspectives*, edited by Richard K. Larson, Viviane Déprez, and Hiroko Yamakido, 115-23. Cambridge: Cambridge University Press.

_____. 2011. *The Recursive Mind: The Origins of Human Language, Thought, and Civilization.* Princeton: Princeton University Press.

Cordain, Loren. 2011. *The Paleo Diet: Lose Weight and Get Healthy by Eating the Foods You Were Designed to Eat.* Boston: Houghton Mifflin.

Coser, Lewis A. 1956. *The Functions of Social Conflict.* New York: Free Press

Costin, Cathy Lynne. 1996. "Exploring the Relationship between Gender and Craft in Complex Societies: Methodological and Theoretical Issues of Gender Attribution." In *Gender and Archaeology*, edited by Rita P. Wright, 111-40. Philadelphia: University of Pennsylvania Press.

_____. 2013. "Gender and Textile Production in Prehistory." In *A Companion to Gender Prehistory*, edited by Diane Bolger, 180-202. Malden, Mass.: Wiley-Blackwell.

Counihan, Carole M. 1999. *The Anthropology of Food and Body*. London: Routledge.

Coutinho, Steve. 2004. *Zhuangzi and Early Chinese Philosophy: Vagueness, Transformation, and Paradox*. Burlington: Ashgate Press

Coyle, Daniel. 1998. "On the *Zhenren*." In *Wandering at Ease in the Zhuangzi*, edited by Roger Ames, 197-210. Albany: State University of New York Press.

Crawford, Gary W. 1992. "Prehistoric Plant Domestication in East Asia." In *The Origins of Agriculture: An International Perspective*, edited by C. Wesley Cowan and Patty Jo Watson, 7-38. Washington, DC: Smithsonian Institution Press.

_____, and Chen Shen. 1998. "The Origin of Rice Agriculture: Recent Progress in East Asia." *Antiquity* 72:858-66.

Csikszentmihalyi, Mihaly. 1990. *Flow: The Psychology of Optimal Experience*. New York: Harper & Row.

Cunnar, Geoffrey. 2013. "A Study of *Lian* Sickles and *Dao* Knives from the Longshan Culture Site of Liangchengzhen in Southeastern Shandong." In *A Companion to Chinese Archaeology*, edited by Anne P. Underhill, 459-72. Malden, Mass.: Wiley-Blackwell.

Damerow, Peter. 1996. "Food Production and Social Status as Documented in Proto-Cuneiform Texts." In *Food and the Status Quest: An Interdisciplinary Perspective*, edited by Polly Wiessner and Wulf Schiefenhövel, 149-70. Oxford: Berghahn Books.

Davenport, Demorest, and Michael A. Jochim. 1988. "The Scene in the Shaft at Lascaux." *Antiquity* 62:558-62.

Davis, Donald D. 2004. "The Tao of Leadership in Virtual Teams." *Science Direct—Organizational Dynamics* 33.1.

Dawkin, Paul. 1976. *The Selfish Gene.* New York: Oxford University Press.

Dean, Kenneth. 2000. "Daoist Ritual Today." In *Daoism Handbook*, edited by Livia Kohn, 659-82. Leiden: Brill.

Despeux, Catherine. 1990. *Immortelles de la Chine ancienne. Taoïsme et alchimie feminine.* Paris: Pardes.

_____. 2000. "Women in Daoism." In *Daoism Handbook*, edited by Livia Kohn, 384-412. Leiden: Brill.

_____. 2007. "Food Prohibitions in China." *The Lantern* 4.1:22-32.

_____, and Livia Kohn. 2003. *Women in Daoism.* Cambridge, Mass.: Three Pines Press.

Diamond, Jared. 1987. "The Worst Mistake in the History of the Human Race." *Discover* May: 64-66.

_____. 1998. *Guns, Germs, and Steel: The Fates of Human Societies.* New York: W. W. Norton.

Diamond, John. 1979. *Behavioral Kinesiology: How to Activate Your Thymus and Increase Your Life Energy.* New York: Harper & Row.

DiCosmo, Nicola. 2002. *Ancient China and Its Enemies: The Rise of Nomadic Power in East Asian History.* Cambridge: Cambridge University Press.

Dietler, Michael. 1996. "Feasts and Commensal Politics in the Political Economy: Food, Power, and Status in Prehistoric Europe." In *Food and the Status Quest: An Interdisciplinary Perspective*, edited by Polly Wiessner and Wulf Schiefenhövel, 187-126 Oxford: Berghahn Books.

_____l. 2001. "Theorizing the Feast: Rituals of Consumption, Commensal Politics, and Power in African Contexts." In *Feasts: Archaeological and Ethonographic Perspectives on Food, Politics, and Power*, edited by Michael Dietler and Brian Hayden, 65-114. Washington, DC: Smithsonian Institution Press.

_____, and Ingrid Herbich. 2001. "Feasts and Labor Mobilization: Dissecting a Fundamental Economic Practice." In *Feasts: Archaeological and Ethonographic Perspectives on Food, Politics, and Power*, edited by Michael Dietler and Brian Hayden, 240-64. Washington, DC: Smithsonian Institution Press.

Domingo, I., P. Garcia-Borja, and C. Roldan. 2012. "Identification, Processing, and Use of Red Pigments (Hematite and Cinnabar) in the Valencian Early Neolithic (Spain)." *Archaeometry* 54.5:868-92.

Donald, Merlin. 2001. *A Mind So Rare: The Evolution of Human Consciousness.* New York: W. W. Norton.

Dor, Daniel. 2014. "The Instruction of Imagination: Language and Its Evolution as a Communication Technology." In *The Social Origins of Language*, edited by Daniel Dor, Chris Knight, and Jerome Lewis, 105-25. New York: Oxford University Press.

_____, and Eva Jablonka. 2014. "Why We Need to Move from Gene-Culture Co-Evolution to Culturally Driven Co-Evolution." In *The Social Origins of Language*, edited by Daniel Dor, Chris Knight, and Jerome Lewis, 15-30. New York: Oxford University Press.

Douglas, Mary. 1973. *Natural Symbols: Explorations in Cosmology*. New York: Pantheon Books.

_____. 1984. "Standard Social Uses of Food: Introduction." In *Food in the Social Order: Studies of Food and Festivities in Three American Communities*, 1-39. New York: Russell Sage Foundation.

_____, and Baron C. Isherwood. 1979. *The World of Goods: Towards an Anthropology of Consumption*. New York: Basic Books.

Down, Bernard. 2000. "Death in Classical Daoist Thought." *Philosophy Now* 27:1-4.

Dowson, Thomas A. and Martin Porr. 2001. "Special Objectes—Special Cultures: Shamanistic Imagery and the Aurignacian Art of South-West Germany." In *The Archaeology of Shamanism*, 165-77. New York: Routledge.

Dreher, Diane. 1996. *The Tao of Personal Leadership*. New York: HarperBusiness.

_____. 2000. *The Tao of Inner Peace*. New York: Penguin Books.

Duarte, Carlos M. 2014. "Red Ochre and Shells: Clues to Human Evolution." *Trends in Ecology and Evolution* 29.10:560-65.

Ducette, Dianna L. 2001. "Decoding the Gender Bias: Inferences of Atlatls in Female Mortuary Context." In *Gender and Chinese Archaeology*, edited by Katheryn M. Linduff and Yan Sun, 159-78. Walnut Creek: Alta Mira Press.

Dunn, Fredrick L. 1968. "Epidemiological Factors: Health and Disease in Hunter-Gatherers." In *Man the Hunter*, edited by Richard B. Lee and Irven DeVore, 221-28. Chicago: Aldine.

Durkheim, Emile. 1961. *The Elementary Forms of the Religious Life*. New York: Free Press.

Earle, Timothy. 1982. "The Ecology and Politics of Primitive Valuables." In *Culture and Ecology: Eclectic Perspectives*, edited by John G. Kennedy and Robert B. Edgerton, 65-83. Washington, DC: American Anthropological Association.

_____. 1991a. "The Evolution of Chiefdoms." In *Chiefdoms: Power, Economy, and Ideology*, edited by Timothy Earle, 1-15. Cambridge: Cambridge University Press.

_____. 1991b. "Property Rights and the Evolution of Chiefdoms." In *Chiefdoms: Power, Economy, and Ideology*, edited by Timothy Earle, 71-99. Cambridge: Cambridge University Press.

_____. 1997. *How Chiefs Come to Power: The Political Economy in Prehistory*. Stanford: Stanford University Press.

Eaton, S. Boyd. 1985. "Paleolithic Nutrition: A Consideration of Its Nature and Current Implication." *England Journal of Medicine* 312:283-89.

_____, Stanley B. Eaton III, and Loren Cordain. 2002. "Evolution, Diet, and Health." In *Human Diet: Its Origin and Evolution*, edited by Peter S. Ungar and Mark F. Teaford, 7-18. Westport, Conn.: Bergin & Garvey.

Edmonson, Amy C. 1987. *A Fuller Explanation: The Synergetic Geometry of R. Buckminster Fuller*. Boston: Birkhäuser.

Edwards, William Ellis. 1967. "The Late-Pleistocene Extinction and Diminution in Size of Many Mammalian Species." In *Pleistocene Extinctions: The Search for a Cause*, edited by Paul S. Martin and Herbert E. Wright, 141-54. New Haven: Yale University Press.

Eibl-Eibesfeldt, Irenäus. 1996. "The Evolution of Nurturant Dominance." In *Food and the Status Quest: An Interdisciplinary Perspective*, edited by Polly Wiessner and Wulf Schiefenhövel, 33-38. Oxford: Berghahn Books.

Eisler, Riane. 1987. *The Chalice and the Blade: Our History, Our Future*. San Francisco: Harper & Row.

_____. 1995. *Sacred Pleasure: Sex, Myth, and the Politics of the Body—New Paths to Power and Love*. San Francisco: HarperSanFrancisco.

Ekengren, Fredrik. 2013. "Contextualizing Grave Goods: Theoretical Perspectives and Methodological Implications." In *The Oxford Handbook of Archaeology of Death and Burial*, edited by Sarah Tarlow and Liv Nielsson Stutz, 173-92. New York: Oxford University Press.

Eliade, Mircea. 1964. *Shamanism: Archaic Techniques of Ecstasy*. Princeton: Princeton University Press, Bollingen Series 76.

_____. 1971. *The Myth of the Eternal Return: Cosmos and History*. Chicago: University of Chicago Press.

_____. 1978. *A History of Religions Ideas: From the Stone Age to the Eleusian Mysteries*. Chicago: University of Chicago Press.

Eller, Cynthia. 2000. *The Myth of Matriarchal Prehistory: Why an Invented Past Won't Give Women a Future*. Boston Beacon Press.

Engelhardt, Ute. 2000. "Longevity Techniques and Chinese Medicine." In *Daoism Handbook*, edited by Livia Kohn, 74-108. Leiden: E. Brill.

_____. 2001. "Dietetics in Tang China and the First Extant Works of *Materia Medica*." In *Innovation in Chinese Medicine*, edited by Elisabeth Hsu, 173-90. Cambridge: Cambridge University Press.

_____, and Rainer Nögel. 2009. *Rezepte der chinesischen Diätetik*. Munich: Urban & Fischer.

Eno, Robert. 1990. *The Confucian Creation of Heaven: Philosophy and the Defense of Ritual Mastery*. Albany: State University of Ne. Albany: State University of New York Press.

Enzinger, Irmgard. 2002. "Bedeutungen des Begriffes "Herz": Das Körper-Denken in *Mengzi* und *Zhuangzi*." *Monumenta Serica* 50:95-170.

Eriksson, Gunilla. 2013. "Stable Isotope Analysis of Humans." In *The Oxford Handbook of Archaeology of Death and Burial*, edited by Sarah Tarlow and Liv Nielsson Stutz, 123-46. New York: Oxford University Press.

Eskildsen, Stephen. 1998. *Asceticism in Early Taoist Religion*. Albany: State University of New York Press.

_____. 2004. *The Teachings and Practices of the Early Quanzhen Taoist Masters*. Albany: State University of New York Press.

Fabbro, D. 1978. "Peaceful Societies: An Introduction." *Journal of Peace Research* 12:67-84.

Falkenhausen, Lothar von. 1994. "Sources of Taoism: Reflections on Archaeological Indicators of Religious Change in Eastern Zhou China." *Taoist Resources* 5.2:1-12.

Fan, T. W., and Y. X. Zhu. 2003. "On Taoist Managerial Psychological Thoughts." *Advances in Psychological Sciences* 11.1:116-19.

Fang, Hui. 2013. "The Eastern Territories of the Shang and Western Zhou: Military Expansion and Cultural Assimilation." In *A Companion to Chinese Archaeology*, edited by Anne P. Underhill, 473-93. Malden, Mass.: Wiley-Blackwell.

Ferguson, Niall. 2013. *The Great Degeneration: How Institutions Decay and Economies Die*. New York: Penguin Press.

Ferguson, R. Brian. 1990. "Explaining War." In *The Anthropology of War*, edited by Jonathan Haas, 26-55. Cambridge: Cambridge University Press.

Ferguson, Yale H. 1991. "Chiefdoms to City-States: The Greek Experience." In *Chiefdoms: Power, Economy, and Ideology*, edited by Timothy Earle, 169-92. Cambridge: Cambridge University Press.

Fernandez-Armesto, Felipe. 2002. *Near a Thousand Tables: A History of Food*. New York: Free Press.

Ferruggia, Mike. 2016. "7 Rules of Taoist Leadership." *Applying the Practice of Tai Chi to Life as a Whole*. www.taichimike.wordpress.com

Fine, Cordelia. 2010. *Delusions of Gender: How Our Minds, Society, and Neurosexism Create Difference*. New York: W. W. Norton.

Finlay, Nyree. 2013. "Gender and Lithic Studies in Prehistoric Archaeology." In *A Companion to Gender Prehistory*, edited by Diane Bolger, 142-60. Malden, Mass.: Wiley-Blackwell.

Fisher, Elizabeth. 1979. *Woman's Creation: Sexual Evolution and the Shaping of Society*. New York: McGraw-Hill.

Flad, Rowan. 2013. "The Sichuan Basin Neolithic." In *A Companion to Chinese Archaeology*, edited by Anne P. Underhill, 125-46. Malden, Mass.: Wiley-Blackwell.

Flannery, Kent V. 1968. "Archaeological Systems Theory and Early Mesoamerica." In *Anthropological Archaeology in the Americas*, edited by Betty J. Meggers, 67-86. Washington, DC: Anthropological Society.

_____. 1969. "Origins and Ecological Effects of Early Domestication in Iran and the Near East." In *The Domestication and Exploitation of Plants and Animals*, edited by Peter J. Ucko and G. W. Dimbleby, 73-100. Chicago: Aldine.

Fogg, Wayne H. 1983. "Swidden Cultivation of Foxtail Millet by Taiwan Aborigines: A Cultural Analogue of the Domestication of *Setaria italica* in China." In *The Origins of Chinese Civilization*, edited by David N. Keightley, 95-115. Berkeley: University of California Press.

Foley, Robert A. 2001. "The Evolutionary Consequences of Increased Carnivory in Hominids." In *Meat Eating and Human Evolution*, edited by Craig B. Stanford and Henry T. Bunn, 305-31. New York: Oxford University Press.

Ford, Julian, and Jon Wortman. 2013. *Hijacked by Your Brain: How to Free Yourself When Stress Takes Over*. Naperville, Ill.: Sourcebooks.

Formicola, Vincenzo, Antonella Pontrandolfi, and Jiri Svoboda. 2001. "The Upper Paleolothic Triple Burial at Dolní Věstonice: Pathology and Funerary Behavior." *American Journal of Physical Anthropology* 115-372-79.

Fox, Michael Allen. 1999. *Deep Vegetarianism: America in Transition.* Philadelphia: Temple University Press.

Franks, David D. 2010. *Neurosociology: The Nexus between Neuroscience and Social Psychology.* New York: Springer.

Fraser, Chris. 2011a. "Emotion and Agency in *Zhuangzi*." *Asian Philosophy* 21.1:97-121.

_____. 2011b. "Wandering the Way: A Eudaimonistic Approach to the *Zhuangzi*." In *Happiness East and West: A Philosophical Dialogue*, edited by T. O'Leary. Hong Kong: Hong Kong University Press.

Fredrickson, Barbara L. 2006. "The Broaden-and-Build Theory of Positive Emotions." In *A Life Worth Living: Contributions to Positive Psychology*, edited by Mihaly Csikszentmihalyi and Isabella Selega Csikszentmihalyi, 85-103. New York: Oxford University Press.

Freeman, L. G., Jr. 1968. "A Theoretical Framework for Interpreting Archaeological Materials." In *Man the Hunter*, edited by Richard B. Lee and Irven DeVore, 262-67. Chicago: Aldine.

Freeman, Michael. 1977. "Sung." In *Food in Chinese Culture*, edited by K. C. Chang, 141-92. New Haven: Yale University Press.

French, Marilyn. 1985. *Beyond Power: On Men, Women, and Morals.* New York: Summit Books.

Freud, Sigmund. 1918. *Totem and Taboo.* New York, Vintage

Fried, Morton H. 1967. *The Evolution of Political Society: An Essay in Political Economy.* New York: Random House.

_____. 1983. "Tribe to State or State to Tribe in Ancient China." In *The Origins of Chinese Civilization*, edited by David N. Keightley, 467-93. Berkeley: University of California Press.

Fuentes, Oscar. 2013. "The Depiction of the Individual in Prehistory: Human Representations in Magdalenian Societies." *Antiquity* 87:985-1000.

Fuller, Buckminster. 1992. *Cosmography: A Posthumous Scenario for the Future of Humanity.* New York: Macmillan.

Fuller, Dorian Q. et al. 2009. "The Domestication Process and Domestication Rate in Rice: Spikelet Bases from the Lower Yangtse." *Science* 323:1607-10.

Fung, C. 2000. "The Drinks Are on Us: Ritual, Social Status, and Practice in Dawenkou Burials, North China." *Journal of East Asian Archaeology* 2:67-92.

Galvany, Albert. 2009. "Distorting the Rule of Seriousness: Laughter, Death, and Friendship in the *Zhuangzi*." *Dao: A Journal of Comparative Philosophy* 8.1:49-59.

_____. 2012. "Death and Ritual Wailing in Early China." *Asia Major* 25.2:15-42.

Gamble, Clive. 1999. *The Palaeolithic Societies of Europe.* Cambridge: Cambridge University Press.

_____. 2007. *Origins and Revolutions: Human Identity in Earliest Prehistory.* Cambridge: Cambridge University Press.

Gao, Xing. 2013. "Paleolithic Cultures in China: Uniqueness and Divergence." *Current Anthropology* 54.8:358-70.

Gazzaniga, Michael S. 2008. *Human: The Science behind What Makes Us Unique.* New York: HarperCollins.

Gedgaugas, Nora T. 2009. *Primal Body, Primal Mind: Beyond the Paleo Diet for Total Health and a Longer Life.* Rochester, VT: Healing Arts Press.

Gero, Joan M. 1991. "Genderlithics." in *Engendering Archaeology: Women in Prehistory*, edited by Joan M. Gero and Margaret W. Conkey, 163-93. Oxford: Basil Blackwell.

Giacobini, Giacomo. 2007. "Richness and Diversity of Burial Rituals in the Upper Paleolithic." *Diogenes* 214-19-39.

Gibson, Kathleen R. 2007. "Putting It All Together: A Constructionist Approach to the Evolution of Human Mental Capacities." In *Rethinking the Human Revolution: New Behavioral and Biological Perspectives on the Origin and Dispersal of Modern Humans*, edited by Paul Mellars, 67-78. Cambridge: McDonald Institute for Archaeological Research.

Gibson, Thomas. 1990. "Raiding, Trading, and Tribal Autonomy in Insular Southeast Asia." In *The Anthropology of War*, edited by Jonathan Haas, 125-45. Cambridge: Cambridge University Press.

Giddens, Anthony. 1984. *The Constitution of Society: Outline of the Theory of Structuration.* Berkeley: University of California Press.

Gilchrist, Roberta.1999. *Gender and Archaeology: Contesting the Past.* New York: Routledge.

Gimbutas, Marija. 1974. *The Goddesses and Gods of Old Europe, 6500-3500 BC: Myths and Cult Images.* Berkeley: University of California Press.

Girardot, Norman. 2008 [1983]. *Myth and Meaning in Early Taoism: The Theme of Chaos (Hundun).* Dunedin, Fla.: Three Pines Press.

Gladwell, Malcolm. 2002. *The Tipping Point: How Little Things Can Make a Big Difference.* Boston: Back Bay Books.

_____. 2005. *Blink: The Power of Thinking without Thinking.* New York: Back Bay Books.

_____. 2015. *David and Goliath: Underdogs, Misfits, and the Art of Battling Giants.* New York: Back Bay Books.

Gleiser, Marcelo. 2010. *A Tear at the Edge of Creation.* New York: Free Press.

Goepper, Roger. 1996. "Precursors and Early Stages of the Chinese Script." In *The Mysteries of Ancient China: New Discoveries from the Early Dynasties*, 273-81. London: British Museum.

Goh, Irving. 2011. "Chuang Tzu's Becoming Animal." *Philosophy East & West* 61.1:110-33.

Goldin, Paul R. 2003. "A Mind-Body Problem in the *Zhuangzi*?" In *Hiding the World in the World: Uneven Discourses on the Zhuangzi*, edited by Scott Cook, 226-47. Albany: State University of New York Press.

Goldman, I. 1970. *Ancient Polynesian Society.* Chicago: University of Chicago Press.

Goodison, Lucy, and Christine Morris. 2013. "Goddesses in Prehistory." In *A Companion to Gender Prehistory*, edited by Diane Bolger, 265-87. Malden, Mass.: Wiley-Blackwell.

Goody, Jack. 1982. *Cooking, Cuisine and Class: A Study in Comparative Sociology*. Cambridge: Cambridge University Press.

Goullart, Peter. 1961. *The Monastery of Jade Mountain*. London: John Murray.

Graham, A. C. 1960. *The Book of Lieh-tzu*. London: A. Murray.

_____. 1981. *Chuang-tzu: The Seven Inner Chapters and Other Writings from the Book of Chuang-tzu*. London: Allan & Unwin.

_____. 1990a. "The *Nung-chia* 'School of the Tillers' and the Origins of Peasant Utopianism in China." In *Studies in Chinese Philosophy and Philosophical Literature*, edited by A. C. Graham, 67-124. Albany: State University of New York Press.

_____. 1990b. "The Origins of the Legend of Lao Tan." In *Studies in Chinese Philosophy and Philosophical Literature*, edited by A. C. Graham, 111-24. Albany: State University of New York Press.

Greenspan, Stanley I., and Stuart G. Shanker. 2004. *The First Idea: How Symbols, Language, and Intelligence Evolved from Our Primate Ancestors to Modern Humans*. Cambridge, Mass.: Da Capo Press.

Gregor, Thomas. 1990. "Uneasy Pease: Intertribal Relations in Brazil's Upper Xingu." In *The Anthropology of War*, edited by Jonathan Haas, 105-24. Cambridge: Cambridge University Press.

Grey, Sir George. 1841. *Journals of Two Expeditions of Discovery in North-West and Western Australia, During the Years 1837, 38, and 39*. 2 vols. London: Boone.

Guilday, John E. 1967. "Differential Extinction during the late Pleistocene and Recent Times." In *Pleistocene Extinctions: The Search for a Cause*, edited by Paul S. Martin and Herbert E. Wright, 121-40. New Haven: Yale University Press.

Gulik, Robert H. van. 1961. *Sexual Life in Ancient China*. Leiden: E. Brill.

Guo, Ruihai, and Li Jun. 2002. "The Nanzhuangtou and Hutouliang Sites: Exploring the Beginnings of Agriculture and Pottery in North China." In *The Origins of Pottery and Agriculture*, edited by Yoshinori Yasuda, 193-204. New Delhi: Roli Books.

Gusinde, Martin. 1961. *The Yamana*. 5 vols. New Haven, Conn.: Human Relations Area Files.

Haas, Jonathan. 1981. "Class Conflict and the State in the New World."In *The Transition to Statehood in the New World*, edited by Grant D. Jones and Robert Kautz, 80-102. Cambridge: Cambridge University Press.

_____. 1982. *The Evolution of the Prehistoric State*. New York: Columbia University Press.

_____. 1990. "Warfare and the Evolution of Tribal Policies in the Prehistoric Southwest." In *The Anthropology of War*, edited by Jonathan Haas, 171-89. Cambridge: Cambridge University Press.

_____. 2001a. "Cultural Evolution and Political Centralization." In *From Leaders to Rulers*, edited by Jonathan Haas, 3-18. New York: Kluwer Academic.

_____. 2001b. "Nonlinear Paths of Political Centralization." In *From Leaders to Rulers*, edited by Jonathan Haas, 235-44. New York: Kluwer Academic.

Hahn, Thomas H. 1988. "The Standard Taoist Mountain and Related Features of Religious Geography." *Cahiers d'Extrême-Asie* 4: 145-56.

_____. 2000. "Daoist Sacred Sites." In *Daoism Handbook*, edited by Livia Kohn, 683-707. Leiden: E. Brill.

Hall, David L. 2001. "From Reference to Deference: Daoism and the Natural World." In *Daoism and Ecology: Ways within a Cosmic Landscape*, edited by Norman Girardot, James Miller, and Liu Xiaogan, 245-64. Cambridge, Mass.: Harvard University Press, Center for the Study of World Religions.

_____, and Roger T. Ames. 1998. *Thinking from the Han: Self, Truth, and Transcendence in Chinese and Western Culture*. Albany: State University of New York Press.

Hanks, L. 1972. *Rice and Man*. Chicago: Aldine.

Hansen, Chad. 1992. *A Daoist Theory of Chinese Thought: A Philosophical Interpretation*. New York: Oxford University Press.

_____. 2010 [1983]. "A Dao of 'Dao' in *Zhuangzi*." In *Experimental Essays on Zhuangzi*, edited by Victor H. Mair, 23-55. Dunedin, Fla.: Three Pines Press.

Harlan, Jack A. 1967. "A Wild Wheat Harvest in Turkey." *Archaeology* 20:197-201.

_____. 1977. "The Origins of Cereal Agriculture in the Old World." In *Origins of Agriculture*, edited by Charles A. Reed, 357-86. The Hague: Mouton.

Harper, Donald. 1998. *Early Chinese Medical Manuscripts: The Mawangdui Medical Manuscripts*. London: Wellcome Asian Medical Monographs.

Harris, David R. 1977. "Alternative Pathways toward Agriculture." In *Origins of Agriculture*, edited by Charles A. Reed, 179-244. The Hague: Mouton.

Harris, Marvin. 1977. *Cannibals and Kings: The Origins of Culture*. New York: Random House.

_____. 1985. *The Sacred Cow and the Abominable Pig: Riddles of Food and Culture*. New York: Simon & Schuster.

_____. 1993. "The Evolution of Human Gender Hierarchies: A Trial Formulation." In *Sex and Gender Hierarchies*, edited by Barbara Diane Miller, 57-79. Cambridge: Cambridge University Press.

Harrold, Francis B. 1980. "A Comparative Analysis of Eurasian Paleolithic Burials." *World Archaeology* 12.2:195-211.

Harrod, Ryan P., Pierre Lienard, and Debra L. Martin. 2012. "Deciphering Violence in Past Societies: Ethnography and a Cast Study." In *The Bioarchaeology of Violence*, edited by Debra Martin, Ryan P. Harrod, and Ventura R. Perez, 63-80. Gainesville: University Press of Florida.

Hart, Donna, and Robert W. Sussman. 2005. *Man the Hunted: Primates, Predators, and Human Evolution*. New York: Westview Press.

Harth, Erich. 1993. *The Creative Loop: How the Brain Makes a Mind*. Reading, Mass.: Addison-Wesley.

Harvati-Papatheodorou, Katerina. 2013. "Neanderthals." In *A Companion to Paleoanthropology*, edited by David R. Begun, 538-56. Malden, Mass.: Wiley-Blackwell.

Hatch, Mallorie A. 2012. "Meaning and the Bioarchaeology of Captivity, Sacrifice, and Cannibalism: A Case Study from the Mississippian Period at Larson, Illinois." In *The Bioarchaeology of Violence*, edited by Debra Martin, Ryan P. Harrod, and Ventura R. Perez, 201-25. Gainesville: University Press of Florida.

Hawkes, David. 1985 [1959]. *Ch'u Tz'u: The Songs of the South*. London: Penguin Books.

Hawkes, Kristen. 2001. "Is Meat the Hunter's Property? Big Game, Ownership, and Explanations of Hunting and Sharing." In *Meat Eating and Human Evolution*, edited by Craig B. Stanford and Henry T. Bunn, 219-36. New York: Oxford University Press.

Hawkins, David R. 2006. *Transcending the Levels of Consciousness: The Stairway to Enlightenment*. Sedona: Veritas.

Hayden, Brian. 1990. "Nimrods, Piscators, Pluckers, and Planters: The Emergence of Food Production." *Journal of Anthropological Archaeology* 9:31-69.

_____. 1995. "A New Overview of Domestication." In *Last Hunters—First Farmers*, edited by Douglas B. Price and Anna B. Gebauer, 273-99. Santa Fe: School of American Research Press.

_____. 1996. "Feasting in Preshistoric and Traditional Societies." In *Food and the Status Quest: An Interdisciplinary Perspective*, edited by Polly Wiessner and Wulf Schiefenhövel, 127-48. Oxford: Berghahn Books.

_____. 2001. "Fabulous Feasts: A Prolegomenon to the Importance of Feasting." In *Feasts: Archaeological and Ethonographic Perspectives on Food, Politics, and Power*, edited by Michael Dietler and Brian Hayden, 23-64. Washington, DC: Smithsonian Institution Press.

_____. 2009. "Funerals as Feasts: Why Are They So Important?" *Cambridge Archaeological Journal* 19.1:29-52.

_____. 2011. "Rice: The First Asian Luxury Food?" In *Why Cultivate? Anthropological and Archaeological Approaches to Foraging-Farming Transitions in Southeast Asia*, edited by Graeme Barker and Monica Janowski, 75-94. Cambridge: McDonald Institute Monographs.

Hays-Gilpin, Kelley. 2013. "Gender and Prehistoric Rock Art." In *A Companion to Gender Prehistory*, edited by Diane Bolger, 122-41. Malden, Mass.: Wiley-Blackwell.

He Jianming 何建明. 2016. "Daojiao 'bugan wei tianxia xian' de lishi chanshi" 道教不敢为天下先的历史阐释. Third International Symposium on Quanzhen Daoism and Lao-Zhuang Studies, 480-90. Wuhan: Huazhong Normal University.

He, Nu. 2013. "The Longshan Period Site of Taosi in Southern Shanxi Province." In *A Companion to Chinese Archaeology*, edited by Anne P. Underhill, 255-77. Malden, Mass.: Wiley-Blackwell.

Heider, John. 1985. *Tao of Leadership: Lao Tzu's Tao te ching Adapted for a New Age*. Atlanta: Humanics New Age.

Heilbrun, Carolyn G. 1973. *Toward a Recognition of Androgyny*. New York: Alfred A. Knopf.

_____. 1981. *Human Sex-Role Behavior*. New York: Pergamon.

Helvenston, Patricia A. 2015. "Psilocybin-Containing Mushrooms, Upper Paleolithic Rock Art, and the Neuropsychological Model." *Rock Art Research* 32.1:84-115.

Hendrischke, Barbara. 1991. "The Concept of Inherited Evil in the *Taiping Jing*." *East Asian History* 2:1-30.

_____. 2000. "Early Daoist Movements." In *Daoism Handbook*, edited by Livia Kohn, 134-64. Leiden: Brill.

_____. 2006. *The Scripture on Great Peace: The Taiping jing and the Beginnings of Daoism.* Berkeley: University of California Press.

_____, and Benjamin Penny. 1996. "*The 180 Precepts Spoken by Lord Lao*: A Translation and Textual Study." *Taoist Resources* 6.2:17-29.

Henrich, Natalie, and Joseph Henrich. 2007. *Why Humans Cooperate: A Cultural and Revolutionary Explanation.* New York: Oxford University Press.

Henry, Donald O. 1985. "Preagricultural Sedentism: The Natufian Example." In *Prehistoric Hunter-Gatherers: The Emergence of Cultural Complexity*, edited by T. Douglas Price and James A. Brown, 365-84. New York: Academic Press.

Henschilwood. Christopher. 2011. "A 100,000 Year Old Ochre-Processing Plant at Blombos Cave, South Africa." *Science* 334.

Herre, Wolf, and Manfred Röhrs. 1977. "Zoological Considerations on the Origins of Farming and Domestication." In *Origins of Agriculture*, edited by Charles A. Reed, 245-80. The Hague: Mouton.

Herrou, Adeline. 2013. *A World of Their Own: Monastics and Their Community in Contemporary China.* St. Petersburg, Fla: Three Pines Press.

Higham, Charles. 1995. "The Transition to Rice Cultivation in Southeast Asia." In *Last Hunters—First Farmers*, edited by Douglas B. Price and Anna B. Gebauer, 127-56. Santa Fe: School of American Research Press.

_____. 2005a. "East Asian Agriculture and Its Impact." In *The Human Past: World Prehistory and the Development of Human Societies*, edited by Chris Scarre, 234-63. London: Thames & Hudson.

_____. 2005b. "Complex Societies of East and Southeast Asia." In *The Human Past: World Prehistory and the Development of Human Societies*, edited by Chris Scarre, 552-94. London: Thames & Hudson.

Hillery, George A. 1992. *The Monastery: A Study in Love, Freedom, and Community.* Westport, CT: Praeger.

Hitchcock, R. 1982. "Patterns of Sedentism among the Basarwa of Eastern Botswana." In *Politics and History in Band Societies*, edited by E. Leacock and Richard B. Lee, 223-68. Cambridge: Cambridge University Press.

Ho, Ping-ti. 1969. "The Loess and the Origin of Chinese Agriculture." *American Historical Review* 75:1-36.

_____. 1975. *The Cradle of the East: An Inquiry into the Indigenous Origins of Techniques and Ideas of Neolithic and Early Historic China, 5000-1000 B.C.* Chicago: University of Chicago Press.

_____. 1977. "The Indigenous Origins of Chinese Agriculture." In *Origins of Agriculture*, edited by Charles A. Reed, 413-84. The Hague: Mouton.

Hodgskiss, Tammy. 2014. "Cognitive Requirements for Ochre Use in the Middle Stone Age at Sibudu, South Africa." *Cambridge Archaeological Journal* 24.3:405-28.

Hodgson, Derek. 2000. "Shamanism, Phosphenes, and Early Art: An Alternative Synthesis." *Current Anthropology* 41.5:866-73.

_____. 2006. "Altered States of Consciousness and Paleo Art: An Alternative Neurovisual Explanation." *Cambridge Archaeological Journal* 16.1:27-37.

Hohmann, Gottfried, and Barbara Fruth. 1986. "Food Sharing and Status in Unprovisioned Bonobos." In *Food and the Status Quest: An Interdisciplinary Perspective*, edited by Polly Wiessner and Wulf Schiefenhövel, 47-68. Oxford: Berghahn Books.

Hold-Cavell, Barbara. 1996. "The Ethological Bases of Status Hierarchies." In *Food and the Status Quest: An Interdisciplinary Perspective*, edited by Polly Wiessner and Wulf Schiefenhövel, 19-32. Oxford: Berghahn Books.

Hopkins, Bobbi Paige. 2013. "The Bible as a Medium for Social Engineering: Jesus as Androgynous Role Model."*Journal of Research in Gender Studies* 3.1:78-87.

Hovers, Erella, Shimon Ilani, Ofer Bar-Yosef, and Bernard Vandermeersch. 2003. "An Early Case of Color Symbolism: Ochre Use by Modern Humans in Qafzeh Cave." *Current Anthropology* 44.4:491-522.

Howells, W. W. 1983. "Origins of the Chinese People: Interpretations of Recent Evidence." In *The Origins of Chinese Civilization*, edited by David N. Keightley, 177-216. Berkeley: University of California Press.

Hrdy, Sarah Blaffer. 1999. *Mother Nature.* New York: Pantheon Books.

Huang, Hsing-Tsung. 2000. *Fermentation and Food Science.* In *Science and Civilisation in China*, vol. VI, part 5. Cambridge: Cambridge University Press.

Huang, Shih-Shan Susan. 2010. "Daoist Imagery of Body and Cosmos, Part 1: Body Gods and Starry Travel." *Journal of Daoist Studies* 3:57-90.

_____. 2011. "Daoist Imagery of Body and Cosmos, Part 2: Body Worms and Internal Alchemy *Journal of Daoist Studies* 4:32-62.

_____. 2012. *Picturing the True Form: Daoist Visual Culture in Traditional China.* Cambridge, Mass.: Harvard University, Center for Chinese Studies.

Huber, Joan. 2007. *On the Origins of Gender Inequality.* Boulder: Paradigm.

Huber, Louisa G. Fitzgerald. 1983. "The Relationship of the Painted Pottery of the Longshan Cultures." In *The Origins of Chinese Civilization*, edited by David N. Keightley, 177-216. Berkeley: University of California Press.

Hunt, Morton. 1973. "Man and Beast." In *Man and Aggression*, edited by Ashley Montagu, 21-38. New York: Oxford University Press.

Hutson, Scott E., Bryan K. Hanks, and K. Anne Pyburn. 2013. "Gender, Complexity, and Power in Prehistory." In *A Companion to Gender Prehistory*, edited by Diane Bolger, 45-67. Malden, Mass.: Wiley-Blackwell.

Ingold, Tim. 1993. The Temporality of the Landscape." *World Archaeology* 25:152-73.

Ip, Po Keung. 1983. "Taoism and the Foundation of Environmental Ethics." *Environmental Ethics* 5:335-43.

Ishida, Hidemi. 1989. "Body and Mind: The Chinese Perspective." In *Taoist Meditation and Longevity Techniques*, edited by Livia Kohn, 41-70. Ann Arbor: University of Michigan, Center for Chinese Studies.

Jackowicz, Stephen. 2006. "Ingestion, Digestion, and Regestation: The Complexities of the Absorption of *Qi*." In *Daoist Body Cultivation*, edited by Livia Kohn, 68-90. Magdalena, NM: Three Pines Press.

Janus, Christopher G. 1975. *The Search for Peking Man.* New York: Macmillan.

Jarzombek, Mark. 2013. *Architecture of First Societies: A Global Perspective.* Hoboken: Wiley.

Jaspers, Karl. 1953. *The Origin and Goal of History.* New Haven, Conn.: Yale University Press.

Jaynes, Julian. 1990 [1976]. *The Origins of Consciousness in the Breakdown of the Bicameral Mind.* Boston: Houghton Mifflin.

_____. 2006. "Verbal Hallucinations and Preconscious Mentality." In *Reflections on the Dawn of Consciousness: Julian Jaynes's Bicameral Mind Theory Revisited*, edited by Marcel Kuijsten, 75-94. Henderson, Nev.: Julian Jaynes Society.

Jèguez-Wolkiewiez, Chantal. 2011. *Sur les chemins étoilés de Lascaux.* Hyères: La Pierre philosphale.

_____l. 2015. *L'ethnoastronomie, nouvelle appréhension de l'art préhistorique: Comment l'art paléolithique révèle l'ordre caché de l'univers.* Cagnes-sur-Mer: Chantal Jèguez-Wolkiewiez.

Jelinek, Arthur J. 1967. "Man's Role in the Extinction of Pleistocene Faunas." In *Pleistocene Extinctions: The Search for a Cause*, edited by Paul S. Martin and Herbert E. Wright, 193-200. New Haven: Yale University Press.

Jia, Jinhua. 2017. *A Career of Their Own: Daoist Priestesses in Tang China (618-907).* New York: Columbia University Press.

Jiang, Leping. 2013. "The Kuahuqiao Site and Culture." In *A Companion to Chinese Archaeology*, edited by Anne P. Underhill, 537-54. Malden, Mass.: Wiley-Blackwell.

Jiang, Yu. 2004. "Ritual Practice, Status, and Gender Identity: Western Zhou Tombs at Baoji." In *Gender and Chinese Archaeology*, edited by Katheryn M. Linduff and Yan Sun, 117-36. Walnut Creek, Calif.: Alta Mira Press.

Jiao, Tianlong. 2001. "Gender Studies in Chinese Neolithic Archaeology." In *Gender and the Archaeology of Death*, edited by Bettina Arnold and Nancy L. Wicker, 51-62. Walnut Creek, Calif.: Alta Mira Press.

_____. 2007. *The Neolithic of Southeast China: Cultural Transformation and Regional Interaction on the Coast.* Youngstown, NY: Cambria Press.

_____. 2013. "The Neolithic Archaology of Southeast China." In *A Companion to Chinese Archaeology*, edited by Anne P. Underhill, 599-611 Malden, Mass.: Wiley-Blackwell.

Jing, Zhichun, Jigen Tang, George Rapp, and James Stoltman. 2013. "Recent Discoveries and Some Thoughts on Early Urbanization at Anyang." In *A Companion to Chinese Archaeology*, edited by Anne P. Underhill, 343-66. Malden, Mass.: Wiley-Blackwell.

Jochim, Chris. 1998. "Just Say No to "No Self" in *Zhuangzi*." In *Wandering at Ease in the Zhuangzi*, edited by Roger Ames, 34-74. Albany: State University of New York Press.

Johnson, Allan G. 2014. *The Gender Knot: Unraveling Our Patriarchal Legacy*. Philadelphia: Temple University Press.

Johnson, Allen. 1982. "Nonreductionist Cultural Ecology." In *Culture and Ecology: Eclectic Perspectives*, edited by John G. Kennedy and Robert B. Edgerton, 18-25. Washington, DC: American Anthropological Association.

Johnson, Craig E. 1999. "Emerging Perspectives in Leadership Ethics." www.academy.umd.edu/ila/publications/proceedings/1999/cjohnson.pdf

Joiner, Bill, and Stephen Josephs. 2007. *Leadership Agility: Five Levels of Mastery for Anticipating and Initiating Change*. Hoboken: John Wiley & Sons.

Jolly, Alison. 1999. *Lucy's Legacy: Sex and Intelligence in Human Evolution*. Cambridge, Mass.: Harvard University Press.

Jones, David, and John Culliney. 1999. "The Fractal Self and the Organization of Nature: The Daoist Sage and Chaos Theory." *Zygon: Journal of Science and Religion* 4:643-54.

Jones, Grant D., and Robert Kautz. 1981. "Issues in the Study of New World State Formation."In *The Transition to Statehood in the New World*, edited by Grant D. Jones and Robert Kautz, 3-34. Cambridge: Cambridge University Press.

Jones, Martin. 2007. *Feast: Why Humans Share Food*. New York: Oxford University Press.

Joordens, Steve. 2011. *Memory and the Human Lifespan*. Chantilly, VA: The Great Courses.

Josephs, Stephen. 2013. *Dragons at Work*. Charleston: Tao Alchemical Press.

Joyce, Rosemary A. 1996. "The Construction of Gender in Classic Maya Monuments." In *Gender and Archaeology*, edited by Rita P. Wright, 167-95. Philadelphia: University of Pennsylvania Press.

______. 2008. *Ancient Bodies, Ancient Lives: Sex, Gender, and Archaeology*. London: Thames & Hudson.

Jullien, François. 1995. *The Propensity of Things: Toward a History of Efficacy in China*. New York: Zone Books.

______. 2007. *Vital Nourishment: Departing from Happiness*. Translated by Arthur Goldhammer. New York: Zone Books.

Jung, Carl Gustav. 1941. *The Integration of the Personality*. London: Kegan Paul.

______. 1949. "The Archetypes and the Collective Unconscious." In *The Collected Works of C. G. Jung*, edited by M. F. Herbert Reed and Gerhard Adler, vol. 9. London: Routledge.

Just, Peter. 1991. "Conflict Resolution and Moral Community among the Dou Donggo." In *Conflict Resolution: Cross-Cultural Perspectives*, edited by Kevin Avruch, Peter W. Black, and Joseph A. Scimecca, 107-44. New York: Greenwood Press.

Kafatos, Menas, and Robert Nadeau. 2000. *The Conscious Universe: Parts and Whole in Modern Physical Theory.* Berlin: Springer Verlag.

Kahn, Miriam. 1986. *Always Hungry, Never Greedy: Food and the Expression of Gender in a Melanesian Society.* Cambridge: Cambridge University Press.

Kaltenmark, Max. 1953. *Le Lie-sien tchouan.* Peking: Université de Paris Publications.

_____. 1979. "The Ideology of the *T'ai-p'ing-ching.*" In *Facets of Taoism*, edited by Holmes Welch and Anna Seidel, 19-52. New Haven: Yale University Press.

Kanter, Rosabeth Moss. 1972. *Commitment and Community: Communes and Utopias in Sociological Perspective.* Cambridge, Mass.: Harvard University Press.

Kaplan, Alexandra G., and Joan P. Bean, eds. 1976. *Beyond Sex-Role Stereotypes: Readings toward a Psychology of Androgyny.* Boston: Little, Brown.

Karetzky, Patricia Eichenbaum. 2015. "The Transformations of Zhenwu/Xuanwu." *Journal of Daoist Studies* 8:70-96.

Keates, Susan G., and Yaroslav V. Kuzmin. 2015. "Shuidonggou Localities 1 and 2 in Northern China: Archaeology and Chronology of the Initial Upper Paleolithic in North-East Asia." Antiquity 89:714-20.

Keeley, Lawrence H. 1995. "Protoagricultural Practices among Hunter-Gatherers: A Cross-Cultural Survey." In *Last Hunters—First Farmers*, edited by Douglas B. Price and Anna B. Gebauer, 243-72. Santa Fe: School of American Research Press.

_____. 1996. *War Before Civilization.* New York: Oxford University Press.

Kei, Yee Mei. 2012. "The Middle Paleolithic in China: A Review of Current Interpretations." *Antiquity* 86:619-26.

Keightley, David N. 1978a. *Sources of Shang History: The Oracle Bone Inscriptions of Bronze Age China.* Berkeley: University of California Press.

_____. 1978b. "The Religious Commitment: Shang Theology and the Genesis of Chinese Political Culture." *History of Religions* 17: 211-25.

_____. 1983. "The Late Shang State: When, Where, What?" In *The Origins of Chinese Civilization*, edited by David N. Keightley, 523-64. Berkeley: University of California Press.

_____. 1987. "Archaeology and Mentality: The Making of China." *Representations* 18:91-128.

_____. 1996. "Art, Ancestors, and the Origins of Writing." *Representations* 56:68-95.

_____. 1998. "Shamanism, Death, and the Ancestors: Religious Mediation in Neolithic and Shang China." *Asiatische Studien* 52:763-831

_____. 1998. "Shamanism, Death, and the Ancestors: Religious Mediation in Neolithic and Shang China." *Asiatische Studien* 52:763-831.

_____. 1999. "Women in Late Neolithic and Shang Period in China." *Nannü* 1:1-63.

_____. 2000. *The Ancestral Landscape: Time, Space, and Community in Late Shang China, ca. 1200-1054 BC.* Berkeley: University of California Press.

Kelly, Raymond C. 2000. *Peaceful Societies and the Origin of War.* Ann Arbor: University of Michigan Press.

Kenton, Leslie, and Susannah Kenton. 1984. *Raw Energy*. New York: Warner Books.

Kenyon, Kathleen M. 1957. *Digging Up Jericho: The Results of the Jericho Excavations, 1952-56*. New York: Praeger.

Keysers, Christian. 2009. "Mirror Neurons: Are We Ethical by Nature?" In *What's Next? Dispatches on the Future of Science*, edited by Max Brockman, 16-24. New York: Vintage Books.

_____. 2011. *The Empathic Brain: How the Discovery of Mirror Neurons Changes Our Understanding of Human Nature*. Lexington, KY: Social Brain Press.

Kimura, Ryosuke. 2015. "Human Migrations and Adaptations in Asia Inferred from Genome Diversity." In *Emergence and Diversity of Human Behavior in Paleolithic Asia*, edited by Yosuke Kaifu, Masami Izuho, Ted Goebel, Hiroyuki Sato, and Akira Ono, 34-50. College Station: Texas A & M University Press.

Kirkland, J. Russell. 2004. *Taoism: The Enduring Tradition*. New York: Routledge.

Klama, John. 1988. *Aggression: The Myth of the Beast Within*. New York: John Wiley & Sons.

Klaus, Haagen D. 2012. "The Bioarchaeology of Structural Violence: A Theoretical Model and a Case Study." In *The Bioarchaeology of Violence*, edited by Debra Martin, Ryan P. Harrod, and Ventura R. Perez, 29-62. Gainesville: University Press of Florida.

Kleeman, Terry F. 1994. "Licentious Cults and Bloody Victuals: Sacrifice, Religious Practice, and Violence in Traditional China." *Asia Major* (3rd Ser.) 7:185-211.

_____. 1998. *Great Perfection: Religion and Ethnicity in a Chinese Millenarian Kingdom*. Honolulu: University of Hawaii Press.

_____. 2002. "Ethnic Identity and Daoist Identity in Traditional China." In *Daoist Identity: History, Lineage, and Ritual*, edited by Livia Kohn and Harold D. Roth, 23-38. Honolulu: University of Hawaii Press.

_____. 2005. "Feasting without the Victuals: The Evolution of the Daoist Community Kitchen." In *Of Tripod and Palate: Food, Politics and Religion in Traditional China*, edited by Roel Sterckx, 140-62. New York: Palgrave MacMillan.

_____. 2016. *Celestial Masters: History and Ritual in Early Daoist Communities*. Cambridge, Mass.: Harvard Yenching Institute.

Klein, R. G., and B. Edgar. 2002. *The Dawn of Human Culture*. New York: John Wiley.

Klein, Richard. 1999. *The Human Career*. Chicago: University of Chicago Press.

_____. 2005. "Hominin Dispersal in the Old World." In *The Human Past: World Prehistory and the Development of Human Societies*, edited by Chris Scarre, 84-123. London: Thames & Hudson.

Knoblock, John, and Jeffrey Riegel. 2000. *The Annals of Lü Buwei*. Stanford: Stanford University Press.

Knott, Cheryl D. 2009. "Orangutans: Sexual Coercion without Sexual Violence." In *Sexual Coercion in Primates and Humans: An Evolutionary Perspective on Male Aggression against Females*, edited by Martin N. Muller and Richard W. Wrangham, 81-111. Cambridge, Mass.: Harvard University Press.

Kobayashi Masayoshi. 1992. "The Celestial Masters under the Eastern Jin and Liu-Song Dynasties." *Taoist Resources* 3.2: 17-45.

Kohn, Livia. 1991. "Taoist Visions of the Body." *Journal of Chinese Philosophy* 18:227-52.

_____. 1996. "The Looks of Laozi." *Asian Folklore Studies* 55.2:193-236.

_____. 1997. "Yin Xi: The Master at the Beginning of the Scripture." *Journal of Chinese Religions* 25:83-139.

_____. 1998a. *God of the Dao: Lord Lao in History and Myth.* University of Michigan, Center for Chinese Studies.

_____. 1998b. "The Beginnings and Cultural Characteristics of East Asian Millenarianism." *Japanese Religions* 23:29-51.

_____. 2000. "The Northern Celestial Masters." In *Daoism Handbook*, edited by Livia Kohn, 283-308. Leiden: Brill.

_____. 2003a. *Monastic Life in Medieval Daoism: A Cross-Cultural Perspective.* Honolulu: University of Hawaii Press.

_____. 2003b. "Monastic Rules in Quanzhen Daoism: As Collected by Heinrich Hackmann." *Monumenta Serica* 51:367-97.

_____. 2004a. *Cosmos and Community: The Ethical Dimension of Daoism.* Cambridge, Mass.: Three Pines Press.

_____. 2004b. *Supplement to Cosmos and Community.* Cambridge, Mass.: Three Pines Press. E-Dao Series (electronic publication).

_____. 2004c. *The Daoist Monastic Manual: A Translation of the Fengdao kejie.* New York: Oxford University Press.

_____. 2005. *Health and Long Life: The Chinese Way.* Cambridge, Mass.: Three Pines Press.

_____. 2006. "Introduction" In *Daoist Body Cultivation*, edited by Livia Kohn, 1-18. Magdalena, NM: Three Pines Press.

_____. 2010a. *Sitting in Oblivion: The Heart of Daoist Meditation.* Dunedin, Fla.: Three Pines Press.

_____. 2010b. *Daoist Dietetics: Food for Immortality.* Dunedin, Fla.: Three Pines Press.

_____. 2011. *Chuang-tzu: The Tao of Perfect Happiness. Selections Annotated and Explained.* Woodstock, VT: Skylight Paths Press.

_____. 2012. *A Source Book in Chinese Longevity.* St. Petersburg, Fla.: Three Pines Press.

_____. 2014. *Zhuangzi: Text and Context.* St. Petersburg, Fla.: Three Pines Press.

_____. 2015a. "Forget or Not Forget? The Neurophysiology of *Zuowang*." In *New Visions of the Zhuangzi*, edited by Livia Kohn, 161-79. St. Petersburg, Fla.: Three Pines Press.

_____. 2015b. "The Inspirational *Laozi*: Poetry, Business, and the Blues." *Journal of Daoist Studies* 8:137-51.

———. 2015c. "Kōshin: Expelling Taoist Demons with Buddhist Means." In *Daoism in Japan: Chinese Traditions and Their Influence on Japanese Religious Culture*, edited by Jeffrey L. Richey, 148-76. New York: Routledge.

———. 2016. *Science and the Dao: From the Big Bang to Lived Perfection.* St. Petersburg, Fla.: Three Pines Press.

Komjathy, Louis. 2007. *Cultivating Perfection: Mysticism and Self-Transformation in Quanzhen Daoism.* Leiden: Brill.

Kondo, Marie. 2014. *The Life-Changing Magic of Tidying Up: The Japanese Art of Decluttering and Organizing.* Berkeley: Ten Speed Press.

Kotani, Yoshinobu. 1981. "Evidence of Plant Cultivation in Jōmon Japan: Some Implications." In *Affluent Foragers: Pacific Coasts East and West*, edited by Shuzo Koyama and David Hurst Thomas, 201-12. Senri: Senri Ethnological Studies.

Koyama, Shuzo, and David Hurst Thomas, eds. 1981. *Affluent Foragers: Pacific Coasts East and West.* Senri: Senri Ethnological Studies.

Kristiansen, Kristian. 1991. "Chiefdoms, States, and Systems of Social Evolution." In *Chiefdoms: Power, Economy, and Ideology*, edited by Timothy Earle, 16-43. Cambridge: Cambridge University Press.

Kroll, Paul W. 1996. "Body Gods and Inner Vision: *The Scripture of the Yellow Court.* In *Religions of China in Practice*, edited by Donald S. Lopez Jr., 149-55. Princeton: Princeton University Press.

Kuhn, Steven L. and Mary C. Stiner. 2007. "Body Ornamentation as Information Technology: Towards an Understanding of the Significance of Early Beads." In *Rethinking the Human Revolution: New Behavioral and Biological Perspectives on the Origin and Dispersal of Modern Humans*, edited by Paul Mellars, 45-54. Cambridge: McDonald Institute for Archaeological Research.

Kupperman, Joel. 1996. "Spontaneity and Education of the Emotions in the *Zhuangzi.*" In *Essays on Skepticism, Relativism, and Ethics in the Zhuangzi*, edited by Paul Kjellberg and Philip J. Ivanhoe, 183-95. Albany: State University of New York Press.

Kuriyama, Shigehisa. 1994. "The Imagination of Winds and the Development of the Chinese Conception of the Body." In *Body, Subject, and Power in China*, edited by Angela Zito and Tani E. Barlow, 23-41. Chicago: University of Chicago Press.

———. 1999. *The Expressiveness of the Body and the Divergence of Greek and Chinese Medicine.* New York: Zone Books.

LaFargue, Michael. 2001. "'Nature' as Part of Human Culture in Daoism." In *Daoism and Ecology: Ways within a Cosmic Landscape*, edited by Norman Girardot, James Miller, and Liu Xiaogan, 45-60. Cambridge, Mass.: Harvard University Press, Center for the Study of World Religions.

Lai, Chi-tim. 2002. "The *Demon Statutes of Nüqing* and the Problem of the Bureaucratization of the Netherworld in Early Heavenly Master Daoism." *T'oung Pao* 88:251-81.

———. 2010. "The Ideas of Illness, Healing, and Morality in Early Heavenly Master Daoism." In *Philosophy and Religion in Early Medieval China*, edited by Alan Chan and Yuet-Keung Lo, 173-202. Albany: State University of New York Press.

Lake, Mark. 1998. "*Homo*: The Creative Genius?" In *Creativity in Human Evolution and Prehistory*, edited by Steven Mithen, 125-42. London: Routledge.

Larsen, Clark Spencer. 2002. "Post-Pleistocene Human Evolution: Bioarchaelology of the Agricultural Transition." In *Human Diet: Its Origin and Evolution*, edited by Peter S. Ungar and Mark F. Teaford, 19-36. Westport, Conn.: Bergin & Garvey.

Laughlin, William S. 1968. "Hunting: An Integrating Beobehavior System and Its Evolutionary Importance." In *Man the Hunter*, edited by Richard B. Lee and Irven DeVore, 304-20. Chicago: Aldine.

Lawlor, Robert. 1991. *Voices of the First Day: Awakening in the Aboriginal Dreamtime*. Rochester, VT: Inner Traditions.

Layton, Robert. 1998. "Creative Thought in Traditional Aboriginal Society." In *Creativity in Human Evolution and Prehistory*, edited by Steven Mithen, 78-89. London: Routledge.

_____. 2000. "Shamanism, Totemism, and Rock Art: *Les chamanes de la prehistoire* in the Context of Rock Art Research." *Cambridge Archaeological Journal* 10.1:169-86.

Leakey, Richard. 1994. *The Origin of Humankind.* New York: Basic Books.

_____, and Roger Lewin. 1977. *Origins: The Emergence and Evolution of Our Species and Its Possible Future.* New York: E. P. Dutton.

Lee, Jung H. 1998. "Disputers of the Tao: Putnam and Chuang-tzu on Meaning, Truth, and Reality." *Journal of Chinese Philosophy* 25.4:447-70.

_____. 2007. "Preserving One's Nature: Primitivist Daoism and Human Rights." *Journal of Chinese Philosophy* 34.4:597-612.

_____. 2014. *The Ethical Foundations of Daoism: Zhuangzi's Unique Moral Vision.* New York: Palgrave-McMillan.

Lee, Richard B. 1968. "What Hunters Do for a Living or, How to Make out on Scarce Resources." In *Man the Hunter*, edited by Richard B. Lee and Irven DeVore, 30-48. Chicago: Aldine.

_____. 1979. *The !Kung San: Men, Women, and Work in a Foraging Society.* Cambridge: Cambridge University Press.

_____., and I. DeVore. 1968. "Problems in the Study of Hunters and Gatherers." In *Man the Hunter*, edited by Richard B. Lee and Irven DeVore, 3-12. Chicago: Aldine.

Lee, Yueh-Ting, Ai-Guo Han, Tammy K. Byron, and Hong-Xia Fan. 2008. "Daoist Leadership: Theory and Application." In *Leadership and Management in China,* edited by Chao-Chuan Chen and Yueh-Ting Lee, 83-107. Cambridge: Cambridge University Press.

Legeza, Laszlo. 1975. *Tao Magic: The Secret Language of Diagrams and Calligraphy.* London: Thames and Hudson.

Legge, James. 1962. *The Sacred Books of China: The Texts of Taoism.* New York: Dover.

_____. 1967. *The Li Ki: Book of Rites.* 2 vols. In *The Sacred Books of China,* Parts 3-4. Delhi: Motilal Barnasidass.

_____. 1969. *The Chinese Classics: The Shoo King or The Book of Historical Documents.* Taipei: Jinwen.

Lei, Congyun. 1996. "Neolithic Sites of Religious Significance." In *The Mysteries of Ancient China: New Discoveries from the Early Dynasties*, 219-24. London: British Museum.

Leroi-Gourhan, Andre. 1993. *Gesture and Speech.* Cambridge, Mass.: MIT Press.

Lévi-Strauss, Claude. 1969. *The Raw and the Cooked: Introduction to a Science of Mythology.* New York: Harper & Row.

Lvi, Jean. 1983. "L'abstinence des céréals chez les taoïstes." *Etudes Chinoises* 1: 3-47.

Levy, Howard S. 1956. "Yellow Turban Rebellion at the End of the Han." *Journal of the American Oriental Society* 76:214-27.

Levy, Jack S., and William R. Thompson. 2011. *The Arc of War: Origins, Escalation, and Transformation.* Chicago: University of Chicago Press.

Lewis-Williams, J. D. 2002. *The Mind in the Cave: Consciousness and the Origins of Art.* London: Thames and Hudson.

______, and D. G. Pearce. 2004. *San Spirituality: Roots, Expression, and Social Consquences.* Walnut Creek, Calif.: Alta Mira Press.

______, and D. G. Pearce. 2005. *Inside the Neolithic Mind: Consciousness, Cosmos, and the Realm of the Gods.* London: Thames & Hudson.

______, and Thomas A. Dowson. 1988. "The Signs of All Times: Entoptic Phenomena in Upper Paleolithic Art." *Current Anthropology* 29.2:201-45.

Lewis, Jerome. 2014. "BaYaka Pygmy Multi-Modal and Mimetic Communication Traditions." In *The Social Origins of Language*, edited by Daniel Dor, Chris Knight, and Jerome Lewis, 77-91. New York: Oxford University Press.

Lewis, Mark Edward. 1990. *Sanctioned Violence in Early China.* Albany: State University of New York Press.

______. 2006a.*The Construction of Space in Early China.* Albany: State University of New York Press.

______. 2006b.*The Flood Myths of Early China.* Albany: State University of New York Press.

Lewis, Mary E. 2007. *The Bioarchaeology of Children: Perspectives from Biological and Forensic Anthropology.* Cambridge: Cambridge University Press. GN799

Li, Feng. 2005. *Landscape and Power in Early China: The Crisis and Fall of the Western Zhou (1045-771BC).* Cambridge: Cambridge University Press.

______. 2008. *Bureaucracy and the State in Early China: Governing the Western Zhou (1045-771BC).* Cambridge: Cambridge University Press.

______. 2013. *Early China: A Social and Cultural History.* Cambridge: Cambridge University Press.

______. 2014. "Fact or Fiction? The Middle Paleolithic in China." *Antiquity* 88:1303-09.

Li, Hui-Lin. 1983. "The Domestication of Plants in China: Ecogeographical Considerations." In *The Origins of Chinese Civilization*, edited by David N. Keightley, 297-319. Berkeley: University of California Press.

Li, Kuang-ti. 2013. "First Farmers and Their Coastal Adaptation in Prehistoric Taiwan." In *A Companion to Chinese Archaeology*, edited by Anne P. Underhill, 612-33. Malden, Mass.: Wiley-Blackwell.

Li, Ling. 1995. "An Archaeological Study of Taiyi (Great One) Worship." *Early Medieval China* 2:1-39.

Li, Xinwei. 2013. "The Later Neolithic Period in the Central Yellow River Valley Area, c. 4000-3000 BC." In *A Companion to Chinese Archaeology*, edited by Anne P. Underhill, 213-35. Malden, Mass.: Wiley-Blackwell.

Li, Yung-ti, and Ming-chorng Hwang. 2013. "Archaeology of Shanxi during the Yinxu Period." In *A Companion to Chinese Archaeology*, edited by Anne P. Underhill, 367-86. Malden, Mass.: Wiley-Blackwell.

Liao, Wen-Kuei. 1959. *The Complete Works of Han Fei Tzu: A Classic of Chinese Political Science.* London: Arthur Probsthain.

Lieberman, Philip. 1989. "The Origins of Some Aspects of Human Language and Cognition." In *The Human Revolution: Behavioral and Biological Perspectives on the Origins of Modern Humans*, 391-414. Edinburgh: Edinburgh University Press.

Lien, Chao-mei. 2015. "Chang-pin Culture of Taiwan and Characteristics of Its Lithic Industry." In *Emergence and Diversity of Human Behavior in Paleolithic Asia,* edited by Yosuke Kaifu, Masami Izuho, Ted Goebel, Hiroyuki Sato, and Akira Ono, 239-49. College Station: Texas A & M University Press.

Linduff, Katheryn M. and Karen S. Rubinson. 2013. "Gender Archaeology in East Asia and Eurasia." In *A Companion to Gender Prehistory*, edited by Diane Bolger, 351-71. Malden, Mass.: Wiley-Blackwell.

Liu, Guanghua. 2005. "Chinese Cinnabar." *Mineralogical Record* 36.1:69-80.

Liu, Li. 1996. "Mortuary Ritual and Social Hierarchy in the Longshan Culture." *Early China* 21:1-46.

_____. 2004. *The Chinese Neolithic: Trajectories to Early States.* Cambridge: Cambridge University Press.

_____, Shaodong Zhai, and Xingcan Chen. 2013. "Production of Gtround Stone Tools at Taosi and Huizui: A Comparison." In *A Companion to Chinese Archaeology*, edited by Anne P. Underhill, 278-99. Malden, Mass.: Wiley-Blackwell.

_____, Sheahan Bestel, Jinming Shi, Yanhua Song, and Xingcan Chen. 2013. "Paleolithic Human Exploitation of Plant Foods during the Last Glacial Maximum in North China." *Proceedings of the National Academy of Sciences* 110.14:5380-85.

_____, and Xingcan Chen. 2003. *State Formation in Early China.* London: Duckworth.

_____, and Xingcan Chen. 2012. *The Archaeology of Ancient China: From the Late Paleolithic to the Early Bronze Age.* Cambridge: Cambridge University Press.

Liu, Xiaogan. 2001. "Nonaction and the Environment Today: A Conceptual and Applied Study of Laozi's Philosophy." In *Daoism and Ecology: Ways within a Cosmic Landscape*, edited by Norman Girardot, James Miller, and Liu Xiaogan, 315-40. Cambridge, Mass.: Harvard University Press, Center for the Study of World Religions.

Liu, Zhengcai. 1990. *The Mystery of Longevity*. Beijing: Foreign Languages Press.

Lo, Vivienne. 2005. "Pleasure, Prohibition, and Pain: Food and Medicine in Traditional China." In *Of Tripod and Palate: Food, Politics and Religion in Traditional China*, edited by Roel Sterckx, 163-85. New York: Palgrave MacMillan.

Lo, Yuet-Keung. 2002. "Wandering and Imaginal Realms in the *Analects* and *Zhuangzi*." *Monumenta Serica* 50:75-93.

Loewe, Michael, and Edward L. Shaughnessy, eds. 1999. *The Cambridge History of Ancient China: From the Origins of Civilization to 221 B.C.* Cambridge: Cambridge University Press.

Lorenz, Konrad. 1966. *On Aggression.* Translated by Marjorie Kerr Wilson. New York: Harvest Books.

Lu, Tracey. 1999. *The Transition from Foraging to Farming and the Origin of Agriculture in China.* Oxford: British Archaeological Reports.

______. 2006. "The Occurrence of Cereal Cultivation in China." *Asian Perspectives* 45:129-58.

Luan, Fengshi. 2013. "The Dawenkou Culture in the Lower Yellow River and Huai River Basin Areas." In *A Companion to Chinese Archaeology*, edited by Anne P. Underhill, 411-34. Malden, Mass.: Wiley-Blackwell.

MacDonald, Dennis R. 1987. *There Is No Male and No Female.* Philadelphia: Fort-ress Press.

Mahdihassan, S. 1987. "History of Cinnabar as Drug: The Natural Substance and the Synthetic Product." *Indian Journal of History of Science* 22.1:63-70.

Maisels, Charles Keith. 1999. *Early Civilizations of the Old World: The Formative Histories of Egypt, the Levant, Mesopotamia, India, and China.* London: Routledge.

Major, John S. 1986. "New Light on the Dark Warrior." *Journal of Chinese Religions* 13/14:65-87.

______. 1993. *Heaven and Earth in Early Han Thought: Chapters Three, Four, and Five of the Huainanzi.* Albany: State University of New York Press.

______, Sarah A. Queen, Andrew S. Meyer, and Harold D. Roth. 2010. *The Huainanzi: A Guide to the Theory and Practice of Government in Early Han China.* New York: Columbia University Press.

Mansvelt-Beck, B. J. 1980. "The Date of the *Taiping jing*." *T'oung Pao* 66:149-82.

______. 1986. "The Fall of Han." In *The Cambridge History of China,* edited by Denis Twitchett and Michael Loewe, 1:317-76. Cambridge: Cambridge University Press.

Maringer, Johannes. 1960. *The Gods of Prehistoric Man.* New York: Alfred A. Knopf.

Markale, Jean. 1999. *The Great Goddess: Reverence of the Divine Feminine from the Paleolithic to the Present.* Rochester, VT: Inner Traditions.

Marlowe, Frank. 2010. *The Hazda: Hunter-Gatherers in Tanzania.* Berkeley: University of California Press.

Marshack, Alexander. 1991. *The Roots of Civilization: The Cognitive Beginnings of Man's First Art, Symbol, and Notation.* London: Moyer Bell Lmited.

Martin, Paul S. 1967. "Prehistoric Overkill." In *Pleistocene Extinctions: The Search for a Cause*, edited by Paul S. Martin and Herbert E. Wright, 75-120. New Haven: Yale University Press.

Maslow, Abraham H. 1954. *Motivation and Personality*. New York: Harper & Row.

_____. 1965. *Eupsychian Management: A Journal*. Homewood, Ill.: Richard Irwin.

Mather, Richard. 1979. "K'ou Ch'ien-chih and the Taoist Theocracy at the Northern Wei Court 425-451." In *Facets of Taoism*, edited by Holmes Welch and Anna Seidel, 103-22. New Haven, Conn.: Yale University Press.

Matsuyama, Toshio. 1981. "Nut Gathering and Processing Methods in Traditional Japanese Villages." In *Affluent Foragers: Pacific Coasts East and West*, edited by Shuzo Koyama and David Hurst Thomas, 117-40. Senri: Senri Ethnological Studies.

Mauss, Marcel. 1967. *The Gift: Forms and Functions of Exchange in Archaic Societies*. New York: W. W. Norton.

_____. 1979. *Sociology and Psychology, Essays*. London: Routledge and Kegan Paul.

Mayer, Daniella E. Bar-Yosef, Bernard Vandermeersch, and Ofer Bar-Josef. 2009. "Shells and Ochre in Middle Paleolithic Qafzeh Cave, Israel: Indications for Modern Behavior." *Journal of Human Evolution* 56: 307-14.

McBrearty, Sally, and Alison Brooks. 2000. "The Revolution That Wasn't." *Journal of Human Evolution* 39:453-563.

McCauley, Clark.1990. "Conference Overview." In *The Anthropology of War*, edited by Jonathan Haas, 1-25. Cambridge: Cambridge University Press.

McGrew, William C. 1996. "Dominance Status, Food Sharing, and Reproductive Success in Chimpanzees." In *Food and the Status Quest: An Interdisciplinary Perspective*, edited by Polly Wiessner and Wulf Schiefenhövel, 39-46. Oxford: Berghahn Books.

_____. 2001. "The Other Faunivory: Primate Insectivory and Early Human Diet." In *Meat Eating and Human Evolution*, edited by Craig B. Stanford and Henry T. Bunn, 160-78. New York: Oxford University Press.

McIntosh, Jane. 2006. *Handbook to Life in Prehistoric Europe*. New York: Oxford University Press.

McNeal, Robin. 2014. "Erligang Contacts South of the Yangzi River: The Expansion of Interaction Networks in Early Bronze Age Hunan." In *Art and Archaeology of the Erligang Civilization*, edited by Kyle Steinke and Dora C. Y. Ching, 173-87. Princeton: Princeton University Press.

McNeill, William H. 1976. *Plagues and Peoples*. Garden City, NY: Anchor Press.

_____. 1982. *The Pursuit of Power: Technology, Armed Force, and Society since 1,000 A.D.* Chicago: University of Chicago Press.

McTaggart, Lynne. 2011. *The Bond: Connecting through the Space between Us*. New York: Free Press.

Meacham, William. 1983. "Origins and Development of the Yüeh Coastal Neolithic: A Microcosm of Culture Change on the Mainland of East Asia." In *The Origins of Chinese Civilization*, edited by David N. Keightley, 147-75. Berkeley: University of California Press.

Meeks, Wayne. 1974. "The Image of the Androgyne: Some Uses of a Symbol in Earliest Christianity." *History of Religions* 13:165-208.

Meighan, Clement W. 1982. "Environment and Explanation in Archaeology." In *Culture and Ecology: Eclectic Perspectives*, edited by John G. Kennedy and Robert B. Edgerton, 84-94. Washington, DC: American Anthropological Association.

Mellars, Paul. 1989. "Technological Changes at the Middle-Upper Paleolithic Transition: Economic, Social, and Cognitive Perspectives." In *The Human Revolution: Behavioral and Biological Perspectives on the Origins of Modern Humans*, 3338-65. Edinburgh: Edinburgh University Press.

_____. 2007. "Rethinking the Human Revolution: Eurasian and African Perspectives." In *Rethinking the Human Revolution: New Behavioral and Biological Perspectives on the Origin and Dispersal of Modern Humans*, edited by Paul Mellars, 1-11. Cambridge: McDonald Institute for Archaeological Research.

_____. 2015. "Some Key Issues in the Emergence and Diversity of 'Modern' Human Behavior." In *Emergence and Diversity of Human Behavior in Paleolithic Asia,* edited by Yosuke Kaifu, Masami Izuho, Ted Goebel, Hiroyuki Sato, and Akira Ono, 3-22. College Station: Texas A & M University Press.

_____, and Chris Stringer. 1989. "Introduction." In *The Human Revolution: Behavioral and Biological Perspectives on the Origins of Modern Humans*, 1-14. Edinburgh: Edinburgh University Press.

Mercer, Calvin, and Thomas W. Durham. 1999. "Religious Mysticism and Gender Orientation." *Journal for the Scientific Study of Religion* 38.1:175-82.

Milcinski, Maja. 1997. "The Notion of Feminine in Asian Philosophical Traditions."*Asian Philosophy* 7.3:195-205.

Miles, Elisabeth. 1998. *The Feng Shui Cookbook: Creating Health and Harmony in Your Kitchen.* Secaucus, NJ: Carol Publishing Company.

Miller, Barbara Diane.1993. "The Anthropology of Sex and Gender Hierarchies." In *Sex and Gender Hierarchies*, edited by Barbara Diane Miller, 3-31. Cambridge: Cambridge University Press.

Milner, George R. and Jesper L. Boldsen. 2012. "Estimating Age and Sex from the Skeleton, a Paleopathological Perspective." In *A Companion to Paleopathology*, edited by Anne L. Grauer, 268-84. Malden, Mass.: Wiley-Blackwell.

Milton, Katherine. 2002. "Hunter-Gatherer Diets: Wild Foods Signal Relief from Diseases of Affluence." In *Human Diet: Its Origin and Evolution*, edited by Peter S. Ungar and Mark F. Teaford, 111-22. Westport, Conn.: Bergin & Garvey.

Mintz, Sidney W. 1985. *Sweetness and Power: The Place of Sugar in Modern History*. New York: Penguin.

_____. 1996. *Tasting Food, Tasting Freedom: Excursions into Eating, Culture and the Past.* Boston: Beacon Press.

Mithen, Steven. 1996. *The Prehistory of the Mind: A Search for the Origins of Art, Religion, and Science.* London: Thames & Hudson.

_____. 1998. "Introduction." In *Creativity in Human Evolution and Prehistory*, 1-15. London: Routledge.

_____. 2004. *After the Ice: A Global Human History, 20,000-5,000 BC.* Cambridge, Mass.: Harvard University Press.

Moeller, Hans-Georg. 2006. *The Philosophy of the Daode jing.* New York: Columbia.

_____. 2015. "Parodoxes of Health and Power in the *Zhuangzi*." In *New Visions of the Zhuangzi*, edited by Livia Kohn, 70-81. St. Petersburg, Fla.: Three Pines Press.

Møllgaard, Eske. 2003. "Zhuangzi's Religious Ethics." *Journal of the American Academy of Religion* 71.2:347-70.

_____. 2005. "Zhuangzi's Notion of Transcendental Life." *Asian Philosophy* 15.1:1-18.

Mollier, Christine. 2000. "Les cuisines de Laozi et du Buddha." *Cahiers d'Extrême-Asie* 11:45-90.

Momigliano, Arnaldo. 1975. *Alien Wisdom: The Limits of Hellenization.* Cambridge: Cambridge University Press.

Montagu, Ashley, 1965. *The Human Revolution.* New York: World Publishing Co.

_____. 1973. "The New Litany of 'Innate Depravity,' or Original Sin Revisited." In *Man and Aggression*, edited by Ashley Montagu, 3-18. New York: Oxford University Press.

Morgan, Christopher, Loukas Barton, Robert Bettinger, Fahu Chen, and Dongju Zhang. 2011. "Glacial Cycles and Paleolithic Adaptive Variability on China's Western Loess Plateau." *Antiquity* 85:365-79.

Morris, Desmond. 1967. *The Naked Ape: A Zoologist's Study of the Human Mind.* New York: McGraw Hill.

Mote, Frederick W. 1977. "Yuan and Ming." In *Food in Chinese Culture*, edited by K. C. Chang, 192-258. New Haven: Yale University Press.

Mountford, Charles P., and R. L. Specht, eds. 1960. *Records of the Australian-American Scientific Expedition to Arnhem Land. Vol. 2: Anthropology and Nutrition.* Melbourne: Melbourne University Press.

Moyer, K. E. 1974. "Sex Differences in Aggression." In *Sex Differences in Behavior*, edited by R. C. Friedman, R. M. Richart, and R. L. Van de Wiele, 335-72. New York: John Wiley & Sons.

Muller, Martin N., Sonya M. Kahlenberg, and Richard W. Wrangham. 2009a. "Male Aggression and Sexual Coercion of Females in Primates." In *Sexual Coercion in Primates and Humans: An Evolutionary Perspective on Male Aggression against Females*, edited by Martin N. Muller and Richard W. Wrangham, 3-22. Cambridge, Mass.: Harvard University Press.

_____. 2009b. "Male Aggression against Females and Sexual Coercion in Chimpanzees." In *Sexual Coercion in Primates and Humans: An Evolutionary Perspective on Male Aggression against Females*, edited by Martin N. Muller and Richard W. Wrangham, 184-217. Cambridge, Mass.: Harvard University Press.

Munroe, Kristen Renwick. 1996. *The Heart of Altruism: Perceptions of a Common Humanity.* Princeton: Princeton University Press.

Murowchick, Robert E. 2013. "'Despoiled of the Garments of Her Civilization:' Problems and Progress in Archaeological Heritage Management in China." In *A Companion to Chinese Archaeology*, edited by Anne P. Underhill, 13-34. Malden, Mass.: Wiley-Blackwell.

Nader, Laura. 1991. "Harmony Models and the Construction of Law." In *Conflict Resolution: Cross-Cultural Perspectives*, edited by Kevin Avruch, Peter W. Black, and Joseph A. Scimecca, 41-60. New York: Greenwood Press.

Nagel, Thomas. 1970. *The Possibility of Altruism*. Oxford: Clarendon Press.

Nanda, Serena. 1994. "*Hijras*: An Alternative Sex and Gender Role in India." In *Third Sex, Third Gender: Beyond Sexual Dimorphism in Culture and History*, edited by Gilbert H. Herdt, 373-418. New York: Zone Books.

Needham, Joseph, et al. 1958. *Science and Civilisation in China*, vol. III: *Mathematics and the Sciences of the Heavens and the Earth*. Cambridge: Cambridge University Press.

_____, Ho Ping-yü, and Lu Gwei-djen. 1976. *Science and Civilisation in China*, vol. V.3: *Spagyrical Discovery and Invention—Historical Survey, from Cinnabar Elixir to Synthetic Insulin*. Cambridge: Cambridge University Press.

Neiman, Madeleine Kegelman, Magdalena Balonis, and Ioanna Kakulli. 2015. "Cinnabar Alteration in Archaeological Wall Paintings: An Experimental and Theoretical Approach." *Applied Physics* 121:915-38.

Nelson, Elke. 2013. "The Paleolithic Diet: A Menu Prescribed by Our Ancestors." *Muscle and Performance* May 2013:49-54.

Nelson, Sarah Milledge. 1991. "The 'Goddess Temple' and the Status of Women at Niuheliang." In *The Archaeology of Gender*, edited by Dale Walde and Noreen D. Willows. Calgary: University of Calgary.

_____. 1993. "Gender Hierarchy and the Queen of Silla." In *Sex and Gender Hierarchies*, edited by Barbara Diane Miller, 297-315. Cambridge: Cambridge University Press.

_____. 1997. *Gender in Archaeology: Analyzing Power and Prestige*. Walnut Creek, Calif.: Alta Mira Press.

_____. 2013. "Gender and Archaeology in Coastal East Asia." In *A Companion to Gender Prehistory*, edited by Diane Bolger, 333-50. Malden, Mass.: Wiley-Blackwell.

_____, and Myriam Rosen-Avalon. 2002. "Ideology, Power, and Gender: Emergence Complexity in Northeastern China." In *Pursuit of Gender: Worldwide Archaeological Approaches*, edited by Sarah Milledge Nelson and Myriam Rosen-Avalon, 73-80. Walnut Creek, Calif.: Alta Mira Press.

Newell, Raymond R. 1973. "The Post-glacial Adaptations of Indigenous Populations of the Northwest European Plain." In *The Mesolithic in Europe*, edited by Stefan Karol Koslowski, 399-440. Warsaw: Warsaw University Press.

Nishida, Masaki. 2002." The Meaning of Agriculture for Humans." In *The Origins of Pottery and Agriculture*, edited by Yoshinori Yasuda, 231-40. New Delhi: Roli Books.

Noble, Vicki. 1991. *Shakti Woman: Feeling Our Fire, Healing Our World*. San Francisco: HarperSanFrancisco.

Noble, William, and Iain Davidson. 1996. *Human Evolution, Language, and Mind: A Psychological and Archaeological Inquiry*. Cambridge: Cambridge University Press.

Northouse, Peter G. 2001. *Leadership: Theory and Practice*. Thousand Oaks, Calif.: Sage Publications.

O'Connell, James, Kristen Hawkes, and Nicholas Blurton Jones. 2002. "Meat-Eating, Grandmothering, and the Evolution of Early Human Diets." In *Human Diet: Its Origin and Evolution*, edited by Peter S. Ungar and Mark F. Teaford, 49-60. Westport, Conn.: Bergin & Garvey.

O'Shea, John. 1984. *Mortuary Variability: An Archaeological Investigation*. New York: Academic Press.

Oakley, Kenneth Page. 1967. *Man the Toolmaker*. Chicago: University of Chicago Press.

Ohnuki-Tierney, Emiko. 1993. *Rice as Self*. Princeton: Princeton University Press.

Olberding, Amy. 2007. "Sorrow and the Sage: Grief in the *Zhuangzi*." *Dao: A Journal of Comparative Philosophy* 6.4:339-59.

Olds, Linda E. 1981. *Fully Human: How Everyone Can Integrate the Benefits of Masculine and Feminine Sex Roles*. Englewood Cliffs: Prentice Hall.

Ong, Walter J. 2002 [1982]. *Orality and Literacy: The Technologizing of the Word*. New York: Routledge.

Oosterzee, Penny Van. 2000. *Dragon Bones: The Story of Peking Man*. Cambridge, Mass.: Perseus Publishing.

Ortner, Donald J. 2012. "Differential Diagnosis and Issues in Disease Classification." In *A Companion to Paleopathology*, edited by Anne L. Grauer, 250-67. Malden, Mass.: Wiley-Blackwell.

Oswalt, Wendell H. 1982. "Material Culture in Anthropology." In *Culture and Ecology: Eclectic Perspectives*, edited by John G. Kennedy and Robert B. Edgerton, 56-66. Washington, DC: American Anthropological Association.

Otterbein, Keith F. 1970. *The Evolution of War: A Cross-Cultural Study*. New Haven: Yale University HRAF Press.

______. 2004. *How War Began*. College Station: Texas A & M University Press.

Outram, Alan K. 2007. "Hunter-Gatherers and the First Farmers: The Evolution of Taste in Prehistory." In *Food: A History of Taste*, edited by Paula Freedman, 35-62. Berkeley: University of California Press.

Overmyer, Daniel L. 1991. "Women in Chinese Religions: Submission, Struggle, Transcendence." In *From Benares to Beijing: Essays on Buddhism and Chinese Religions in Honour of Prof. Jan Yün-hua*, edited by Koichi Shinohara and Gregory Shopen, 91-120. Oakville, Ont.: Mosaic Press.

Pagel, Mark. 2012. *Wired for Culture: Origins of the Human Social Mind*. New York: W. W. Norton.

Palacio-Pérez, Eduardo, and Aitor Ruiz Redondo. 2014. "Imaginary Creatures in Paleolithic Art: Prehistoric Dream or Prehistorians' Dreams?" *Antiquity* 88:259-66.

Pankenier, David W. 2004. "A Brief History of Beiji (Northern Culmen), with an Excursus on the Origin of the Character *Di*." *Journal of the American Oriental Society* 124.2:229-35.

______. 2010. "Cosmic Capitals and Numinous Precincts in Early China." *Journal of Cosmology* 9:2030-40.

______. 2013. *Astrology and Cosmology in Early China: Conforming Earth to Heaven*. Cambridge: Cambridge University Press.

Panksepp, Jaak. 1998. *Affective Neuroscience: The Foundation of Human and Animal Emotions*. New York: Oxford University Press.

______. 2008. "The Affective Brain and Core Consciousness: How Does Neural Activity Generate Emotional Feelings?" In *Handbook of Emotions*, edited by Michael Lewis, Jeannette M. Haviland-Jones, and Lisa Feldman Barrett, 47-66. New York: Guilford Press.

Paoli, Tommaso. 2009. "The Absence of Sexual Coercion in Bonobos." In *Sexual Coercion in Primates and Humans: An Evolutionary Perspective on Male Aggression against Females*, edited by Martin N. Muller and Richard W. Wrangham, 410-23. Cambridge, Mass.: Harvard University Press.

Parker, Richard A. 1950. *The Calendars of Ancient Egypt*. Chicago: University of Chicago Press.

Pearson, Richard. 1981. "Social Complexity in Chinese Coastal Neolithic Sites." *Science* 213:1081-85.

______. 1983. "The Ch'ing-lien-kang Culture and the Chinese Neolithic." In *The Origins of Chinese Civilization*, edited by David N. Keightley, 119-45. Berkeley: University of California Press.

______. 1988. "Chinese Neolithic Burial Patterns: Problems of Method and Interpretation." *Early China* 13:1-45.

______. 2006. "The Social Context of Early Pottery in the Lingnan Region of China." *Antiquity* 38:239-58.

Pechenkina, Kate, Ma Xiaolin, and Fan Wenquan. 2013. "Trajectories of Health in Early Farming Communities of East Asia." In *Bioarchaeology of East Asia: Movement, Contact, Health*, edited by Kate Pechenkina and Marc Oxenham, 444-81. Gainesville: University Press of Florida.

______, Ma Xiaolin, Fan Wenquan, Wei Dong, and Zhang Quanchao. 2013. "Yangshao Oral Health from West to East: Effects of Increasing Complexity and Contacts with Neighbors." In *Bioarchaeology of East Asia: Movement, Contact, Health*, edited by Kate Pechenkina and Marc Oxenham, 288-322. Gainesville: University Press of Florida.

______, Robert A. Benfer, Jr., and Stanely H. Ambrose. 2000. "Diet and Health Changes at the End of the Chinese Neolithic: The Yangshao/Longshan Transition in Shaanxi." *American Journal of Physical Anthropology* 117.1:15-36.

Pei, Anping. 2002. "Rice Paddy Agriculture and Pottery from the Middle Reaches of the Yangtze River." In *The Origins of Pottery and Agriculture*, edited by Yoshinori Yasuda, 167-81. New Delhi: Roli Books.

______. 2013. "The Pengtoushan Culture in the Middle Yangzi River Valley." In *A Companion to Chinese Archaeology*, edited by Anne P. Underhill, 497-509. Malden, Mass.: Wiley-Blackwell.

Penny, Benjamin. 1996. "Buddhism and Daoism in 'The 180 Precepts Spoken by Lord Lao'." *Taoist Resources* 6.2: 1-16.

Perez, Ventura R. 2012. "The Politicization of the Dead: Violence as Performance, Politics as Usual." In *The Bioarchaeology of Violence*, edited by Debra Martin, Ryan P. Harrod, and Ventura R. Perez, 13-28. Gainesville: University Press of Florida.

Perlmutter. David, with Kristin Loberg. 2013. *Grain Brain: The Surprising Truth about Wheat, Carbs, and Sugar—Your Brain's Silent Killers.* New York: Little, Brown, and Co.

Peterson, Christian E., and Xueming Lu. 2013. "Understanding Hongshan Period Social Dynamics." In *A Companion to Chinese Archaeology*, edited by Anne P. Underhill, 55-80. Malden, Mass.: Wiley-Blackwell.

_____, Robert D. Drennan, and Kate L. Bartel. 2016. "Comparative Analysis of Neolithic Household Artifact Assemblage Data from North China." *Journal of Anthropological Research 72.2*:200-25.

Pettitt, Paul. 2005. "The Rise of Modern Humans." In *The Human Past: World Prehistory and the Development of Human Societies*, edited by Chris Scarre, 124-73. London: Thames & Hudson.

_____. 2011. *The Paleolithic Origins of Human Burial.* New York: Routledge.

Petzinger, Genvieve von. 2015. *The First Signs: Unlocking the Mysteries of the World's Oldest Symbols.* New York: Atria Books.

Pfeiffer, John E. 1982. *The Creative Explosion: An Inquiry into the Origins of Art and Religion.* New York: Harper & Row.

Pilling, Arnold R. 1968. "Southeastern Australia: Level of Social Organization." In *Man the Hunter*, edited by Richard B. Lee and Irven DeVore, 138-45. Chicago: Aldine.

Ponting, Clive. 1982. *A Green History of the World: The Environment and the Collapse of Great Civilizations.* New York: St. Martin's Press.

Poo, Mu-chou. 2005. "A Taste of Happiness: Contextualizing Elixirs in Baopuzi." In *Of Tripod and Palate: Food, Politics and Religion in Traditional China*, edited by Roel Sterckx, 123-39. New York: Palgrave MacMillan.

Pope, G. 1988. "Recent Advances in Far Eastern Paleoanthropology." *Annual Review of Anthropology* 17:43-77.

Power, Camilla. 2014a. "Signal Evolution and the Social Brain." In *The Social Origins of Language*, edited by Daniel Dor, Chris Knight, and Jerome Lewis, 47-55. New York: Oxford University Press.

_____. 2014b. "The Evolution of Ritual as a Process of Sexual Selection." In *The Social Origins of Language*, edited by Daniel Dor, Chris Knight, and Jerome Lewis, 47-55. New York: Oxford University Press.

Powers, William K., and Marla M. N. Powers. 1984. "Metaphysical Aspects of an Oglala Food System." In *Food in the Social Order: Studies of Food and Festivities in Three American Communities*, 40-96. New York: Russell Sage Foundation.

Pregadio, Fabrizio. 2004. "The Notion of 'Form' and the Ways of Liberation in Daoism." *Cahiers d'Extrême-Asie* 14:95-130.

_____. 2006. *Great Clarity: Daoism and Alchemy in Early Medieval China.* Stanford: Stanford University Press.

_____, ed. 2008. *The Encyclopedia of Taoism.* 2 vols. London: Routledge.

Pribram, Karl H., and F. T. Melges. 1969. "Psychophysiological Basis of Emotion." In *Handbook of Clinical Neurology*, edited by P. J. Vinken and T. M. Powledge, 49-140. New York: Wiley Interscience.

Price, Douglas B., and Anna B. Gebauer. 1995. "New Perspectives on the Transition to Agriculture." In *Last Hunters—First Farmers*, edited by Douglas B. Price and Anna B. Gebauer, 3-20. Santa Fe: School of American Research Press.

Price, Neil S. 2001. "An Archaeology of Altered States: Shamanism and Material Culture Studies." In *The Archaeology of Shamanism*, 3-16. New York: Routledge.

Price, T. Douglas, and James A. Brown. 1985. "Aspects of Hunter-Gatherer Complexity." In *Prehistoric Hunter-Gatherers: The Emergence of Cultural Complexity*, edited by T. Douglas Price and James A. Brown,3-20. New York: Academic Press.

Price, Weston A. 1989 [1939]. *Nutrition and Physical Degeneration.* New Canaan, Conn.: Keats Publishing.

Primack, Joel R., and Nancy Ellen Abrams. 2006. *The View from the Center of the Universe: Discovering Our Extraordinary Place in the Cosmos.* New York: Riverhead Books.

Puett, Michael. 2002. *To Become a God: Cosmology, Sacrifice, and Self-Divinization in Early China.* Cambridge, Mass.: Harvard University Press.

_____. 2003. "Can Nothing Overcome Heaven? The Notion of Spirit in the *Zhuangzi.*" In *Hiding the World in the World: Uneven Discourses on the Zhuangzi*, edited by Scott Cook, 248-62. Albany: State University of New York Press.

_____. 2005. "The Offering of Food and the Creation of Order: The Practice of Sacrifice in Early China." In *Of Tripod and Palate: Food, Politics and Religion in Traditional China*, edited by Roel Sterckx, 75-95. New York: Palgrave MacMillan.

Pyborn, K. Anne. 2004. "Rethinking Complex Society." In *Ungendering Civilization*, edited by K. Anne Pyborn, 1-46. London: Routledge.

Qin, Ling. 2013. "The Liangzhu Culture." In *A Companion to Chinese Archaeology*, edited by Anne P. Underhill, 574-96. Malden, Mass.: Wiley-Blackwell.

Raja, Rabina. 2015. *A Companion to the Archaeology of the Ancient World.* Chichester: John Wiley & Sons.

Ramachandran, V. S. 2011. *The Tell-Tale Brain: A Neuroscientist's Quest for What Makes Us Human.* New York: W. W. Norton & Co.

Rapoport, Anatol. 1995. *Origins of Violence: Approaches to the Study of Conflict.* New York: Paragon House.

Ratey, John J. 2002. *A User's Guide to the Brain: Perception, Attention, and the Four Theaters of the Brain.* New York: Vintage Books.

Rawson, Jessica. 1996a. "Unknown China." In *The Mysteries of Ancient China: New Discoveries from the Early Dynasties*, 31-84. London: British Museum.

______. 1996b. "The Ritual Bronze Vessels of the Shang and the Zhou." In *The Mysteries of Ancient China: New Discoveries from the Early Dynasties*, 248-65. London: British Museum.

Raz, Gil. 2008. "The Way of the Yellow and the Red: Re-examining the Sexual Initiation Rite of Celestial Master Daoism." *Nannü: Men, Women and Gender in China* 10:86-120.

Reed, Barbara E. 1987. "Taoism." In *Women in World Religions*, edited by Arvind Sharma, 161-80. Albany: State University of New York Press.

Reed, Charles A. 1977. "Origins of Agriculture: Discussion and Some Conclusions." In *Origins of Agriculture*, edited by Charles A. Reed, 879-953. The Hague: Mouton.

Rees, Martin. 2000. *Just Six Numbers: The Deep Forces That Shape the Universe.* New York: Basic Books.

Renfrew, Jane M. 1973. *Paleoethnobotany: The Prehistoric Food Plants of the Near East and Europe.* London: Methuen.

Réquéna, Yves. 2012. "The Biochemistry of Internal Alchemy: Decapitating the Red Dragon." *Journal of Daoist Studies* 5:141-52.

Richard, Natalie. 2013. "Did Prehistoric Man Bury His Dead? Early Debates on Paleolithic Burials in a National Context." In *The Oxford Handbook of Archaeology of Death and Burial*, edited by Sarah Tarlow and Liv Nielsson Stutz, 27-46. New York: Oxford University Press.

Riches, David. 1986. *The Anthropology of Violence.* New York: Basil Blackwell.

Rickett, W. Allyn. 1985. *Kuan-tzu: Political, Economic, and Philosophical Essays from China.* Vol. 1. Princeton: Princeton University Press.

Ridley, Matt. 1997. *The Origins of Virtue: Human Instincts and the Evolution of Cooperation.* New York: Viking.

Riel-Salvatore, Julien, and Claudine Gravel-Miguel. 2013. "Upper Paleolithic Burial Practices in Eurasia: A Critical Look at the Burial Record." In *The Oxford Handbook of Archaeology of Death and Burial*, edited by Sarah Tarlow and Liv Nielsson Stutz, 303-46. New York: Oxford University Press.

Rifkin, Riaan. 2011. "Assessing the Efficacy of Red Ochre as a Prehistoric Hide-Tanning Ingredient." *Journal of African Archaeology* 9:131-58.

Rindos, David. 1984. *The Origins of Agriculture: An Evolutionary Perspective.* Orlando, Fla.: Academic Press.

Ringrose, Kathryn M. 1994. "Living in the Shadows: Eunuchs and Gender in Byzantium." In *Third Sex, Third Gender: Beyond Sexual Dimorphism in Culture and History*, edited by Gilbert H. Herdt, 89-110. New York: Zone Books.

Robarchek, Clayton. 1990. "Motivations and Material Causes: On the Explanation of Conflict and War." In *The Anthropology of War*, edited by Jonathan Haas, 56-76. Cambridge: Cambridge University Press.

Robbins, Martha M. 2009. "Male Aggression against Females in Mountain Gorillas: Courtship or Coercion?" In *Sexual Coercion in Primates and Humans: An Evolutionary Perspective on Male Aggression against Females*, edited by Martin N. Muller and Richard W. Wrangham, 112-27. Cambridge, Mass.: Harvard University Press.

Roberts, Charlotte. 2013. "The Bioarchaeology of Health and Well-Being: Its Contribution to Understanding the Past." In *The Oxford Handbook of Archaeology of Death and Burial*, edited by Sarah Tarlow and Liv Nielsson Stutz, 79-98. New York: Oxford University Press.

Robinet, Isabelle. 1989. "Visualization and Ecstatic Flight in Shangqing Taoism." In *Taoist Meditation and Longevity Techniques*, edited by Livia Kohn, 159-91. Ann Arbor: University of Michigan, Center for Chinese Studies.

_____. 1993. *Taoist Meditation: The Mao-shan Tradition of Great Purity*. Translated by Norman Girardot and Julian Pas. Albany: State University of New York Press.

_____. 1997. *Taoism: Growth of a Religion*. Translated by Phyllis Brooks. Stanford: Stanford University Press.

Robson, James. 2009. *Power of Place: The Religious Landscape of the Southern Sacred Peak in Medieval China*. Cambridge, Mass: Harvard University Asia Center.

Rodman, Peter S. 2002. "Plants of the Apes: Is There a Hominid Model for the Origins of Human Diet?" In *Human Diet: Its Origin and Evolution*, edited by Peter S. Ungar and Mark F. Teaford, 77-110. Westport, Conn.: Bergin & Garvey.

Roebroeks, Wil, et al. 2012. "Use of Red Ochre by Early Neadertals." *Proceedings of the National Academy of Sciences* 109.6:1889-94.

Roscoe, Will. 1994. "How to Become a Berdache: Toward a Unified Analysis of Gender Diversity." In *Third Sex, Third Gender: Beyond Sexual Dimorphism in Culture and History*, edited by Gilbert H. Herdt, 329-72. New York: Zone Books.

Rose, Lisa M. 2001. "Meat and the Early Human Diet: Insights from Neotropical Primate Studies." In *Meat Eating and Human Evolution*, edited by Craig B. Stanford and Henry T. Bunn, 141-59. New York: Oxford University Press.

Roth, Harold D. 1990. "The Early Taoist Concept of *Shen*: A Ghost in the Machinery?" In *Sagehood and Systematizing Thought in the Late Warring States and Early Han*, edited by Kidder Smith, 11-32. Brunswick, Maine: Bowdoin College.

_____. 1999. *Original Tao: Inward Training and the Foundations of Taoist Mysticism*. New York: Columbia University Press.

Rubin, Jeffrey Z, Dean G. Pruitt, and Sung Hee. Kim. 1994. *Social Conflict: Escalation, Stalemate, and Settlement*. New York: McGraw Hill.

Ryan, Lyndall. 1981. *The Aboriginal Tasmanians*. Vancouver: University of British Columbia Press.

Ryan, Mary Kay. 2011. "Infusing Chinese Medicine with Spirit: Daoism, Shamanism, and Chinese Medicine in the Modern World." *Journal of Daoist Studies* 4:175-89.

Ryan, Robert E. 1999. *The Strong Eye of Shamanism: A Journey into the Caves of Consciousness*. Rochester, VT: Inner Traditions.

Sahlins, Marshall. 1972. *Stone Age Economics*. London: Tavistock.

Salviati, Filippo. 1997a. "The Age of Jade." In *Virtual Archaeology: Great Discoveries Brought to Life through Virtual Reality*, edited by Arnoldo Mondadori, 216-19. London: Thames & Hudson.

_____. 1997b. "The Shang Dynasty: New Disoveries." In *Virtual Archaeology: Great Discoveries Brought to Life through Virtual Reality*, edited by Arnoldo Mondadori, 220-21. London: Thames & Hudson.

Sarkassian, Hagop. 2010. "The Darker Side of Daoist Primitivism." *Journal of Chinese Philosophy* 37.2:312-29.

Saso, Michael. 1972. *Taoism and the Rite of Cosmic Renewal.* Seattle: Washington University Press.

_____. 1978. *The Teachings of Taoist Master Chuang.* New Haven: Yale University Press.

_____. 1994. *A Taoist Cookbook*. Boston: Charles E. Tuttle.

Sato, Yo-Ichiro. 2002. "Origin of Rice Cultivation in the Yangtze River Basin." In *The Origins of Pottery and Agriculture*, edited by Yoshinori Yasuda, 143-50. New Delhi: Roli Books.

Sauer, Carl Ortwin. 1952. *Agricultural Origins and Dispersals.* New York: American Geographical Society.

Sauvet, Georges, et al. 2009. "Thinking with Animals in Upper Paleolithic Rock Art." *Cambridge Archaeological Journal* 19.3: 319-36.

Sawyer, Ralph D. 1993. *The Seven Military Classics of Ancient China.* Boulder: Westview Press.

Saxe, Arthur. 1970. *Social Dimensions of Mortuary Practice.* Ann Arbor: University of Michigan Press.

Scarpari, Maurizio. 2000. *Ancient China: Chinese Civilization from Its Origins to the Tang Dynasty.* New York: Barnes & Noble Books.

Scarre, Chris. 2005. "The World Transformed: From Foragers and Farmers to States and Empires." In *The Human Past: World Prehistory and the Development of Human Societies*, edited by Chris Scarre, 176-99. London: Thames & Hudson.

Schafer, Edward H. 1977a. "T'ang." In *Food in Chinese Culture*, edited by K. C. Chang, 85-140. New Haven: Yale University Press.

_____. 1977b. "The Restoration of the Shrine of Wei Hua-ts'un at Lin-ch'uan in the Eighth Century." *Journal of Oriental Studies* 15:124-38.

_____. 1977c. *Pacing the Void.* Berkeley: University of California Press.

_____. 1978. "The Capeline Cantos: Verses on the Divine Love of Taoist Priestesses." *Asiatische Studien/Etudes Asiatiques* 32:5-65.

Schick, Kathy, and Nicholas Toth. 1993. *Making Silent Stones Speak: Human Evolution and the Dawn of Technology.* New York: Simon & Schuster.

_____. 2013. "The Origins and Evolution of Technology." In *A Companion to Paleoanthropology*, edited by David R. Begun, 265-89. Malden, Mass.: Wiley-Blackwell.

Schipper, Kristofer M. 1978. "The Taoist Body." *History of Religions* 17:355-87.

_____. 1984. "Le monachisme taoïste." In *Incontro di religioni in Asia tra il terzo e il decimo secolo d. C.*, edited by L. Lanciotti, 199-215. Firenze: Leo S. Olschki.

_____. 1994. *The Taoist Body.* Translated by Karen C. Duval. Berkeley: University of California Press.

______. 2001. "Daoist Ecology: The Inner Transformation. A Study of the Precepts of the Early Daoist Ecclesia." In *Daoism and Ecology: Ways within a Cosmic Landscape,* edited by Norman Girardot, James Miller, and Liu Xiaogan, 79-94. Cambridge, Mass.: Harvard University Press, Center for the Study of World Religions.

______, and Franciscus Verellen, eds. 2004. *The Taoist Canon: A Historical Companion to the Daozang.* 3 vols. Chicago: University of Chicago Press.

Schmandt-Besserat, Denise. 2001. "Feasting in the Ancient Near East." In *Feasts: Archaeological and Ethonographic Perspectives on Food, Politics, and Power*, edited by Michael Dietler and Brian Hayden, 391-403. Washington, DC: Smithsonian Institution Press.

Schmid, Ron. 1987. *Primal Nutrition: Paleolithic and Ancestral Diets for Optimal Health*. Rochester, VT: Healing Arts Press.

Schmookler, Andrew Bard. 1995. *The Parable of the Tribes: The Problem of Power in Social Evolution.* Albany: State University of New York Press.

Schoeninger, Margaret J, Henry T. Bunn, Shawn Murray, Travis Pickering, and Jim Moore. 2001. "Meat-Eating by the Fourth African Ape." In *Meat Eating and Human Evolution*, edited by Craig B. Stanford and Henry T. Bunn, 179-95. New York: Oxford University Press.

Schwartz, David M., and Victor Englebert 1995. *Yanomami: People of the Amazon.* New York: Lothrop, Lee, and Shepard.

Scott, Eleanor. 2001. "Killing the Female? Archaeological Narratives of Infanticide." In *Gender and the Archaeology of Death*, edited by Bettina Arnold and Nancy L. Wicker, 1-22. Walnut Creek: Calif.: Alta Mira Press.

Scott, John. 2001. *Power.* Malden: Blackwell Publishers.

Scranton, Laird. 2014. *China's Cosmological Prehistory: The Sophisticated Science Encoded in Civilizations' Earliest Symbols.* Rochester, VT: Inner Traditions.

Seidel, Anna. 1984. "Taoist Messianism." *Numen* 31:161-74.

Sept, Jeanne. 2001. "Modeling the Edible Landscape." In *Meat Eating and Human Evolution*, edited by Craig B. Stanford and Henry T. Bunn, 73-98. New York: Oxford University Press.

Service, Elman R. 1963. *Profiles in Ethnology.* New York: Harper & Row.

______. 1971. *Primitive Social Organization: An Evolutionary Perspective.* New York: Random House.

______. 1975. *Origins of the State and Civilization: The Process of Cultural Evolution*. New York: W. W. Norton.

Shahar, Meir, and Robert P. Weller, eds. 1996. *Unruly Gods: Divinity and Society in China.* Honolulu: University of Hawaii Press.

Shao, Wangping. 2005. "The Formation of Civilization: The Interaction Sphere of the Longshan Period." In *The Formation of Chinese Civilization: An Archaeological Perspective*, edited by Sarah Allan, 85-124. New Haven, Conn.: Yale University Press.

Shelach-Levi, Gideon. 2015. *The Archaeology of Early China: From Prehistory to the Han Dynasty.* Cambridge: Cambridge University Press.

Shelach, Gideon. 2004. "Marxist and Post-Marxist Paradigms for the Neolithic." In *Gender and Chinese Archaeology*, edited by Katheryn M. Linduff and Yan Sun, 11-28. Walnut Creek, Calif.: Alta Mira Press.

_____, and Mingyu Teng. 2013. "Earlier Neolithic Economic and Social Systems of the Liao River Region, Northeast China." In *A Companion to Chinese Archaeology*, edited by Anne P. Underhill, 37-54. Malden, Mass.: Wiley-Blackwell

Sheldon, Natasha. 2014. "The Use of Colours and the Brave Show They Make: Pigments of Roman Frescoes." www.decodethepast.com.

Shinde, Vasant. 2002. "The Emergence, Development and Spread of Agricultural Communities in South Asia." In *The Origins of Pottery and Agriculture*, edited by Yoshinori Yasuda, 89-115. New Delhi: Roli Books.

Silk, Joan B. 1993. "Primatological Perspectives on Gender Hierarchies." In *Sex and Gender Hierarchies*, edited by Barbara Diane Miller, 212-35. Cambridge: Cambridge University Press.

Simoons, Frederick J. 1991. *Food in China: A Cultural and Historical Inquiry*. Boca Raton, Fla.: CRC Press.

Singer, June. 2000. *Androgyny: The Opposites Within*. York Beach, ME: Nicolas-Hays.

Sinha, Chris. 2014. "Niche Construction and Semiosis: Biocultural and Social Dynamics." In *The Social Origins of Language*, edited by Daniel Dor, Chris Knight, and Jerome Lewis, 31-46. New York: Oxford University Press.

Skar, Lowell, and Fabrizio Pregadio. 2000. "Inner Alchemy (*Neidan*)." In *Daoism Handbook*, edited by Livia Kohn, 464-97. Leiden: Brill.

Slaughter, Bob H. 1967. "Animal Ranges as a Clue to Late Pleistocene Extinctions." In *Pleistocene Extinctions: The Search for a Cause*, edited by Paul S. Martin and Herbert E. Wright, 155-67. New Haven: Yale University Press.

Slingerland, Edward. 2003. *Effortless Action: Wu-wei as a Conceptual Metaphor and Spiritual Ideal in Ancient China*. New York: Oxford University Press.

Smith, Bruce D. 1995. *The Emergence of Agriculture*. New York: Scientific American Library.

Smith, Noel W. 1992. *An Analysis of Ice Age Art: Its Psychology and Belief System*. New York: Peter Lang.

Smith, Richard J. 1991. *Fortune-tellers and Philosophers: Divination in Traditional Chinese Society*. Boulder: Westwood Press.

Smuts, Barbara B. 1987. "Gender, Aggression, and Influence." In *Primate Societies*, edited by Barbara B. Smuts, 400-12. Chicago: University of Chicago Press.

Sommer, Deborah. 2008. "Boundaries of the *Ti* Body." *Asia Major* (3rd ser.) 21.3:293-324.

_____. 2010. "Concepts of the Body in the *Zhuangzi*." In *Experimental Essays on Zhuangzi*, edited by Victor H. Mair, 212-27. Dunedin, Fla.: Three Pines Press.

Soothill, William E. 1952. *The Hall of Light: A Study of Early Chinese Kingship*. New York: Philosophical Library.

Sørensen, Marie Louise Stig. 2000. *Gender Archaeology*. Malden, Mass.: Blackwell.

Spence, Jonathan. 1977. "Qing." In *Food in Chinese Culture*, edited by K. C. Chang, 259-94. New Haven: Yale University Press.

Spencer, Colin. 1993. *Vegetarianism: A History.*New York: Four Walls Eight Windows.

Speth, John D., and Eitan Tchernov. 2001. "Neandertal Hunting and Meat-Processing in the Near East: Evidence from Kebara Cave (Israel)." In *Meat Eating and Human Evolution*, edited by Craig B. Stanford and Henry T. Bunn, 52-72. New York: Oxford University Press.

Staal, Julius. 1984. *Stars of Jade: Calendar Lore, Mythology, Legends and Star Stories of Ancient China.* Decatur: Writ Press.

Standford, Craig B. 2001. "A Comparison of Social Meat-Foraging by Chimpanzees and Human Foragers." In *Meat Eating and Human Evolution*, edited by Craig B. Stanford and Henry T. Bunn, 122-40. New York: Oxford University Press.

Stein, Gil. 2001. "Who Was King? Who Was Not King? Social Group Composition and Competition in EarlyMesopotamian State Societies." In *From Leaders to Rulers*, edited by Jonathan Haas, 205-31. New York: Kluwer Academic.

Stein, Rolf A. 1963. "Remarques sur les mouvements du taoisme politico-religieux au IIe siecle ap. J.-C." *T'oung-pao* 50: 1-78.

Stein, Stephan. 1999. *Zwischen Heil und Heilung: Zur frühen Tradition des Yangsheng in China.* Uelzen: Medizinisch-Literarische Verlagsgesellschaft.

Sterckx, Roel. 2005. "Food and Philosophy in Early China." In *Of Tripod and Palate: Food, Politics and Religion in Traditional China*, edited by Roel Sterckx, 34-61. New York: Palgrave MacMillan.

_____. 2011. *Food, Sacrifice, and Sagehood in Early China.* Cambridge: Cambridge University Press.

Sternberg, Esther M. 2009. *Healing Spaces: The Science of Place and Well-Being.* Cambridge, Mass.: Harvard University Press.

Stevelny, Kim. 2012. *The Evolved Apprentice: How Evolution Made Us Human.* Cambridge, Mass.: MIT Press.

Steward, Julian H. 1968. "Causal Factors and Processes in the Evolution of Pre-farming Societies." In *Man the Hunter*, edited by Richard B. Lee and Irven DeVore, 321-34. Chicago: Aldine.

Strickmann, Michel. 1978. "A Taoist Confirmation of Liang Wu-ti's Suppression of Taoism." *Journal of the American Oriental Society* 98:467-74.

_____. 1980. "History, Anthropology, and Chinese Religion." *Harvard Journal of Asiatic Studies* 40:201-48.

_____. 1981. *Le taoïsme du Mao chan: chronique d'une révélation.* Paris: Collège du France, Institut des Hautes Etudes Chinoises.

Stuart, G. A. 1976. *Chinese Materia Medica.* Taipei: Southern Materials Center.

Stutz, Liv Nielsson, and Sarah Tarlow. 2013. "Beautiful Things and Bones of Desire: Emerging Issues in the Archaeology of Death and Burial." In *The Oxford Handbook of Archaeol-*

ogy of Death and Burial, edited by Sarah Tarlow and Liv Nielsson Stutz, 1-14. New York: Oxford University Press.

Sullivan, Lawrence E. 1990. "Body Works: Knowledge of the Body in the Study of Religion." *History of Religions* 30.1:86-99.

Sun, Bo. 2013. "The Longshan Culture of Shandong." In *A Companion to Chinese Archaeology*, edited by Anne P. Underhill, 435-58. Malden, Mass.: Wiley-Blackwell.

Sun, Guoping. 2013. "Recent Research on the Hemudu Culture and the Tianluo-shan Site." In *A Companion to Chinese Archaeology*, edited by Anne P. Underhill, 555-72. Malden, Mass.: Wiley-Blackwell.

Sun, Hua. 2013. "The Sanxingdui Culture of the Sichuan Basin." In *A Companion to Chinese Archaeology*, edited by Anne P. Underhill, 147-69. Malden, Mass.: Wiley-Blackwell.

Sun, Yan, and Hongyu Yang. 2004. "Gender Ideology and Mortuary Practice in Northwestern China." In *Gender and Chinese Archaeology,* edited by Katheryn M. Linduff and Yan Sun, 29-46. Walnut Creek: Alta Mira Press.

Sunday, Suzanne R. 1991. "Biological Theories of Animal Aggression." In *Genes and Gender VI: On Peace, War, and Gender—A Challenge to Genetic Explanation*, edited by Anne E. Hunter, 50-63 New York: City University of New York Press.

Suttles, Wayne. 1968. "Coping with Abundance: Subsistence on the Northwest Coast." In *Man the Hunter*, edited by Richard B. Lee and Irven DeVore, 56-68. Chicago: Aldine.

Svoboda, Jiri. 2015. "Early Modern Human Dispersal in Central and Eastern Europe." In *Emergence and Diversity of Human Behavior in Paleolithic Asia,* edited by Yosuke Kaifu, Masami Izuho, Ted Goebel, Hiroyuki Sato, and Akira Ono, 23-33. College Station: Texas A & M University Press.

Swinne, Brian Thomas, and Mary Evelyn Tucker. 2011. *Journey of the Universe: The Epic Story of Cosmic, Earth, and Human Transformation.* New Haven, Conn.: Yale University Press.

Tangney, June Price. 2009. "Humility." In *Oxford Handbook of Positive Psychology*, edited by C. R. Snyder and Shane J. Lopez, 483-90. New York: Oxford University Press.

Taussig, Michael T. 1987. *Shamanism, Colonialism, and the Wildman: A Study in Terror and Healing.* Chicago: University of Chicago Press.

Tavakolian, Bahram. 1982. "A Cultural Analysis of Sheikhanzai Economic Behavior." In *Culture and Ecology: Eclectic Perspectives*, edited by John G. Kennedy and Robert B. Edgerton, 95-109. Washington, DC: American Anthropological Association.

Taylor, Ken. 2012. *Celestial Geometry: Understanding the Astronomical Meanings of Ancient Sites.* London: Watkins Publications.

Teaford, Mark F., and Peter S. Ungar. 2000. "Diet and the Evolution of the Earliest Human Ancestors." *Proceedings of the National Academy of Science* 97:13506-11.

_____, and Frederick E. Grine. 2002. "Paleontological Evidence for the Diets of African Plio-Pleistocene Hominins with Special Reference to Early *Homo*." In *Human Diet: Its Origin and Evolution*, edited by Peter S. Ungar and Mark F. Teaford, 143-66. Westport, Conn.: Bergin & Garvey.

Temple, Daniel H., and Clark Spencer Larson. 2013. "Bioarchaeological Perspectives on Systemic Stress during the Agricultural Transition in Prehistoric Japan." In *Bioarchaeology of East Asia: Movement, Contact, Health*, edited by Kate Pechenkina and Marc Oxenham, 344-67. Gainesville: University Press of Florida.

Thompson, Melissa Emery. 2009. "Human Rape: Revising Evolutionary Perspectives." In *Sexual Coercion in Primates and Humans: An Evolutionary Perspective on Male Aggression against Females*, edited by Martin N. Muller and Richard W. Wrangham, 346-76. Cambridge, Mass.: Harvard University Press.

Thorp, Robert L., and Richard Ellis Vinograd. 2001. *Chinese Art and Culture*. New York: Harry N. Abrams.

Tomasello, Michael. 1999. *The Cultural Origins of Human Cognition*. Cambridge, Mass.: Harvard University Press.

Toth, Nicholas, and Kathy Schick. 2005. "African Origins." In *The Human Past: World Prehistory and the Development of Human Societies*, edited by Chris Scarre, 46-83. London: Thames & Hudson.

Toyama, Shuichi. 2002. "The Origin and Spread of Rice Cultivation as Seen from Rice Remains." In *The Origins of Pottery and Agriculture*, edited by Yoshinori Yasuda, 263-72. New Delhi: Roli Books.

Tributsch, Helmut. 2016. "Ochre Bathing of the Bearded Vulture: A Bio-Mimetic Model for Early Humans towards Smell Prevention and Health." *Animals* 6/7:1-17.

Trinkaus, Eric, et al. 2014. *The People of Sunghir: Burials, Bodies, and Behavior in the Earlier Upper Paleolithic*. New York: Oxford University Press.

Trout, Paul A. 2011. *Deadly Powers: Animal Predators and the Mythic Imagination*. Amherst, NY: Prometheus Books.

Tsien, Tsuen-Hsuin. 1985. *Science and Civilisation in China*, vol. V.1: *Spagyrical Discovery and Invention—Paper and Printing*. Cambridge: Cambridge University Press.

Tsuchiya, Masaaki. 2002. "Confession of Sins and Awareness of Self in the *Taiping jing*." In *Daoist Identity: History, Lineage, and Ritual*, edited by Livia Kohn and Harold D. Roth. Honolulu: University of Hawaii Press.

Tsutsumi, Takashi. 2002. "Origins of Pottery and Human Strategies for Adaption during the Termination of the Last Glacial Period in the Japanese Archipelago." In *The Origins of Pottery and Agriculture*, edited by Yoshinori Yasuda, 241-62. New Delhi: Roli Books.

Turner, Bryan. 1997. "The Body in Western Society." In *Religion and the Body*, edited by Sarah Coakley, 15-41. Cambridge: Cambridge University Press.

Turner, Victor W. 1967. *The Forest of Symbols: Aspects of Ndembu Ritual*. Ithaca: Cornell University Press.

______. 1969. *The Ritual Process: Structure and Anti-Structure*. Chicago: Aldine.

______. 1974. *Dramas, Fields, and Metaphors: Symbolic Action in Human Society*. Ithaca, NY: Cornell University Press.

Twist, Lynne. 2003. *The Soul of Money: Transforming Your Relationship with Money and Life*. New York: W. W. Norton.

Underhill, Anne P. 2002. *Craft Production and Social Change in Northern China.* New York: Kluwer Academic.

_____. 2013. "Introduction: Investigating the Development and Nature of Complex Societies in Ancient China." In *A Companion to Chinese Archaeology*, edited by Anne P. Underhill, 3-12. Malden, Mass.: Wiley-Blackwell.

Ungar, Peter S., and Mark F. Teaford. 2002. "Perspectives on the Evolution of Human Diet." In *Human Diet: Its Origin and Evolution*, edited by Peter S. Ungar and Mark F. Teaford, 1-6. Westport, Conn.: Bergin & Garvey.

Upex, Beth, and Keith Dobney. 2012. "More than Just Mad Cows: Exploring Human-Animal Relationships through Animal Paleopathology." In *A Companion to Paleopathology*, edited by Anne L. Grauer, 191-213. Malden, Mass.: Wiley-Blackwell.

Valkenburgh, Blaire Van. 2001. "The Dog-Eat-Dog World of Carnivores: A Review of Past and Present Carnivore Community Dynamics." In *Meat Eating and Human Evolution*, edited by Craig B. Stanford and Henry T. Bunn, 101-21. New York: Oxford University Press.

Vervoorn, Aat Emile. 1983. "Boyi and Shuqi: Worthy Men of Old?" *Papers in Far Eastern History* 29:1-22.

_____. 1984. "The Origins of Chinese Eremitism." *Xianggang zhongwen daxue Zhongguo wenhua yanjiu suo xuebao* 香港中文大學中國文化研究所學報 15:249-95.

_____. 1990. *Men of the Cliffs and Caves: The Development of the Chinese Eremitic Tradition to the End of the Han Dynasty.* Hong Kong: Chinese University Press.

Villa, Paolo, et al. 2015. "A Milk and Ochre Paint Mixture Used 49,000 Years Ago at Sibudu, South Africa." www.PlosOne 10(6):e0131273.

Wager, Tor D., et al. 2008. "The Neuroimaging of Emotion." In *Handbook of Emotions*, edited by Michael Lewis, Jeannette M. Haviland-Jones, and Lisa Feldman Barrett, 249-71. New York: Guilford Press.

Wagner, Philip L. 1977. "The Concept of Environmental Determinism in Cultural Evolution." In *Origins of Agriculture*, edited by Charles A. Reed, 49-74. The Hague: Mouton.

Wallace, Leslie V. 2012. "Betwixt and Between: Depictions of Immortals (*Xian*) in Eastern Han Tomb Reliefs. *Ars Orientalis* 41:73-101.

Wallman, Sandra. 1978. "The Epistemologies of Sex." In *Female Hierarchies*, edited by Lionel Tiger and Heather T. Fowler. Chicago: Beresford Book Service.

Walsh, Roger. 2007. *The World of Shamanism: New Views of an Ancient Tradition.* Woodbury, Minn.: Llewellyn Publications.

Walter, Chip. 2006. *Thumbs, Toes, and Tears: And Other Traits That Make Us Human.* New York: Walker & Company.

Wang, Aihe. 2000. *Cosmology and Political Culture in Early China.* Cambridge: Cambridge University Press.

Wang, Bo. 2014. *Zhuangzi: Thinking through the Inner Chapters.* Translated by Livia Kohn. St. Petersburg, Fla.: Three Pines Press.

Wang, Chuan-Chao, Yunzhi Huang, Shao-Qing Wen, Chun Chen, Li Jin, and Hui Li. 2016. "Agriculture Driving Male Expansion in Neolithic Times." *Science China—Life Science*, April 2016:1-4. www. link.springer.com/article/ 10.1007%2Fs11427-016-5057-y

Wang, Fen. 2013. "The Houli and Beixin Cultures." In *A Companion to Chinese Archaeology*, edited by Anne P. Underhill, 389-410. Malden, Mass.: Wiley-Blackwell.

Wang, Haicheng. 2014. "China's First Empire? Interpreting the Material Record of the Erligang Expansion." In *Art and Archaeology of the Erligang Civilization*, edited by Kyle Steinke and Dora C. Y. Ching, 67-98. Princeton: Princeton University Press.

Wang, Lixin. 2013. "The Lower Xiajiadian Culture of the Western Liao River." In *A Companion to Chinese Archaeology*, edited by Anne P. Underhill, 81-102. Malden, Mass.: Wiley-Blackwell.

Wang, Ningsheng. 1987. "Yangshao Burial Customs and Social Organization: A Comment on the Theory of Yangshao Matrilineal Society and Its Methodology." Translated by David N. Keightley. *Early China* 11/12:6-32.

Wang, Robin R. 2012. *Yinyang: The Way of Heaven and Earth in Chinese Thought and Culture*. Cambridge: Cambridge University Press.

Wang, Ying. 2004. "Rank and Power among Court Ladies at Anyang." In *Gender and Chinese Archaeology*, edited by Katheryn M. Linduff and Yan Sun, 95-116. Walnut Creek, Calif.: Alta Mira Press.

Wang, Youping. 2015. "New Evidence of Modern Human Behavior in Paleolithic Central China." In *Emergence and Diversity of Human Behavior in Paleolithic Asia*, edited by Yosuke Kaifu, Masami Izuho, Ted Goebel, Hiroyuki Sato, and Akira Ono, 250-58. College Station: Texas A & M University Press.

Wang, Zhongjiang. 2015. *Daoism Excavated: Cosmos and Humanity in Early Manuscripts*. Translated by Livia Kohn. St. Petersburg, Fla.: Three Pines Press.

Wann, Dave. 2009. "Finding Real Wealth: Twice the Value for Half the Resources." In *Less Is More: Embracing Simplicity for a Healthy Planet, a Caring Economy, and Lasting Happiness*, edited by Cecile Andrews and Wanda Urbanska, 41-46. Gabriola Island: New Society Publishers.

Ware, James R. 1933. "The *Wei-shu* and the *Sui-shu* on Taoism." *Journal of the American Oriental Society* 53:215-50.

_____. 1966. *Alchemy, Medicine and Religion in the China of AD 320*. Cambridge, Mass.: MIT Press.

Washburn, Sherwood L. and C. S. Lancaster. 1968. "The Evolution of Hunting." In *Man the Hunter*, edited by Richard B. Lee and Irven DeVore, 293-303. Chicago: Aldine.

Watson, Aaron. 2001. "The Sounds of Transformation: Acoustics, Monuments, and Ritual in the British Neolithic." In *The Archaeology of Shamanism*, 178-92. New York: Routledge.

Watson, Ben. 2012. "The Body and the Brain: Neuroscience and the Representation of Anthropomorphs in Paleoart." *Rock Art Research* 29.1:3-18.

Watson, Burton. 1968. *The Complete Works of Chuang-tzu*. New York: Columbia University Press.

Watson, Patty Jo. 1995. "Explaining the Transition to Agriculture." In *Last Hunters—First Farmers*, edited by Douglas B. Price and Anna B. Gebauer, 21-38. Santa Fe: School of American Research Press.

Watson, Richard A., and Patty Jo Watson. 1969. *Man and Nature: An Anthropological Essay in Human Ecology*. New York: Harcourt, Brace & World.

Watts, Ian. 2009. "Red Ochre, Body Painting, and Language: Interpreting the Blombos Ochre." In *The Cradle of Language*, edited by Rudolf Botha and Chris Knight, 62-92. New York: Oxford University Press.

_____. 2014. "The Red Thread: Pigment Use and the Evolution of Collective Ritual." In *The Social Origins of Language*, edited by Daniel Dor, Chris Knight, and Jerome Lewis, 208-27. New York: Oxford University Press.

_____, Michael Chazan, and Jayne Wilkins. 2016. "Early Evidence for Brilliant Ritualzed Display: Specularite Use in the Northern Cape (South Africa) between ~500 and ~300 Ka." *Current Anthropology* 57.3:287-310.

Watts, Joseph, Oliver Sheehan, Quentin D. Atkinson, Joseph Bulbulia, and Russell D. Grey. 2016. "Ritual Human Sacrifice Promoted and Sustained the Evolution of Stratified Societies. *Nature* 532:228-31.

Weckman, George. 1987. "Monasticism: An Overview." In *Encyclopedia of Religion*, edited by Mircea Eliade, 10: 35-41. New York: Macmillan.

Weglian, Emily. 2001. "Grave Goods Do Not a Gender Make: A Case Study from Singen am Hohentwie, Germany." In *Gender and the Archaeology of Death*, edited by Bettina Arnold and Nancy L. Wicker, 137-55. Walnut Creek, Calif.: Alta Mira Press.

Welch, J. L. 1996. "Cross-Dressing and Cross-Purposes: Gender Possibilities in the Acts of Thecla." In *Gender Reversals and Gender Culture: Anthropological and Historical Perspectives*, edited by Sabrina Petra Ramet, 66-78. London: Routledge.

Welker, Wolfgang. 2016. "First Paleolithic Rock Art in Germany: Engravings on Hunsrück Slate." *Antiquity* 349:32-47.

Wheatley, Paul. 1971. *The Pivot of the Four Quarters: A Preliminary Enquiry into the Origins and Character of the Ancient Chinese City*. Chicago: University of Chicago Press.

White, Joyce. 1995. "Modeling the Development of Early Rice Agriculture." *Asian Perspectives* 34:37-68.

White, Randall. 1989. "Beyond Art: Towards an Understanding of the Origins of Material Representation in Europe." In *The Human Revolution: Behavioral and Biological Perspectives on the Origins of Modern Humans*, edited by Paul Mellars and Chris Stringer, 366-90. Edinburgh: Edinburgh University Press.

Whitehead, Charles. 2014. "Why Humans and Not Apes: The Social Preconditions for the Emergence of Language." In *The Social Origins of Language*, edited by Daniel Dor, Chris Knight, and Jerome Lewis, 157-70. New York: Oxford University Press.

Whitley, David S. 2009. *Cave Paintings and the Human Spirit: The Origins of Creativity and Belief.* Amherst, NY: Prometheus Books.

_____., and James D. Keyser. 2003. "Faith in the Past: Debating an Archaeology of Religion." *Antiquity* 77:385-93.

Whyte, Robert Orr. 1983. "The Evolution of the Chinese Environment." In *The Origins of Chinese Civilization*, edited by David N. Keightley, 3-20. Berkeley: University of California Press.

Wiessner, Polly. 1996a. "Introduction: Food, Status, Culture, and Nature." In *Food and the Status Quest: An Interdisciplinary Perspective*, edited by Polly Wiessner and Wulf Schiefenhövel, 1-18. Oxford: Berghahn Books.

_____. 1996b. "Leveling the Hunter: Constraints on the Status Quest in Foraging Societies." In *Food and the Status Quest: An Interdisciplinary Perspective*, edited by Polly Wiessner and Wulf Schiefenhoevel, 171-92. Oxford: Berghahn Books.

_____. 2001. "Of Feasting and Value: Enga Feasts in a Historical Perspective (Papua New Guinea)." In *Feasts: Archaeological and Ethonographic Perspectives on Food, Politics, and Power*, edited by Michael Dietler and Brian Hayden, 115-43. Washington, DC: Smithsonian Institution Press.

Wightman, Gregory J. 2015. *The Origins of Religion in the Paleolithic.* Lanham, MD: Rowman & Littlefield.

Wilber, Ken. 1993. *The Spectrum of Consciousness.* Wheaton, Ill.: Quest Books.

Wilhelm, Richard. 1950. *The I Ching or Book of Changes.* Princeton: Princeton University Press, Bollingen Series XIX.

Williams, B. J. 1968. "The Birhor of India and Some Comments on Band Organization." In *Man the Hunter*, edited by Richard B. Lee and Irven DeVore, 126-31. Chicago: Aldine.

Williams, Pat. 2012. *Leadership Excellence.* Uhrichsville, OH: Barbour Publishing.

Wilmsen, E. N. 1989. *Land Filled with Flies: A Political Economy of the Kalahari.* Chicago: University of Chicago Press.

Wilson, Edward O. 1975. *Sociobiology: The New Synthesis.* Cambridge, Mass.: Harvard University Press.

Winkelman, Michael. 2002. "Shamanism and Cognitive Evolution." *Cambridge Archaeological Journal* 12.1:71-101.

Winterhalder, Bruce. 2001. "Intragroup Resource Transfers: Comparative Evidence, Models, and Implication for Human Evolution." In *Meat Eating and Human Evolution*, edited by Craig B. Stanford and Henry T. Bunn, 279-301. New York: Oxford University Press.

Wolf, Eric R. 1982. *Europe and the People without History.* Berkeley: University of California Press.

Wolpert, Lewis. 2007. "Causal Belief Makes Us Human." In *What Makes Us Human?* edited by Charles Pasternak, 164-81. New York: Oxford University Press.

Woodburn, James. 1968a. "An Introduction to Hazda Ecology." In *Man the Hunter*, edited by Richard B. Lee and Irven DeVore, 49-55. Chicago: Aldine.

_____. 1968b. "Stability and Flexibility in Hazda Residential Groupings." In *Man the Hunter*, edited by Richard B. Lee and Irven DeVore, 103-10. Chicago: Aldine.

_____. 1982. "Egalitarian Societies." *Man* 17:431-51.

Worne, Heather, Charles R. Cobb, Giovanna Vidoli, and Dawnie Wolfe Steadman. 2012. "The Space of War: Connecting Geophysical Landscapes with Skeletal Evidence of Warfare-Related Trauma." In *The Bioarchaeology of Violence*, edited by Debra Martin, Ryan P. Harrod, and Ventura R. Perez, 141-59. Gainesville: University Press of Florida.

Wrangham, Richard W. 2009. *Catching Fire: How Cooking Made Us Human.* New York: Basic Books.

_____, and Dale Peterson. 1996. *Demonic Males: Apes and the Origins of Human Violence.* Boston: Houghton Mifflin.

Wren, J. Thomas. 1995. *The Leader's Companion: Insights on Leadership through the Ages.* New York: Free Press.

Wright, Herbert E. 1977. "Environmental Change and the Origin of Agriculture in the Old and New Worlds." In *Origins of Agriculture*, edited by Charles A. Reed, 281-318. The Hague: Mouton.

Wright, Patricia Chapple. 1993. "Variations in Male-Female Dominance and Offspring Care in Non-Human Primates." In *Sex and Gender Hierarchies*, edited by Barbara Diane Miller, 127-45. Cambridge: Cambridge University Press.

Wright, Rita P. 1991. "Women's Labor and Pottery Production." In *Engendering Archaeology: Women and Prehistory*, edited by Joan M. Geor and Margaret W. Conkey, 194-223. Oxford: Basil Blackwell.

_____. 1996. "Technology, Gender, and Class: Worlds of Difference in Ur III Mesopotamia." In *Gender and Archaeology*, edited by Rita P. Wright, 79-110. Philadelphia: University of Pennsylvania Press.

Wright, Robert. 1994. *The Moral Animal: The New Science of Evolutionary Psychology.* New York: Pantheon Books.

_____. 2000. *NonZero.* New York: Pantheon Books.

Wrong, Dennis H. 1995. *Power: Its Forms, Bases, and Uses.* New Brunswick: Transaction Publishers.

Wu, Jui-man. 2004. "The Late Neolithic Cemetery at Dadianzi, Inner Mongolia Autonomous Region." In *Gender and Chinese Archaeology*, edited by Katheryn M. Linduff and Yan Sun, 47-91. Walnut Creek, Calif.: Alta Mira Press.

Xu, Hong. 2013. "The Erlitou Culture." In *A Companion to Chinese Archaeology*, edited by Anne P. Underhill, 300-22. Malden, Mass.: Wiley-Blackwell.

Yan, Wenming. 2002. "The Origins of Rice Agriculture, Pottery and Cities." In *The Origins of Pottery and Agriculture*, edited by Yoshinori Yasuda, 151-56. New Delhi: Roli Books.

_____. 2005. "The Beginning of Farming." In *The Formation of Chinese Civilization: An Archaeological Perspective*, edited by Sarah Allan, 27-42. New Haven, Conn.: Yale University Press.

_____, and Youping Wang. 2005. "Early Humans in China." In *The Formation of Chinese Civilization: An Archaeological Perspective*, edited by Sarah Allan, 11-26. New Haven, Conn.: Yale University Press.

Yang, Rur-Bin. 2003. "From 'Merging the Body with the Mind' to 'Wandering in Unitary *Qi*': A Discussion of Zhuangzi's Realm of the True Man and Its Corporeal Basis." In *Hiding the World in the World: Uneven Discourses on the Zhuangzi*, edited by Scott Cook, 88-127. Albany: State University of New York Press.

Yang, Yang. 1996. "The Chinese Jade Culture." In *The Mysteries of Ancient China: New Discoveries from the Early Dynasties*, 225-31. London: British Museum.

Yao, Alice. 2013. "Engendering Ancestors through Death Ritual in Ancient China." In *The Oxford Handbook of the Archaeology of Death and Burial*, edited by Sarah Tarlow and Liv Nilsson Stutz, 581-96. New York: Oxford University Press.

Yao, Ted. 2000. "Quanzhen—Complete Perfection." In *Daoism Handbook*, edited by Livia Kohn, 567-93. Leiden: Brill.

Yasuda, Yoshinori. 2002a. "The Second East Side Story: Origin of Agriculture in West Asia." In *The Origins of Pottery and Agriculture*, edited by Yoshinori Yasuda, 15-38. New Delhi: Roli Books.

______. 2002b. "Origins of Pottery and Agriculture in East Asia." In *The Origins of Pottery and Agriculture*, edited by Yoshinori Yasuda, 119-42. New Delhi: Roli Books.

Yates, Robin D. S. 1997. *Five Lost Classics: Tao, Huang-Lao, and Yin-Yang in Han China.* New York: Ballentine Books.

Yearley, Lee. 2010 [1983]. "The Perfected Person in the Radical *Zhuangzi*." In *Experimental Essays on Zhuangzi*, edited by Victor H. Mair, 122-36. Dunedin, Fla.: Three Pines Press.

Yengoyan, Aram A. 1968. "Demographic and Ecological Influences on Aboriginal Australian Marriage Sections." In *Man the Hunter*, edited by Richard B. Lee and Irven DeVore, 185-99. Chicago: Aldine.

Yoshioka, Yoshitoyo. 1979. "Taoist Monastic Life." In *Facets of Taoism*, edited by Holmes Welch and Anna Seidel, 220-52. New Haven, Conn.: Yale University Press.

Yü, Ying-shih. 1977. "Han." In *Food in Chinese Culture*, edited by K. C. Chang, 53-84. New Haven: Yale University Press.

Yuan, Guangkuo. 2013. "The Discovery and Study of Early Shang Culture." In *A Companion to Chinese Archaeology*, edited by Anne P. Underhill, 323-42. Malden, Mass.: Wiley-Blackwell.

Yuan, Jiarong. 2002. "Rice and Pottery 10,000 Years BP at Yuchanyan, Dao County, Hunan Province." In *The Origins of Pottery and Agriculture*, edited by Yoshinori Yasuda, 157-66. New Delhi: Roli Books.

Yudkin, John. 1969. "Archaeology and the Nutritionist." In *The Domestication and Exploitation of Plants and Animals*, edited by Peter J. Ucko and G. W. Dimbleby, 547-52. Chicago: Aldine.

Zhang, Changping. 2014. "Erligang: A Perspective from Panlongcheng." In *Art and Archaeology of the Erligang Civilization*, edited by Kyle Steinke and Dora C. Y. Ching, 51-63. Princeton: Princeton University Press.

Zhang, Chi. 2013. "The Qujialing-Shijiahe Culture in the Middle Yangzi River Valley." In *A Companion to Chinese Archaeology*, edited by Anne P. Underhill, 510-34. Malden, Mass.: Wiley-Blackwell.

Zhang, Ji, 2002. "Early Pottery and Rice Phytolith Remains from Xianrendong and Diaotongshan Sites, Wannian, Jiangxi Province." In *The Origins of Pottery and Agriculture*, edited by Yoshinori Yasuda, 185-92. New Delhi: Roli Books.

Zhang, Juzhong, and Yun Kuen Lee. 2005. "The Magic Flutes." *Natural History* 114.7:42-47.

_____, Xinghua Xiao, and Yun Kuen Lee. "2005. The Early Development of Music: Analysis of the Jiahu Bone Flutes." *Antiquity* 78:769-78.

_____, and Qilong Cui. 2013. "The Jiahu Site in the Huai River Area." In *A Companion to Chinese Archaeology*, edited by Anne P. Underhill, 194-212. Malden, Mass.: Wiley-Blackwell.

Zhang, Zhongpei. 1985. "The Social Structure Reflected in the Yuanjunmiao Cemetery." *Journal of Anthropological Archaeology* 4:19-33.

_____. 2005. "The Yangshao Period: Prosperity and the Transformation of Prehistoric Society." In *The Formation of Chinese Civilization: An Archaeological Perspective*, edited by Sarah Allan, 43-84. New Haven, Conn.: Yale University Press.

Zhao, Chunqing. 2013. "The Longshan Culture in Central Henan Province, c. 2600-1900 BC." In *A Companion to Chinese Archaeology*, edited by Anne P. Underhill, 236-54. Malden, Mass.: Wiley-Blackwell.

Zheng, Zhenxiang. 1996. "The Royal Consort Fu Hao and Her Tomb." In *The Mysteries of Ancient China: New Discoveries from the Early Dynasties*, 240-47. London: British Museum.

Zhou, Dianzeng. 1996. "The Sacrificial Pits at Sanxingdui." In *The Mysteries of Ancient China: New Discoveries from the Early Dynasties*, 232-39. London: British Museum.

Zhou, Zuyan.2003. *Androgyny in Late Ming and Early Qing Literature*. Honolulu: University of Hawaii Press.

Zhu, Yanping. 2013. "The Early Neolithic in the Central Yellow River Valley, c. 7000-4000 BC." In *A Companion to Chinese Archaeology*, edited by Anne P. Underhill, 171-93. Malden, Mass.: Wiley-Blackwell.

Zihlman, Adrienne L. 1993. "Sex Differences and Gender Hierarchies among Primates: An Evolutionary Perspective." In *Sex and Gender Hierarchies*, edited by Barbara Diane Miller, 32-56. Cambridge: Cambridge University Press.

_____. 1997. "The Paleolithic Glass Ceiling: Women in Hunting Evolution." In *Women in Human Evolution*, edited by Lori D. Hager, 91-113. London: Routledge.

_____. 2013. "Engendering Human Evolution." In *A Companion to Gender Prehistory*, edited by Diane Bolger, 23-44. Malden, Mass.: Wiley-Blackwell.

Zillmann, Dolf. 1984. *Connections between Sex and Aggression*. Hillsdale, NJ: Lawrence Erlbaum Associates.

Zohary, Daniel, Maria Hopf, and Ehud Weiss. 2012. *Domestication of Plants in the Old World: The Origin and Spread of Cultivated Plants in West Asia, Europe, and the Mediterranean Basin*. New York: Oxford University Press.

Zukav, Gary. 2002. *Soul Stories*. New York: Simon & Schuster.

Index